F
215
J86
2000   Jumpin' Jim Crow.

$17.95

BAKER & TAYLOR

Jumpin' Jim Crow

Jumpin' Jim Crow

Southern Politics from Civil War to Civil Rights

EDITED BY

JANE DAILEY

GLENDA ELIZABETH GILMORE

AND BRYANT SIMON

PRINCETON UNIVERSITY PRESS

PRINCETON AND OXFORD

Library of Congress Cataloging-in-Publication Data
Jumpin' Jim Crow : southern politics from Civil War to
civil rights / edited by Jane Dailey, Glenda Elizabeth Gilmore,
and Bryant Simon.
p.   cm.
Includes bibliographical references and index.
ISBN 0-691-00192-8 (cloth : alk. paper)
ISBN 0-691-00193-6 (paper : alk. paper)
1. Southern States—Politics and government—1865–
2. Southern States—Race relations.   3. Southern States—
Social conditions.   4. Afro-Americans—Civil rights—
Southern States—History.   5. Sex role—Southern States—History.
I. Dailey, Jane Elizabeth, 1963–   II. Gilmore, Glenda Elizabeth.
III. Simon, Bryant.
F215 .J86 2000
975'.04—dc21   00-027861

This book has been composed in Janson.

The paper used in this publication meets the minimum
requirements of ANSI/NISO Z39.48-1992 (R 1997)
(*Permanence of Paper*)

www.pup.princeton.edu

Printed in the United States of America

10 9 8 7 6 5 4 3 2 1

10 9 8 7 6 5 4 3 2 1
(pbk.)

To Jacquelyn Dowd Hall and Nell Irvin Painter,
who taught us and brought us together,
and who continue to amaze and inspire us.

In memory of C. Vann Woodward, 1908–1999.

Contents

Preface

A PREFACE is something usually written by the author or authors of a work that follows. It is the very nature of what follows in this instance, however, that prompted the main doubts in the mind of the present writer about his qualifications for this assignment. Here is a book filled with splendid examples of the way history has come to be written at the end of the twentieth century: whereas the writer of the preface began his writing back toward its beginning—in the 1930s. Naturally his publications reflected fashions of their period. Fashions change, and over the next six decades, to some extent so did his writing, but that does not make him the precursor or inspirer of the new school. Among the things that the writer of any preface and the authors of the essays in this collection *do* have in common, however, is by all odds the most fascinating field of American history, the southern part.

Older generations of historians filled long shelves with books and monograph series about the Reconstruction period. But not until recently did historians include such vital struggles as those the freedpeople made for legal protections, rights, and privacy of their marriages, their families, and the custody of their own children, legal rights that only whites enjoyed in the old order and rights that they sought to deny free blacks afterward. Violence was, of course, commonly acknowledged to be extensive during Reconstruction. But it was usually attributed to "mobs" of poor whites or explained by the need to "restore order," prevent black domination, or maintain white supremacy by white "militia" and Klansmen. Only lately has serious attention been focused upon those who benefited and used for their purposes the reign of racist terrorism, lynching, torture, murder, and massacres. It was not the poor whites but the white elite who as a result gained domination not only of the blacks but over whites of the lower order as well. White elite supremacy did not go unchallenged by political combinations of whites and blacks in several southern states during the years following Reconstruction. One such movement was that of the Readjusters of Virginia. They did win power briefly in the name of a free ballot and human rights, but they were soon undermined by propaganda against "miscegenation."

Paternalism was a lasting heritage from the old order, and males generally continued to take charge and have things their own way. An odd exception was control over the prevailing conceptions of the South's past. That proved to be women's work in the last two decades of the nineteenth century and the first two of the twentieth. It was therefore the white ladies, not the white gentlemen, who bore primary responsibility for the myths glorifying the old order, the Lost Cause, and white supremacy. It was the United Daughters of the Confederacy (UDC), and the Daughters of the American Revolution (DAR), Daughters of Pilgrims, and Daughters of Colonial Governors who were "guardians of the past." Non-daughters were excluded. White women took over the shaping, methodology, and writing of what is now called public history, but of an elite sort.

Our new historians, men and women, are of a quite different order. The representatives in the essays that follow also write about race, segregation, and politics, but not in celebration of the past. Only a few illustrative examples can be offered here.

One of them deals with political history of the traditional kind, but in order to make important corrections in prevailing views. A striking and well-known reversal of political allegiances of the races took place in the early decades of the twentieth century when southern Democrats became Republicans and southern Republicans became Democrats, thus reversing traditional allegiances that had lasted since Lincoln and the Civil War. The common explanation was the New Deal and what happened in two presidential elections, those of 1932 and 1936. For blacks it was the appeal of Roosevelt reforms, the promise of jobs, relief, and hope for the future. For southern whites it was the appeal of conservative Republicans and their fight against the New Deal. It was that simple. A far more complex and satisfactory explanation comes from one of our new historians. It considers *push* factors as well as *pull* factors. For black voters the push came from the racism of the Lily White Republicans during the 1920s. For southern whites the push was from northern New Dealers. Other factors are so numerous that only a few can be mentioned here: the NAACP, woman suffrage, black migrants in the North, white primaries in the South, and black intellectuals and writers, to mention only a few.

Defiance could take ugly forms in the modern South—defiance of the law, the federal government, and the elemental human rights to life, liberty, and property. One example is the violence of the Second Reconstruction, which sometimes equaled or even exceeded that of the First. The new outburst followed the Supreme Court's *Brown* decision against segregated schools in 1954. The poor whites revived the Ku Klux Klan; white elites founded the White Citizens Councils and proclaimed "massive resistance," and 101 of 128 southern Congressmen signed the "Southern Manifesto"—all in defiance of the law. If any single act ignited the fuse of violence it was that of President Dwight Eisenhower, who on September 25, 1957, ordered federal troops into Little Rock to control the mob preventing nine black children from entering school in that city. Reactions to the first intervention of federal troops since the Compromise of 1877 were numerous. One example must suffice.

Just a week after the Little Rock incident there appeared a pamphlet entitled *South Carolinians Speak: A Moderate Approach to Race Relations.* Sponsored by five Episcopalian ministers of the state, it consisted of twelve essays that were certainly moderate by any reasonable standard even though treasonous heresy by then current standards. One of the essays was by Claudia Thomas Sanders, a Charleston blueblood of high intelligence, wife of a prominent physician, and mother of two children. They lived in a large handsome house in the small city of Gaffney. A few weeks after the pamphlet appeared five Klansmen set out to dynamite the house. The earlier of several bombs that failed to ignite contained enough dynamite to destroy the whole house and much of the neighborhood. The one that finally did explode was smaller but big enough to damage the house severely. One of the five Klansmen confessed fully and identified the others, with eight police officers as witnesses. The FBI investigated and confirmed the evidence entirely. The case against the Klansmen was solid. Then the Klansman who confessed suffered a mysterious accident and was crushed to death under his own car. A local magistrate ruled the dead man's confessions inadmissible as "hearsay" and dismissed the case against two of the accused. A jury of white men acquitted the other two. Hooded Klansmen paraded the streets and cheered a showing of the old film, "Birth of a Nation." The state press applauded the outcome and the Charleston *News and Courier* suggested secession and armed resistance to federal intervention. The five clergymen who had sponsored the "moderate" pamphlet fled the state, and Mrs. Sanders, ostracized by all, left her bombed house for an extended vacation up North.

None of the last several generations of southern historians could ignore such subjects as race, slavery, Civil War, Reconstruction, violence, segregation, and politics. What distinguishes the new history is not only its inclusion of subjects that the old history neglected, but the new questions it raises and the way it treats the traditional subjects. That includes attention to the roles played and leadership provided by a race, a gender, or a class, that had heretofore been treated by historians not as participants, but as helpless spectators or victims.

C. VANN WOODWARD
Hamden, Conn.

Acknowledgments

WE WOULD like to thank our editor at Princeton University Press, Brigitta van Rheinberg, for suggesting this collection and for sending the manuscript to three incredibly generous and insightful readers, whose comments strengthened this book: Gail Bederman, Drew Faust, and Vernon Burton. Thanks, too, to our contributors, who endured our occasionally rough editorial interventions with good cheer and unparalleled punctuality. Our eternal gratitude goes to Robin Kelley for moderating—literally—the raucous "New Directions in Southern Political History" session at the Southern Historical Meeting in Atlanta in 1998, and to Beth Hale and Robert Hinton for standing up for us that day. This book gained a whole new meaning that afternoon and later that night and the next morning. Many thanks also to the always brilliant and patient Pete Daniel. And thanks finally to Anne Scott, who loaned us her house in Chapel Hill, even if we couldn't always keep track of the keys, for several all-night and all-day editing sessions. Without her generosity, we would have met exclusively in smoky bars during conferences. At that rate, we were never going to finish the book.

Jumpin' Jim Crow

Introduction

I jump jis'so, An' ev'y time I turn about I jump Jim Crow
—Thomas "Daddy" Rice

In 1955, on the very eve of the modern Civil Rights Movement, African American novelist James Baldwin remarked that "the history of the American Negro problem is not merely shameful, it is also something of an achievement. For even when the worst has been said, it must also be added that the perpetual challenge posed by this problem was always, somehow, perpetually met." Assuming an ironic tone of grudging admiration, Baldwin highlighted the contested nature of southern race relations. Far from being static, the South's "Negro problem" was instead lively, slippery, a "perpetual challenge" that had to be repeatedly "met."[1]

The ways in which white southerners "met" the race "problem" have intrigued historians writing about post–Civil War southern politics since at least 1928, when Ulrich B. Phillips pronounced race relations the "central theme" of southern history. What contemporaries referred to as "the race question" may be phrased more bluntly today as the struggle for white domination. Establishing and maintaining this domination—creating the system of racial segregation and African American disfranchisement known as Jim Crow—has remained a preoccupation of southern historians. From our vantage point on the far side of the Civil Rights Movement, it is easy to understand why: just as the questions we ask about German state formation in the nineteenth century are grounded by events in the twentieth, so too was it difficult to comprehend the dissolution of the Jim Crow South without looking back to its foundations. Southern political history's best narratives focus on the frenzied efforts of the champions of white supremacy—whether the button-down booster, the "feather-legged" demagogue, or the good ol' boy populist—to erect and defend an institutional and ideological edifice capable of repelling challenges from within as well as from without.

In recognizing white supremacy as the "central theme" of southern history, however, historians have sometimes minimized variations on that theme in ways that impoverish our appreciation of the complexities of racism and power. Stunned by the sheer magnitude and obscenity of the

---

[1] James Baldwin, *Notes of a Native Son* (Boston: Beacon Press, 1955), 175.

Jim Crow South, historians often emphasize the power of white supremacists and their tools—violence, economic oppression, electoral fraud, and manipulation of the social structure—and minimize the contingent nature of white supremacist ideas and regimes. In this collection, the "central theme" of southern history remains central, but white supremacy is not seen as an overwhelming force. Rather, it is a precarious balancing act, pulled in all directions by class, gender, and racial tensions. As the epigraph from Daddy Rice suggests, Jim Crow was at bottom a social relationship, a dance in which the wary partners matched their steps, bent, and whirled in an unending series of deadly serious improvisations.

To point to the dynamism of white supremacy is not to underestimate either its thoroughness or its potency. Jim Crow looked anything but precarious to those who tried to fight it in 1880 or 1930 or 1955. But stressing the contingent nature of Jim Crow by seeing it as dependent on individual actions through time helps to denaturalize white supremacy. Jim Crow was not the logical and inevitable culmination of civil war and emancipation, but rather the result of a calculated campaign by white elites to circumscribe all possibility of African American political, economic, and social power.

These essays explore white supremacy's balancing act from a number of analytical and narrative perspectives. All turn on politics. Many investigate the broad spectrum of African American resistance to white supremacist ideas and regimes. Some emphasize the agency of white and black women in crafting or resisting (as the case may be) a coherent system of white racial domination. To complicate white electoral politics and to uncover sites of resistance, these essays often turn away from the polling place and voter returns toward a broader definition of the political. Some find contestation in the creation and interpretation of law, in the rhetoric and structure of political parties, and in governmental agencies and the courts. Borrowing from cultural studies, anthropology, and feminist theory, others find the political in more unlikely spaces: in the household; in the overflowing aisles of a dime store; on the street. The notion of politics that informs this collection extends from the polling station to the front porch, and bridges the distance between public and private contests for power and dignity.

The expanded definition of politics and the attention paid to African American actions in these essays suggest a conclusion to one of the most drawn-out debates of southern historiography: the "continuity/change" argument. For forty years, southern historians have argued over to what degree, and in what ways, the Civil War and emancipation represented a rupture in the history of the South. Traditionally, this debate has analyzed white electoral politics, landownership, and patterns of economic change to determine exactly which white men got on top and how they stayed there. Continuarians insist that despite changes in personnel, traditional values—particularly the value of elite white social, political, and economic domination—persevered through Reconstruction and the turn of the twentieth century. Those who emphasize change argue that the New South of factories, white tenant farmers, and cities called for a new white supremacy in a revolutionary context.

Shifting the focus from white to black southerners reveals a new definition of continuity and change. Black resistance, not white supremacy, was continuous, while white supremacy remodeled itself to meet any challenge. In every decade from emancipation through the 1960s, black people in the South resisted white elite domination. Despite the fact that fighting for civil rights could spark civil war, African Americans in the South looked continuously for room to jump Jim Crow. Sometimes they found it in alliances with whites disenchanted with parts of their region's "traditions." Other times they resisted white definitions of black rights and prerogatives through the courts, or on the streets, or in the dressing room of a department store. In this way, the actions of black southerners and their white allies both molded the articulation of white supremacy and suggested strategies of resistance to it. The essays in this collection trace channels that began at emancipation to cut paths through the dam of white supremacy. While these individual streams often ran dry for decades, taken as a whole these essays demonstrate the continuous contest between southern blacks determined to assert their civil rights and whites determined to deny blacks that power.

Uncovering resistance to segregation undermines the traditional periodization of postwar southern history at the same time that it strips Jim Crow of the sense of inevitability and invulnerability traditionally ascribed to it. In viewing the "Age of Segregation" as constantly beleaguered, the essays in this book collectively make the point that the grid lines of power were never drawn neatly on the ground, and no single event marked either the birth or the death of Jim Crow. At the same time, by placing black southerners, white dissidents, and women of both races at the center of southern history, we begin to rewrite the history of the "backward" South—that miasma of reactionary politics, poverty, and violence—and focus instead on those portions of the South that served as an incubator for one of the most extraordinary social justice movements in the history of the United States. Strom Thurmond was not simply a reincarnation of Ben Tillman. Rosa Parks was not the first black woman to challenge segregation. Martin Luther King, Jr., did not emerge *sui generis* to advocate political equality from the pulpit. Just as white supremacy made and remade itself over a century, Parks and King continued a long tradition of African American activism. By revealing the history of racism and resistance central to the southern experience, this collection, we hope, will enable students to understand not just the Second Reconstruction but how racism continues to thrive and be thwarted today. It is our hope that the gathering together of these essays in *Jumpin' Jim Crow* will spotlight the many turnabouts in what remains the central dance of southern history.

Chapter 1

LAURA F. EDWARDS

The Politics of Marriage and Households in North Carolina during Reconstruction

IN THE FALL of 1865,[1] North Carolina lawmakers gathered at the state-house in Raleigh to draw up a new constitution. The unenviable job of opening this difficult session fell to Edwin G. Reade, who tried to set a reassuring, positive tone. "Fellow-citizens," he began, *"we are going home."* Despite recent events, the Union still stood as an "old homestead . . . built upon a rock . . . [that] . . . weathered the storm." Defeated Confederates simply needed to "grasp hard again the hand of friendship which stands at the door . . . [and] . . . enjoy together the long, bright future which awaits us."[2] With this imagery of this Union as a domestic haven, Reade intended to blunt the conflicts that had torn the nation apart and divided the Con-federacy. While Unionists and Confederates had faced off on battlefields and in statehouses, their old homesteads stood unchanged, waiting to en-fold them in domestic tranquility when they returned. Now they just had to open the door and enter.

Reade's homecoming metaphor drew praise both within and outside the South. Not everyone, however, greeted his invitation with enthusiasm. At the very same time that North Carolina's lawmakers were listening to Edwin Reade, a group of African American delegates gathered across town and called to order the first statewide Freedmen's Convention. Their final report also featured domestic issues and imagery. But their destination could not have been more different than Reade's. The delegates wanted "education for our children," protection for "our family relations," provi-sion for "orphan children," and support for "the re-union of families which have long been broken up by war or by the operations of slavery." Unlike Reade and other white lawmakers who longed to "go home" to the house-holds they had left behind in 1860, black delegates had no intention of returning to their ex-masters' "old homesteads." They and the African Americans they represented wanted households of their own.[3]

In the history of Reconstruction, Edwin Reade's domestic vision has taken precedence over the African American delegates' claims. Even as historians of the period carefully questioned every other aspect of politi-cal and social conflict, they left this one, highly gendered image in place. Like Reade, they assumed a distinction between "private" and "public": the public sphere, a dynamic and contentious place, was where history happened; it did not happen in the quiet isolation of "private," domestic space. Traditional political historians occasionally noted sentimental attachments to the "old homestead," but then passed it by to locate the dynamics of change in coalitions, elections, legislation, and organized acts of violence. Social historians extended the public realm to include fields, streets, and work places and to cover the battles waged by African Americans and poor whites over labor and race. Yet, for the most part, they too ignored the domestic sphere. The household may have provided support and motivation for political action, but it was not actually part of that arena. By either standard, Edwin Reade's metaphoric homestead seemed historically accurate and the domestic issues raised by the North Carolina Freedmen's Convention appeared politically inconsequential.

Recent work that uses gender, in combination with race and class, has challenged this view. Emphasizing the institutional connections between the "private" and "public" spheres, these studies have revealed the extent to which public power was deeply rooted in domestic relations and underscored the centrality of southern households to social and political change.[4] As this new work has shown, the antebellum household was far more than a collection of people or a place of residence. It also defined private obligations and mediated the distribution of public power. Before emancipation, heads of household assumed economic, legal, and moral responsibility for a range of dependents, who included African American slaves as well as white women and children. Heads of household also shouldered the duty of representing their dependents' interests in the public arena of politics. In this way, private authority translated directly into public rights and power.[5]

The exemplary household head was an adult, white, propertied male. To those who held the reins of power in the antebellum South, this was the only kind of person capable of the responsibilities of governance, whether in private households or public arenas. Because women, children, and African Americans were considered to lack both self-control and the capacity for reason, they were thought to require the protection and guidance of white men. But white men claimed power on their ability to fulfill the duties of household head, not on the basis of their race and sex alone. Not every man measured up. Dependency tainted all those who lacked sufficient property to control their own labor and maintain their own households. Nevertheless, all propertyless white men possessed the potential to head independent households. In this sense, their position was always different from that of white women and African Americans, who could step out of their proper place and even step into the role of household head, but could never fully embody the power of that role.[6]

War and emancipation shook the antebellum household to its foundations and shattered the configurations of power it supported. Freed from their dependent position as slaves, African American men could, theoretically, take on the role of household head with all its private and public privileges. Although African American women would find it difficult to claim the same rights as their menfolk, they might well demand privileges previously reserved for white women as dependent wives and daughters. At the same time, many white men faced the loss of their property and, in the case of slaveholders, most of their dependents as well. Not only did the borders of their households shrink but also the very basis of their mastery there was called into question, a situation that also undermined their exclusive claims to public power. The household thus became a highly contested political issue. After all, political and civil rights still hinged on how households were defined, who qualified as a household head, and what rights they and their dependents could exercise.[7]

Nowhere was the political content of the household more evident than in conflicts over marriage in the early years of Reconstruction. As the institution that created households, marriage lay at the very center of the postemancipation political structure.[8] Perhaps more than any other issue in Reconstruction, the questions raised by the status of freedpeople's marriages show how domestic relations structured civil status and political rights. Immediately following emancipation, conservative whites imposed legal marriage on freedpeople as a way to consolidate state power over them and compel them to support their families. African Americans, however, turned legal marriage to their advantage, using it to buttress their claims to civil and political rights while also trying to maintain their own vision of marital relations. But the laws governing marriage allowed them only so much room for maneuver. The rules of marriage formed the central support in a patriarchal legal framework that had subordinated poor white and African American men as well as women before the war and could still be mobilized to serve the same ends.

As conflicts over marriage are connected to traditional political issues through gender, the politics of Reconstruction begin to look different. New issues come into focus: Edwin Reade's homestead becomes far less tranquil, while the domestic claims of the first Freedmen's Convention begin to look far more significant. The actions of people excluded from formal political arenas take on new immediacy as well. Ultimately, their efforts to remake the domestic sphere meant that Edwin Reade and other elite white southerners could never "go home" to a place untouched by political conflict or historical change.

With the abolition of slavery, the legal burden of constituting households fell to marriage alone. As a Mississippi judge explained in 1873: "The superstructure of society rests upon marriage and the family as its foundation. The social relations and rights of property spring out of it and attach to it."[9] Without marriage, there were no legally recognized fathers, and without fathers, there were no legally recognized parents, since mothers had no formal rights to their children. In this situation, the transfer of property across generations became more complex. Inheritance laws, designed to keep property in the legitimate male line of the family, supplied little guidance in a world where fathers had no legally recognized male heirs. Marriage also framed the rules for the distribution of property and authority within households. In its absence, women no longer surrendered to their husbands their property, their wages, their children, and their ability to contract in their own name. Laws did exist to deal with children who were born out of wedlock and lived outside a legally recognized family; they became wards of the state and were apprenticed to a responsible master. But there were no comparable mechanisms to deal with unmarried women, whose number multiplied as a result of wartime casualties and emancipation. They were simply on their own, accountable for their own material needs, political interests, and moral destiny. The prospect of self-supporting women called the allocation of public power into question as well. Household heads represented the interests of their wives and children in the public sphere because they were legally liable for them. In the absence of this relationship, former dependents moved in the public world on their own. Within existing legal and political structures, of course, those people assumed to be dependents had few rights and little power. But without marriage, the rationale for this situation also dissolved.

Given the importance of marriage, it is not surprising that North Carolina's Supreme Court buttressed the institution against change in the years directly following emancipation. The first effort to do so came in 1868 with *State v. Rhodes*, a case of wife beating. A lower court had found Benjamin Rhodes innocent, basing the ruling in generations of legal precedent that allowed a husband to whip his wife as long as the switch was no larger in diameter than his thumb. In a decision written by Justice Edwin Reade, the same man who offered the homecoming metaphor at the 1865 constitutional convention, the North Carolina Supreme Court upheld the verdict but questioned the reasoning. For Reade, the issues in *Rhodes* extended beyond wife beating or even the civil status of married women. At stake was the relationship between the household and the state, which emancipation had destabilized. The state, Reade flatly declared, did not "recognize the right of the husband to whip his wife." Nonetheless, the sanctity of the private sphere shielded the husband's actions from public scrutiny. However loath the court was to condone violence within the domestic sphere, Reade believed that far greater evils "would result from raising the curtain and exposing to public curiosity and criticism the nursery and the bed chamber." "Family government," Justice Reade declared, "being in its nature as complete in itself as the State government is in itself, the Courts will not attempt to control, or interfere with it, in favor of either party." In practice, this meant that the court assumed a household head innocent until proven guilty, since it was his governance that was in question. Given the court's reluctance to interfere, guilt was nearly impossible to prove.[10]

Despite the rhetoric of domestic privacy, *Rhodes* also established the public dimension of the household. For the state's conservative elite, marriage and the households it created were too important to their notions of social order to be left entirely to the discretion of the people, most of whom they neither respected nor trusted. Marriage, as Justice Reade later explained in defending the state's right to prohibit interracial unions, "is more than a civil contract; it is a *relation*, an *institution*, affecting not merely the parties, like business contracts, but offspring particularly, and society generally." Because marriage contained such wide-ranging social and political implications, the state had a right—indeed a duty—to make sure the institution took forms that served the public interest. The same logic shaped Reade's decision in *Rhodes*. Even as he drew a veil around relations within the household, Reade planted that private sphere squarely in the public realm. Household heads derived their power from the state, and family government was ultimately subordinate to state government. Although the state would never meddle with "trivial complaints arising out of the domestic relations," it would intervene if a husband, father, or master "grossly abuse[d] his powers." The state reserved for itself the power to decide what constituted gross abuse.[11]

In *Rhodes*, Reade confronted a world without slavery by reaffirming the household's boundaries and its connection to public power. Emancipation lurked, unstated, between the lines. Focusing on "family government" and "domestic relations," Reade explicitly extended the logic of his decision to other domestic relationships—namely, those of parent/child and master/apprentice. If not for emancipation, the relationship of master and slave would have been included. The fact that it was not made the others unstable. After all, if one domestic relationship could be dissolved with the stroke of a pen, then what was so inviolable about the rest? At the very least, they might be subject to alteration. *Rhodes*, however, ruled out this possibility, establishing precedent that would shape subsequent cases for the remainder of the century.[12]

But *Rhodes* did not resolve all the questions posed by emancipation. It made no mention of ex-slaves' relation to legal marriage or whether legally married freedpeople acquired the same rights and duties that fell to legally married whites. Antebellum law had not recognized slave marriages, and emancipation did not make ex-slaves' marriages legal. During the war, some northern officials found the absence of legal marriage among slave couples troubling and promoted "the sacred nature and binding obligations of marriage." In some cases, their efforts were well received by African Americans who had their own reasons for formalizing their domestic relations.[13] As long as slavery was in force, white southerners did not share these concerns. After emancipation, many southern whites began to view freedpeople's domestic relations with alarm. Marriage figured prominently in William W. Holden's recommendations to freedpeople in his first address as North Carolina's provisional governor on June 13, 1865. In order "to enter upon the pursuit of prosperity and happiness," Holden advised three things: marriage, hard work, and education. Marriage topped the list, coming even before discussions about the control of labor. Other white lawmakers shared Holden's priorities. While squabbling continually over the terms of peace, delegates to the 1865 constitutional convention could agree on one issue: freedpeople had to be married.[14]

White commentators often expressed their concerns about freedpeople and marriage in moral terms. But more was at stake than morality, as an editorial by B. F. Moore, a strong Unionist and perhaps the most instrumental figure in the creation of the state's Black Code, reveals. Freedpeople had to assume responsibility for themselves and their families, Moore argued, since the responsibility for their welfare no longer fell to their masters. Yet he doubted that they would assume these obligations without coercion, and coercion was impossible without marriage. Marriage, as Moore pointed out, institutionalized family relationships in the form of the "legal responsibilities of husbands and wives" and "parents and children." Where indigent women and children became wards of the state in the absence of marriage, they became the legal responsibility of individual household heads in its presence. As such, marriage compelled ex-slaves to take charge of their families by allowing the state to "enforce the performance of all these duties as it does in the case of the white race."[15]

Marriage, however, also carried the potential to increase freedpeople's authority within the state. During slavery, North Carolina's Supreme Court had categorically denied slaves marriage precisely because it was a civil contract that served as the entering wedge into a broad range of other civil rights.[16] After the war, conservatives downplayed the relationship of marriage and civil rights, emphasizing instead marriage's obligations. The other provisions in the Black Code, of which the marriage act was a part, underscored the point, severely limiting African Americans' civil rights and denying them any political rights whatsoever.[17]

To put it another way, the Black Code's provisions left African Americans without rights to protect the families that they were now obligated to maintain. The apprenticeship section was the most blatant. While stating that white and black children were to be bound out in the same manner, the measure singled out black children for apprenticeship "when the parents with whom such children may live do not habitually employ their time in some honest, industrious occupation." With this clause, the rights of African American parents to their children became conditional. If challenged, black parents had to prove themselves "industrious" and "honest," no easy task when so many whites saw all blacks as lazy and dishonest by nature. In practice, county courts made liberal use of the clause to apprentice children at will. The act privileged ex-masters' custody claims over those of everyone else, including relations and friends. As other historians have pointed out, former masters wanted the labor of these "children"— some of whom were well beyond childhood. But such claims rested on the assumption that African American parents did not have legally recognized households or rights to their children. If the abolition of slavery forced ex-masters to concede that they could no longer compel adult freedpeople to live as dependents within their households, many were unwilling to admit that freedom made African Americans competent to form households of their own. A few "industrious" and "honest" freedpeople might be able to raise their own children; but many, if not most, black children belonged within the households of a white propertied man. Given the restrictions of apprenticeship, marriage did not make African American men household heads with the power to protect the interests of their dependents. It simply obliged them to support their dependents when it was inconvenient and unprofitable for white planters to do so.[18]

The notion that marriage was more about obligations than rights was not new. Antebellum courts had defined marriage in these terms before emancipation. Legal marriage alone had not been sufficient to claim other civil and political rights, and it certainly did not lead to social or political equality. The fact that free blacks could marry, for instance, did not enhance their civil status. In fact, North Carolina's conservative lawmakers thought that the laws limiting the rights of free blacks during slavery provided the ideal model for newly freed slaves and created the Black Code directly from them. After all, emancipation only eliminated slavery, not the inequalities that had always existed among free people in southern society. Confident in their ability to control freed slaves as they had free blacks, the possibility that marriage might convey more rights to freedpeople than it had to free blacks did not seem to occur to white lawmakers.[19]

It was a major oversight. Slavery had actually anchored the status of antebellum free blacks. The logic behind the denial of rights to free blacks depended on the assumption that all African Americans should properly be dependent slaves, and that all slaves were denied full civil and political rights. Without the legal reference point of slavery, the status of African Americans was not so easily contained. In this context, marriage also took on new meanings. However much conservative whites might emphasize responsibilities, they could not avoid the fact that marriage also implied rights for all free people.

African Americans seized on this opening and turned the laws of marriage and domestic relations to their advantage. In fact, they began establishing their own households and claiming domestic autonomy long before state lawmakers even thought to consider the legal status of their marriages. During the war, many slaves undermined their masters' households from within by slowing their work pace, sabotaging the production process, appropriating property, and abandoning the plantations altogether. Emancipation then opened new opportunities to bring scattered families back together, and some ex-slaves traveled long distances to search for family members who had been sold away. But even for those families whose members had lived on neighboring plantations, the act of consolidating loved ones under one roof was highly symbolic. It meant rejecting their position as their masters' dependents and asserting the right to form their own households.[20]

Among African Americans' first demands as free people was the legal recognition of their family ties. Many had married legally during the war behind Union lines. After Confederate surrender, others followed suit. In July 1865, a year before passage of the legislative act requiring ex-slaves to register their marriages, an Episcopal minister in Warren County married 150 African American couples in the course of just two days. Over the county line in Granville, many of the 878 couples who registered their unions in compliance with the legislative act may have already formalized their vows, just as their Warren neighbors had done. The majority recorded their unions in July and August of 1866, well before the legal deadline mandated in the Black Code.[21]

The popularity of legal marriage lay in its affirmation of African Americans' new status as free people. Not only did it bring new security to their family ties, it also demonstrated their place as citizens with direct ties to the state. Even sympathetic whites did not fully grasp the meanings freedpeople attached to legal marriage. Many commended the popularity of marriage among ex-slaves, interpreting it as a sign of their moral improvement. Some even mistakenly assumed that freedpeople were accepting marriage as a relationship of "obligations" and "responsibilities." All these interpretations missed the mark, as the words of one black corporal in the U.S. Colored Troops suggest. Explaining to his troops the implications of Virginia's 1866 act legitimating slave marriages, he maintained: "The Marriage Covenant is at the foundation of all our rights. In slavery we could not have *legalised* marriage: *now* we have it . . . and we shall be established as a people." If the prohibition of marriage had underscored slaves' dependent position and the precariousness of their family ties in slavery, legal marriage now symbolized their rejection of the slave status. To freedpeople, marriage was about rights.[22]

Marriage could also be used to claim rights. Resistance to apprenticeship provides a particularly striking example. If North Carolina's apprenticeship system looked bad on paper, it was even worse in practice. The situation infuriated African Americans. How could they be free if their children could still be taken from them as easily as they had been in slavery? The uproar echoed across the South, as denunciations mounted in frequency and intensity between 1865 and 1867. But while black leaders attacked the system verbally, it was the actions of poor black parents that dealt the most telling blows to apprenticeship.

Black parents went to great lengths to keep their children out of the hands of former masters. When evasion failed, they challenged apprenticeship directly, through the courts. As early as 1866, African Americans were filing suits in local courts all across North Carolina, demanding the cancellation of apprentice contracts. When the courts proved unresponsive, freedpeople enlisted the aid of the Freedmen's Bureau. Indeed, the sheer number of complaints to the Bureau testifies to African Americans' persistence and the role they played in making apprenticeship a political issue.

The Bureau and many agents were initially ambivalent about apprenticeship. At first, some officials believed that apprenticeship could be useful training for children who might otherwise receive no instruction at home, although the Bureau officially objected to racial distinctions in the treatment of white and black children. As time went on, however, more agents worried about the way the apprenticeship laws were applied. Some regularly shepherded cases through the local courts and sometimes cancelled indentures themselves. But even sympathetic officers would not have been so aware of the system's inequities if not for the freedpeople themselves, who kept agents' attention riveted on the issue, whether they liked it or not. One bureau agent, for instance, cancelled seventy-seven indentures in his three-county district during the first eight months of 1867 alone.[23]

The case of Richard Hester reveals the logic of African Americans' resistance. Hester, a former slave, tried to obtain custody of his two grandsons in 1867. Unable to block their apprenticeship in court, he turned to the Freedmen's Bureau and solicited Daniel Paschall, a sympathetic white planter and local magistrate, to write on his behalf. As Paschall explained, "My course on the bench of our county court has been to bind the colored children to colored friends where it was in proof that they were capable and had the means of feeding and clothing, but in many instances was overruled, if this case was before me on the bench, I should give these boys to Richard Hester." Paschall, however, did not question the right of the court to apprentice black children. But Hester did. He did not want the court's permission to apprentice his grandchildren; he believed he already had custody rights as their grandfather. He thus challenged the court's guardianship power and its right to apprentice his grandchildren to anyone at all. Ultimately, Hester was able to proceed with the case on his own terms. With the backing of the Freedmen's Bureau, he filed a motion in the local court, asking that the contracts "be cancelled" and that his grandsons "be placed in the custody and care of him, the said Dick Hester."[24]

Legal marriage gave freedpeople the materials necessary to construct a wall of privacy around their domestic relations and to draw their children and grandchildren within their own households. Like Richard Hester, legally married African American men could claim the position of household head and the attendant rights to their children and their kin. When women filed appeals, they often did so as married women who were attached to a legally recognized male household head. Kate Durham's children, for instance, had been apprenticed before the war. Afterward, when she sued for custody, her claims rested on her legal marriage to London Brame. Brame may have been the father of Durham's children, but the court was less interested in paternity than in Kate Durham's marital status. It was Durham's position as a wife assured of male supervision and economic maintenance that convinced the court to return her children. Of course, this meant that women still could not claim their children in their own right. If Kate Durham had not been legally married, her case would have been treated much differently.[25]

But even as freedpeople wielded legal marriage to defend the boundaries of their lives from the encroachments of outsiders, they refused to surrender their own definitions of the marital relation. To be sure, the marital concepts of propertied and professional African Americans conformed more closely to those in law and the social practices of elite whites. And many black leaders trumpeted the virtues of legal marriage and middle-class domesticity as a way to elevate the race. But most poor freedpeople did not understand marriage primarily as a legal contract, nor did they accept the gender roles or the complete separation of private and public space established by it.[26]

For slaves, marriage had been a relationship governed by custom and the community. After emancipation, poor African Americans continued to adhere to these culturally sanctioned rules and rejected the idea that a legal contract was necessary to initiate, maintain, or end a marriage. As the pension records of black Civil War veterans indicate, the community recognized a couple as husband and wife when they took on certain responsibilities for each other: the woman washed, cleaned, cooked, and tended the house, while the man contributed to her and her children's maintenance. Although unions could be legalized, it was ultimately the substance of the relationship and community recognition of it, not the legal contract, that constituted the marriage. Both men and women could sever the marital bond if their partners abandoned their responsibilities or otherwise mistreated them. Irvin Thompson, for instance, married his first wife in a legal ceremony soon after the war, and lived with her for about a year. "Then she associated with other men and left me," he told a pension examiner. "No I did not get any divorce. She just went off . . . and I lost track of her." Soon afterward, he married another woman in a legal ceremony that the community accepted as a valid marriage.[27]

Two divorce cases illuminate both the internal dynamics of freed-people's definition of marriage and the confusion these standards generated among elite whites. In 1876, Smith Watkins filed for divorce on the grounds that his wife, Dink, had been sleeping with other men. He gave a long list of offenses, which included his discovery of her having sex with another man in the lot of the black Baptist church. When confronted by Smith, Dink responded: "I am my own woman and will do as I please." According to E. B. Bullock, another African American man, his wife Jane defended her unfaithfulness in a similar manner. To court officials, these were straightforward cases. The men's statements "proved" adultery on the part of the wife, one of the legal grounds for divorce. While not sufficient proof in and of themselves, the bold words of these two women lent credence to the charges against them by underscoring their malicious intent.[28]

In their own communities, however, the statements of Dink Watkins and Jane Bullock conveyed very different meanings. Instead of claiming their freedom to do as they pleased within marriage, it is more likely that these women were marking the end of their relationships with their husbands. As far as Dink Watkins and Jane Bullock were concerned, they now had the right to select new partners because they were no longer married. As such, their former husbands had no right to interfere in their lives at all. The court records suggest that Smith Watkins and E. B. Bullock understood their wives' words in this way. Adultery, in and of itself, was not necessarily the reason the men filed for divorce, even though their cases hinged on the sexual transgressions of their wives. At the time E. B. Bullock initiated his suit, for instance, he and Jane had not lived together as man and wife for many years. In court, he used his wife's subsequent liaisons to prove that fact. As he explained to the court, he had waited so long to file for a legal divorce because he was unaware that he needed to obtain one.[29]

As these two cases suggest, poor African Americans reserved the right to form and maintain marriages and households as they saw fit, even when they married legally. Others saw no advantage in legalizing their unions at all. Even Herbert Gutman's figures, which he used to establish near universal acceptance of legal marriage among freedpeople following emancipation, suggest that as many as 50 percent of ex-slaves in North Carolina chose not to formalize their relationships in law. Although saturated with

racism, the comments of contemporary white observers also suggest as much. According to one, many freedpeople "refuse to be married, preferring the system of concubinage brought out from slavery."[30] Such complaints held a grain of truth. What white observers noted were deviations from their own marital standards. What they did not understand was the internal logic of a culture that defined the marital relationship differently than they did.

Poor African Americans could define the substance of marital relations while they remained within their own families and communities. But the law mediated and shaped their claims to domestic autonomy as soon as they stepped into the courtroom. When Richard Hester demanded custody of his grandchildren, for instance, he argued that he was their grandfather and they were rightly his. In court, his arguments were translated into the legal claim that he was a household head with legitimate ties to his children and, by extension, his grandchildren. It is probably safe to assume that Hester was unaware of the body of law marshaled in his defense or its wider implications for family relations. If he had been, he probably would have disagreed with many of its provisions. Nonetheless, Hester's own claims fit neatly enough within the existing legal framework to allow him to use it for his own ends. Kate Durham used the courts in the same way. It is unlikely that she would have agreed that mothers had no established rights to their children, and she may well have objected to other legal restrictions placed on wives as well. Yet, when Durham tried to get her children back, the fact that she was married to a man who was legally bound to support them made her case. In this context, she could turn her position as a dependent wife to her own benefit.

Whether conservative whites liked it or not, legal marriage could now legitimize rights as well as obligations for free African Americans. Apprenticeship cases underscored the inability of conservative legislators to control the political situation around them, as freedpeople flooded the courts with challenges to the system as laid out in the Black Code. Legally denying parental privileges to freedpeople did not stop them from claiming what they believed to be one of their most basic rights. To the contrary, they did so with exhausting persistence. Successes at the local level suggest that at least a few officials found freedpeople's demands convincing. If not, they apparently found it hard to refute such claims within the existing structure of the law. Indeed, the Supreme Court's position on the household made it difficult to maneuver around African Americans' parental rights. Although decided in 1868, *Rhodes* is nonetheless revealing because it affirmed the existing principle of the inviolable nature of domestic government. If freedpeople were now husbands and wives, then, by implication, the concept of domestic government should extend to their households as well. After all, how could the court intervene to take children away if family government was "in its nature as complete in itself as the State government is in itself"?[31] In this context, the very legal principles used to coerce freedpeople into marriage and allow the state greater control over them also legitimized African Americans' own claims to greater autonomy.

By the time Congress entered the fray and struck down southern Black Codes, freedpeople had already chipped away enough of the existing system to expose its weaknesses. Congressional Reconstruction then bolstered their position. The Fourteenth and Fifteenth Amendments prohibited racial discrimination in the construction and exercise of the law and granted full political rights to African American men. The resulting Republican-authored state constitution of 1868 restructured North Carolina's governing structure, not only sweeping away the impediments that kept African Americans from enjoying the same rights under the law as whites, but also democratizing local courts by making the key positions of magistrate and judge elective.[32]

Historians of Reconstruction have documented how profoundly disturbing elite white southerners found these changes and how they tried to overturn them in desperate battles over economic independence, civil rights, and universal manhood suffrage. But the legal principle of domestic privacy also buttressed the independence of all poor and politically marginalized people, with its protective "curtain" that shielded large portions of their lives from state interference. After the war, African Americans used this legal right with great success to protect their families from the intrusion of meddling outsiders. It is no coincidence, for instance, that apprenticeship cases all but disappeared from the court dockets after 1868. African Americans also mobilized the legal principle of domestic privacy to justify demands for a more equitable distribution of economic resources and political power. As they argued, women and children could not perform their role as dependents unless their menfolk could protect and provide for them; men could not meet these responsibilities without the necessary economic and political power; and families—the cornerstone of society—would disintegrate unless men and women could fulfill their proper roles.[33]

Yet defeat lurked just beneath the surface. This patriarchal legal structure could easily accommodate racial and class hierarchies, and the courts could easily turn the gendered arguments of African Americans and Republican officials against them. As Peter Bardaglio has argued, southern courts and other state institutions increased their power to oversee and regulate the domestic sphere throughout the late nineteenth century, transferring key elements of patriarchal power from the hands of individual men to the state. In so doing, the courts built on another legal principle central to *Rhodes*: the state's right to intervene in domestic space. The results gave agents of the state the latitude to pass judgment on a wide range of family issues affecting poor white as well as black families. To this end, North Carolina judges delved into the character of litigants to ferret out the "worthy" husbands, wives, and children who deserved the court's protection from the "unworthy" ones who did not. An 1877 divorce case, *Taylor v. Taylor*, illuminates the court's new role. Citing frequent evidence of violent abuse, Sarah Taylor maintained that her husband David had made her life intolerable, which constituted grounds for divorce. The antebellum court would have refused to intervene on the basis that this was a private conflict that should be settled within the domestic arena. But now the court saw fit to adjudicate the matter.[34]

As long as poor whites and all African Americans retained their hold on public power, they could use their access to the system and their clout with Republican officials to include themselves among those considered "suitable" and "worthy." But these decisions acquired far more ominous meanings as the tide of Republican influence ebbed and conservatives flooded back into the judicial system in the mid-1870s. The legal curtain surrounding the domestic sphere began lifting at the same time that poor whites and African Americans lost power within governmental institutions, exposing both groups to unprecedented state regulation at the moment of their greatest vulnerability. Justice Bynum's decision in *Taylor v. Taylor* is suggestive. Making racial and class distinctions through gendered standards of men's and women's ability to fill certain domestic roles, he noted that "among the lower clases [*sic*], blows sometimes pass between married couples who in the main are very happy and have no desire to part; amidst very coarse habits such incidents occur almost as freely as rude or reproachful words." In this particular case, however, the court could not overlook such behavior because both the husband and wife belonged to "respectable walks of life." Although the logic of this decision would seem to remove the households of poor whites and African Americans from public scrutiny, it did not. While obstructing "unrespectable" women's claims to protection from their husbands, it labeled "lower classes" as coarse, rude, violent, and uncivilized people in need of state supervision. From this perspective, it was no coincidence that the domestic autonomy of African Americans and poor whites came under attack at the same time that their public rights did.[35]

Undercutting African American men and women's position within the domestic realm had profound political implications for their civil and political status. Nowhere were the insidious results more graphically illustrated than in the 1875 attempted rape case, *State v. Alexander Neely*. In July of 1874, a young white woman got off the railroad at an isolated country crossroads, said goodbye to a friend, and began to walk home alone. A short distance down the road, she heard Alexander Neely, a black man, "'holler' to her to stop." Turning around to see him running toward her, she took off with Neely following behind. Only when she turned into the lane to her brother-in-law's house did the black man disappear into the woods. In court, Neely's guilt turned on his intent. His defense argued that intent could not possibly be deduced from Neely's actions, because he could have been pursuing the woman for any number of reasons. But Justice Pearson disagreed. As he explained, "I see a chicken-cock drop his wings and take after a hen: my experience and observation assure me that his purpose is sexual intercourse; no other evidence is needed." Just for good measure, he offered another analogy, "I see a dog in hot pursuit of a rabbit; my experience and observation assure me the intent of the dog is to kill the rabbit; no doubt about it." Pearson then applied his logic to Neely, arguing that black men's instincts meant they pursued white women for one reason—rape. No evidence was necessary because "experience" proved it.[36]

Justice Rodman issued a ringing dissent. Cutting straight to the heart of the matter, he rejected Pearson's direct analogies between "brute animals" and human beings. The analogy that Neely "is a brute, or so like a brute that it is safe to reason from the one to the other; that he is governed by brutish and, in his case, vicious passions unrestrained by reason or moral sense," was false, Rodman insisted. Neely was a man, and "he must be presumed to have the passions of a man, and also the reason and moral sense of a man." As such, Rodman continued, "he is entitled to be tried as a man, and to have his acts and intents inquired into and decided upon by the principles which govern human conduct, and not brutish conduct." Otherwise, "what need of court and jury?" If Neely were no more than an animal, the law did not apply. Anyone could destroy him, as they did other unruly animals, "without legal ceremony." Justice Bynum joined Rodman in arguing that Pearson had pushed the "lower classes" too far down the scale of humanity. At this time, however, they were outnumbered. Instead, Pearson's depiction of black men as brutes, completely enslaved to their passions, prevailed.[37] Unfit to govern themselves and their families, they were also unable to participate as citizens in the public arena.

This is the same argument that conservative white Democratic leaders used to overturn the changes of Reconstruction. Drawing distinctions among men on the basis of race and class and couching those distinctions in the gendered imagery of the household, Democrats argued that they, as the "best men," represented everyone's interests. African American and dissident white men, by contrast, were "unmanly" men who, like minors and women, should be excluded from politics. Democrats thus used the gendered relationship between men and women within the household to legitimize hierarchies among men in the public arena. The logic worked because it had such a strong structural foundation in existing systems of governance. Ultimately these Democratic leaders made good on Edwin

Reade's invitation to return "home" to a world where African Americans and even poor whites were excluded from participation in formal political institutions. But they had to rebuild and remodel their fathers' houses before they could move in.[38]

ACKNOWLEDGMENTS

The author would like to thank Peter Bardaglio, Ben Brown, Vikki Bynum, Noralee Frankel, Glenda Gilmore, Jacquelyn Hall, Dirk Hartog, Nancy Hewitt, Tera Hunter, Bob Ingalls, John McAllister, and Dave Roediger for their invaluable comments on various drafts of this piece. Special thanks go to Jane Dailey, whose insightful reading clarified the arguments and greatly strengthened the presentation in this version.

NOTES

1. Material presented here is drawn from "'The Marriage Covenant Is at the Foundation of All Our Rights': The Legal and Political Implications of Marriage in Postemancipation North Carolina," *Law and History Review* 14 (spring 1996): 81–124.

2. *Journal of the Convention of North Carolina at Its Session of 1865* (Raleigh, 1865), 7.

3. *Journal of Freedom*, 7 October 1865.

4. Peter Bardaglio, *Reconstructing the Household: Families, Sex, and the Law in the Nineteenth-Century South* (Chapel Hill: University of North Carolina Press, 1995); Nancy Bercaw, "The Politics of Household: Domestic Battlegrounds in the Transition from Slavery to Freedom in the Yazoo-Mississippi Delta, 1850–1860," Ph.D. dissertation, University of Pennsylvania, 1996; Victoria Bynum, *Unruly Women: The Politics of Social and Sexual Control in the Old South* (Chapel Hill: University of North Carolina Press, 1992); Jane Dailey, "The Limits of Liberalism in the New South: The Politics of Race, Sex, and Patronage in Virginia, 1879–1883," in this volume; Laura F. Edwards, *Gendered Strife and Confusion: The Political Culture of Reconstruction* (Urbana: University of Illinois Press, 1997); Drew Gilpin Faust, *Mothers of Invention: Women of the Slaveholding South in the American Civil War* (Chapel Hill: University of North Carolina Press, 1996); Elizabeth Fox-Genovese, *Within the Plantation Household: Women in the Old South* (Chapel Hill: University of North Carolina Press, 1988); Noralee Frankel, *Freedom's Women: African-American Women in Mississippi, 1860–1870* (Bloomington: University of Indiana Press, forthcoming 1999); Martha Hodes, *White Women, Black Men: Illicit Sex in the Nineteenth-Century South* (New Haven: Yale University Press, 1997); Tera W. Hunter, *To 'Joy My Freedom: Southern Black Women's Lives and Labors after the Civil War* (Cambridge: Harvard University Press, 1997), 4–97; Stephanie McCurry, *Masters of Small Worlds: Yeoman Households, Gender Relations, and the Political Culture of the Antebellum South Carolina Low Country* (New York: Oxford University Press, 1995); Leslie A. Schwalm, *A Hard Fight for We: Women's Transition from Slavery to Freedom*

in South Carolina (Urbana: University of Illinois Press, 1997); LeeAnn Whites, *The Civil War as a Crisis in Gender: Augusta, Georgia, 1860–1890* (Athens: University of Georgia Press, 1995). The works of the authors in this book are on the forefront of applying gender to race and politics in southern history for the late-nineteenth and twentieth centuries.

5. In particular, see Bardaglio, *Reconstructing the Household*; Fox-Genovese, *Within the Plantation Household*; McCurry, *Masters of Small Worlds*.

6. In particular, see Bardaglio, *Reconstructing the Household*, 3–112; Bynum, *Unruly Women*; McCurry, *Masters of Small Worlds*. For propertyless whites, see Edwards, *Gendered Strife and Confusion*, 66–80, 185–87.

7. For an elaboration of these themes, see Edwards, *Gendered Strife and Confusion*. Also see: Bardaglio, *Reconstructing the Household*, 137–228; Bercaw, "The Politics of Household"; Dailey, "The Limits of Liberalism"; Frankel, *Freedom's Women*; Martha Hodes, "The Sexualization of Reconstruction Politics: White Women and Black Men in the South after the Civil War," *Journal of the History of Sexuality*, vol. 3, no. 3 (1993): 402–17; and Hodes, "Wartime Dialogues on Illicit Sex: White Women and Black Men," in *Divided Houses: Gender and the Civil War*, edited by Catherine Clinton and Nina Silber (New York: Oxford University Press, 1992), 230–42; Hunter, *To 'Joy My Freedom*, 21–97; Schwalm, *A Hard Fight for We*, 147–268.

8. On the centrality of marriage to the legal and political structure of the South, see also McCurry, "The Two Faces of Republicanism: Gender and Proslavery Politics in Antebellum South Carolina," *Journal of American History* 78 (March 1992): 1245–64. For the nation as a whole, see: Nancy F. Cott, "Giving Character to Our Whole Civil Polity: Marriage and the Public Order in the Late Nineteenth Century," in *U.S. History as Women's History: New Feminist Essays*, edited by Linda K. Kerber, Alice Kessler-Harris, and Kathryn Kish Sklar (Chapel Hill: University of North Carolina Press, 1995), 107–21; Amy Dru Stanley, "Conjugal Bonds and Wage Labor: Rights of Contract in the Age of Emancipation," *Journal of American History* 75 (September 1988): 477–82.

9. Quoted in Michael Grossberg, *Governing the Hearth: Law and the Family in Nineteenth-Century America* (Chapel Hill: University of North Carolina Press, 1985), 99.

10. *State v. Rhodes*, 61 N.C. 453 (1868). For the position of the antebellum North Carolina Supreme Court on wife-beating, see Bynum, *Unruly Women*, 70–72.

11. *State v. Hairston and Williams*, 63 N.C. 451 (1869); *State v. Rhodes*, 61 N.C. 453 (1868). For a discussion of the legal regulation of "fit" marital unions in the U.S. as a whole, see Grossberg, *Governing the Hearth*, 103–52. See also Hendrik Hartog, "Marital Exits and Marital Expectations in Nineteenth-Century America," *Georgetown Law Journal* 80 (October 1991): 95–129. Hartog emphasizes the legal conception of marriage as a public relationship and the simultaneous reluctance to interfere in its actual dynamics.

12. *State v. Rhodes*, 61 N.C. 453 (1868). Although the Court later repudiated a husband's right to physically chastise his wife and increased its own powers to intervene in the domestic sphere, it maintained the separation of private from public established in *Rhodes* throughout the late nineteenth century.

13. Quote from Chaplain of a Louisiana Black Regiment to the Regimental Adjutant in Ira Berlin, Joseph P. Reidy, and Leslie S. Rowland, eds., *Freedom: A Documentary History of Emancipation, 1861–1867*, series 2: *The Black Military Experience* (New York: Cambridge University Press, 1982), 624; see also 623, 660–61.

14. For Holden's address, see *Raleigh Daily Record*, 13 June 1865; for a similar message, see *North Carolina Standard*, 17 October 1866. After the abolition of slavery, marriage was the first issue involving freedpeople to be discussed by the legislature; *Journal of the Convention of the State of North Carolina at Its Session of 1865* (Raleigh, 1865), 41–47. Delegates delayed action temporarily until the 1866 legislative session for procedural reasons. But when the matter did come to the floor, the brief debate revealed a general consensus on the issue, with concerns centering on how best to implement the measure and how to make it as broadly inclusive as possible. For the final bill, see *Public Laws of the State of North Carolina . . . 1866* (Raleigh, 1866), chap. 40, sec. 5. For the debate, see: *Raleigh Sentinel*, 1 February, 10 February, 12 February, and 22 February 1866; *North Carolina Standard*, 7 February 1866. For the eagerness of southern conservative legislators to legalize slave unions generally, see: Rebecca Sue Alexander, *North Carolina Faces the Freedmen: Race Relations during Presidential Reconstruction, 1865–67* (Durham: Duke University Press, 1985), 47–48; Grossberg, *Governing the Hearth*, 133.

15. *Sentinel*, 29 Aug. 1865. This position was also written into the recommendations of the commission, headed by Moore, that drew up the draft of the state's Black Code; see *Sentinel*, 31 January 1866.

16. In the antebellum case of *Howard v. Howard*, 51 N.C. 235 (1858), for instance, Justice Richmond Pearson ruled that two slaves who had been married according to the customs of their community did not become legally married just because they had been freed from slavery's restraints and lived as free blacks. He first established that slaves could claim no civil rights, including the right to contract marriage. Without the right to contract, there was no marriage and the emancipation of the couple did not change that fact. To conclude otherwise, Pearson argued, would be to accept the "idea of civil rights being merely *dormant* during slavery." Such a conclusion was untenable—so much so that Pearson dismissed it out of hand as "a fanciful conceit." When post-emancipation legislators retroactively acknowledged all slave marriages to be civil contracts, they affirmed the "fanciful conceit" that the civil rights of slaves had been dormant in slavery. If the institution of slavery was what had kept slaves from claiming civil rights, then there was nothing to keep freedpeople from them now.

17. The Black Code recognized freedpeople's right to contract and allowed them access to the criminal and civil courts. But within the context of its other provisions and the overarching assumption that equal access did not mean equality in the eyes of the law, these rights meant little. African Americans were not allowed to testify against whites, except in cases that directly involved their own interests, and they were barred from sitting on juries. The vagrancy section required freedpeople to work and limited their freedom of movement, while other provisions denied them the right to bear arms and encumbered their ability to enter into contracts and to buy and sell property. The Black Code did not ever refer to African Americans as citizens; they acquired only the duties and obligations, not the

rights of freedom. *Public Laws of the State of North Carolina Passed by the General Assembly at the Session of 1866* (Raleigh, 1866), chapter 40.

18. Quoted in Alexander, *North Carolina Faces the Freedmen*, 45; see 112–19 for a discussion of apprenticeship. See also Barbara Jeanne Fields, *Slavery and Freedom on the Middle Ground: Maryland during the Nineteenth Century* (New Haven: Yale University Press, 1985), 139–42; Eric Foner, *Reconstruction: America's Unfinished Revolution* (New York: Harper and Row, 1988), 201–2; Rebecca Scott, "The Battle over the Child: Child Apprenticeship and the Freedmen's Bureau in North Carolina," *Prologue* 10 (Summer 1978): 101–13.

19. For the status of free blacks, see Ira Berlin, *Slaves without Masters: The Free Negro in the Antebellum South* (New York: Pantheon, 1974); John Hope Franklin, *The Free Negro in North Carolina, 1790–1860* (Chapel Hill: University of North Carolina Press, 1943; reprint edition, New York: Russell and Russell, 1969); Guion Griffis Johnson, *AnteBellum North Carolina: A Social History* (Chapel Hill: University of North Carolina Press, 1937), 597–606. As Grossberg describes the situation in *Governing the Hearth*, 350, n. 69, free blacks could marry, "but this right was couched in terms that ensured that their marriages posed no threat to the slave system." As Charles Brantner Wilson argues in *The Black Codes of the South* (Tuscaloosa, Ala.: University of Alabama Press, 1965), 13–41, southern lawmakers based their states' Black Codes in the laws relating to free blacks before the war with the express purpose of making the position of ex-slaves like that of free blacks. The intent is clear in the "Report of the Commission . . . to Prepare a Code for the Freedmen of this State," *Sentinel*, 31 Jan. 1866; continued in 1 Feb. 1866.

20. Herbert G. Gutman, *The Black Family in Slavery and Freedom, 1750–1925* (New York: Pantheon Books, 1976), 204–7. Also see Berlin, Reidy, and Rowland, eds., *The Black Military Experience*; Ira Berlin, Barbara J. Fields, Thavolia Glymph, Joseph P. Reidy, and Leslie S. Rowland, eds., *Freedom: A Documentary History of Emancipation, 1861–1867*, series 1, vol. 1: *The Destruction of Slavery* (New York: Cambridge University Press, 1985); Fields, *Slavery and Freedom on the Middle Ground*, 100–130; Joseph P. Reidy, *From Slavery to Agrarian Capitalism in the Cotton Plantation South: Central Georgia, 1800–1880* (Chapel Hill: University of North Carolina Press, 1992), 108–35; Schwalm, *A Hard Fight for We*, 75–144, 234–68. (See note 4.)

21. *New York Tribune*, 8 Sept. 1865. Register of the Marriages of Free People, vols. 1 and 2, Granville County. For the symbolic importance of marriage and its popularity among freedpeople, see *The Black Family in Slavery and Freedom*, 412–18. The number in Granville County comes to 41 percent of the marriageable African American population, a figure far less than the 70 percent for nearby Warren County, but one that still nears Gutman's average. Also see Berlin, Reidy, and Rowland, eds., *The Black Military Experience*, 604–5, 623–24, 660–61, 709–12. Other scholars, however, emphasize freedpeople's caution; see note 30.

22. Quoted in Berlin, Reidy, and Rowland, eds., *The Black Military Experience*, 672. See also Schwalm, *A Hard Fight for We*, 234–68. Jim Cullen, "'I's a Man Now': Gender and African American Men," in *Divided Houses*, edited by Clinton and Silber, 76–91, is also suggestive on this point.

23. Assistant Superintendent Thomas W. Hay to Lieutenant Colonel Jacob W. Chur, 25 September 1867, Annual Reports of Operations Received from Staff and

Subordinate Officers, ser. 2463, Bureau of Refugees, Freedmen, and Abandoned Lands (BRFAL), RG 105, National Archives. The Sub-District of Warren included Warren, Franklin, and Granville Counties, all with sizeable black populations. Examples of complaints can be found in abundance in all levels of the Freedmen's Bureau and in the Apprentice Bonds of county courts, North Carolina Division of Archives and History (NCDAH). See also Ira Berlin, Stephen F. Miller, and Leslie S. Rowland, eds., "Afro-American Families in the Transition from Slavery to Freedom," *Radical History Review* 42 (1988): 107–11. For the development of the Bureau's position on apprenticeship in North Carolina, see Alexander, *North Carolina Faces the Freedmen*, 112–19; Scott, "The Battle over the Child." The Bureau's policies elsewhere in the South were similar. See Donald G. Nieman, *To Set the Law in Motion: The Freedmen's Bureau and the Legal Rights of Blacks, 1865–1868* (Millwood, New York: KTO Press, 1979), 78–82, 137–38.

24. Daniel A. Paschall to Major General Miles, 17 Sept. 1867, Letters Received, Records of the Assistant Commissioner for the State of North Carolina, BRFAL, National Archives Microfilm Publication M843. *Dick Hester* v. *William S. Hester*, Nov. 1867, Apprentice Bonds, Granville County, NCDAH. See also Schwalm, *Hard Fight for We*, 249–54. For the contrast to the antebellum period, see Victoria Bynum, "On the Lowest Rung: Court Control over Poor White and Free Black Women," *Southern Exposure* 12 (November-December 1984): 40–44.

25. *Kate Durham* v. *H.H. Rowland*, Aug. 1866 and Sept. 1866; see also *Sally Hicks* v. *Samuel R. Hunt and James P. Hunt*, letter and subpoena, February 1868, Apprentice Bonds, Granville County, NCDAH. See also Berlin, Miller, and Rowland, eds., "Afro-American Families," 116–18; Gutman, *The Black Family in Slavery and Freedom*, 409–10.

26. Hartog, "Marital Exits and Expectations," also notes the disjuncture between individuals' conceptions of marriage and legal definitions of it. Many African American leaders were quite aware that whites used marriage as a barometer of their people's fitness for freedom, and urged blacks to adopt the domestic patterns common among wealthier whites to convince the nation that ex-slaves deserved the rights and privileges of freedom. See Foner, *Reconstruction*, 87. For the importance of respectability to middle-class African Americans' reform agenda, see: Glenda Elizabeth Gilmore, *Gender and Jim Crow: Women and the Politics of White Supremacy in North Carolina, 1896–1920* (Chapel Hill: University of North Carolina Press, 1996); Evelyn Brooks Higginbotham, *Righteous Discontent: The Women's Movement in the Black Baptist Church, 1880–1920* (Cambridge: Harvard University Press, 1993).

27. Irvin Thompson alias Cherry Thompson, 37th Regiment, Company K, U.S. Colored Troops, Infantry, Civil War Pension Records, RG 15, National Archives. Also see Noralee Frankel, *Freedom's Women*; Schwalm, *A Hard Fight for We*, 234–68.

28. *Smith Watkins* v. *Dink Watkins*, Fall Term 1876; *E.B. Bullock* v. *Jane Bullock*, Fall Term 1876; both in Divorce Records, Granville County, NCDAH.

29. Ibid.

30. Quoted in Ira Berlin, Thavolia Glymph, Steven F. Miller, Joseph P. Reidy, Leslie S. Rowland, and Julie Saville, eds., *Freedom: A Documentary History of Emancipation, 1861–1867*, series 1, vol. 3: *The Wartime Genesis of Free Labor: The Lower*

South (New York: Cambridge University Press, 1991), 859. In *The Black Family in Slavery and Freedom*, 415–16, Gutman estimated the percentage of couples who registered their unions by comparing the number of registered marriages with the slave population aged twenty and over in 1860. Surveying fourteen counties in North Carolina, he concluded that the number of recorded marriages represented about 47 percent of all possible marriages. Of course, the figure is really a "guesstimate." Comparing registered unions to the entire slave population twenty and older presumes that all these people would be married and all adults are never married at any given time. Moreover, there is no way of knowing whether or not existing records are complete. Still, the estimate suggests that many freedpeople did not rush to legalize their marriages. For the reluctance of freedpeople to accept legal marriage, see Frankel, *Freedom's Women*; Schwalm, *A Hard Fight for We*, 244–48.

31. *State v. Rhodes*, 61 N.C. 453 (1868).

32. For discussions of this process in North Carolina, see William McKee Evans, *Ballots and Fence Rails: Reconstruction on the Lower Cape Fear* (Chapel Hill: University of North Carolina Press, 1966); Paul D. Escott, *Many Excellent People: Power and Privilege in North Carolina, 1850–1900* (Chapel Hill: University of North Carolina Press, 1985).

33. For an expanded discussion of these issues, see Edwards, *Gendered Strife and Confusion*. In the 1890s, apprenticeship resurfaced again with the "discovery" of the widespread abuse of apprentices by their masters. Still, black children were no longer taken from parents to be apprenticed to more "suitable" guardians. See *Second Annual Report of the Bureau of Labor Statistics of the State of North Carolina for the Year 1888* (Raleigh, 1888), 211–35.

34. *Taylor v. Taylor*, 76 N.C. 433 (1877). See also Peter Bardaglio, *Reconstructing the Household*, esp. 115–228. In *Governing the Hearth*, Grossberg makes a similar argument for the antebellum North.

35. *Taylor v. Taylor*, 76 N.C. 433 (1877).

36. *State v. Neely*, 74 N.C. 425 (1875).

37. *State v. Neely*, 74 N.C. 425 (1875).

38. Gilmore, *Gender and Jim Crow*; Dailey, "The Limits of Liberalism." Beginning in the late 1870s, conservative Democrats in North Carolina began to argue openly that the interests of African American and poor white men were dependent on and subsumed by the interests of white elite men. See Edwards, *Gendered Strife and Confusion*, 218–54.

Negotiating and Transforming the Public Sphere: African American Political Life in the Transition from Slavery to Freedom

On April 15, 1880, Margaret Osborne, Jane Green, Susan Washington, Molly Branch, Susan Gray, Mary A. Soach and "over two hundred other prominent sisters of the church" petitioned the Richmond, Virginia, First African Baptist Church's business meeting to allow women to vote on the pastor:

> We the sisters of the church feeling that we are interested in the welfare of the same and also working hard to finish the house and have been working by night and day . . . We know you have adopted a law in the church that the business must be done by the male members. We don't desire to alter that law, nor do we desire to have anything to do with the business of the church, we only ask to have a vote in electing or dismissing him. We whose names are attached to this petition ask you to grant us this privilege.[1]

The circumstances surrounding these women's petition suggest the kinds of changes taking place internally in late-nineteenth- and early-twentieth-century black Richmond and other southern black communities. In the immediate post–Civil War era women had voted in mass meetings and Republican Party conventions held at First African, thus contradicting gender-based assumptions within the larger society about politics, political engagement and appropriate forms of political behavior. Now, women sitting in the same church were petitioning for the right to vote in an internal community institution, couching the petition in terms designed to minimize the request and avoid a challenge to men's authority and position.

Scholars' assumptions of an unbroken line of exclusion of African American women from formal political associations in the late nineteenth century has obscured fundamental changes in the political understandings within African American communities in the transition from slavery to freedom. Women in First African and in other arenas were seeking in the late nineteenth century not a new authority but rather a lost authority, one they now often sought to justify on a distinctively female basis. As these women petitioned for their rights within the church and as other women formed voluntary associations in turn-of-the-century Richmond they were not, as often depicted in the scholarly literature, emerging into the political arena through such actions. Rather, these women were attempting to retain space they traditionally had held in the immediate post-emancipation period. This essay explores the processes of public discourse within Richmond and other southern black communities and the factors that led to increasingly more clearly gendered and class spaces within those communities to understand why women by the 1880s and 1890s needed to create their own pulpits from which to speak—to restore their voices to the community. This exploration suggests how the ideas, process, meanings, and practice of freedom changed within the late-nineteenth-century southern African American communities and what the implications of those changes may be for our visions of freedom and for the possibilities of African American community in the late twentieth century.

After emancipation, African American men, women, and children, as part of black communities throughout the South, struggled to define on their own terms the meaning of freedom and in the process to construct communities of struggle. Much of the literature on Reconstruction portrays freed African Americans as rapidly and readily adopting a gendered private-public dichotomy.[2] Much of the literature on the nineteenth-century public sphere constructs a masculine liberal bourgeois public with a female counterpublic.[3] This essay, focusing on the civic geography of post–Civil War black Richmond suggests the problematic of applying such generalizations to African American life in the late-nineteenth-century South. In the immediate post-emancipation era black Richmonders enacted their understandings of democratic political discourse through mass meetings attended and participated in (including voting) by men, women, and children and through mass participation in Republican Party conventions. They carried these notions of political participation into the state capitol, engaging from the gallery in the debates on the constitutional convention floor.

Central to African Americans' construction of a fully democratic notion of political discourse was the church as a foundation of the black public sphere.[4] In the post-slavery era, church buildings also served as meeting halls and auditoriums as well as educational and recreational facilities, employment and social service bureaus, and bulletin boards. First African, especially, with a seating capacity of nearly four thousand, was the site of large political gatherings. Schools such as Richmond Theological Seminary and Richmond Colored High and Normal School held their annual commencement exercises at First African Baptist, allowing these events to become community celebrations. Other groups, such as the Temperance Union, were regularly granted the church for their meetings or rallies. As a political space occupied by men, women, and children, literate and nonliterate, ex-slave and formerly free, church members and nonmembers, the availability and use of First African for mass meetings enabled the construction of political concerns in democratic space. This is not to suggest that official versions and spokespersons were not produced, but these official versions were the product of a fairly egalitarian discourse and, therefore, represented the conditions of black Richmonders of differing classes, ages, and genders. Within black Richmonders' construction of the public sphere, the forms of discourse varied from the prayer to the stump speech to the testimonies regarding outrages against freedpeople to shouted interventions from the galleries into the debates on the legislative floor. By the very nature of their participation—the inclusion of women and children, the engagement through prayer, the disregard of formal rules for speakers and audience, the engagement from the galleries in the formal legislative sessions—Afro-Richmonders challenged liberal bourgeois notions of rational discourse. Many white observers considered their unorthodox political engagements to be signs of their unfamiliarity and perhaps unreadiness for politics.[5]

In the decades following emancipation as black Richmonders struggled to achieve even a measured amount of freedom, the black public sphere emerged as more fractured and perhaps less democratic at the end of the nineteenth century, yet even then it retained strong elements of a democratic agenda. This essay examines the changing constructions of political space and community discourse in the post-emancipation era.

ENVISIONING FREEDOM

In April 1865, when Union troops marched into Richmond, jubilant African American men, women, and children poured into the streets and crowded into their churches to dance, kiss, hug, pray, sing, and shout. They assembled in First African, Third Street African Methodist, Ebenezer, and Second African not merely because of the need to thank God for their deliverance but also because the churches were the only institutional spaces, and in the case of First African certainly the largest space, owned by African Americans themselves.[6] As the process of reconstruction unfolded, black Richmonders continued to meet regularly in their churches, now not merely to rejoice. If Afro-Richmonders had thought freedom would accompany emancipation, the events of the first few weeks and months of Union occupation quickly disabused them of such ideas. Throughout the summer and fall of 1865 black Richmonders reported numerous violations of their rights. Among them were pass and curfew regulations designed to curtail black mobility and force African American men and women out of the city to labor in the rural areas. Pass and curfew violators (eight hundred in the first week of June) were detained in bullpens—one for women and children, a separate one for men—away from and often unknown to family members. Black Richmonders also detailed numerous incidents of disrespectful treatment, verbal abuse, physical assault, and torture. "Many poor women" told "tales of their frights and robberies"; vendors told of goods destroyed by military police. Private homes were not immune to the intrusions of civilian and military white men. One couple was confronted by soldiers, one of whom stood over them in bed "threatening to blow out their brains if they moved" while others "pillage[d] the house of money, watches, underclothing, etc."[7] Many spoke of the sexual abuse of black women: "gobbling up of the most likely looking negro women, thrown into the cells, robbed and ravished at the will of the guard." Men and women in the vicinity of the jail testified "to hearing women scream frightfully almost every night."[8]

The regular meetings in the African churches, originally ones of jubilation, quickly became the basis for constructing a discourse about freedom and organizing large-scale mass protest. On June 10, 1865, over three thousand assembled at First African to hear the report of the investigating committee that had conducted hearings and gathered the evidence and depositions necessary to present black Richmonders' case directly to Governor Francis H. Pierpoint and to the "chief head of all authority," the president of the United States. The protest memorial drawn up during the meeting was ratified at meetings in each of the other churches and money was raised through church collections to send six representatives (one from each church in Richmond and one from First Baptist, Manchester) to Washington. On Friday, June 16, these delegates delivered the mass meeting's protest directly to President Andrew Johnson:[9] "Mr. President: We have been appointed a committee by a public meeting of the colored people of Richmond, Va., to make known . . . the wrongs, as we conceive them to be, by which we are sorely oppressed." In their memorial, as in their meetings, black Richmonders recounted not merely the abuses but they also used their individual stories to construct a collective history and to combat the idea of being "idle negroes" unprepared for freedom.[10]

We represent a population of more than 20,000 colored people, including Richmond and Manchester . . . more than 6,000 of our people are members in good standing of Christian churches, and nearly our whole population constantly attend divine services. Among us there are at least 2,000 men who are worth $200 to $500; 200 who have property valued at from $1,000 to $5,000, and a number who are worth from $5,000 to $20,000. . . .

The law of Slavery severely punished those who taught us to read and write, but, not withstanding this, 3,000 of us can read, and at least 2,000 can read and write, and a large number of us are engaged in useful and profitable employment on our own account.

The community they described was one based in a collective ethos; it was not merely their industry but also their responsibility that was the basis on which they claimed their rights.

> None of our people are in the alms-house, and when we were slaves the aged and infirm who were turned away from the homes of hard masters, who had been enriched by their toil, our benevolent societies supported while they lived, and buried when they died, and comparatively few of us have found it necessary to ask for Government rations, which have been so bountifully bestowed upon the unrepentant Rebels of Richmond.

They reminded Johnson of the efforts black men and women in Richmond had taken to support the Union forces against the Confederacy.

> During the whole of the Slaveholders' Rebellion we have been true and loyal to the United States Government. . . . We have given aid and comfort to the soldiers of Freedom (for which several of our people, of both sexes, have been severely punished by stripes and imprisonment). We have been their pilots and their scouts, and have safely conducted them through many perilous adventures.

They declared themselves the loyal citizens of the United States, those the federal government should be supporting. And finally they invoked the religious destiny that emancipation had reaffirmed, reminding the president of a "motto once inscribed over the portals of an Egyptian temple, *'Know all ye who exercise power, that God hates injustice!'*"[11]

Mindful of others' versions of their history, standing, and entitlements, black Richmonders also moved to have their own story widely circulated. When local white newspapers refused to publish their account, they had it published in the *New York Tribune*.[12] Throughout 1865 and 1866 black Richmonders continued to meet regularly in mass meetings where men, women, and children collectively participated in constructing and announcing their own story of community and freedom.[13] The story told in those mass meetings, published in northern white newspapers, carried in protest to Union officials, was also carried into the streets as black Richmonders inserted themselves in the pre-existing national political traditions and at the same time widened those traditions. John O'Brien has noted that in the immediate aftermath of emancipation, black Richmonders developed their own political calendar, celebrating four civic holidays: January 1; George Washington's Birthday; April 3 (Emancipation Day); and July 4.[14] White Richmonders were horrified as they watched former slaves claim civic holidays and traditions they believed to be the historical possession of white Americans and occupy spaces, like Capitol Square, which had formerly been reserved for white residents.[15]

The underlying values and assumptions that would pervade much of black people's political struggles in the city were forged in slavery and war and in the weeks following emancipation. Military regulations that limited black mobility and made finding and reunifying family members even more difficult placed the economic interests of white men and women above the material and social interests of African Americans. The bullpens, which detained many away from their families, and the raids on black homes, which made all space public and subject to the interests of the state, obliterated any possible distinctions between public and private spheres. Demanding passes and evidence of employment denied black Richmonders the right to act and to be treated not as economic units and/or property but as social beings and family members. The difficulty of finding decent housing at affordable prices further impeded freedpeople's efforts to bring their families together. All of these obstacles to and expectations of family life were part of what Eric Foner speaks of as the "'politicization' of every day life."[16]

These political issues underpinned Afro-Richmonders' petition to Johnson and would continue to underpin their political struggles in late-nineteenth-century Richmond. Even as they fashioned individual stories into a collective history, black Richmonders could and did differ on the means by which they might secure freedom—vigorously debating issues such as the necessity of confiscation.[17] But they also understood freedom as a collective struggle. When they entered the formal political arena through Republican Party politics in 1867, this understanding was the foundation for their initial engagement with issues of suffrage and democracy. As Julie Saville has observed for South Carolina, freedpeople in Richmond "were not so much converted to the Republican Party as they were prepared to convert the Republican Party to themselves."[18] The post–Civil War southern black public sphere was forged in jubilation and struggle as African American men, women, and children claimed their own history and set forth their own political ideals.

All the resources of black Richmonders became elements in their political struggles. The *Richmond Whig*, intending to ridicule the inappropriateness of freedpeople's behaviors and assumptions, highlighted the politicized nature of all aspects of black life during Reconstruction; the freedpeople's "mass meetings, committee meetings, and meetings of the different societies all have political significance. The superstitions of the colored people are availed on, and religion and Radicalism are all jumbled together. Every night they have meetings and musterings, harangues and sermons, singing and praying—all looking to political results."[19] Similarly the *Richmond Dispatch* reported an 1867 Republican meeting which began with "Harris, colored" offering "the most remarkable" prayer "we have ever heard. It was frequently interrupted by laughter and manifestations of applause":

Oh, Lord God, bless our enemies—bless President Johnson. We would not even have him sent to hell. Come, oh come, good Lord, and touch his heart even while I am talking with you here to-night. [Amen.] Show him the error of his ways. Have mercy upon our 'Moses,' [Sarcastic, Great laughter and amens.] who, like Esau, has sold his birthright for a morsel of pottage—took us in the wilderness and left us there. Come down upon him, oh Lord, with thy blessing. God bless us in our meeting to-night, and help us in what we do. God forbid that we should choose any Conservative that has the spirit of the devil in his heart, and whose feet take hold on hell. God bless our friend—true and tried—Mr. Hunnicut, who has stood a great many sorrows and I think he can stand a great many more. [Laughter.] Bless our judge, Mr. Underwood, who is down here among us, and don't let anything harm a hair of his head.[20]

What the *Whig* and the *Dispatch* captured was a political culture in which the wide range of institutional and noninstitutional resources of individuals and the community as a whole became the basis for defining, claiming, and securing freedom in post-emancipation Richmond. The church provided more than physical space, financial resources, and a communication network; it also provided a cultural base that validated emotion and experience as ways of knowing, and drew on a collective call and response, encouraging the active participation of all.[21]

Virginia's rejection of the Fourteenth Amendment brought the state under the Reconstruction Act of 1867; a constitutional convention became prerequisite for full restoration to the Union. Black men, enfranchised for the delegate selection and ratification ballots, were to have their first opportunity to engage in the political parties and legislative chambers of the state. The struggles in which they had engaged in the two years since emancipation influenced the manner of black Richmonders' initial participation in the formal political arena of conventions and voting. On August 1, 1867, the day the Republican state convention opened in Richmond to adopt a platform for the upcoming state constitutional convention, thousands of African American men, women, and children absented themselves from their employment and joined the delegates at the convention site, First African Baptist Church.[22] Tobacco factories, lacking a major portion of their workers, were forced to close for the day.

This pattern persisted whenever a major issue came before the state and city Republican conventions held during the summer and fall of 1867, or the state constitutional convention that convened in Richmond from December 1867 to March 1868. A *New York Times* reporter estimated that "the entire colored population of Richmond" attended the October 1867 local Republican convention where delegates to the state constitutional convention were nominated. Noting that female domestic servants were a large portion of those in attendance, the correspondent reported: "as is usual on such occasions, families which employ servants were forced to cook their own dinners, or content themselves with a cold lunch. Not only had Sambo gone to the Convention, but Dinah was there also."[23]

These men and women did not absent themselves from work just to be onlookers at the proceedings, but to be active participants. They assumed as equal a right to be present and participate as the delegates themselves, a fact they made abundantly clear at the August 1867 Republican state convention. Having begun to arrive four hours before the opening session, African American men and women had filled the meeting place long before the delegates arrived. Having shown up to speak for themselves, they did not assume delegates had priority in discussion or in seating. Disgusted at the scene, as well as unable to find a seat, the conservative white Republican delegates removed to the Capitol Square to convene an outdoor session. That was quite acceptable to the several thousand additional African American men and women who, unable to squeeze into the church, were now still able to participate in the important discussions and to vote down the proposals of the conservative faction.[24]

Black men, women, and children were also active participants throughout the state constitutional convention. A *New York Times* reporter commented on the tendency for the galleries to be crowded "with the 'unprivileged,' and altogether black." At issue was not just these men's and women's presence but also their behavior. White women, for example, certainly on occasion sat in the convention's gallery as visitors silently observing the proceedings; these African Americans, however, participated from the gallery, loudly engaging in the debates. At points of heated controversy, black delegates turned to the crowds as they made their addresses on the convention floor, obviously soliciting and relying upon mass participation. Outside the convention hours, mass meetings were held to discuss and vote on the major issues. At these gatherings vote was either by voice or rising and men, women, and children voted. These meetings were not mock assemblies; they were important gatherings at which the community made plans for freedom. The most radical black Republican faction argued that the major convention issues should actually be settled at these mass meetings with delegates merely casting the community's vote on the convention floor. Though this did not occur, black delegates were no doubt influenced by both the mass meetings and the African American presence in the galleries, both of which included women.[25]

Black Richmonders were operating in two separate political arenas: an internal one and an external one. While these arenas were related, they each proceeded from different assumptions, had different purposes, and therefore operated according to different rules. Within the internal political process women were enfranchised and participated in all public forums—the parades, rallies, mass meetings, and the conventions themselves.[26] Richmond was not atypical in this regard.[27]

It was the state constitutional convention, however, that would decide African American women's and men's status in the political process external to the African American community. When the Virginia convention began its deliberation regarding the franchise, Thomas Bayne, a black delegate from Norfolk, argued the inherent link between freedom and suffrage, and contended that those who opposed universal suffrage were actually opposing the freedom of African American people. In rejoinder, E. L. Gibson, a conservative white delegate, enunciated several principles of republican representative government. Contending that "a man might be free and still not have the right to vote," Gibson explained the fallacy of assuming that this civil right was an inherent corollary to freedom: if the right were inherent then it would belong to both sexes and to all from "the first moment of existence" and to foreigners immediately. This was "an absurdity too egregious to be contemplated."[25] And yet, this "absurd" notion of political rights was what was in practice in the Richmond black community—males and females voted without regard to age, the thousands of rural migrants who came into Richmond suffered no waiting period but immediately possessed the full rights of the community. What was absurd to Gibson and most white men—Republican or Democrat—was obviously quite rational to many black Richmonders. Two very different conceptions of freedom and public participation in the political process were in place.

In the end only men obtained the legal franchise. The impact of this decision is neither inconsequential nor fully definitive. African American women were by law excluded from the formal political arena external to their community. Yet this does not mean that they were not active in that arena; witness Richmond women's participation in the Republican and the constitutional conventions. Southern black men and women debated the issue of women's suffrage in both the external and internal political arenas. In Nansemond County, Virginia, for example, the mass meetings resolved that women should be granted the legal franchise; in Richmond, while a number of participants in a mass meeting supported female suffrage, the majority opinion swung against it.[29] But the meaning of that decision was not as straightforward as it may seem. The debate as to whether women should be given the vote in the external political arena occurred in internal political arena mass meetings where women participated and voted not just before and during, *but also after* the negative decision regarding legal enfranchisement. This maintained the status quo in the external community; ironically enough, the status quo in the internal community was maintained as well—women continued to have the vote. African American men and women clearly operated within two distinct political systems.

Focusing on formal disfranchisement obscures women's continued participation in the external political arena. In Richmond and throughout the South exclusion from legal enfranchisement did not prevent African American women from shaping the vote and the political decisions. Throughout the late 1860s and 1870s women continued to participate in political meetings in large numbers and to organize political societies. Some like the Rising Daughters of Liberty and the Daughters of the Union Victory in Richmond or the United Daughters of Liberty organized by coal miners' wives living outside Manchester had all-female memberships. Others, like the two-thousand-member National Political Aid Society, the Union League of Richmond, and the Union Equal Rights League of Manchester had male and female members. Even though white Republicans made efforts to exclude them from further participation in political meetings by the late 1860s, African American women in Virginia, South Carolina, Louisiana, and elsewhere were still attending these meetings in the 1870s.

Women's presence at these meetings was anything but passive. In the violent political atmosphere of the last years of Reconstruction, they had an especially important and dangerous role. In South Carolina, for example, while the men participated in the meeting, the women guarded the guns—thus serving in part as the protectors of the meeting. For those women and men who lived in outlying areas of Richmond and attended outdoor meetings, political participation was a particularly dangerous matter, a fact they clearly recognized. Meetings were guarded by posted sentinels with guns who questioned the intent of any suspicious people, usually white men, coming to the meeting. A reporter for the *Richmond Daily Dispatch* described one such encounter when he attempted to cover a political meeting of fifty women and twenty-five men.[30]

Women as well as men took election day off from work and went to the polls. Fraud, intimidation, and violence became the order of election days. White newspapers and politicians threatened loss of jobs, homes, and lives. Afro-Richmonders countered with a group presence. Often even those living within the city and short distances from the polling places went early, even the night before, and camped out at the polls, hoping that their early presence would require the acceptance of their vote and that the group presence would provide protection from violence and intimidation. In the highly charged political atmosphere of late-nineteenth-century Richmond it was no small matter for these women and men to participate in political meetings and to show up at the election sites. The reasons for the group presence at the polls were varied. African American women in Virginia, Mississippi, South Carolina, and elsewhere understood themselves to have a vital stake in African American men's franchise. The fact that only men had been granted the vote did not at all mean that only men should exercise the vote. Women throughout the South initiated sanctions against men who voted Democratic; some went along to the polls to insure a properly cast ballot. As increasing white fraud made black men's voting more difficult, early arrival at the polls was partly intended to counter such efforts.

Although election days in Richmond were not as violent as they were elsewhere throughout Virginia and other parts of the South, guns were used to intimidate and defraud. It is also probable that in Richmond, as elsewhere throughout the South, when black men went to camp out overnight at the polls, households feared leaving women and children unprotected at home. Thus the women's presence, just as the group presence of the men, may have been a sign of the need for collective protection. If Richmond women were at all like their sisters in South Carolina and Danville, they may have carried weapons with them—to protect themselves and/or help protect the male voters.[31] Women and children's presence reflects their excitement about the franchise but also their understanding of the dangers involved in voting. The necessity for a group presence at the polls reinforced the sense of collective enfranchisement. Women's presence at the polls was both a negative sanction and a positive expression of the degree to which they understood the men's franchise to be a new political opportunity for themselves as well as their children.

In the dangerous political atmosphere of the late nineteenth century, the vote took on a sacred and collective character. Black men and women in Richmond, as throughout the South, initiated sanctions against those black men perceived as violating the collective good by supporting the conservative forces. Black Democrats were subject to the severest exclusion: disciplined within or quite often expelled from their churches and mutual benefit societies; denied board and lodging with black families. Additionally, mobs jeered, jostled, and sometimes beat black Democrats or rescued those who were arrested for such acts. Women were often reported to be in the forefront of this activity. Similarly, black women were said to have "exercised a positive influence upon some men who were inclined to hesitate or be indifferent" during the early 1880s Readjuster campaigns.[32]

All of this suggests that African American women and men understood the vote as a collective, not an individual, possession; and furthermore, that African American women, unable to cast a separate vote, viewed African American men's vote as equally theirs. They believed that franchise should be cast in the best interest of both. This is not the nineteenth-century patriarchal notion that men voted on behalf of their wives and children. By that assumption women had no individual wills; rather men operated in women's best interest because women were assumed to have no right of input. African American women assumed the political rights that came with being a member of the community even though they were denied the political rights they thought should come with being citizens of the state.

To justify their political participation Richmond and other southern black women in the immediate post–Civil War period did not need to rely on arguments of superior female morality or public motherhood. Their own cultural, economic, and political traditions provided rationale enough. An understanding of collective autonomy was the basis on which African Americans reconstructed families, developed communal institutions, constructed schools, and engaged in formal politics after emancipation. The participation of women and children in the external and internal political arenas was part of a larger political worldview of ex-slaves and free men and women, a worldview fundamentally shaped by an understanding that freedom, in reality, would accrue to each of them individually only when it was acquired by all of them collectively. Such a worldview contrasted sharply with the "possessive individualism" of liberal democracy.[33] This sense of suffrage as a collective, not an individual, possession was the foundation for much of African American women's political activities in the post–Civil War era.[34] Within these understandings the boundary lines between men's and women's political behavior were less clearly drawn and active participation in the political arenas—internal or external—seldom required a retreat into womanhood or manhood as its justification.

Even in the organization of militia units, post-emancipation black Richmonders, at least for a time, rejected the liberal bourgeois ideal of a solely male civic domain. By 1886 black men had organized three militia companies. By the late 1870s black women had also organized a militia company, although apparently only for ceremonial purposes; it reportedly was active only before and during emancipation celebrations. Its members conducted preparatory drills on Broad Street, one of Richmond's main thoroughfares. Frank Anthony, the man who prepared and drilled the women's company, demanded military precision and observance of regular military commands.[35] Unlike the men participating in the militias, who came from working-class, artisan, business, and professional backgrounds, the women were probably working-class. Although they served no self-defense role, their drilling in Richmond streets and marching in parades challenged ideas and assumptions about appropriate public behavior held by both white southerners and white Unionists. The women's unit not only challenged, as did the men's, the idea of black subservience, but also suggested wholly new forms and meanings of respectable female behavior. There is no evidence concerning how long this women's unit survived or the causes of its demise. We can speculate that, besides horrifying whites, such a unit may have also become unacceptable to a number of black Richmonders. Increasingly, concerns about respectable behavior were connected to the public behavior of the working class and of women. This black women's militia, however, suggests the fluidity of gender notions in the early years of emancipation. The brevity of its appearance suggests how questions of public behavior became integral within black Richmond, just as they had been within the larger society. Yet for a time the actions of these women declared that perhaps no area of political participation or public ceremony was strictly a male domain.

RENEGOTIATING PUBLIC LIFE

The 1880 First African women's petition followed three contentious church meetings, some lasting until two or three o'clock in the morning, at which the congregants considered dismissing and/or excluding the pastor, the Reverend James H. Holmes. This discussion was initiated at a 5 April meeting where two women were charged with fighting about the pastor. The 6 April meeting considered charges of "unchristian conduct" on the part of Holmes; those men present voted to exclude Holmes. A meeting on 11 April endorsed a protest signed by all but two of the deacons against the earlier proceedings. The protest charged the anti-Holmes faction with trying to "dispose of the deacons, take charge of prayer meetings, the Sunday school and revolutionize things generally." The discussions that ensued over the next two months split the congregation; the May and June church business meetings were "disorderly" and "boisterous." Holmes and the deacons called in the mayor, city court judge, and chief of police to support the pastor and the police to remove or arrest those members of the congregation designated as "rebellious." After the anti-Holmes faction was removed from the church, the June meeting expelled forty-six men for "rebelliously attempting to overthrow and seize upon the church government." It also excluded the two women initially charged, one for fighting and the other for tattling; exonerated Holmes "from all false" accusations; and thanked the civil officers who attended the meeting and restored order. Only after these actions did the church consider the women's petition, which had been presented in the midst of the controversy more than two months earlier.

First African's records do not adequately reveal the nature of gender relations within the church in the late 1860s and 1870s. We do know that the pre–Civil War sex-segregated seating patterns were abandoned by Richmond black Baptist churches immediately after the Civil War and that by the late 1860s women "not only had a voice, but voted in the business meetings" of Ebenezer Baptist Church.[37] Women who voted in political meetings held in First African in the late 1860s and 1870s may have carried this participation over to church business meetings. Often in the immediate post–Civil War period, business and political meetings were not clearly distinguishable.

The petition of the women of First African makes clear, however, that by the early 1880s, while women attended and apparently participated in church meetings, the men had "adopted a law in the church that the business must be done by the male members." Whether Margaret Osborne, Jane Green, and others thought that their voices and interests were being inadequately represented, even ignored, by the deacons, or wanted to add their voices to those, including the deacons, who were struggling to retain Holmes and control of First African, these women understood that they would have to defend their own rights. The women argued their right to decide on the pastor, justifying their petition by both their work on behalf of the church and the importance of their economic support to the church's ongoing activities and to the pastor's salary. Not until after the matter of Holmes's exclusion was settled were the petitioners granted their request. Since they apparently remained within First African, the petitioners' organization probably indicates that they were not among those dissatisfied with Holmes. It does suggest, however, their dissatisfaction with church procedure and the place of women in church polity. Still, the petition was conservative and the women denied any intention to demand full voting rights in church matters. The petition was not taken as a challenge to church authority, as were the actions of the anti-Holmes faction. When brought up for a vote in the June meeting, the women's petition was adopted by a vote of 413 to 16.[38]

The women's petition and the vote in favor of it suggest the tenuous and ambiguous position that women had come to occupy both within First African and within the internal political arena more generally. They participated actively in church meetings but the authority for that participation and the question of limiting women's role resurfaced throughout the late nineteenth century. In the 1890s the women of First African would again have to demand their rights, this time against challenges to their very presence at church meetings, when a deacon sought to prohibit women from even attending First African business meetings. The women protested and the church responded quickly by requiring the deacon to apologize to the women and assure them that they were welcome at the meetings. The degree of women's participation and decision-making powers, however, remained ambiguous.

In 1901–1902 during another crisis period in First African, a number of men sought to blame the problems on women. John Mitchell, Jr., a member of First African and editor of the *Richmond Planet*, cited the active participation of women ("ladies who knew nothing of the machinery at work or the deep laid plans on foot") and children ("Sunday School scholars from 8 years of age upward") in church affairs, suggesting that they did not comprehend the proceedings and had been easily misled or manipulated by male factions. Deacon J. C. Farley cited women's active participation in church meetings as the problem, reminding the congregation that "it was the rule of the church" that women were only allowed to vote on the pastor but had extended their participation far past that. And the new minister, the Reverend W. T. Johnson, admonished the women, saying that "the brethren could almost fight in the church meeting and when they went out they would shake hands and laugh and talk. But the sisters would talk about it going up Broad St. and everybody would know what they had done." First African women rejected these assessments of their church's problems. A significant number walked out rather than have their participation censured; those who remained reportedly refused to be silent but continually "talked out in the meeting." Sister Margaret Hewlett later sought out the editor of the *Richmond Planet* to voice her opposition to the men's denunciation of women's roles and to make clear that the women thought the church's problems lay in the male leadership, saying specifically "the deacons were the cause of all the trouble anyway."[39]

In the early 1890s, the *Virginia Baptist* publicized its belief that women, in exceeding their proper places in the church by attempting to preach, and in the community by their "deplorable" efforts to "exercise the right of suffrage," would lose their "womanliness."[40] The complexity of gender relations within the African American community was such that at the same time First African was debating women's attendance at church meetings and the *Virginia Baptist* was advocating a severely restricted women's role, other women such as Alice Kemp were known throughout the community as the authors of prominent male ministers' sermons and women such as the Reverend Mrs. Carter were establishing their reputations as "soul-stirring" preachers. The *Richmond Planet* reported these women's activities without fanfare, as if they were commonplace. The debate over women's roles also had become commonplace. The Reverend Anthony Binga, pastor of First Baptist (Manchester), noted the debate in his sermon on Church Polity: Binga supported women teaching Sunday School, participating in prayer-meetings and voting "on any subject pertaining to the interest of the church" including the pastor; but he interpreted the Bible as forbidding women "throwing off that modesty that should adorn her sex, and taking man's place in the pulpit." The subject received community-wide attention in June 1895 when Ebenezer Baptist Church staged a debate between the ministers of Second Baptist (Manchester) and Mount Carmel, judged by other ministers from Fourth Baptist, First African, First Baptist (Manchester) and others on the subject. "Resolved that a woman has every right and privilege that a man has in the christian church."[41]

The debates within First African and other churches over women's roles were part of a series of political struggles within black Richmond in the late nineteenth and early twentieth centuries. As formal political gains, initially secured, began to recede and economic promise became less certain and less surely tied to political advancement, the political struggles over relationships between the working class and the newly emergent middle class, between men and women, between literate and nonliterate, increasingly became issues among Afro-Richmonders. Briefly examining how the sites of public discourse changed and how discussions regarding qualifications for and nature of individual participation developed suggests the degree to which debates over space and relationships represented important changes in many black Richmonders' assumptions about freedom itself.

The authority of the church in personal and civil matters decreased over the late nineteenth and early twentieth centuries. The church quietly acknowledged these changes without directly confronting the issue of its changed authority. The use of civil authorities to resolve the church dispute, especially since individual members continued to face censure if they relied on civil rather than church sanctions in a dispute with another member, suggests the degree to which First African tried to maintain its traditional authority over its members while acknowledging the limitations of its powers. First African turned outside not only itself but also the black community by inviting the intervention of the mayor, police chief and judge.[42] The decreasing authority of the church, however, accompanied a shrinking sphere of influence and activity for the church and the development of secular institutions and structures to take over, compete for, or share functions traditionally connected to the church as institution and structure. The changing church axis suggests important developments in the structures, nature, and understandings of community in black Richmond.

After the Reverend James Holmes and the deacons of First African survived the 1880 challenge to their leadership, one of their first actions was to establish a regulation that church business meetings be closed to all but members. They had argued that it was ouside agitators who had instigated and sustained the disorder and opposition. While this reflects concerns about internal church business, the closing off of the church was reflected in other central ways that potentially had more far-reaching consequences, and suggests the particularization of interests, concerns, and functions of internal community institutions, and the changed nature of internal community politics. Having completed, at considerable expense, their new edifice, First African worried about avoiding damage and excess wear and tear. In November 1882 the church adopted regulations designed to eliminate the crowds of people attending weddings in the church by requiring guest lists and tickets, and to deny entirely the use of the main auditorium with the largest capacity for "programmes, closing of public schools, political meetings or feasts." In February 1883 when the Acme Lyceum requested use of the main auditorium for a lecture by Frederick Douglass, the church, following its new regulations, refused to grant the request, although it did offer as a substitute the use of its smaller lecture room. That same year it denied the use of the church for the Colored High and

Normal closing. The paucity of facilities available to black Richmonders meant that these activities now had to be held in much smaller facilities and the possibilities for the large mass meetings that First African had previously hosted were now reduced. Political meetings and other activities moved to other, smaller church sites or to some of the new halls being erected by some of the societies and businessmen. The latter, however, were more expensive to obtain since their rental was a major source of revenue for the group or individual owner; it also often particularized the meeting or occasion to a specific segment of the community. Without the large facility of First African, graduations and school closings could no longer be the traditional community-wide mass celebrations. Denied the use of First African and barred from the Richmond Theatre where the white high school students had their graduation, the 1883 Colored High and Normal graduation class held their exercises in a small classroom where very few could attend.[43]

First African did not initiate and was not singly responsible for the changing nature of Republican Party participation, but its actions reinforced the narrower sense of party politics that white Republicans had already tried to enforce. Disturbed at black influence over Republican meetings, beginning in 1870 white Republican officials had taken steps to limit popular participation and influence in party deliberations. First they moved the party conventions from First African to the United States courtroom, a facility that held many fewer people and was removed from the black community; then they closed the gallery, thus allowing none but official delegates to attend and participate. In such a setting they were able to adopt a more conservative platform. Black Republicans had continued, however, to hold mass meetings, often when dissatisfied with the official Republican deliberations. When they were dissatisfied with Republican nominees for municipal office that came from the 1870 closed party convention, for example, black Republicans agreed to convene their own sessions and make their own nominations.[44]

In increasingly delimiting the church's use, distinguishing more clearly between sacred and secular activities as when it began to disallow certain kinds of entertainments in its facilities or on its behalf, and attempting to reserve the church for what was now designated as the "sacred," First African contributed to the increasing segmentation of black Richmond.[45] With the loss of the largest capacity structure some black Richmonders recognized the need to reestablish a community space. Edward A. Randolph, founder and first editor of the *Richmond Planet*, used Acme Literary Association meetings to argue regularly throughout 1883 and 1884 for the construction of a hall, a public meeting place within the community. His call was reinforced when the Choral Association was denied use of the Richmond Theatre and had to have its production in a small mutual benefit society hall, an inadequate facility for such a production. The construction of a large auditorium on the top floor of the Grand Fountain, United Order of True Reformers' bank and office building when it opened in 1890 was an effort to provide that space. It could hold larger gatherings than the other halls and most churches but still had only a small percentage of the seating capacity of First African.[46] A mass meeting on the scale common in the 1860s and 1870s could be held only outside the community, and the facilities for such were often closed to African Americans. As political meetings moved to private halls rather than church buildings, they became less mass meetings not only in the numerical sense; they also became more gatherings of an exclusive group of party regulars. This signaled not only a change in the role of the church but also a change in the nature of politics in black Richmond. The emerging format gave business and professional men, especially, greater control over the formal political process. First African's prohibitions against mass meetings, school closings, and other programs did not last long; the need and desire of members and other Afro-Richmonders for a space that could truly contain a community-wide activity eventually led members to ignore their prohibition. But instituting the prohibition had not only significantly affected community activities in the early 1880s; it also meant that, even after strict enforcement was curtailed, decisions about using the church for graduation exercises, political meetings, and other activities were now subjects of debate. Afro-Richmonders could no longer assume the church as a community meeting place; instead they had to argue such. The church remained an important community institution, but it increasingly shared power with both civil authorities and other community institutions such as mutual benefit and fraternal societies.

The efforts by white Republican officials to limit popular decision-making and the decreased accessibility of First African as a community-wide meeting place affected a politics that had been based in mass participation. Mass meetings were still held throughout the late nineteenth century, but they were now less regular. These changes were exacerbated by the struggle to retain the vote and office-holding and the necessity, therefore, to counter various tactics of both white Republicans and Democrats. The fraudulent tactics employed to eliminate black voters, for example, led some black Republicans, like John Mitchell, who continued to argue against literacy qualifications for voting, in the 1890s to encourage nonliterate black men to abstain from voting. Difficulty with many of the election officials' questions and with the ballots could not only delay the line but also the nonliterate voter's rights and/or ballot would more likely be challenged. Mitchell thought it important to get those least likely to be challenged or disqualified, and most capable of correctly marking the ballots, through the lines first before polls closed on them. While Mitchell argued for a temporary change in practice—not perspective—regarding the right of all to vote, his and other prominent black Republicans' prioritizing of the literate voter significantly changed the makeup of the presumed electorate.

As the divisions between black and white Republicans became deeper in the 1890s, Mitchell and other black Republicans began to hold small Republican caucuses in selected homes, in essence attempting to control ward conventions by predetermining nominees and issues. The ward conventions themselves were often held in halls rather than the larger churches. The organization in 1898 of a Central Republican League, which would oversee black Republican activities through sub-Leagues in all the city's wards, reinforced the narrowing party politics framework. Republican Party decision-making was now more clearly limited to Party regulars; the mass of black voters and other election activists were expected to support these channels of decision-making.[47] These changes, consistent with democratic politics and republican representative government as practiced in late-nineteenth-century United States, served to limit the power and influence of most black Richmonders in the electoral arena. If many black men abandoned electoral politics even before formal disfranchisement, it was in large measure due to the effectiveness of the extralegal disfranchisement efforts of white men. The exclusion from real decision-making power within the Republican Party and, in this respect within the community, was also decisive.

The increasingly limited notion of political decision-makers that these changes encouraged is also evident in other ways. In 1896, during a factional dispute among black Republicans, John Mitchell challenged the decisions made in one meeting by noting that a substantial portion of those attending and participating were not even "legal voters," that is, they were women. Although he espoused feminine dress and comportment, Mitchell supported women's rights and championed Dr. Sarah G. Jones's success as a physician as evidence of women's equality. He also endorsed women's suffrage while advising black women to understand the racism of the white women's suffrage movement and not to align themselves with it. Despite these personal convictions, Mitchell could dismiss or minimize opposing factions by a reference to the participation of women, suggesting the ways in which the meanings and understandings of politics, of appropriate political actors, and even of the ownership of the franchise had changed in the late nineteenth century.[48]

Questions of qualifications for participation in the external political arena and internal community institutions were now frequent. During the conflictual 1901 business meeting at First African, for example, John Mitchell, Jr., questioned his opponents' right to participate even though they were all church members by pointing out their unfamiliarity with parliamentary procedure or their inelegant ways of speaking. The women, who were the targets of much of Mitchell's challenge, refused to accept these as criteria for their participation and even denigrated what he put forth as his formal qualifications by talking out when he got up to speak, saying derisively, "Don't he look pretty."[49] Questions of formal education had already affected the congregation in fundamental ways, most obviously in the late-nineteenth-century debate over song, a debate that represented a significant change in the basis of collective consciousness.

The antiphonal nature of the traditional church service at First African and many black churches reinforced a sense of community. The services included spontaneous verbal and nonverbal interaction between minister and prayer, speaker, and congregation, thus allowing for the active participation of everyone in the worship service. It was this cultural discourse that was carried over into the political meetings. One important element that bound the congregation together was song; as Lawrence Levine has noted, through their collective song churchgoers "meld[ed] individual consciousness into the group consciousness."[50] However, the practice of lining hymns, which was basic to collective song, was one that white visitors often referred to when they described what they perceived as the unrefined black church services. Some black churchgoers saw the elimination of this practice as part of the work of uplifting the religious style and uplifting the race. But with the elimination of this practice, those unable to read and follow the lyrics in a song book were now unable to participate, to be fully a part of the community, the collective. It was the equivalent of being deprived of a voice, all the more significant in an oral culture. Daniel Webster Davis, a member of First African and pastor of Second Baptist (Manchester) as well as public school teacher, suggested such in his poem, "De Linin' Ub De Hymns":

> Dar's a mighty row in Zion, an' de debbil's gittin' high,
>
> . . . .
>
> 'Twuz 'bout a berry leetle thing—de linin' ub a hymn.
> De young folks say 'tain't stylish to lin' um out no mo';
> Dat dey's got edikashun, an' dey wants us all to know
> Dey likes to hab dar singin'-books a-holin' fore dar eyes,
> An' sing de hymns right straight along "to manshuns in de skies."
>
> . . . .
>
> An' ef de ol' folks will kumplain 'cause dey is ol' an' blin',
> An' slabry's chain don' kep' dem back frum larnin' how to read—
> Dat dey mus' take a corner seat, an' let de young folks lead.
>
> . . . .
>
> We don' edikate our boys an' gals, an' would do de same again;
>
> . . . .

De sarmon's highfalutin', an' de church am mighty fin';

. . . .

De ol'-time groans an' shouts an' moans am passin' out ub sight—
Edikashun changed all dat, an' we belebe it right,
We should serb God wid 'telligence; fur dis one thing I plead:
Jes' lebe a leetle place in church fur dem ez kin not read.[51]

The debates about women's roles in the church and in the more formal political arenas, like the debate over lining the hymns, were part of widespread discussions about the nature of community, of participation and of freedom.

The proliferation of scholarly works centered on the flowering of black women's political activity in the late nineteenth and early twentieth centuries[52] has perhaps left the impression that this was the inaugural moment or even height of black women's participation in politics. Overt or not, the suggestion seems to be that black women came to political prominence as (because) black men lost political power.[53] In much of this scholarship the reasons for black women's "emergence" are usually tied to external factors. For example, the development of black women's clubs in the late nineteenth century and their important roles in the political struggles of the twentieth century most often have been seen by historians as the result of the increasing development of such entities in the larger society and as reactions to vitriolic attacks on the morality of black women. Such a perspective explains this important political force solely in terms of external dynamics, but external factors alone cannot account for this development.[54] The internal political arena, which in the immediate post–Civil War era was grounded in the notion of a collective voice that gave men, women, and children a platform and allowed them all participation, came increasingly in the late nineteenth century to be shaped by a narrowing notion of politics and appropriate political behavior.

While mass meetings continued to be held, the more regular forums for political discussions were literary societies, ward meetings, mutual benefit society and fraternal society meetings, women's clubs, labor organizations, newspapers, streetcorners, kitchens, washtubs, and saloons. In the development of literary societies as a primary venue for public discussion, one can see the class and gender assumptions that by the turn of the century came to be central to the political organization of black Richmond. While some, as the Langston Literary Association, had male members only, most of the literary societies founded in the 1880s and 1890s had middle-class and working-class men and women members. Despite the inclusive nature of the membership and often of the officers, the form of discussion that developed privileged middle-class males. Unlike mass meetings where many people might take the floor in planned and unplanned expositions and attendees might freely interrupt or talk back to speakers, thus allowing and building mass participation, literary forums announced discussion topics in advance; charged individual members, apparently almost always male, to prepare a paper on the subject; and designated specific, also male, members to reply.

The discussions that then ensued were open to all present, but the structure privileged those familiar with the conventions of formal debate. Women, who served as officers and attended in large numbers, may have joined in the discussion but their official roles were designated as the cultural arm of the forum—reading poetry, singing songs, often with political content appropriate to the occasion. The questions under consideration at the meetings often betrayed the class bias of the forum. Even when the discussions centered on some aspect of working-class life and behavior, the conversation was conducted by middle-class men. The purpose of the forums, as articulated by the Acme Literary Society, suggested the passive observer/learner position that most were expected to take: to hold "discussions, lectures, and to consider questions of vital importance to our people, so that the masses of them may be drawn out to be entertained, enlightened, and instructed thereby."[55] Given the exclusionary nature of the discussion in these literary forums, even though welcoming a wide audience, it is understandable that far more working-class black men and women saw the Knights of Labor as their principal political vehicle in the late 1880s.[56]

In the changing circumstances of the late nineteenth century, working-class men and women and middle-class women were increasingly disfranchised within the black community, just as middle-class black men were increasingly disfranchised in the larger society. Men and women, working-class and middle-class, at the turn of the century were struggling to move back to a political authority they once had—internally and externally. As they did so they each often justified such authority along distinctively gendered and class-based lines.

African American men countered the image of themselves as uncivilized, beastly rapists—an image white southerners used to justify disfranchisement, segregation, and violence—with efforts to demonstrate their own manhood and to define white males as uncivilized and savage.[57] While white Richmonders told stories of black barbarity, John Mitchell, Jr., inverted the tale. The *Richmond Planet*, for example, repeatedly focused on the sexual perversions of white men with cases of rape and incest and spoke of white men in terms designed to suggest their barbarism: "Southern white folks have gone to roasting Negroes, we presume the next step will be to eat them."[58] In the process of unmanning white males, however, Mitchell and others developed a narrative of endangered black women. Urban areas, once sites of opportunity for women, became sexually dangerous places for the unprotected female, easy prey to deceitful and barbarous white males.[59] Black men's political rights were essential so that they could do as men should—protect their communities, homes, families, women. The focus on manhood could, initially, be the venue for discussing domestic violence as well. For example, the Reverend Anthony Binga, sermonizing against physical abuse of one's wife, drew on the discourse of manhood: "I have never seen a man whip his wife. I mean a *man*. Everyone who wears a hat or a coat is not a *man*. I mean a *man*." And the members of First African took as a serious issue of concern the case of a husband who had infected his wife with syphilis.[60] Concurrent with the narrative of sexual danger in the city and the larger society was an implied corollary narrative of protection within one's own community. Thus the discourse on manhood could keep the concern with violence against women in the public discussion while at the same time setting the stage for issues of domestic abuse and other forms of intraracial violence, which could be evidence of the uncivility of black men, to be silenced as politically dangerous.

In drawing on the new narrative of endangered women, middle-class black women, increasingly disfranchised by the connections between manhood and citizenship in the new political discourse, turned the focus from themselves and on to the working class, enabling middle-class women to project themselves as the protectors of their less fortunate sisters. In this manner they reinserted themselves into a public political role.[61] Autonomous women's organizations, such as the Richmond Women's League (later the Richmond Mothers' Club), or women's divisions within other organizations, such as the Standing Committee on Domestic Economy of the Hampton Negro Conference, developed to serve these functions. These associations promulgated class-specific ideas of respectability, in part justifying their public role through the need to impart such protective measures to working-class women. Specific constructions of womanhood, as manhood, thus became central to the arguments for political rights. Through discussions of manhood and womanhood, middle-class men and women constructed themselves as respectable and entitled, and sought to use such constructions to throw a mantle of protection over their working-class brothers and sisters. By increasingly claiming sexual violence as a women's issue, middle-class black women claimed a political/public space for themselves but they also contributed to an emerging tendency to divert issues of sexual violence to a lesser plane and to see them as the specific interest of women, not bound up in the general concerns and struggle for freedom. This set the stage for the masculine conception of liberation struggle, which would emerge in the twentieth century.[62]

COLLECTIVE HISTORY/COLLECTIVE MEMORY

In July 1895 three black women—Mary Abernathy, Pokey Barnes, and her mother, Mary Barnes—were convicted in Lunenberg County, Virginia, of murdering a white woman. When the women were moved to the state penitentiary in Richmond their case became a cause célèbre in the black community there. For over a year black men and women in Richmond struggled to keep the Lunenberg women from being hanged or returned to Lunenberg County for a retrial, fearing that a return to Lunenberg would mean death, the women lynched at the hands of an angry white mob. The community succeeded and the three women were eventually released.

The organization of black Richmonders in defense of these women partly illustrates the increasingly gendered nature of internal community politics. Men and women were portrayed as having decidedly different roles in the defense; one avenue of defense was to draw on ideas of motherhood in defending these three women; and the Lunenberg women's release called forth very particular discussions of respectability and womanhood. John Mitchell, Jr., portrayed himself as the militant defender of the women. Women, led by schoolteacher Rosa Dixon Bowser, organized the Richmond Women's League for the purposes of raising funds for the women's defense, visiting them in jail and supporting their husbands and families. Through her column in the *Woman's Era* and her participation in the National Federation of Afro-American Women, Bowser, as did Mitchell, brought the case to national attention. The front page stories in Mitchell's *Planet* emphasized the Lunenberg women as mothers, especially reporting on Mary Abernathy's pregnancy and the birth of her child in her jail cell. While the pictures and stories during the fourteen-month struggle for their release portrayed the women as simply clad, barefoot, farm women, the announcement of Pokey Barnes's final victory was accompanied by a photograph of her now transformed into a true Victorian woman with an elegant balloon-sleeved dress, a symbol of respectable womanhood. Later descriptions of Barnes, on speaking engagements, emphasized her dress: "a neat fitting, changeable silk gown and . . . a black felt hat, trimmed with black velvet and ostrich plumes." Mitchell emphasized the importance of this transformation: "The picture showing what Pokey Barnes looked like when brought to Richmond the first time and what she appears to-day will be a startling revelation to the public and will fill with amazement the conservative people everywhere when they realize what a terrible blunder the execution of this young woman would have been." He thus suggested that it was her ability to be a respectable woman (signified superficially by a class-based standard dress) that was the justification for his and others' protection of her.[63]

But the year-long discussion of these women's fates (the front page of nearly every issue of the *Richmond Planet* from July 1895 through early fall 1896 was devoted to these cases and included pictures of the women and sketches of their cabins) occurred alongside stories about lynchings or near lynchings of black men. Importantly, therefore, when black Richmonders spoke of lynching in the late nineteenth century, they had no reason to assume the victim to be male. When a freed Pokey Barnes rode as "mascot" in the 1896 Jackson Ward election rally parade, the idea of Mitchell and other black men as defenders was reinforced. But also affirmed was the underlying understanding that violence, including state repression, was a real threat to African American women as much as men. This meant that the reconstruction of clearly delineated notions of womanhood and manhood as the basis for political activism remained relatively ambiguous in late-nineteenth-century black Richmond. But issues of class and gender were increasingly evident, as when Pokey Barnes and Mitchell accepted public speaking engagements—ones in which she was clearly expected to be the silent symbol of oppression and he the vocal proponent of resistance. Barnes, countering that assumption, set forth her own understandings of her role and qualifications, contradicting the class and gender assumptions of Mitchell and of those who invited them: "she said that she was not an educated lecturer and did not have any D.D.'s or M.D.'s to her name, but she was simply Pokey Barnes, c.s. (common sense)." Her two-hour lecture on her ordeal, while giving credit to Mitchell, established herself not only as victim but also as heroine.[64]

The rescue of the Lunenberg women by black Richmonders brought women's struggles to the fore of black rights and reaffirmed violence against women as part of their collective history and struggle. At the same time black Richmonders struggled to create a new category of womanhood that would be respected and protected, and of middle-class womanhood and manhood that could protect.[65] The plight of the Lunenberg women reaffirmed the collective history of black men and women at the same time as it invigorated increasingly distinct political vehicles for middle-class black men and women.

Just as disfranchisement, segregation, lynching, and other violence denied the privileges of masculinity to African American men; segregation, lynching, sexual violence, and accusations of immorality denied the protections of womanhood to African American women. Increasingly, black women relied on constructing not only a respectable womanhood but, in large measure, an invisible womanhood. Hoping that a desexualized persona might provide the protection to themselves and their communities that seemed otherwise unobtainable, many black women carefully covered up all public suggestions of sexuality, even of sexual abuse. In the process issues specific to black women were increasingly eliminated from public discussion and collective memory.[66] In the late twentieth century therefore many African Americans have come to link a history of repression and racial violence exclusively to challenges to black masculinity and thus to establish a notion of freedom and black liberation that bifurcates public discussion and privileges men's history and experiences. In 1991 when Supreme Court justice nominee Clarence Thomas challenged his questioners by calling the Senate Judiciary Committee hearings a "high-tech lynching," black Americans were divided in their response. Some men and women supported his analysis; others opposed either Thomas's analogy or his right to, in using such, assume the mantle of black manhood that he had so often rejected. Few people, however, questioned the assumption basic to Thomas's analogy that lynching and other forms of violence had historically been a masculine experience. Similarly, when black people across the country responded to the video of Los Angeles policemen's brutal beating of Rodney King, a narrative of state repression against black men followed.[67] The masculine focus is most evident in the widespread public discussion of "endangered" black men. While appropriately focusing attention on the physical, economic, and social violence that surrounds and engulfs many black men in the late-twentieth-century United States, much of this discussion trivializes, or ignores, the violence of many black women's lives—as victims of rape and other forms of sexual abuse, murder, drugs and alcohol, poverty, and the devastation of AIDS. Seldom are discussions of rape and domestic violence included in summits on black-on-black crime. The masculinization of race progress that this implies often has some black leaders looking for ways to improve the lot of men, not only omitting women from the picture but often even accepting the violence against women. What else can explain how Mike Tyson, even before he was charged with the rape of an eighteen-year-old black woman, would have been projected by ministers of the National Baptist Convention as a role model for young black men? By what standards would a man who had already publicly acknowledged that he enjoyed brutalizing women have been put forward as a role model—unless rescuing black men from poverty and inner-city death at any price, including violence against women, was the standard by which the good of the race was being defined?

Such is the long-term consequence of political strategies developed in the late nineteenth century to empower black men and black women. Understandable and necessary in their day, they served to maintain a democratic agenda even as black political life became more divided. Eventually, however, the experiences of men were remembered as central to African Americans' struggles but the experiences of women, including the physical violence—lynchings, rapes, sexual and other forms of physical abuse as employees in white homes, domestic abuse—as well as the economic and social violence, which has so permeated the history of black women in the United States, were not as vividly and importantly retained in our memory. We give life and validity to our constructions of race, community, and politics by giving those constructions a history. Those who construct masculine notions of blackness and race progress and who claim only some forms of violence as central to African American liberation struggles are claiming/remembering a particular history. African American collective memory in the late twentieth century often appears partial, distorted, and dismembered. The definitions and issues of political struggle that can come from that partial memory are limited. Before we can construct truly participatory discussions around a fully democratic agenda where the history and struggles of women and men are raised as issues of general interest necessary to the liberation of all, we have some powerful lot of reremembering to do.[68]

NOTES

An earlier version of this paper was presented at the Black Public Sphere in the Reagan-Bush Era Conference, Chicago Humanities Institute, University of Chicago, in October 1993, where I benefited from the comments of Kenneth Warren and the discussion of the conference participants. Thanks also to Carol A. Breckenridge and to two anonymous reviewers for their comments, and to Nataki H. Goodall for her critical eye and unflagging support. The writing of this essay was facilitated by a research leave from the University of Michigan and research fellowships at the W. E. B. DuBois Institute for Afro-American Research, Harvard University; and the Virginia Center for the Humanities.

1. Petition of Mrs. Margaret Osborne et al. to the deacons and members of the First Baptist Church, April 15, 1880, recorded in First African Baptist Church, Richmond City, Minutes, Book II, June 27, 1880 (microfilm), Archives, Virginia State Library and Archives, Richmond, Virginia (hereafter cited as FABC).

2. The idea of the immediate adoption of a gendered public-private dichotomy pervades much of the historical literature on post–Civil War black communities. It is most directly argued by Jacqueline Jones: "the vitality of the political process, tainted though it was by virulent racial prejudice and violence, provided black men with a pubilc forum distinct from the private sphere inhabited by their womenfolk. Black men predominated in this arena because, like other groups in nineteenth-century America, they believed that males alone were responsible for—and capable of—the serious business of politicking," *Labor of Love, Labor of Sorrow: Black Women, Work, and the Family from Slavery to the Present* (New York: Basic Books, 1985), 66. But it is also an accepted tenet of otherwise rigorous analyses such as Eric Foner, *Reconstruction: America's Unfinished Revolution 1863–1877* (New York: Harper and Row, 1988), esp. 87.

3. Many recent discussions of the public sphere among U.S. scholars have orbited around the work of Jürgen Habermas, whose 1962 *Strukturwandel der Öffentlichkeit* was published in 1989 in English as *The Structural Transformation of the Public Sphere: An Inquiry into a Category of Bourgeois Society*, trans. Thomas Burger with assistance of Frederick Lawrence (Cambridge: MIT Press). See also Jürgen Habermas, "The Public Sphere: An Encyclopedia Article (1964)," *New German Critique* 1 (Fall 1974): 49–55. Critics who have emphasized the masculine bias in the liberal bourgeois public sphere and posited a female counterpublic include Nancy Fraser, "Rethinking the Public Sphere: A Contribution to the Critique of Actually Existing Democracy" and Mary Ryan, "Gender and Public Access: Women's Politics in Nineteenth-Century America," both in *Habermas and the Pub-*

lic Sphere, ed. Craig Calhoun (Cambridge: MIT Press, 1992), 109–142 and 259–289, respectively. See also Nancy Fraser, "What's Critical About Critical Theory? The Case of Habermas and Gender," in Nancy Fraser, ed., *Unruly Practices: Power, Discourse, and Gender in Contemporary Social Theory* (Minneapolis: University of Minnesota Press, 1989); Mary Ryan, *Women in Public: Between Banners and Ballots, 1825–1880* (Baltimore: Johns Hopkins University Press, 1990): Joan B. Landes, *Women and the Public Sphere in the Age of the French Revolution* (Ithaca: Cornell University Press, 1988); Rita Felaki, *Beyond Feminist Aesthetics: Feminist Literature and Social Change* (Cambridge: Harvard University Press, 1989), 154–182. Focusing on contemporary politics, Iris Marion Young offers a critique of an ideal public sphere in which the universal citizen is not only masculine but also white and bourgeois, *Justice and the Politics of Difference* (Princeton: Princeton University Press, 1990).

4. For a study that conceptualizes the history of the black church in relation to Habermas's theory of the public sphere, see Evelyn Brooks Higginbotham, *Righteous Discontent: The Women's Movement in the Black Baptist Church, 1880–1920* (Cambridge: Harvard University Press, 1993), esp. 7–13. Higginbotham describes "the black church not as the embodiment of ministerial authority or of any individual's private interests and pronouncements, but as a social space for discussion of public concerns" (1993: 10).

5. Similar negotiations and pronouncements occurred in other post-emancipation societies. For a discussion of the ways in which British colonial officers sought to impose ideas of a liberal democratic moral and political order, with its attendant gender relations, on former slaves in the West Indies and then pronounced these ex-slaves incapable of responsible citizenship when they failed to wholly adopt such, see Thomas C. Holt, "'The Essence of the Contract': The Articulation of Race, Gender, and Political Economy in British Emancipation Policy, 1838–1866," paper presented at the Black Public Sphere in the Reagan-Bush Era Conference, Chicago Humanities Institute, The University of Chicago, October 1993 (cited with permission of Holt).

6. The question of ownership was one of the first issues Afro-Richmonders addressed, as antebellum law had required that the titles be in the names of white-male supervising committees although the black congregants had themselves bought and paid for the buildings. Through a series of struggles black churchgoers had by the end of 1866 obtained titles to all of their church buildings. See *New York Tribune*, June 17, 1865; Peter Randolph, *From Slave Cabin to Pulpit* (Boston: Earle, 1893), 94–95; John Thomas O'Brien, Jr., "From Bondage to Citizenship: The Richmond Black Community, 1865–1867" (Ph.D. diss., University of Rochester, 1974), 273–275.

7. Statement of Jenny Scott, wife of Ned Scott, colored, June 6, 1865; Statement of Richard Adams, colored, June 8, 1865; Statement of Nelson E. Hamilton, June 9, 1865; Statement of Lewis Harris, June 9, 1865; Statement of Wm. Ferguson, June 9, 1865; Statement of Albert Brooks, colored, June 10, 1865; Statement of Thomas Lucas, colored, June 12, 1865; Statement of Washington Hutchinson, summer 1865; Statement of Edward Davenport, n.d.; Statement of Bernard H. Roberts, n.d.; Statement of Albert Williams, n.d.; Statement of Thos. J. Wayer, n.d.; Statement of Harry R. Jones, n.d.; Statement of Wellington Booker, n.d.;

Statement of Stephen Jones, n.d.; Statement of John Oliver of Mass., n.d.; Wm. M. Davis to Col. O. Brown, June 9, 1865, all in Records of the Assistant Commissioner for the State of Virginia, Bureau of Refugees, Freedmen and Abandoned Lands, 1865–1869, Record Group 105, M1048, reel 59, National Archives, Washington, D.C.; *New York Tribune*, June 12, 17, August 1, 8, 1865; *Richmond Times*, July 26, 1865; S.E.C. (Sarah Chase) to Mrs. May, May 25, 1865, in Henry L. Swint, ed., *Dear Ones at Home: Letters from Contraband Camps* (Nashville: Vanderbilt University Press, 1966), 159–160; Julia A. Wilbur in *The Pennsylvania Freedman's Bulletin* 1 (August 1865), 52, quoted in John T. O'Brien, "Reconstruction in Richmond: White Restoration and Black Protest, April–June 1865," *Virginia Magazine of History and Biography* 89, 3 (July 1981): 273, 275.

8. *New York Tribune*, August 1, 8, 1865. One of the most neglected areas of Reconstruction history and of African American history in general, is that of violence against women. This has led to the still prevalent assumption that black women were less likely to be victims of racial violence and the generalization that this reflects the fact that black women were less threatening than black men. Historian W. Fitzhugh Brundage, for example, concludes that black women had "greater leeway" to "voice their opinions and anger without suffering extralegal violence themselves." *Lynching in the New South: Georgia and Virginia, 1880–1930* (Urbana: University of Illinois Press, 1993), 80–81, 322–323n. This reflects both the emphasis on lynching as the major form of racial violence, and the limited historical attention to the black women who were lynched (at least fifteen between 1889 and 1898; at least seventy-six between 1882 and 1927). Even those ostensibly attuned to issues of gender and sexuality still assume that "the greatest violence was reserved for black men"; see, for example, Martha Hodes, "The Sexualization of Reconstruction Politics: White Women and Black Men in the South after the Civil War," *Journal of the History of Sexuality* 3 (January 1993): 404. Yet the evidence from Richmond and elsewhere suggests that the extent of violence against black women is greater than previously recognized, even greater than reported at the time. One North Carolina man, Essic Harris, giving testimony to the Senate committee investigating Ku Klux Klan terror, reported the rape of black women was so frequent as to be "an old saying by now." Essic Harris testimony, July 1, 1871, in U.S. Congress, *Testimony Taken by the Joint Select Committee to Inquire into the Condition of Affairs in the Late Insurrectionary States* Vol.: *North Carolina* (Washington: GPO, 1872), 100. Only recently have historians begun to uncover and analyze sexual violence against black women as an integral part of Reconstruction history. See, for example, the dissertation-in-progress by Hannah Rosen, University of Chicago, which examines the rapes connected with the 1866 Memphis race riot. See also, Catherine Clinton, "Reconstructing Freedwomen," *Divided Houses: Gender and the Civil War*, eds. Catherine Clinton and Nina Silber (New York: Oxford University Press, 1992), chapter 17.

9. *New York Tribune*, June 12, 17, 1865.

10. The *Richmond Times* (May 24, 1865), in refusing to publish black Richmonders' statements of protest, reasoned that they were mistaken in believing that they were all oppressed by the military and civilian officials; only the "idle negroes" were targets of military restrictions and inspections. Throughout the early months of emancipation both white southerners and white Unionists defined freedpeople's

mobility in search of family or better jobs and in expression of their newfound freedom as evidence of an unwillingness to work. Similarly, those who chose to vend goods on city streets rather than signing work contracts with white employers were seen as lazy or idle. See O'Brien, "From Bondage to Citizenship," 117–131; see also various communications among the military command reprinted in U.S. War Department, *The War of the Rebellion: A Compilation of the Official Records of the Union and Confederate Armies*, Series I, Volume XLV, Part III–*Correspondence, Etc.* (Washington: GPO, 1894), 835, 932–933, 1005–1006, 1091, 1094–1095, 1107–1108, 1131–1132.

11. *New York Tribune*, June 17, 1865.

12. Black Richmonders were countering the very different image of their community put forth not only by white southerners but also by Union officers. Major-General H. W. Halleck, for example, emphasized the goodwill between Rebel and Union soldiers, both "brave and honest men, although differing in opinion and action"; justified the military restrictions on African Americans; and reported a lack of marriage relationships among African Americans "and the consequent irresponsibility of the parents for the care and support of their offspring." He argued that "colored females," especially, needed legal restrictions, supervision, and suitable punishments, because "being released from the restraints imposed by their former masters and mistresses, . . . naturally fall into dissolute habits." H. W. Halleck, Major-General, Commanding, Headquarters Military Division of the James, Richmond, Va., to Hon. E. M. Stanton, Secretary of War, June 26, 1865, in U.S. War Department, *The War of Rebellion*, 1295–1297. Halleck was one of the Union officers who was reassigned to a different command as a result of the June protest.

13. O'Brien details these meetings in "From Bondage to Citizenship," chapters 6–9.

14. O'Brien, "From Bondage to Citizenship," 326.

15. See, for example, *Richmond Enquirer*, February 23, 1866; *Richmond Dispatch*, July 6, 1866; *Richmond Times*, July 6, 1866.

16. Foner, *Reconstruction*, 122.

17. *Richmond Dispatch*, April 19, 1867; *New York Times*, April 19, 1867.

18. Julie Saville, "A Measure of Freedom: From Slave to Wage Laborer in South Carolina, 1860–1868" (Ph.D diss., Yale University, 1986), 273.

19. *Richmond Whig*, April 1, 1867.

20. *Richmond Dispatch*, October 5, 1867.

21. Aldon Morris makes a similar argument regarding the church and the modern civil rights movement, emphasizing the ways in which the church served as a physical, financial, and cultural resource, with its sermons, songs, testimonies, and prayers becoming political resources in the mobilization of participants and in the construction and communication of political ideology. *The Origins of the Civil Rights Movement: Black Communities Organizing for Change* (New York: Free Press, 1984). See also Robin D. G. Kelley, "Comrades, Praise Gawd for Lenin and Them!": Ideology and Culture Among Black Communists in Alabama, 1930–1935," *Science and Society* 52, 1 (spring 1988): 59–82; Brenda McCallum, "Songs of Work and Songs of Worship: Sanctifying Black Unionism in the Southern City of Steel," *New York Folklore* 14, 1 & 2 (1988): 9–33. For an argument that eliminating emotions and aesthetics from acceptable forms of public discourse becomes a

means to eliminate particular groups of people from active participation in public life, see Iris Marion Young, "Impartiality and the Civic Public: Some Implications of Feminist Critiques of Moral and Political Theory," in *Feminism as Critique: On the Politics of Gender*, eds. Seyla Benhabib and Drucilla Cornell (Minneapolis: University of Minnesota, 1987), 56–76.

22. The following discussion of collective enfranchisement as the basis for black women's political activism in the post–Civil War era is drawn from Elsa Barkley Brown, "To Catch the Vision of Freedom: Reconstructing Southern Black Women's Political History, 1865–1880," in *To Be a Citizen*, eds. Arlene Avakian, Joyce Berkman, John Bracey, Bettye Collier-Thomas, and Ann Gordon (Amherst: University of Massachusetts Press, forthcoming).

23. *Richmond Dispatch*, August 1, 2, September 30, October 9, 1867; *New York Times*, August 1, 2, 6, October 18, 1867. My discussion of these events follows closely Peter J. Rachleff, *Black Labor in the South: Richmond, Virginia, 1865–1890* (Philadelphia: Temple University Press, 1984), 45–46. See also Richard L. Morton, *The Negro in Virginia Politics, 1865–1902*. Publications of the University of Virginia Phelps-Stokes Fellowship Papers Number Four (Charlottesville: University of Virginia Press, 1919), 40–43. Similar reports issued from other areas throughout the South, causing one chronicler to report that "the Southern ballot-box" was as much "the vexation of housekeepers" as it was of farmers, businessmen, statesmen, or others: "Elections were preceded by political meetings, often incendiary in character, which all one's servants must attend." Election Day itself could also be a problem. As one Tennessean reported in 1867, "Negro women went [to the polls], too: my wife was her own cook and chambermaid," Myria Lockett Avary, *Dixie After the War: An Exposition of Social Conditions Existing in the South, During the Twelve Years Succeeding the Fall of Richmond* (New York: Doubleday, Page and Co., 1906; reprint, New York: Negro Universities Press, 1969), 282–284. See also Susan Bradford Eppes for similar occurrences in Florida, *Through Some Eventful Years* ([1926], reprint ed., Gainesville: University of Florida Press, 1968).

24. *Richmond Dispatch*, August 1, 2, 1867; *New York Times*, August 2, 6, 1867; see also Rachleff, *Black Labor in the South*, 45; Morton, *Negro in Virginia Politics*, 40–43.

25. The October 1867 city Republican ward meetings and nominating convention adopted the practice common in the black community's mass meetings: a voice or standing vote which enfranchised men, women, and children. See, for example, the October 8 Second Ward meeting for delegate selection: "All who favored Mr. Washburne were first requested to rise, and forty were found on the floor, including women." *Richmond Dispatch*, September 20, October 9, 1867; January 2, 4, 14, 23, 24, February 15, 25, April 3, 8, 25, 1868; *New York Times*, August 6, October 15, 18, 1867: January 11, 1868; Rachleff, *Black Labor in the South*, 45–49: Avary, *Dixie After the War*, 229–231, 254.

The issue of children's participation is an interesting one, suggestive of the means by which personal experience rather than societal norms shaped ex-slaves' vision of politics. A similarly telling example was in the initial proposal of the African National Congress that the new South African constitution set the voting age at fourteen, a testament to those young people, as those in Soweto, who experienced the ravages of apartheid and whose fight against it helped bring about the political negotiations to secure African political rights and self-determination.

26. Compare black women's active participation in Richmond's formal politics—internal and external—in the first decades after the Civil War to Michael McGerr's assessment that nineteenth-century "women were allowed into the male political realm only to play typical feminine roles—to cook, sew, and cheer for men and to symbolize virtue and beauty. Men denied women the central experiences of the popular style: not only the ballot but also the experience of mass mobilization." McGerr's analysis fails to acknowledge the racial basis of his study, i.e., it is an assessment of white women's political participation. Michael McGerr, "Political Style and Women's Power, 1830–1930," *Journal of American History* 77 (December 1990): 864–885, cap. 867. My analysis also differs substantially from Mary P. Ryan, *Women in Public*. Ryan gives only cursory attention to African Americans but finds black women's political expression in the Civil War and Reconstruction eras restricted "with particular severity" and "buried beneath the surface of the public sphere," see 146–147, 156, *passim.*

27. For women's participation in political parades in Louisville, Kentucky, Mobile, Alabama, and Charleston, South Carolina, see Herbert G. Guttman, *The Black Family in Slavery and Freedom*, 380; *Liberator*, July 21, 1865 and *New York Daily Tribune*, April 4, 1865, both reprinted in *The Trouble They Seen: Black People Tell the Story of Reconstruction*, ed. Dorothy Sterling (Garden City, N.Y.: Doubleday, 1976), 2–4. In other areas of Virginia besides Richmond and in South Carolina and Louisiana men and women participated in the political meetings. See, for example, Vincent Harding, *There Is a River: The Black Struggle for Freedom in America* (New York: Harcourt Brace Jovanovich, 1981), 294–297; Rupert Sargent Holland, ed., *Letters and Diary of Laura M. Towne Written from the Sea Islands of South Carolina 1862–1884* (Cambridge: Riverside Press, 1912; reprint ed., New York: Negro Universities Press, 1969), 183; Testimony of John H. Burch given before a Senate committee appointed to investigate the exodus of black men and women from Louisiana, Senate Report 693, 46th Congress, 2nd Session, part 2, 232–233 reprinted in *A Documentary History of the Negro People in the United States*, 2 vols., ed. Herbert Apetheker (New York: Citadel Press, 1951), 2: 721–722; Thomas Holt, *Black Over White: Negro Political Leadership in South Carolina during Reconstruction* (Urbana: University of Illinois Press, 1977), 34–35. Graphic artists recognized the participation of women as a regular feature of parades, mass meetings, and conventions as evidenced by their illustrations. See "The Celebration of Emancipation Day in Charleston" from *Leslie's Illustrated Newspaper* reprinted in Francis Butler Simkins and Robert Hilliard Woody, *South Carolina During Reconstruction* (Chapel Hill: University of North Carolina Press, 1932; reprint ed., Gloucester, Mass.: Peter Smith, 1966), facing 364; "Electioneering at the South, *Harper's Weekly*, July 25, 1868, reprinted in Foner, *Reconstruction*, fol. 386; "Colored People's Convention in Session" reprinted in Sterling, *The Trouble They Seen*, 65.

28. *New York Times*, January 11, 22, 1868. *The Debates and Proceedings of the Constitutional Convention of the State of Virginia. Assembled at the City of Richmond* (Richmond, 1868). 505–507, 524–527.

29. *Richmond Dispatch*, June 18, 1867; Rachleff, *Black Labor in the South*, 48.

30. Rachleff, *Black Labor in the South*, 31–32; *Richmond Daily Dispatch*, May 10, 1867; *New Nation*, November 22, 29, December 6, 1866; Holt, *Black Over White*, 35; Avary, *Dixie After the War*.

31. Barkley Brown, "To Catch the Vision of Freedom"; *Richmond Enquirer*, October 22, 1867; *Richmond Whig*, October 19, 1867; Robert E. Martin, "Negro Disfranchisement in Virginia," *The Howard University Studies in the Social Sciences*, I (Washington, D.C., 1938): 65–79; *Richmond Afro-American*, December 2, 1962; Mrs. Violet Keeling's testimony before Senate investigating committee, February 18, 1884, Senate Report No. 579, 48th Congress, 1st Session, reprinted in Aptheker, *Documentary History*, 2: 739–741.

32. Barkley Brown, "To Catch the Vision of Freedom"; Howard N. Rabinowitz, *Race Relations in the Urban South, 1865–1880* (New York: Oxford University Press, 1978), 222: Airutheus Ambush Taylor, *The Negro in the Reconstruction of Virginia* (Washington, D.C.: The Association for the Study of Negro Life and History, 1926), 181, 269; Michael B. Chesson, "Richmond's Black Councilmen, 1871–96," in *Southern Black Leaders of the Reconstruction Era*, ed. Howard N. Rabinowitz (Urbana: University of Illinois Press, 1982), 219n; Peter J. Rachleff, "Black, White and Gray: Working-Class Activism in Richmond, Virginia, 1865–1890" (Ph.D. diss., University of Pittsburgh, 1981), 473, 488n; *Richmond Dispatch*, October 25, 26, 1872; September 14, 1874; Avary, *Dixie After the War*, 285–286, 347; Thomas J. Evans, Alexander Sands, N. A. Sturdivant et al., Richmond, to Major-General Schofield, October 31, 1867, reprinted in *Documents of the Constitutional Convention of the State of Virginia* (Richmond: Office of the *New Nation*, 1867), 22–23; John H. Gilmer to Gen. Schofield reprinted in *New York Times*, October 30, 1867; *New York Times*, November 3, 1867; Wendell P. Dabney, "Rough autobiographical sketch of his boyhood years," (typescript, n.d.), 98–99, microfilm copy in Wendell P. Dabney Papers, Cincinnati Historical Society, Cincinnati, Ohio; Proceedings before Military Commissioner, City of Richmond, 26 October 1867 in the case of Winston Jackson filed as G-423 1867 Letters Received, ser. 5068, 1st Reconstruction Military District, Records of the U.S. Army Continental Commands, Record Group 393, Pt. 1, National Archives [SS-1049] (bracketed numbers refer to files in the Freedmen and Southern Society Project, University of Maryland; I thank Leslie S. Rowland, project director, for facilitating my access to these files); George F. Bragg, Jr., Baltimore, Maryland, to Dr. Woodson, August 26, 1926, reprinted in "Communications," *Journal of Negro History* 11 (1926), 677.

33. See Thomas C. Holt, "An Empire over the Mind": Emancipation, Race, and Ideology in the British West Indies and the American South," in *Religion, Race, and Reconstruction: Essays in Honor of C. Vann Woodward*, ed. J. Morgan Kousser and James M. McPherson (New York: Oxford University Press, 1982), 283–314; also David Montgomery, *The American Civil War and the Meanings of Freedom: An Inaugural Lecture delivered before the University of Oxford on 24 February 1987* (Oxford: Clarendon Press, 1987), 11–13.

34. This is not to suggest that African American women did not desire the vote nor that they did not often disagree with the actions taken by some black men. One should, however, be careful about imposing presentist notions of gender equality on these women. Clearly for them the question was not an abstract notion of individual gender equality but rather one of community. That such a vision might become over time a lead into a patriarchal conception of gender roles is not a reason to dismiss the equity of its inception.

35. Dabney, "Rough autobiographical sketch," 17–18.

36. FABC, II, April 5, 6, 11, May 3, June 27, 1880.

37. First African minutes for 1841–1859 and 1875–1930, are available at First African and on microfilm in Archives, Virginia State Library. The Civil War and immediate post-emancipation minutes apparently have not survived. Peter Randolph, who came to Richmond from Massachusetts within weeks of emancipation and became the first black man elected pastor of Ebenezer Baptist, attributed both the change in seating patterns and the formal inclusion of women as voters in church business meetings to his own progressivism. Whether or not he initiated such measures, it is unlikely either change would have been effected without wide acceptance within the congregation. Randolph, *From Slave Cabin to Pulpit*, 89.

38. FABC, II, June 27, 1880.

39. FABC, III, November 7, 20, 1899; *Richmond Planet*, July 6, 20, August 10, 31, 1901, March 8, 15, 1902. Similar debates must have occurred in Ebenezer Baptist Church as well. In approving the conduct of business at Ebenezer, Mitchell noted that "only the male members were permitted to vote" on the appointment of a new pastor, *Richmond Planet*, September 14, 1901. Those debates over gender roles within black churches occurred on congregational and denominational levels. For studies which examine these debates at the state and/or national level, see, for example, Higginbotham, *Righteous Discontent*; Glenda Gilmore, "Gender and Jim Crow: Women and the Politics of White Supremacy in North Carolina, 1896–1920" (Ph.D. diss., University of North Carolina at Chapel Hill, 1992); Cheryl Townsend Gilkes, "'Together and in Harness': Women's Traditions in the Sanctified Church," *Signs: Journal of Women in Culture and Society* 10 (summer 1985): 678–699.

40. *Virginia Baptist* cited in *Woman's Era* 1 (September 1894), 8.

41. *Richmond Planet*, July 26, 1890; June 8, 1895; September 17, 24, November 19, 1898; September 9, 1899; Anthony Binga, Jr., *Sermons on Several Occasions*, I (Richmond, 1889), 97–99. Both Kemp and Carter were Baptist. A few women also conducted services in the Methodist church. Evangelist Annie E. Brown, for example, conducted two weeks of revival services at Leigh Street Methodist Episcopal Church in 1900, *Richmond Planet*, April 28, 1900. Even when one "female preacher . . . took up station" outside a Manchester barbershop and preached against the male members, claiming they were "leading the young down to perdition," the *Planet's* Manchester correspondent did not denounce her right to preach but rather suggested that if she "is called to preach the gospel, and is sanctified, as some say, why not organize a church of sanctification," rather than stand on street corners issuing "broad and uncalled for" attacks upon other ministers, *Richmond Planet*, December 12, 1896.

42. In July 1880 a council representing nine Richmond black Baptist churches censured First African for having called the police. "The First African Baptish Church, Richmond, Virginia, to the Messengers & Churches in General Ecclesiastical Council Assembled," in FABC, II, following April 3, 1881, minutes. For late-nineteenth-century disciplinary procedures with regard to members who got civil warrants against other members, see for example, FABC, II, January 7, October 6, 1884; February 3, 1890.

43. FABC, II, June 27, November 6, 1882; February 5, April 2, 1883. Wendell P. Dabney, a member of that 1883 graduating class, remembered the students

as having met in early June and "determined not to go to any church. That we would go to the Richmond Theatre or no where." He calls this "the first school strike by Negro pupils on record in the United States!" First African had, however, already denied the use of its facilities because of its new regulation. There is some evidence that, subsequent to the students' action, other black churches may have supported the young people by denying their facilities as well. Dabney. "Rough autobiographical sketch of his boyhood years," 107–109; Wendell P. Dabney, *Maggie L. Walker and the I. O. of Saint Luke: The Woman and Her Work* (Cincinnati: Dabney Publishing Co., 1927), 32–33, *New York Globe*, June 23, 1883.

44. Rachleff, "Black, White, and Gray," 307–309.

45. See, for example, the discussion of the reconfiguration of leisure space, including the barring of cakewalks and other dancing from the church, in Elsa Barkley Brown and Gregg D. Kimball, "Mapping the Terrain of Black Richmond," *Journal of Urban History* (forthcoming).

46. *New York Globe*, October 1883–January 1884. Estimates of the True Reformers' auditorium's seating capacity range from 900 to 1,500 to 2,000. Nearly 4,000 people had been able to attend the March 1867 mass meeting held in First African in support of the Federal Sherman Bill. With their new edifices erected in 1890, Sixth Mount Zion and Sharon Baptist Churches had seating capacity of 1,400 and 1,200 respectively; most churches seated far fewer, Rachleff, *Black Labor in the South*, 40: *Richmond Planet*, March 14, May 31, 1890.

47. For information on the Central Republican League, see *Richmond Planet*, August–September 1898; *Richmond Evening Leader*, August 6, 16, 24, 27, 30, September 1, 28, October 12, 1898; *Richmond Times*, August 3, September 3, 11, 1898; *Richmond Dispatch*, September 14, 1898.

48. *Richmond Planet*, January 26, 1895; October 17, 1896. Similarly, when black Republican men formed the Negro Protective Association in 1898 to organize to retain their vote and political influence, one of the most controversial discussions concerned whether to allow a women's auxiliary, the main purpose of which would be to raise monies for electoral activities. Because of heated opposition the proposal was abandoned. *Proceedings of the Negro Protective Association of Virginia, Held Tuesday, May 18th, 1897, in the True Reformers' Hall, Richmond, Va.*

49. *Richmond Planet*, July 6, 1901.

50. Lawrence Levine, *Black Culture and Black Consciousness: Afro-American Folk Thought from Slavery to Freedom* (New York: Oxford University Press, 1977).

51. Daniel Webster Davis, "De Linin' Ub De Hymns," *'Weh Down Souf and Other Poems* (Cleveland: The Helman-Taylor Company, 1897), 54–56.

52. The scholarly emphasis on this latter period is not merely a reflection of available sources. It also reflects the conceptual paradigms that have guided the investigation of black women's politics: a focus on the national level, often with minimal attention to different patterns within the North and the South; the acceptance of what Suzanne Lebsock has called the "consensus . . . that for women the standard form of political participation" in the nineteenth century "was the voluntary association"; an emphasis on autonomous women's organizations; and a focus on excavating political (and feminist) texts. This scholarly emphasis has produced a number of insightful works about the period; among them are Higginbotham, *Righteous Discontent*; Gilmore, "Gender and Jim Crow"; Hazel V. Carby, *Recon-*

structing Womanhood: The Emergence of the Afro-American Woman Novelist (New York: Oxford University Press, 1987): Claudia Tate, *Domestic Allegories of Political Desire: The Black Heroine's Text at the Turn of the Century* (New York: Oxford University Press, 1992). Quote is from Suzanne Lebsock, "Women and American Politics, 1880–1920," in *Woman, Politics, and Change*, eds. Louise A. Tilly and Patricia Gurin (New York: Russell Sage Foundation, 1990), 36.

53. Seeing the 1880–1920 period as "the greatest political age for women (including black women)," Suzanne Lebsock raises the question "what does it signify" that such occurred at "the worst" age for black people; "an age of disfranchisement and increasing legal discrimination." "Women and American Politics," 59, 37. Glenda Gilmore, in an otherwise thoughtful and nuanced study, contends that black women in North Carolina gained political prominence at the turn of the century as (because) black men vanished from politics—either leaving the state altogether or sequestering themselves in a nonpolitical world, "Gender and Jim Crow," chapter 5. It is an idea, however, that is often unstated but implicit in much literature which imagines black women's turn-of-the-century club movement as their initial emergence into politics. Such a narrative contributes to the fiction that black women were safer in the Jim Crow South than were black men.

54. I am indebted to Stephanie J. Shaw for making the point that it was internal community dynamics more so than external factors which gave rise to the black women's clubs in the late nineteenth century. See Stephanie J. Shaw, "Black Club Women and the Creation of the National Association of Colored Women," *Journal of Women's History* 3 (1991): 10–25. In the end, my analysis of what those internal factors were differs somewhat from Shaw's; she attributes their rise to migration and the resultant presence of a newly migrated group within the community in the 1890s, who sought to recreate in these communities the associational life they had left in their home communities.

55. *New York Globe*, 1883 and 1884, *passim*; Acme quote is June 23, 1883; *Richmond Planet*, July 26, 1890; January 12, 1895; 1890–1895, *passim*.

56. For a discussion of black Richmonders' participation in the Knights of Labor, see Rachleff, *Black Labor in the South*, chapters 7–12.

57. Efforts to demonstrate manhood increasingly took on class and status dimensions. For an example of this, see the discussion of black militias and the military ritual taken on by black fraternal orders such as the Knights of Pythias, in Barkley Brown and Kimball, "Mapping the Terrain."

58. See for example, *Richmond Planet*, June 11, 1891; February 24, September 22, 1900; February 16, 1901; October 25, November 1, December 20, 1902. Ida Wells-Barnett, in her struggle against the violence aimed at black women and black men, also challenged the links between white supremacy and manliness. For a discussion of Wells-Barnett's writings in this regard, see Gail Bederman, "'Civilization,' the Decline of Middle-Class Manliness, and Ida B. Well's Antilynching Campaign (1892–94)," *Radical History Review* 52 (winter 1992): 5–30. Similarly, Frances Ellen Watkins Harper and Anna Julia Cooper associated Anglo-Saxon "imperialism with unrestrained patriarchal power," depicting white males as bestial devourers "of lands and peoples." Hazel V. Carby, "'On the Threshold of Woman's Era': Lynching, Empire, and Sexuality in Black Feminist Theory," *Critical Inquiry* 12 (autumn 1985): 265.

59. The idea of sexual danger had been a part of the Reconstuction era discourse, as evidenced in the mass indignation meetings and testimonies. Then, however, it was constructed as a matter of general interest, part of the general discussion of repression of African Americans. Now a more clearly gendered discourse developed where violence against men was linked to state repression and the struggle against it to freedom and violence against women became a matter of specific interest, increasingly eliminated from the general discussions.

60. First African also excluded men found to have physically abused their wives. Binga, "Duty of Husband to Wife," in Binga, *Sermons on Several Occasions*, I, 304–305 (emphasis in original); FABC, II, August 6, September 3, November 5, 1883, April 7, 1884. Ultimately the members of First African were at a loss as to how to deal with the sexually transmitted disease but the persistence of the church's efforts to take it up suggests the degree to which some members considered this a serious issue.

61. It is important to note the constructed nature of this narrative. Suzanne Lebsock has taken the development of women's clubs with these concerns as possible evidence of the increased instances of exploitation of women, "Women and American Politics," 45. I suggest that the exploitation is not increased or even of greater concern, but that the venues for expressing and acting on that concern and the ideology through which this happens—both the narrative of endangerment and the narrative of protection—are the new, changed phenomenon. While the emphasis on motherhood and womanly virtues which undergirded the ideology of middle-class women as protectors may resonate with much of the work on middle-class white women's political activism in this period, it is important to bear in mind two distinctions: African American women's prior history of inclusion, not exclusion, shaped their discourse of womanhood and their construction of gender roles; they did so not in concert with ideas in the larger society but in opposition as white Americans continued to deny African Americans the privileges of manhood or the protections of womanhood, reinforcing the commonality rather than the separateness of men's and women's roles.

62. James Oliver Horton and Lois E. Horton suggest that a masculine conception of liberation, based on violence as an emancipatory tool available principally to men, developed within African American political rhetoric in the North in the antebellum period. "Violence, Protest, and Identity: Black Manhood in Antebellum America," in James Oliver Horton, *Free People of Color: Inside the African American Community* (Washington, D.C.: Smithsonian Institution Press, 1993), chapter 4.

63. Abernathy's and the Barnes' trials, incarceration, retrials, and eventual releases can be followed in the *Richmond Planet*, July 1895–October 1896; *Richmond Times*, July 23, 1895; *Richmond Dispatch*, September 13–19, October 2, 23, November 8, 9, 12, 14, 16, 21, 23, 24, 27, 28, 1895; July 5, 1896. For Bowser's discussion of the formation of the Women's League to protect the Lunenberg women, see *Woman's Era*, October and November 1895; Charles Wesley, *History of the National Association of Colored Women*. The first photographs of the women in the *Planet* appear August 3, 1895. The first picture of "Mary Abernathy and Her Babe" was published February 15, 1896. The post-release photograph of Pokey Barnes and Mitchell's comment regarding it appeared June 27, 1896. For a description of

Barnes' attire, see March 6, 1897. Discussions of the case can be found in Brundage, *Lynching in the New South*; and Samuel N. Pincus, *The Virginia Supreme Court, Blacks and the Law 1870–1902* (New York: Garland Publishing, 1990), chapter 11. Brundage emphasizes the role of Governor O'Ferrall, and Samuel Pincus emphasizes the legal maneuverings that prevented the women's certain lynching. While emphasizing the importance of Mitchell's stands against lynching, Ann Alexander dismisses the prolonged front page coverage of the Lunenberg case in the *Richmond Planet* as mere sensationalism. "Black Protest in the New South: John Mitchell, Jr., (1863–1929) and the *Richmond Planet*" (Ph.D. diss., Duke University, 1973), 152–153. Yet it is certain that it was the continuous efforts of black men and women in Richmond which created the climate of protection for Pokey Barnes, Mary Abernathy, and Mary Barnes, keeping their cases in the public eye, encouraging government and judicial officials to intervene, and providing the financial resources necessary to acquire a team of prominent white men as defense attorneys and advocates for the Lunenberg women. Pamela Henry has pointed to the focus on motherhood as a central point of the *Planet's* defensive strategy and suggested the futility of such a strategy in an era when black women were denied the protections of Victorian womanhood. Pamela J. Henry, "Crime, Punishment and African American Women in the South, 1880–1940," paper for Research Seminar in African American Women's History, University of Michigan, Fall 1992 (cited by permission of Henry). I am uncomfortably cognizant of the fact that my narrative also, for the most part, silences Mary Abernathy and Pokey and Mary Barnes. This reflects my primary interest in understanding what this case illuminates about black Richmond. Abernathy and the Barneses, their lives and their cases, are certainly worthy of investigation in their own right; Suzanne Lebsock is currently undertaking such a study.

64. *Richmond Planet*, March 6, 1897.

65. The narrative of class and gender, protectors and protected, was not uncontested. For example, the women of the Independent Order of Saint Luke offered a counternarrative that emphasized the possibilities of urban life not only for the middle class but importantly the possibilities of urban life for single, working-class black women who, through their collective efforts, could be their own protectors. Still further, they suggested that women—working-class and middle-class—through their political and economic resources, could become men's protectors. Reinterpreting the standards for "race men" to require support for women's rights, they thus reinserted women's condition and rights as a barometer of freedom and progress. Some aspects of the Saint Lukes' ideas regarding the relationship between the well-being of women and the well-being of men and the community as a whole are traced in Elsa Barkley Brown, "Womanist Consciousness: Maggie Lena Walker and the Independent Order of Saint Luke," *Signs: Journal of Women in Culture and Society* 14, 3 (spring 1989): 610–633.

66. It is important to understand this desexualization of black women as not merely a middle-class phenomenon imposed on working-class women. Many working-class women resisted and forged their own notions of sexuality and respectability. But many working-class women also, independent of the middle class and from their own experiences, embraced a desexualized image. Who better than a domestic worker faced with the sexual exploitation of her employer might hope

that invisibility would provide protection? Histories that deal with respectability, sexuality, and politics in all its complexity in black women's lives have yet to be written. For beginning discussions see Darlene Clark Hine, "Rape and the Culture of Dissemblance: Preliminary Thoughts on the Inner Lives of Black Midwestern Women," *Signs: Journal of Women in Culture and Society* 14 (summer 1989): 919–920; Elsa Barkley Brown, "'What Has Happened Here': The Politics of Difference in Women's History and Feminist Politics," *Feminist Studies* 18 (summer 1992): 295–312; Paula Giddings, "The Last Taboo," in *Race-ing Justice, En-gendering Power: Essays on Anita Hill, Clarence Thomas, and the Construction of Social Reality*, ed. Toni Morrison (New York: Pantheon Books, 1992), 441–463.

67. Bytches With Problems, "Wanted," is one effort by young black women to democratize the discussion of repressive violence. Focusing on the often sexualized nature of police brutality against black women, they remind us that such is often less likely to be included in statistics or acknowledged in the public discussion. *The Bytches* (Noface Records, 1991).

68. Elsa Barkley Brown, "Imaging Lynching: African American Women, Communities of Struggle, and Collective Memory," in *African American Women Speak Out: Responses to Anita Hill-Clarence Thomas*, ed. Geneva Smitherman (Detroit: Wayne State University, forthcoming).

One Man's Mob Is Another Man's Militia: Violence, Manhood, and Authority in Reconstruction South Carolina

A "MOB" WAS not an easy thing to define in Reconstruction South Carolina. As Republican militias composed almost entirely of black men clashed with white "rifle clubs" led by former Confederate officers, each group claimed to represent legitimate authority against the riotous criminals on the other side. It was a contest both of armies and of appearances. The Republicans, supported by constitutional and electoral victories, ought to have had a substantial advantage in the clash of claims, for Klansmen and "red-shirts" who harassed, beat, and murdered black and white Carolinians posed a direct threat to the rule of law. Yet the insurgents won. Former slave-holders and Confederate officers re-established their political authority on a foundation of white men's fears and expectations, convincing many white men that their armed struggle against a democratically elected government was legitimate, and perhaps inevitable.

In this struggle, the identification of a group of men as "the mob" could serve multiple purposes. The leaders of the campaign against Reconstruction asserted that black men's right to vote and bear arms in collective struggle represented a revolutionary challenge to white patriarchal authority. Reconstruction, they argued, was in essence a slave revolt, and nearly all white men had a common, legitimate interest against this sort of "mob."[1] But they simultaneously aimed a very different argument at northern Republicans. The Democratic challengers frequently blamed the violence of their campaign on poor white men whom they described as outraged and impoverished by Reconstruction policies. Pushed beyond endurance and denied the thoughtful guidance of their historic leaders, these men had devolved into a murderous mob. White elites intimated that they could hold that lower-class savagery in check, but only if Republicans would acknowledge the authority of "respectable" whites. So even as black Republicans reeled under the rifle-club leadership's repeated assaults, that leadership was persuading local and national audiences to look elsewhere for the mob.

These spurious analyses masked the white leadership's straightforward but constitutionally unacceptable intention: to restore as much as possible of the world they had lost. In that lost antebellum world, white men's responsibilities as citizens extended to every sphere of individual and collective activity. As solitary masters of independent households, white men were responsible for dependent white women and children, and for black slaves. Collectively, they bore responsibility for enforcing their authority through the militia, slave patrols, and grand and petit juries. Sometimes white men exercised this authority through less formal channels—the mass mobilization that accompanied an insurrection scare, or the committee of citizens that waited upon visitors suspected of abolitionist activities, or slaveholders, who behaved so brutally that they undermined the institution's legitimacy.[2] In any case, armed collective action, with or without formal legal sanction, had been a crucial aspect of white men's responsibilities as citizens.[3] When confronted with a danger of sufficient seriousness, a true citizenry would arise spontaneously.

There were no mobs in the slave South, explained South Carolina planter James Henry Hammond in 1845, only the "habitual vigilance" of a citizenry "concerned in the maintenance of order." "[T]he people" might "assemble to chastise" a trespassing abolitionist, but this was "no more of a mob, than a rally of shepherds to chase a wolf out of their pastures would be one."[4] If abolition were forced upon it, this society would immediately collapse: former slaves would wander the land, idle except to plunder. This, however, would provoke a reaction among "the people" that would, for Hammond, again demonstrate white southern superiority. "'[A]rmed police' . . . would immediately spring into existence" through a sort of social spontaneous generation. They would know and do their duty as citizens without the need of formal sanction because they were defending their social order as surely as any officially constituted patrol. Before long, "the African race would be exterminated, or reduced again to Slavery."[5]

Slaves might have quarreled with Hammond's analysis. They probably would have defined the patrols and vigilante parties that broke up their meetings and murdered them, as "mobs." But slaves had no authority to name the actions of white men. Slaveowners sought a form of rule that did not require the perpetual use of force. The notion of a hierarchical but organic unity among a "family, black and white," predicated on a master's paternal responsibility for all of his dependents, offered an alternative. But this paternalist gentility was hollow at the core; the reciprocal terrors of punishment and insurrection, not paternalist myths of reciprocal obligation, lay at the heart of antebellum Southern life. Very few masters and even fewer slaves ever forgot that the essence of slavery was physical domination, or that a bullwhip carried in a velvet bag was a bullwhip just the same.[6]

After emancipation stripped the elite of its human property, congressional Reconstruction established that property as part of a redefined citizenry. In South Carolina, former slaves and other black men constituted a majority of the electorate after 1867. This new political climate encouraged the formation of interest-based coalitions. One possibility was a union of poor black and white men. Another, mutually exclusive, alternative was building white unity across class lines. Although many white households stood to benefit from Republican policies such as public education, most white men experienced occupation by black troops, or freedpeople's aspirations to land ownership, as evidence of a world out of joint. Black southerners established independent households, stark refutations of landowners' right to control black labor and white men's collective right to monitor and limit black activities.

While black voters frightened white men, African American militias terrified them. In the eyes of many white men, black men were inherently unfit for citizenship. Black men could not constitute a legitimate body of "the people," fitted for public meetings, political rallies, or military service. When black men did take on these roles, whites portrayed them as comical and ignorant, or more often as impudent and riotous—as a mob. Reconstruction consisted of corrupt "misrule" and "taxation without representation" by the "voting power" of "an impressible people, whose passions and prejudices [are] easily excited."[7] To many whites, the elevation of such unsuitable citizens to this position of authority created chaos masquerading as order, a polity that those committed to a white male monopoly on citizenship must oppose as fundamentally illegitimate.[8] Black women's participation in the early stages of Reconstruction electoral politics— including, most famously, guarding the weapons during a meeting—struck some white observers as further evidence of how chaotic politics had become.[9] Men and women, laborers, renegades, and aliens, the Republicans represented all the forces of disorder. When the Republicans swept into power in the 1868 elections, it seemed to many white men in South Carolina that the "mob" had taken over the state.

Former slaveholders and Confederate officers rebelled. They opposed the new government's tax and labor policies and its composition. They also sought to regain the status of first-among-equals that they had had as white men. After coalition and peaceful protest movements failed to dislodge the Republicans from power, Hammond's political descendants sought to make good on his prophecy by taking up arms against Reconstruction's radical redefinition of "the people."[10] These elite white men had two powerful historical expectations on their side. First, most white men understood manhood and citizenship to be essentially white. Among white men, elites would naturally assume leadership positions in politics and armies. Elite white men sought to reestablish older forms of order, and to present their rebellion against black freedom and black male citizenship as a reflexive exercise of the republican "vigilance" Hammond described.

Former slaveholders seemed to understand that their greatest weakness was the transparency of their disdain for the democracy of the new order. Black Republican spokesmen, including former slaves and Union veterans Prince Rivers and Robert Smalls, denounced the planter class as "that most dangerous of oligarchies, a landed aristocracy," and as the source of secession and war.[11] Such rhetoric had an appeal for ordinary white men who had experienced the elite's exercise of power as dangerous to their lives and liberties. If elites could not mask their antidemocratic ideology, they risked a return to federal occupation. Their "spontaneous" uprising, they knew, had to be carefully planned and carefully represented. It had to seem to emerge from deep within the mass of white men and not from the plotting of a dethroned elite. Otherwise, they might appear to be nothing more than a violent faction, one the federal government could and must suppress. To do this, elites used the language of "the mob" to distance themselves from the very acts of violence they promoted, claiming that these were carried out by disreputable white men—by mobs, in short, from which only respectable white men could protect black Southerners.

The Ku Klux Klan constituted the first major offensive of elite white men and their allies against Republican Reconstruction. Between their initial attacks in 1868 and the federal government's intervention in 1871, Klansmen lashed out against various manifestations of the new order, flogging black and white Republican activists, attacking black landowners, and burning churches and schools. When the United States Senate began to investigate Klan violence in South Carolina, they knew who to call.[12]

One of the South Carolinian federal authorities summoned was former Confederate general Matthew Butler, a wealthy planter from Edgefield County. In his testimony, Butler denied any role in the Klan, but he emphasized how much influence he had with the white men of his county. Indeed, he suggested that his own authority was in some respects more legitimate than that of the state's Republican elected officials. Butler explained that he represented a group of "men who have a right to know and be heard. . . . There is always a moral power with that class of people which entitles them to respect." When he had raised a military company and offered its services to the state, the Republican governor had refused the offer. This suggested to Butler that Republican governor Robert K. Scott had misunderstood the relationship between the state and men of a certain class. Until Scott treated the best men with respect, Butler explained, he could not expect their cooperation. Here Butler laid out the philosophical underpinning of the elite-led rebellion against Reconstruction: certain men were entitled to pass judgment on state policies and veto those they disapproved.[13]

Butler understood that this assertion did not by itself entitle him to set up his own militia—or at least, to claim that right in front of hostile congressmen. Instead of threatening violence, he focused on the other half of the dialectic of authority, emphasizing his capacity for forbearance. Here as always, though, the capacity for violence was implicit in the declaration of restraint. "Last summer," he told the committee, "I could easily have provoked a riot in ten minutes, but I have taken legal rather than violent means."[14] Although he denied organizing Klan activity, he could not resist asserting once again his capacity to organize and mobilize white men through less formal understandings—what he called "a touching of elbows to be ready for any emergency."[15] He dismissed a Klan raid at Laurens as "a sort of spontaneous thing," but added that he had "advised some young men to go."[16]

Elite white men sought to present their opponents with a choice: well-considered and surgical acts of violence, or more random and bloodier conflicts with white mobs. In a speech to an 1874 convention of wealthy white "tax-payers," one delegate presented the now-defunct Klan as a justifiable response to "outrage[s] against justice" in which black criminals went unpunished. White men had banded together "for mutual protection," he said. But in the climate of lawlessness fostered by Reconstruction, an organization like the Klan could develop in two directions: either "revolution or brigandage, according to the relative numbers, intelligence, or morality participating." The "outrage and abuses" of black South Carolinians had occurred because in certain cases "the Ku-Klux appears to have been mainly a body of ignorant men, and devoid of justice as they were of judgment."[17] Had they been revolutionaries rather than brigands, had their ignorance been tempered with the greater "intelligence" of more respectable whites, they would not have done violence to the black pawns of Reconstruction but would instead have "dealt with the white persons that organized the frauds and violence of which they justly complained and made an example in high quarters in Columbia." In other words, lower-class white men could not be expected to know who were their real enemies. They sought justice, but in doing so they acted like a mob. A better class of white men would have aimed directly at the leaders of the illegitimate party.[18] More than a retrospective apology for Klan excesses, this was an outline for future assaults on Republican governance.

Republicans understood the seriousness of the challenge that the Klan presented, and raised a large state militia to put down any future guerrilla activity. This militia recruited a few whites, but it was mainly composed of black officers and men. This ambitious act of self-defense and citizenship faced many obstacles. First, most of the state's adult white men had extensive military experience, whereas a much smaller proportion of its black men had served for any length of time during the war. Second, Reconstruction had not reversed the historic racial divide in wealth; many black families worked land owned by whites. In short, white men held most of the land and most of the guns, and both could be powerful tools of coercion.

During the mid-1870s, the same former slaveholders and Confederates who had organized the Klan set their sights on the black militias. In Matthew Butler's home county, the planter leadership urged that black militiamen be denied land or employment, and that whites who ignored this prohibition be ostracized. Planters saw nothing improper in using economic power to achieve political ends. Many Edgefield blacks complained of being driven off lands they had leased or of having their labor contracts broken because they belonged to the state militia or voted Republican.[19]

Planters faced the difficult task of establishing white unity while disciplining renegade whites.[20] White terrorists burned the buildings of white race-traitors "who had refused to unite with others in the recent proscriptions against the colored people."[21] Nightriders singled out white men who took a more direct part in the Republican militias. Joe Crews, a white man who led a state militia company in Laurens, was assassinated in 1875.[22] A year later, former Confederate general Martin W. Gary warned that when making reprisals for Republican depredations, his party planned on "beginning first with the white men."[23] So when Democratic leaders declared their determination to have "white government," they were not talking only about skin color but also about ideology. According to the emerging tenets of a planter-defined "white supremacy," only those who supported a return to planter rule under the Democratic Party were truly white.

In 1874 and 1875, white rifle clubs provoked confrontations with local black militia units. Sometimes they rallied a thousand men or more to chase down their outnumbered opponents. During one of these chases, black Republican militia leader Ned Tennant defused a potentially calamitous situation by guiding his men through and around the rifle-club lines and delivering his company's weapons to his commander before the rifle-club partisans could engineer a direct confrontation.[24] This brazen defiance of the civil order provoked the moderate Republican governor, Massachusetts native Daniel Chamberlain, to investigate. He sent U.S. Colonel Theodore Parmele to Edgefield in February 1875 to recover the arms collected from Tennant's men and report back to Chamberlain on the local situation.

Parmele interpreted the conflict before him very much as Matthew Butler would have wished, never seeing the connections between elite rhetoric and militia violence. After three weeks in the county, he praised local whites as "a highly cultivated, industrious, law-abiding class" and blacks as "industrious, respectable, and opposed to any act of lawlessness." He believed that the troubles in Edgefield were caused by "a disturbing element in the minority of both races." Parmele concluded that the tensions arose because of "a class of [white] young men who hold human life at little value," who were "habitually armed and ready to resent any assertion of equality as a citizen when coming from a colored man." The black "disturbing element," by contrast, Parmele described as "a class who do not wish to labor and are known as habitual thieves, or disturbers of the peace by making incendiary remarks or suggested threats, in retaliation for acts or language perpetrated or used by white people against them."[25] But even in Parmele's "balanced" account, the inequality of the two sides' offenses was obvious: black ne'er-do-wells faced white murderers. If in the mind of the governor's agent these constituted equivalent threats to the social order, then black Republicans could count on little meaningful aid from their state government.

Parmele's analysis, which saw political violence as the result of a clash between black and white criminal classes, proved that the Republicans lacked the will to confront the state's white elite and protect black civil rights. Although he brought African Americans' protests back to the capital, Parmele left the militia's weapons locked in the Edgefield jail, from which they were soon stolen.[26] Governor Chamberlain, who hoped to harness the votes of moderate Democratic men of means to the Republican Party in 1876, supported Parmele. Neither man knew that the rifle-club leaders were already mobilizing to polarize politics along racial and partisan lines for the coming election. Their failure to understand the crisis in Edgefield foreshadowed the disaster soon to come in Hamburg.

The turning point in the war against Reconstruction in South Carolina came on the nation's hundredth birthday. On July 4, 1876, a recently reconstituted militia unit drilled in the streets of Hamburg, a town on the Savannah River. A local center of black Republican POWs, Hamburg was also home to one of Matthew Butler's white rifle clubs. Still, most town officials were black men. The city's trial justice was former slave and Union veteran Prince Rivers, who was also a major general of the militia. The men who drilled that day under local activist Dock Adams were celebrating the centennial with a show of force, fitting themselves for the duties of armed male citizenship. On a wide Hamburg street, overgrown with weeds except in its wagon ruts, the company encountered a buggy occupied by Thomas Butler and Henry Getzen, two young white planter men from a household just outside the town's limits. The two parties stopped, face to face, each claiming the right of way. They exchanged demands and threats before the militia men gave way. The parties later swore out warrants against each other, and Prince Rivers set a hearing for July 8.[27]

The very date of the initial conflict, July 4, reflected the underlying conflict over race and citizenship. Planters' unwillingness to accept black men as citizens no doubt contributed to Butler and Getzen's hostility. According to one planter, the observance of Independence Day by black men generated "intense anger among the whites."[28] Such men could hardly accept that the revolution honored by Independence Day offered any legitimate cause for black American celebration. This made it doubly important for Adams' militia to assert their right to parade.[29]

Competing narratives of the July 4 confrontation exemplified how little room existed for compromise between white men who identified with the old planter elite and black men who assumed the roles of citizenship. Expectations of deference and assertions of democracy came into direct conflict on the streets of Hamburg. Getzen and Butler were furious that black men, even a uniformed militia on parade, had failed to move out of their way. Adams, for his part, noted that there was ample room on either side of the company for the white men to pass. Thomas Butler and his father Robert considered the road, which led to their plantation gate, to be their private property. They stressed that it was their wagon that had worn the ruts along the road. At first, they denied that the road was a public way. Although the elder Butler admitted, when pressed, that it was indeed "a common road," his son continued to refer to it as "my father's street."[30]

Disagreements over the character of the street and the town symbolized the larger political conflict. For Adams and his colleagues, Hamburg's largely black population, militia, and government made the town a symbol of black independence. For planters and former Confederate officers like Matthew Butler, these same factors made Hamburg a "lawless den."[31] The contest was a microcosm of the conflict at the state and regional level: it demonstrated that the planter elite did not recognize the legitimacy of democratically elected black leadership, the right of black men to participate in the arms-bearing rites of citizenship, or, indeed, to walk the common streets as equals.[32]

Hamburg's whites argued that the militia was in fact no militia at all, but an illegitimate body of armed men—in short, a mob. In fact, it was unclear whether the men had been officially commissioned by the state, were reactivating a dormant unit, or had simply taken up arms in response to growing white rifle-club activity in the area. If the latter case, they would have indeed lacked legal standing—though this should not in itself have served as a powerful argument for men who themselves claimed the right to rebel against intolerable conditions. These ambiguities did not trouble the rifle clubs. "We looked upon them as nothing more than a parcel of men—not as militia," explained Robert Butler; they had "no right to those guns."[33] Butler may have meant to indicate the actual firearms, which were the property of the state militia, or the illegitimacy of armed black struggle generally. In any case, the hostility to the militia was based not in a deep regard for the written law, but in former slaveholders' expectations of personal and collective authority. They questioned the validity of Adams' charter, but their skepticism ran much deeper. A black militia, they implied, was an oxymoron.

On July 8, Getzen and Butler appeared in Hamburg for their hearing accompanied by Matthew Butler, their legal representative, and a host of armed white men from the surrounding counties. This was no accident, since Butler was a leader in the rifle-club movement. The men had clearly arrived to do more than legal business. Dock Adams and his men, fearing for their safety, refused to appear in court, at which point Matthew Butler and Prince Rivers began an uneasy colloquy. Butler demanded that the militia surrender its arms to him, symbolically asserting his right to control collective martial activity. He also demanded an apology. His demand was militarily real and politically symbolic. It sought to reduce the militia as a counterforce to the rifle clubs while simultaneously establishing Butler in a position of quasi-legal authority—as the representative of a white Democratic shadow-government. However Adams responded, Butler did not believe he could lose. If the militia men acquiesced, they would lose face. More importantly, they would lose their arms and the rifle-clubs would have won local control without firing a shot. If the men refused, they would provide Butler with the pretext he needed to move his troops against them.

Finding themselves for the moment at a significant tactical disadvantage, local black leaders sought to defuse the conflict. Rivers set himself somewhat apart from the men he nominally commanded, holding Dock Adams in contempt for his nonappearance and offering to take the weapons into his own custody. Cotton factor Samuel Spencer offered his services as a mediator between the militia men and the rifle-club leaders. Both black men's overtures were refused: the red-shirts sought confrontation and submission, not negotiation. They had arrived in Hamburg that day wearing red shirts, a uniform that at once suggested military discipline and bloody intentions. In the months and years after, such rifle clubs would be referred to as "red-shirts." Even on their first day of existence, their message to black South Carolinians was clear. "Sam," Butler told Spencer, "there is not any use in parleying any longer. Now, by God, I want [the militia's] guns, and I'll be God damned if I ain't going to have them." As if to underline that subordination was the point, one of Butler's aides then pointed a pistol at Spencer.[34]

Fearing for their lives, the militia men barricaded themselves in their drill-room. Butler then made a brief trip across the river to neighboring Augusta, Georgia, and told white men there that he "would not be surprised at any time if a riot were to break out" in Hamburg.[35] Butler did not report saying the other, more pointed words attributed to him by an Augusta newspaper: "Things over in Hamburgh [sic] look squally; young men, we may want you over there this evening; get yourselves in readiness."[36]

Soon, joined by white men from Augusta, Butler's red-shirts surrounded the militia men in their drill room and demanded their surrender. Shots broke out, and one of the white attackers was killed. At that, the red-shirts and their allies used a cannon brought from Augusta to break down the walls of the building. The militia men tried to flee, but many were caught and taken prisoner. After some discussion, the red-shirt leaders identified a number of the Republican activists and officials whom they considered particularly "offensive," all of them black men who had dared to exercise authority over white men. One by one, the red-shirts led these men out from the circle of prisoners and executed them with a bullet to the head. After killing at least six of their opponents, they told the rest to run and then fired on them as they fled.[37]

Although this killing landed many of the participants in jail and brought more federal troops to South Carolina, the red-shirts won this battle. Red-shirts sought to frame the conflict in such a way as to minimize their culpability, justify their actions, and establish the necessity for their return to power. Many red-shirts referred to the violence as the "Hamburg Riot," suggesting an unforeseen outbreak. Faced with intolerable conditions, white men spontaneously rebelled. The responsibility for the chaos and violence lay with the state authorities who had allowed the social order to deteriorate.

The men Butler and his red-shirts sought to displace saw matters rather differently. For them, the nature of the Hamburg militia mattered less than the brazen lawlessness of the rifle club members. Leading black Republicans argued that white citizens had "neglected and refused" to fulfill their duty to serve in the militia, leaving it an "almost exclusively" black institution. It was white noncompliance, not black, that marred the militia.[38] For whites then to establish themselves as a revolutionary counterforce was to make an outrageous and premeditated challenge to lawful government. The "slaughter of American citizens" at Hamburg, leading colored citizens concluded, was "an assault upon our right to exercise our privilege as a part of the arms-bearing population of our country."[39]

Black Republicans struggled to counter this challenge to their independent manhood. Not to resist would constitute submission, the most dreaded word in the lexicon of southern manhood. It was better to go down fighting like men. But white violence had already taken its toll. White men had already demonstrated such hypersensitivity to black self-assertion that violent retribution was better hinted at than threatened. A committee of genteel black Columbians put it most circumspectly: "although conscious of our rights, we have manifested a spirit of patience and endurance unheard of and unknown in the history of the most servile population. We ask that we be not cruelly goaded on to madness and desperation."[40] Black men were peaceful, dutiful citizens, but these spokesmen implied that they could be pushed only so far. At some point, they would give in to their own version of the mob: the slave who would rather die—or kill—than remain in chains. The recourse to such threats, though, revealed the dilemma faced by black militants. If they failed to react to the rifle clubs' murderous challenge, they would be swept aside, but when they drew on their tradition of armed resistance, they risked activating many whites' long-standing fears of black insurrection.

Even some elite Democrats denounced the violence. Francis W. Dawson, editor of the influential *Charleston News and Courier*, denounced the massacre at Hamburg as "a wholly unjustifiable affray" and called the red-shirts "barbarous in the extreme."[41] In retaliation, Butler and the other red-shirt leaders instigated a boycott of his newspaper and challenged him to a duel. Dawson held his ground for a time but soon realized he had been outflanked. After a few weeks, he changed his position. Like the orator at the 1874 "tax-payer's" convention, he expressed regret that the victims had been from "the humblest class of negroes," rather than from the men truly responsible, the Republican leadership class.[42] Dawson now accepted that white men who failed to close ranks, whether Democratic editors or Republican officials, risked becoming victims of the red-shirts' white supremacy campaign.

Governor Chamberlain condemned the massacre's instigators. In letters of protest to President Grant and Secretary of War Simon Cameron, Chamberlain argued that the violence in Hamburg had been premeditated and was "only the beginning of a series of similar race and party collisions in our State, the deliberate aim of which is . . . the political subjugation and control of this State."[43] He asked for and received federal troops to respond to this challenge.[44]

Chamberlain's interpretation of the conflict suggested that he still accepted the same social fiction offered by Colonel Parmele the year before. Chamberlain insisted that "the better and more conservative classes of society" did not approve of the "daring, lawless, reckless white men, accustomed to arms and deeds of violence . . . who are inspired by an intense and brutal hatred of the Negro as a free man, and more particularly as a voter and a republican."[45] Taking some planters' genteel manners and organic social metaphors at face value, he failed to understand that this way of life and thought had always relied, in the last instance if not always in the first, on physical force. Yet Chamberlain saw something deeper at work: something savage and primal that filled him with fear. Writing to another South Carolina Republican, he expressed outrage at the "atrocity of barbarism" and "the murderous and inhuman spirit" he saw in the Hamburg massacre. "Shame and disgust must fill the breast of every man who respects his race or human nature," he exclaimed. But Chamberlain's shame and disgust moved him to despair, not resolve. "What hope can we have when such a cruel and blood thirsty spirit waits in our midst for its hour of gratification?" he wondered. "Is our civilization so shallow? Is our race so wantonly cruel?"[46]

Matthew Butler offered yet another interpretation of the violence in Hamburg, one which emphasized its spontaneity as well as its lower-class origins. Butler denied that his party of white South Carolinians had been responsible for whatever excesses had taken place. The red-shirts, he explained, were "generally of a class of people who do not commit outrages of that sort." They had not met in Hamburg by any concerted plan. They had forborne for hours despite outrageous Republican actions. He claimed to have left Hamburg before the murders took place. Responsibility for the murders lay with the hundreds of Augustans present, men he described as drunken "factory people" and "Irish" who had crossed the bridge "for the purpose of plunder." Butler could hardly be blamed for the violence: "I had no more control over that mob than I would have over a northeast hurricane."[47] Here, Butler (again like the "tax-payer" orator of a few years earlier) was reinventing the spurious and complicated protection racket that had undergirded the slave system: black men had to decide whether they preferred to submit to genteel, upper-class whites or to become the victims of a bloodthirsty white mob no longer under elite control.

In their accelerating campaign against the Republicans throughout the next months, the red-shirts in fact offered no such choice. They sought to destroy their enemies simultaneously from the bottom up and from the top down. In defiance of the governor's order to disband, rifle clubs continued to ride against militia units, the militant grassroots of black Republican power. They also introduced a new tradition to the state's political culture: masses of armed red-shirts arrived at Republican rallies and demanded that their opponents "divide time" with them, allowing Democrats to address the audience. In practice, this furnished an excuse for Democrats to "howl down" their opponents, provoke physical conflicts, and break up the rally. In effect, Democrats transformed a peaceful political meeting—an assembly whose legitimacy was difficult to challenge, and whose goal was a unified, energized Republican electorate—into a riot. They used one of the staples of democracy—equal time in public speaking—to subvert their enemies' claims to participate in that democracy. They denied them the right to organize separately, much as slaveholders had formally prohibited slaves from assembling without a white man present.

Red-shirts also targeted leading Republicans.[48] Red-shirt leader and former Confederate general Gary even urged the assassination of Republican officials and activists. "Never threaten a man individually if he deserves to be threatened," he wrote in a "plan of campaign" for red-shirt clubs. "The necessities of the time," he added, "require that he should die."[49] Red-shirts assassinated Republican activists throughout the upcountry. In the fall of 1876 in a swamp near Ellenton, red-shirts killed dozens of black militia men. Only the arrival of federal troops stopped the slaughter.[50] More limited violence could be effective when the victim was highly visible. When Governor Chamberlain arrived in Edgefield for a Republican rally in August, so many red-shirts climbed up on the speaker's stand that it collapsed. They then menaced Chamberlain and other Republicans until they hurriedly departed by train. Gary explained that the intention had been to humiliate Chamberlain in public, to show that he could not defend himself, let alone the men he claimed as constituents.[51]

This kind of targeted political violence and assassination was a very practical matter: a party whose local activists had been murdered would have a difficult time mobilizing for an election. But for participants, observers, and those who heard or read accounts of violent episodes, such actions were also a form of political theater, dramas in which the wild and threatening energy of a mob of partisans was held in check, barely, by the ex-Confederate officers who had brought them together and set them in motion. Taking control of the event was a demonstration of the kind of power that a ruling party should wield; failing to prevent such a takeover was evidence of some deep inadequacy and perhaps a source of demoralization. Republicans understood what Democrats intended. "The entire Democratic party of the State," wrote a Republican editor, "is fully armed and organized and disciplined to carry the State on the Mississippi plan— more dependence is placed in the shotgun than argument."[52] But as Matthew Butler announced to his interrogators, "If I am the red-handed ruffian and bloodhound that I have been accused of being, either [the Republican] government is imbecile and utterly worthless, or I should have been put in the penitentiary long before this."[53] In other words, Butler's ability to get away with murder was proof that black and white Republicans could not maintain law and order.

This sort of "humiliation" constituted a social and economic claim as much as a political one. Men of Butler and Gary's class would not long accept a definition of political citizenship and a system of suffrage "by which the white man has been robbed of his influence, and the African race, unaccustomed to the duties of a statesman, have been transferred from scenes of daily labor in the fields, and assigned to discharge the functions of the legislator."[54] In this version of events, blacks became passive actors, unwillingly (or at least unwittingly) "transferred" and "assigned" duties by scheming carpetbaggers, or white southern race-traitors. Here, black men (all militia activity notwithstanding) were not independent citizens, but were rather the dependents of corrupt and misguided white men, illegitimate patriarchs. By making Chamberlain appear weak, ineffective, or even ridiculous, Democrats hoped to sow fear among his "dependents" and send them running "to lean upon those with whom they played in their childhood"—"their former owners."[55] Assassination and massacres of militia men served a double purpose here, eliminating black men who could not be forced into this model of permanent dependence while limiting the options available to those who remained.

In their campaign against the Republicans, as during slavery, leading whites offered black people incentives for acquiescence while ruthlessly beating down those who refused. In the black majority counties of the lowcountry, Democratic gubernatorial candidate Wade Hampton stumped for black votes, promising honest government, equal protection of the laws, and equal funding for public schools. This was a pragmatic course: when Democrats pressed the well-organized and militant lowcountry Republicans too hard, those Republicans tended to press back: "riots" at Charleston and Cainhoy late in the fall campaign produced more white victims than black.[56] In the lowcountry, at least, there were limits to what white coercion unaccompanied by concessions could accomplish.

Hampton faced Chamberlain in November in an election marked by fraud, intimidation, and violence. Both men claimed victory and a standoff ensued. Chamberlain, the incumbent, remained nominally in power, but Hampton asked his supporters to withhold their tax payments and to send a portion to him. In January, Democrats refused to renew the land and labor contracts of men who continued to support the Republican Party, thus starving out both the nominal government and its constituency. This situation of competing governments was finally brought to an end by a series of compromise arrangements that put a Republican in the White House, withdrew federal troops from Southern capitols, and abandoned the last few Southern Republican governments to the mercies of their adversaries.[57]

As governor, Wade Hampton denounced red-shirt violence as distasteful and unnecessary. He had come a long way from his position during the Klan rising, when he had funded the defense of accused Klansmen. As governor, he now promised black voters "protection," public education, and a safe, subordinate place in a peaceful world of one-party politics. What Hampton envisioned was not a nonracial citizenship so much as a paternalism characterized less by reciprocal obligation than by noblesse oblige. He welcomed black voting so long as it was Democratic, not democratic. White manhood was not by itself a license to rule; rather, power should be controlled by the "wealth and intelligence" of the state, by those men whose political judgment remained unclouded by ignorance, poverty, or dependence.[58]

By contrast, men like Martin Gary celebrated the white violence of 1876 and envisioned an inherently racialized conflict over power. Gary believed that where once there had existed an "irrepressible conflict between free labor and slave labor," there was now only "a conflict between the Caucasian and African races."[59] He argued that Hampton had misunderstood the meaning of 1876. According to Gary, politics was essentially "a question of race or struggle for supremacy between the races and not a mere contest for honest government as has been alleged."[60]

The stylistic and rhetorical differences between these men have led historians and popular interpreters of southern history to see them as representing real alternatives rather than as complementary, mutually necessary policies. These alternatives have been seen by historians as alternate "roads" facing the postbellum generation, or as rival subcategories of the "white mind," one "radical" in its commitment to the violent racialization of society, the other "conservative," concerned with restoring proper relationships of deference and social place not limited to racial hierarchy.[61]

But this duality is misleading, for the roots of both lay in the social and labor system of slavery, where paternalism and violence had functioned as carrot and stick. Gary and Butler sought to cut Republicanism off at the knees, driving black voters into retreat or to the Democratic Party. Hampton promised black citizens "protection" from the very men who were ensuring his victory in the upcountry. No gangster's racket could have functioned more effectively. Indeed, one of the Democratic legislature's first acts after it took power in 1877 was to organize a new state military force into which the red-shirt companies could be absorbed. Whatever Hampton might say about the mob that had put him in power, it was now a militia.[62]

As this suggests, violence and accommodation did not lie at opposite poles of a spectrum of political possibilities. Rather, as Matthew Butler's artful rhetorical dances suggest, they were tactics. Yet generations of observers of southern society have sought to reduce the complexities of class, race, and violence to a simple binary: a confrontation between violent lower-class white men and aristocratic paternalists. From this misprision emerged two theories of white supremacist violence. Violence might be presented as the actions of groups of disreputable men, lawless mobs who did not have the support of "respectable" members of society. Parmele, Butler, and others had offered this line of argument. Or violence might come from somewhere deep inside all white men, in part a racial instinct not to accept black men as citizens; Chamberlain had leaned this way in his revulsion at the Hamburg massacre.

The first argument, that violence was the work of a lawless few, was altogether self-serving, for many of the men making this argument were themselves the eminently "respectable" citizens who planned, recruited, and carried out the Klan and red-shirt campaigns. These men, schooled in slaveholding and in Civil War military service, were the ones whose thoroughgoing campaign of terror finally destroyed the Reconstruction state.

But the second argument, that white men harbored a racial instinct to rule black men, was more insidious. White men did have specific, historically rooted expectations of authority and autonomy. In an era long before biological race became a suspect category of social analysis, this history might seem to indicate something more deeply real about "Anglo-Saxon civilization" or whiteness more generally. The recourse to race as an explanation validated the red-shirts' vision. The red-shirts had quite literally fought to make black male and Republican authority seem weak and illegitimate. While claiming an identity of interest among white men, they had terrorized those white men who opposed their means or ends. The red-shirt terror had been no spontaneous eruption, but the product of a well-established political culture in which a leadership class had certain powerful prerogatives when white men assembled in arms. So when Chamberlain bemoaned the cruelty of a "race" and "civilization," and, more, when President Grant expressed his weariness with "annual autumnal outbreaks" of violence in the South, they allowed the red-shirts their discursive victory, reading a triumph of terrorist tactics as the upswelling of an irrepressible instinct, almost a force of nature.

A generation later, these explanations vied for primacy. Northern and southern reformers denounced lynching as the work of uneducated "poor whites" and appealed to the "better elements" for help. Meanwhile, a former leader of the South Carolina red-shirts, now serving his second term in the U.S. Senate, justified the lynching of black men accused of rape as a matter of racial instinct. "If you scratch the white man too deep," Ben Tillman told his Senate colleagues, "you will find the same savage whose ancestry used to roam wild in Britain. . . . I have seen the very highest and best men we have, lose all semblance of Christian human beings in their anger and frenzy when some female of their acquaintance or one of their daughters had been ravished, and they were as wild and cruel as any tiger of the jungle."[63]

Neither explanation had the chilling plausibility of the scenario Tillman offered a few years later, as he addressed the audience at a "Red-Shirt Reunion" in the South Carolina upcountry. There, his narrative of the "struggles of 1876" contained no mindless mobs, no explosion of white savagery, but careful military mobilization and discipline. No racial instinct was at work, but a "settled purpose" on the part of "the leading white men . . . to provoke a riot and teach the negroes a lesson . . . [by] having the whites demonstrate their superiority by killing as many of them as was justifiable."[64] In their "excitement and anger," a few white men forgot

could, and strengthen the d
leaders murdered during the
lease, *White Terror*, 11: W
57–8; *U.S. House Misc. Doc.*

17. "Proceedings of the
(Charleston, 1874), pamphle
18. Ibid.
19. Benjamin Ryan Tillm
Delivered from Carpet-bag a
Anderson. Personal Reminis
phlet at SCL; Zuczek, *State*

20. Tillman, "Struggles o
21. Parmele to Chamberl
South Carolina Dept. of Arc
22. On Crews' career, see
rept., Freeport, N.Y.: Books
South Carolina during Reconstr
Reconstruction (c. 1957; rept.,

23. Simkins and Woody, *S*
24. Tillman, "Struggles o
25. There was a grain of
their foes directly, and aband
did indeed resort to such clan
Carolina communities, leadin
nection between their activiti
his campaign against the mili
mysterious circumstances. Pa
Chamberlain Papers, DAH;
1876."

26. "My Childhood Days,
mon pattern: see Trelease, *W*
27. For various perspectiv
8 July 1876, see, in addition to
1876"; untitled volume, ca. 1
Days," Tillman Papers, SCL;
1st Sess., reprinted as *South Car*
chise . . . by the United States S
No. 48, Forty-Fourth Congress
Fourth of July Democratic Ce
at Hamburg, S.C. . . . Debate
Representatives," pamphlet at

28. "My Childhood Days
1876."

29. On Independence day
Transforming the Public Sphe
30. *U.S. Senate Misc. Doc.*

themselves. But most killings were cold-blooded assassinations, carried out against particular men in order to frighten and deter others, and to decapitate the opposition. Here, finally, was a red-shirt's true social vision: the mass of white men neither as a mob nor as a true democracy, but as a standing reserve army that could be called to battle by "the leading white men."

NOTES

1. Key works on Reconstruction in South Carolina include: Francis Butler Simkins and Robert Hilliard Woody, *South Carolina During Reconstruction* (c. 1932; rept. Gloucester, Mass., 1966); Joel Williamson, *After Slavery: The Negro in South Carolina During Reconstruction, 1861–1877* (Chapel Hill: University of North Carolina Press, 1965); Orville Vernon Burton, "Ungrateful Servants? Edgefield's Black Reconstruction: Part I of the Total History of Edgefield County, South Carolina" (Ph.D. dissertation, Princeton University, 1976); Thomas F. Holt, *Black Over White: Negro Political Leadership in South Carolina During Reconstruction* (Urbana: University of Illinois Press, 1977); Julie Saville, *The Work of Reconstruction: From Slave to Wage Laborer in South Carolina, 1860–1870* (New York: Cambridge University Press, 1994); Richard Zuczek, *State of Rebellion: Reconstruction in South Carolina* (Columbia: University of South Carolina Press, 1996).

2. On democracy, consensus, and conflict among whites in the nineteenth-century South, see especially: Stephanie McCurry, *Masters of Small Worlds: Yeoman Households, Gender Relations, and the Political Culture of the Antebellum South Carolina Low Country* (New York: Oxford University Press, 1995); Eugene Genovese, "Yeoman Farmers in a Slaveholders' Democracy," *Agricultural History* 49 (1975): 331–42; Steven Hahn, *The Roots of Southern Populism: Yeoman Farmers and the Transformation of the Georgia Upcountry, 1850–1890* (New York: Oxford University Press, 1983); Lacy K. Ford, Jr., *Origins of Southern Radicalism: The South Carolina Upcountry, 1800–1860* (New York: Oxford University Press, 1988).

3. On the roots of arms-bearing as an aspect of citizenship in slave society, see Kathleen M. Brown, *Good Wives, Nasty Wenches, and Anxious Patriarchs: Gender, Race, and Power in Colonial Virginia* (Chapel Hill: University of North Carolina Press, 1996), esp. 174–79.

4. James Henry Hammond, "Letter to an English Abolitionist," in Drew Gilpin Faust, ed., *The Ideology of Slavery: Proslavery Thought in the Antebellum South, 1830–1860* (Baton Rouge: Louisiana State University Press, 1981), 177–79.

5. Ibid., 201–02.

6. I have elaborated on this subject in the following essay: "The Two Faces of Domination in North Carolina, 1800–1898," in David Cecelski and Timothy B. Tyson, eds., *Democracy Betrayed: The Wilmington Race Riot of 1898 and Its Legacy* (Chapel Hill: University of North Carolina Press, 1998).

7. "Proceedings of the Tax-Payers' Convention of South Carolina . . . 1871" (Charleston, 1871), pamphlet at South Caroliniana Library, University of South Carolina, Columbia (hereafter SCL), 59, 66–67.

8. Women's expanded rights of property and contract during Reconstruction

represented a comple
see Suzanne D. Lebs
Southern Women," *Jo*
Bardaglio, *Reconstructi*
Century South (Chapel

9. On black wome
Brown, "Negotiating a
litical Life in the Trar
107–46. Half a centur
during Reconstruction
woman suffrage: "They
ple more hideous," ass
of the campaign again
would be even more "
Telegraph, 19 April 191
Collections. Even a pr
participation in politics
had children stripped
Manichean terms; "[t]h
Report on the Denial of th
Election of 1876, by the U
leges and Elections [to ac
Congress, Second Session]

10. Zuczek, *State of I*
campaign against Recor

11. "Counter-statem
No. 234, 43d Cong., 1s

12. On the Klan in
Ku Klux Klan Conspiracy
University Press, 1995);
Carolina Up-Country, 1
Herbert Shapiro, "The
Episode," *Journal of Neg*
lion, 55–134; Lou Falkn
1871–1872 (Athens: Un

13. "The Condition
Report No. 41, 42d Con

14. Ibid., IV: 1209.

15. Ibid., IV: 1208.

16. On spontaneity ir
Indiana University Press
ties throughout the state
planter D. Wyatt Aiken
elected black Republican
shot dead at the Abbevil
the goals of Klan terror

31. Tillman, "Struggles of 1876."

32. Racialized conflicts over notions of "public space" receive exemplary theoretical and empirical analysis in Jane Dailey, "Deference and Violence in the Postbellum Urban South: Manners and Massacres in Danville, Virginia," *Journal of Southern History* 63 (August 1997): 553–90.

33. *U.S. Senate Misc. Doc.* No. 48, 44th Cong., 2d Sess., I:1057.

34. Ibid., I: 710.

35. Ibid., II: 240–1.

36. Quoted in "A Centennial Four of July Democratic Celebration: The Massacre of Six Colored Citizens of the United States at Hamburg, S.C." (n.p, n.d.), pamphlet at SCL, 4.

37. Tillman, "Struggles of 1876," and "My Childhood Days."

38. "An Address to the People of the United States, Adopted at a Conference of Colored Citizens, Held at Columbia, S.C., July 20 and 21st, 1876" (Columbia, 1876), pamphlet at SCL, 3–5.

39. Ibid., 9–10.

40. Ibid., 10–11.

41. *Charleston News and Courier*, 10, 11 July 1876.

42. Ibid., 21 July 1876.

43. Chamberlain to Grant, *U.S. Senate Ex. Doc.* No. 85, 44th Cong., 1st Sess., 3.

44. Ibid.; Chamberlain to Cameron, 12 July 1876, Gov. Chamberlain Letterbooks, DAH.

45. Chamberlain to Grant, *U.S. Senate Ex. Docs.* No. 85, 44th Cong., 1st Sess., 3.

46. Chamberlain to Robertson, 13 July 1876, Gov. Chamberlain Letterbooks, DAH.

47. *U.S. Senate Misc. Doc.* No. 48, 44th Cong., 2d Sess., II: 243–7.

48. Alfred B. Williams, *Hampton and His Red Shirts: South Carolina's Deliverance in 1876* (Charleston, 1935), 66.

49. Simkins and Woody, *South Carolina during Reconstruction*, appendix, 568–9.

50. For assassinations, see e.g., *U. S. Senate Misc. Doc.* No. 48, 44th Cong., 2d Sess., I: 719–23; Tillman, "Struggles of 1876." On the Ellenton "riot," in which at least several dozen black men were murdered, see Tillman, *ibid.*

51. Greenville *Enterprise and Mountaineer*, quoted in *Keowee Courier*, 29 August 1878.

52. Port Royal *Standard and Commercial*, 5 October 1876.

53. *U.S. Sen. Misc. Doc.* No. 48, 44th Cong., 2d Sess., II: 247.

54. "Proceedings of the Taxpayers' Convention . . . 1871," 34.

55. Ibid., 36–7.

56. Williamson, *After Slavery*, 271–3.

57. Simkins and Woody, *South Carolina during Reconstruction*, 514–41.

58. On Hampton and his successors, see William J. Cooper, Jr., *The Conservative Regime: South Carolina, 1877–1890* (Baltimore: Johns Hopkins University Press, 1968).

59. Burton, "Ungrateful Servants?" 101–2, citing *Edgefield Advertiser*, 10, 24 June, 1 July 1868.

60. "Saxon," "The Philosophy of Straightout Democracy," undated clipping from *Abbeville Medium* (ca. 1880–1882) in Fitz William McMaster and Mary Jane Macfie McMaster Papers, SCL.

61. South Carolina's historiography is particularly rich in "roads": see especially Hampton M. Jarrell, *Wade Hampton and the Negro: The Road Not Taken* (Columbia: University of South Carolina Press, 1949); also Lewis Pinckney Jones, *Stormy Petrel: N. G. Gonzales and His State* (Columbia: University of South Carolina Press, 1973) and Jones, "Two Roads Tried—And One Detour," *South Carolina Historical Magazine* 79 (July 1978): 207–18. On racial radicalism and conservatism as "mentalities," see Joel Williamson, *The Crucible of Race: Black-White Relations in the American South Since Emancipation* (New York: Oxford University Press, 1984) or the abridged version, *A Rage for Order: Black-White Relations in the American South Since Emancipation* (New York: Oxford University Press, 1986). Williamson's effort to embody distinct "white minds" in the persons of particular historical figures—including South Carolina red-shirt Ben Tillman—offers some compelling insights, but it amplifies the underlying methodological problems of works such as George Fredrickson, *The Black Image in the White Mind: The Debate on Afro-American Character and Destiny, 1817–1914* (c. 1971; rept., Middletown, Conn.: Wesleyan University Press, 1987).

62. Some black militia units persisted in the lowcountry until the turn of the century, but their role was limited to ceremonial occasions such as reviews by the governor. They never again served as a fighting force. Williams to Hampton, 23 February 1877, Benjamin S. Williams papers, Perkins Library, Duke University; George Brown Tindall, *South Carolina Negroes, 1877–1900* (c. 1952; rept., Baton Rouge: Louisiana State University Press, 1966), 286–8.

63. Benjamin Ryan Tillman, "'The Race Problem,' Speech in the Senate of the United States, February 23–24, 1903" (Washington, 1903), pamphlet at SCL.

64. Tillman, "Struggles of 1876."

Chapter 4

JANE DAILEY

The Limits of Liberalism in the New South: The Politics of Race, Sex, and Patronage in Virginia, 1879–1883

THE SOUTH has never been short on liberals. Many southerners have called themselves liberals, and historians have identified a number of others who never claimed the title. Most discussions of liberalism in the post–Civil War South have focused on race relations, although their authors have rarely included more than a token reference to black southern liberals. (As one historian put it frankly in 1977, "I have used the terms 'racial liberals,' 'white liberals,' 'white Southern liberals,' and 'Southern liberals' inter-changeably.")[1] Dated conventionally to George Washington Cable's 1885 defense of black civic liberty, "The Freedmen's Case in Equity," post-bellum southern liberals remain personified by a small group of white in-tellectuals such as Cable and Lewis Harvie Blair of Richmond who consid-ered preservation of African Americans' constitutional rights compatible with white social and political dominance.[2] But even those white southern-ers rarely applied liberalism in its broadest sense: as a variety of related positions centered on freedom of contract and individual rights.[3]

In the twentieth century, white southern "liberals" became even less lib-eral. Gunnar Myrdal, the noted Swedish sociologist engaged in a massive survey of mid-twentieth-century southern race relations, remarked on the incongruence of white southern liberal support for the Jim Crow system of racial segregation and subordination in 1944. "Southern liberalism is not liberalism as it is found elsewhere in America or the world," Myrdal de-clared. "It is a unique species."[4]

Given this distance between liberal ideal and practice, it is not surprising that historians of southern liberalism tend to be apologetic about their subject, whether they are demonstrating how liberalism's sanctification of private property could be utilized to defend the traffic in human beings or revealing the way liberal notions of individual rights could prop up the oxymoronic post–Civil War system of "separate but equal." Assuming, as Myrdal did, that there is a stable taxonomy of liberalism against which the southern variant can be measured and found wanting does not help solve the problem of southern liberalism.

We can make better sense of southern liberalism by not thinking of it in ideal terms. We should instead take a bifurcated view of liberalism, viewing it first as a complicated political philosophy that contains its own possibilities of inequalities that gravitate around the axis of gender. Liberalism is predicated on the contract rights of men, and we will see some of the implications of this for southern politics later in the essay. Second, southern liberalism may be considered a language, not always coherent, in which a number of positions can be drawn on, either wholly or in part. Seen in this way, liberalism in the South makes sense only when placed in counterposition to other ideological constructions (for example, conservatism).

One place to see the inner workings of southern liberalism is by looking at the Readjuster Party of Virginia—or, as it was known after 1881, the Liberal Party. One of the most successful practitioners of biracial political alliance in the post–Civil War South, the Readjusters were an independent coalition of black and white Republicans and white Democrats that governed Virginia from 1879 to 1883. During this period a Readjuster governor occupied the statehouse, two Readjusters represented the Old Dominion in the United States Senate, and Readjusters served six of Virginia's ten congressional districts. Led by former Confederate general, slaveholder, and railroad magnate William Mahone, the coalition controlled the state legislature and the courts, and distributed the state's many coveted federal patronage positions. A black-majority party, the Readjusters legitimated and promoted African American citizenship and political power by supporting black suffrage, officeholding, and jury service. To a degree previously unseen in Virginia, the Readjusters became an institutional force for the protection and advancement of black rights and interests. In this capacity they inspired both hope and foreboding outside the borders of the Commonwealth.[5]

Liberal ideals and rhetoric were central to the Readjusters' success. Self-consciously defining themselves as liberals committed to civic equality among men, the Readjusters borrowed from another idea at the core of nineteenth-century American liberalism, that of the separate spheres doctrine. According to the separate spheres doctrine, the world could be divided into a public sphere of justice and equality and an associational private sphere that allowed discrimination. These two spheres were explicitly gendered and considered complementary: the public world of commerce and politics belonged to men, whereas to women was left the home and its occupants.[6] Making use of liberalism's gendered separation and opposition of public and private space, the Readjusters created room for biracial political alliance among men by stressing the possibility of public and private spheres sharply delineated along lines of race as well as gender. Incorporating black men into the polity but not into the parlor, white Readjusters worked to protect and profit from the political rights and activities of African American men without at the same time eroding excessively the privileges of whiteness.

But drawing the color line parallel to the division between public and private space had dangers of its own. By attempting to trump a racial hierarchy in the public sphere by retaining a gendered one in private, the Readjusters became vulnerable to political attacks by conservative critics who used gender to combat the racially progressive aspects of liberalism. A dramatic example of this may be seen in the collapse of the Readjuster coalition over issues of miscegenation manifested not through any epidemic of interracial sex or marriage but through the distribution of public offices to black Readjusters. When the Readjusters appointed two African American men to the Richmond school board in the spring of 1883, Democrats protested. Asserting a fundamental connection between black political and sexual power, Democrats argued that issues of public authority and private influence were related. There is nothing intrinsically obvious about the logic of such a claim, although that logic eventually became the cornerstone of racial politics in the New South. By investigating how that logic was constructed and resisted in Readjuster Virginia, we may reveal some of the processes that made the equation of black political power and sexual power seem both obvious and natural.

The Readjuster coalition in Virginia arose out of a struggle over the distribution of state resources. As the main battleground for all four years of the Civil War, in 1865 Virginia was in financial and physical ruin. Yet, disregarding the devastation of agriculture, the disorganization of labor, and the disruption of commerce, the Virginia legislature declared in 1870 that it would honor the state's entire antebellum debt. By the late 1870s, the only way to meet interest payments on the debt was to appropriate public monies designated for other state services. Outraging a majority of white and black voters, Virginia's Conservative Democrats violated the 1868 constitution and diverted funds from the new public school system to pay interest to bondholders. By 1879 half the state's schools failed to open. In that year, the opponents of full funding of the debt—those who favored its "readjustment"—challenged the Conservatives successfully for control of the state.[7]

The Readjusters gained control of the Virginia legislature in 1879. Their success was a victory for the perceived community of interest between white and black citizens organized around the school crisis. Scarcely had the Readjusters settled into their leadership role in the Virginia legislature, however, before the 1880 presidential election confronted them. By forcing the coalition to identify itself with one national party or another, the presidential election threatened to sunder the alliance along lines of support for the executive. This is precisely what happened: Democratic Readjusters cast Democratic ballots, whereas Republican Readjusters supported successful GOP candidate James A. Garfield. The Readjusters, who fielded an independent third ticket pledged to the Democratic presidential candidate, trailed a miserable third.[8] Among the many lessons of the 1880 election in Virginia, the importance of demography loomed large: in a white-majority state such as Virginia, defeat of the Democrats required almost unanimous Republican—meaning African American—electoral support combined with a sizeable minority of white Democratic voters. Confronting their electoral disaster in 1880, Readjuster leaders conceded for the first time the importance of the black vote to the coalition. It was suddenly clear to white Readjusters that the future of the coalition turned, in the words of one local leader, on the actions of "our Republican friends."[9]

Looking for a way to ally with black Republicans without seeming to threaten white dominance, in 1881 the Readjusters recast themselves as "Liberals."[10] This renaming did not signal an embrace of laissez-faire economic theory, but rather a commitment to an essentially rights-oriented political language and program. Sounding more like Tom Paine than John Locke, the Readjusters trumpeted the rights of man. The first right, and the necessary precondition for liberalism in Virginia, was, as Mahone put it in April 1881, "a free and priceless ballot."[11] Although decried by the Readjusters then and by a good many historians since as backward and unimaginative, Virginia's Conservative Democrats were at the forefront in one arena: suffrage restriction. Callously manipulating the desire of ordinary Virginians to educate their children, the Conservatives made prepayment of the dollar capitation tax, which was the main source of public school funding, a prerequisite for voting in 1876.[12] Still largely unreconciled to popular democracy, Conservative leaders exploited the effects of the depression of the 1870s on state revenue to limit the right to vote. A burden at any time, a hardship in the midst of a depression, the capitation tax effectively barred many Virginia men, especially black men, from the polls.[13]

Black assemblymen in the House of Delegates had made separation of the capitation tax from the suffrage a condition of their alliance with the Readjusters in 1879.[14] Equal access to the suffrage was a pillar of African American politics everywhere, and the black Republicans of Rockingham County spoke for many when they recognized "the removal of the restrictions to suffrage as the supreme issue" of Virginia politics in the spring of 1881.[15] Separation of the capitation tax from the suffrage was also a class issue capable of spanning the color line. Equal representation issues were the traditional focus of voter discontent in Virginia's western counties, the original Readjuster stronghold. The western white yeomanry well remembered the tidewater elite's antebellum opposition to equal white manhood suffrage (gained only in 1851) and sectional political equity. The color-blind nature of the poll tax issue was reflected in the response elicited from one Tidewater black. When asked by a northern reporter if the poll tax was a grievance to the African American community the black Virginian replied, "As many white men as colored men don't want this tax, or any other, for that matter."[16]

In the spring of 1881 Mahone honored his part of the bargain and declared that the fall canvass would be fought on the issue of a free and equal suffrage. The anti-Readjuster *New York Times* noted the change in Virginia politics in the summer of 1881. "The debt question has receded to the background," wrote the *Times*'s Virginia correspondent, "and questions affecting the rights of citizens, the purity of elections and a generally progressive policy have come to the front."[17] In addition to satisfying the demand of black Readjusters, a commitment to free suffrage and an honest count softened the resistance of national Republican Party leaders protesting the alliance with debt repudiators.[18]

The 1881 Readjuster Party platform enunciated the coalition's commitment to liberal notions of civic equality for men and cast the issues of free public education and tax relief in terms of equity. In an address to the members of the coalition, Mahone pronounced the party dedicated to "the complete liberation of the people, the preservation and improvement of the public schools, the final readjustment of the public debt and restoration of the public credit, the overthrow of race prejudices, the removal of unnecessary causes for sectional contention, the liberalization and equalization of the laws."[19] By June the coalition's gubernatorial candidate, William E. Cameron of Petersburg, proclaimed, "I am going forward to preach Liberalism."[20]

As the Readjusters ventured further into the realm of progressive politics, the national media portrayed them as more than merely repudiationist. The *New York Evening Post* slipped from quoting Readjuster self-assertions to editorializing in their favor, showing how the coalition's agenda had expanded beyond the issue of debt settlement to denounce the traditional nemeses of liberalism: "They say they are fighting caste. They assert that they represent the dignity of labor. Their hero is a man of the people. . . . They champion the rights of man against the privileges of an aristocracy of office-holding families."[21] Even the antirepudiationist *New York Times* conceded that the Readjusters stood for "the securing of human rights to the poor whites and the poor blacks" and cheered the coalition's "formation of politics on other than the color line." "It becomes more and more evident every day," the *Times* continued, "that the Readjuster party in Virginia is engaged in a cause that is broader than that State and deeper than the debt question. . . . The main contest is against the old intolerant and proscriptive conservatism which will not accept the doctrine of equal rights, but connives at all manner of iniquity and injustice in order to perpetuate its own ascendancy."[22]

Urged from within by farmer and worker interest groups, the Readjusters moved in the 1881 gubernatorial campaign beyond their original focus on debt settlement to consider broader reforms. The Readjusters' 1881 platform was designed to solidify the support of workingmen and small farmers, and it reflected both local concerns and the national context of rising workingmen's power.[23] In addition to calling for the uncoupling of the capitation tax from the suffrage, the 1881 platform advocated a protective tariff to encourage industry in the New South, a mechanic's lien law to favor workers over creditors, and Granger proposals for railroad regulation and fertilizer inspection. These planks were shrewdly designed to maintain the sympathy of rural voters while encouraging urban white workers to desert the Democrats, and they mirrored the resolutions passed by a convention of black Republicans in Petersburg in March 1881.[24] Beyond the inducements to workers and farmers, the Readjusters broadened their vision to consider such reforms as corporate taxation, federal aid to mining and manufacturing, and increased state funding of hospitals, asylums, and penitentiaries. The general thrust of the entire Readjuster program was both populist and statist, and it caused concern at the national Republican level as well as among Virginia Conservatives.[25]

While the Readjusters urged white workingmen to follow their class interests, Democrats paraded the specter of Negro domination, warning white voters to remain unified against the threat of a black electorate that would exploit any breach in white ranks.[26] But Democratic hopes that white voters would privilege race chauvinism over economic and educational self-interest withered under blistering Readjuster pronouncements on class bias. Readjuster speakers blasted Democratic proclamations of race solidarity as hypocritical and reminded voters that "the lines of demarcation are as distinct between whites as between whites and colored."[27] Many white men found this line of argument so compelling that by October 1881 Democrats were changing their tune. John W. Daniel, a Democratic candidate for Congress from the party that in April had fulminated against governance by "illiterate, non-tax-paying voters," was now selling himself as "the friend of the laboring man."[28] Increasingly desperate, the Democrats designated class-consciousness a "false doctrine" and admonished white voters to fight against "all the low arts of the demagogue, against the race prejudice of the negro and the class prejudice of the white man, which [had] been incited, fomented and stimulated" by the Readjusters.[29]

Successful repression of the race issue combined with the "false doctrine" of class interest led the Readjusters to their greatest electoral victory. The coalition elected its ticket by a majority of twelve thousand votes. The Readjusters retained control of both houses of the state legislature and added the governor to their ranks. The election of William E. Cameron of

Petersburg as governor eliminated the final obstacle to the passage of debt reduction legislation and thus represented the achievement of the Readjusters' original call to arms. The very success of the coalition at biracial politics repelled attempts aimed at race solidarity from both the Democrats and the rump Republicans and remained crucial to the successful practice of biracial politics in Virginia.[30]

The Readjusters quickly interpreted their victory as the rejection by white men of race as a political issue. After the election, the *Culpeper Times* denounced the Democrats for their position "that there could be no honest ground for agreement between black and white citizens" and interpreted William Cameron's election as evidence of the dismissal by reflective white Virginians of the racial divide in politics. "[S]uch a verdict as that given to Cameron by the great Democratic strongholds of Southwestern Virginia and the Shenandoah Valley proves that the white people of Virginia have thrown off the shackles of the narrow party tyranny," the editor of the *Times* lectured, "and have endorsed the principles of Liberalism and Nationalism which our speakers and our platform have proclaimed to them."[31] For the coalition as a whole, whose fate was ever more enmeshed with that of Virginia's African American minority, liberalism had come to mean the repudiation of the race issue in politics. Interested outside observers drew the same conclusion and announced optimistically that "[t]he triumph of the Readjuster and Republican coalition in Virginia shows that with time the prejudice of the Southern whites against Negro suffrage, is fast giving way and disappearing in practical politics."[32] Playing off national concern about the Readjusters' plan to scale down the state debt, the partisan *Norfolk Review* insisted that "[i]f there is repudiation in Virginia by the Liberal Party, it is the repudiation of sectional hate and race prejudices."[33]

The new governor reflected these sentiments in his inaugural speech, which was a virtual paean to liberalism. "Virginia, always in the van of great national events, furnishes a grave upon her soil for the vexed question of [the] color line in politics. Today Virginia stands before the world offering all the blessings of free citizenship, of absolute freedom in politics and religion, to those who may seek her borders. . . . The laws of Virginia guarantee equal protection and privilege to every citizen; and the people of the commonwealth have ordered that all departments of the government shall execute the spirit and letter of those laws."[34] The "Liberal revolution" appeared triumphant.

At the core of the Readjusters' conception of "liberalism" lay a commitment to equal rights. Even so, liberalism still meant different things to different people. Indeed, part of the usefulness of liberal idiom to the

Readjusters was its ability to bind together coalitionists with divergent goals and provide a common language within which to pursue those goals. In Virginia, Readjuster liberalism allowed blacks and whites with radically different a priori assumptions about fundamental rights to cooperate politically and to participate in a common discourse of equality.

Liberal political theorists of their time or ours would not necessarily recognize any carefully articulated Readjuster philosophy of liberalism. Rather than concern themselves with outlining a consistent liberal ideology, Readjuster leaders turned to a liberal vocabulary because it offered them a way of expressing positions that made the coalition politically viable.[35] Future state school superintendent Richard R. Farr was one of the first white Readjusters to define the party's mission in "liberal" terms. According to Farr, the party's mission was "contending for human rights—liberalism—and a break up in the Solid South." Notwithstanding Farr's espoused commitment to human rights, he did not embrace a definition of liberalism as encompassing complete equality before the law. For Farr, liberalism meant "maintaining all those rights, which are guaranteed to all, by laws adopted by the people."[36] This was equality hedged around the edges. While black Readjusters saw in liberalism absolute parity of manhood rights, white Readjusters believed they had found a political philosophy and rhetoric capable of separating some rights from others.

This separation was crucial because of one highly contested "right" in particular, that of masculine sex right and the related question of black men's sexual access to white women. Recently, southern political historians have begun to reconceptualize the postbellum political struggle between black and white southerners as revolving around competing definitions of masculinity and manhood rights.[37] At the core of this discussion lies the question of control over women. As Martha Hodes and others have argued, the issue of black men's sexual authority underlay congressional debates over emancipation, and the elusive definition of African American "equality" plagued supporters of black suffrage.[38] From the moment of emancipation, white men and women conflated the political and sexual power of black men, insisting that black suffrage would lead to sexual liaisons between white women and African American men. Republican congressional leaders countered the association between sexual and political equality among men, wondering how marriage with a white woman would result "because a colored man is allowed to drop a little bit of paper in a box."[39] Nevertheless, throughout the postwar era southern white supremacists continued to press the connection between black suffrage and sex. These connections had deep roots. For example, on the eve of secession in 1860 a South Carolina minister warned white men that emancipation would not only liberate the slave, making him "his own master," but would also make him the equal of every white man. The logical next step, he argued, would be the arrival of "Abolition preachers" to "consummate the marriage of your daughters to black husbands."[40]

The rhetorical link between black suffrage and interracial sex has been denounced as "the *reductio ad absurdum* of the congressional debates," but the logic was far from absurd.[41] We might dub this issue the Othello problem: once the black man has been admitted to the republic, is there any way to limit his rights in private? Definitions of political rights that tied them to manhood, as the Fourteenth and Fifteenth Amendments did, suggested that there was not.[42] The conflation of masculine sexual and political identity in the postwar South meant that white men who hoped to channel the political power of African American men had to find a language of politics that promised sufficient rights to black men to gain their votes at the same time that it quarantined the suffrage from the right of sexual access to white women.

This is what liberal language and ideology, particularly the separate spheres doctrine, did for the Readjuster coalition. White Readjusters relied on the separate spheres ideology to differentiate between civil or political rights and social rights. The rights that most white Readjusters considered bound to liberalism were, in the words of one Abingdon Readjuster, "all constitutional provisions in relation to political or civil rights."[43] This translated in practical terms into a guarantee of black suffrage, office-holding, and jury service. Regarding the question of where, precisely, to locate the line dividing private and public rights, the coalition relied on Virginia's laws forbidding sex and marriage across the color line to mark the outer boundaries of black civil equality and to serve as the barrier to the white private sphere. As the collective voice of the coalition, the *Richmond Whig*, explained in 1883, "Our party . . . encourages each race to develop its own sociology separately and apart from unlawful contamination with each other, but under a government which recognizes and protects the civil rights of all."[44] Joseph Porter, an 1883 candidate for the legislature, was more specific: "I am opposed to Mixed Schools, Mixed Marriages, Miscegenation, or ANY AND ALL PROMISCUOUS MIXING OF TWO DISTINCT RACES OF PEOPLE; believing these things to be injurious to the morals and repulsive to the better instincts of both," he explained. But, Porter continued, "still claiming for each equal and exact justice before the Law," he left black and white Virginians "to work out their appointed destinies under a common government."[45]

White Readjusters admitted that the Reconstruction amendments to the Constitution guaranteed black men equal civic rights. Interracial marriage, however, was regarded as outside the bounds of civic rights. White Readjusters defined the private sphere as contiguous with the laws of sex and marriage, just as southern jurists did. This theoretical move, as legal historian Michael Grossberg has noted, "forestalled the classification of marriage as a political rather than a social right."[46]

Black Readjusters, who deployed the same liberal idiom as their white coalition partners, nonetheless differed radically in their approach to the antimiscegenation laws and hence drew different lines between the public and private spheres. When white Readjusters insisted that the boundary between the spheres necessarily paralleled the color line, black Readjusters disagreed. Black Readjusters considered marriage a political right, with the marriage contract itself serving as the boundary between spheres that were fully integrated.[47]

This definition of the spheres centered on a vision of liberalism that saw the ideal of "equal rights before the law" as founded in masculinity. Drawing on constructions of liberalism by such African American political leaders as Frederick Douglass and Virginian John Mercer Langston, black Republican Readjusters defended equality as grounded in citizenship and manhood. As Langston put it in 1874, black men demanded, and the Fourteenth and Fifteenth Amendments guaranteed, "complete equality before the law, in the protection and enjoyment of all those rights and privileges which pertain to manhood, enfranchised and dignified."[48] This sentiment was echoed in 1882 by Readjuster George F. Bragg, Jr., who edited Petersburg's black newspaper, *The Lancet*. After the war, Bragg wrote, "The slave . . . was made a freeman and a citizen[;] while, before, he was a mere chattel, or thing, he was left a man and a sovereign."[49]

When southern blacks defined their political rights and individual autonomy as rooted in their masculinity, they asserted their commonality with white men through their essential difference from and superiority to women, and established themselves as citizen-patriarchs. As Laura Edwards has argued, African American men after the Civil War "harnessed a traditional definition of the household" and their place in it to serve the radical end of black enfranchisement and civic power.[50] An assembly of Alabama freedmen articulated these principals as early as 1865. "We claim exactly *the same rights, privileges and immunities as are enjoyed by white men*," they declared, because "the law no longer knows white or black, but simply men."[51] That African American political leaders could use the Fourteenth and Fifteenth Amendments to justify their participation in the polity in terms of their manliness testifies to the diversity of political ideology and vocabulary in the post–Civil War South. The Reconstruction Amendments, which stood as the guarantors of African American equality within the liberal polity, were themselves links with the past through their grounding of political right in sexual identity and men's implied domestic majesty.

The foundation of domestic sovereignty was marriage, an institution that bore the weight of a world of symbolic meanings in the nineteenth century. Understood as the basis of society as well as its reproductive unit, marriage also served as a crucial boundary marker of the intersection between the private world of the household and the public world of the state, with the husband and father serving as intermediary. It was through this interrelated role of husband and father that matrimony established a clear relationship between sexual self-determination and civic power, and the nineteenth-century definition of the masculine citizen as independent, decisive, and forceful was, as German historian Isabel Hull has argued, a civil translation of analogous sexual qualities.[52]

Along with negotiating contracts, voting, and exploring their legal rights through the court system, black southerners after the Civil War used marriage to signify their new identity as civic co-equals.[53] Marriage may be easily seen as constituting a recognition of equality: not between the partners but between the families of the betrothed. Indeed, marriage is such a recognition of equality that the definition of equality itself has become bound up over the years with that of marriage so that, as the anthropologist Edmund Leach has argued, cultures determine the standing of a group by asking, "Do we intermarry with them?"[54] As far as black Readjusters were concerned, laws that limited the right to marry limited a free exchange of property (sexual and material) as well as social alliances among families, thus fencing in equality itself.

Against the wishes of white Readjusters, black Readjusters in the General Assembly introduced bills to repeal the state's ban on interracial marriage. Practically, black legislators were concerned with protecting black women already in common-law marriages with white men and the mixed-race children of those unions. More abstractly, black Readjusters acted out of dedication to their vision of public equality *before the law* as enunciated in the Readjuster party platforms. At the 1879 Colored Citizens Convention in Richmond, delegates denounced the state's antimiscegenation law as an oppressive abridgement of "our privileges as citizens of the State." Threatening to emigrate from Virginia to other American states or territories "where there is no distinction on account of color," the convention expressed its sympathy for and solidarity with Edmund Kinney and his wife Mary, currently performing hard labor in the state penitentiary for marrying in defiance of the ban on interracial unions.[55]

White coalitionists refused to support black Readjusters' attempts to repeal the antimiscegenation laws. Black assemblyman Shed Dungee's 1880 resolution to revoke the law fell by a 77–10 margin, and Petersburg leader Armistead Green's 1881 bill to repeal the law languished in committee.[56] The antimiscegenation law stood, and for a time the Readjusters proved capable of countering Democratic accusations that the coalition stood for interracial sex and marriage.

In 1883, however, the Readjuster coalition collapsed in the midst of a miscegenation panic. The anxiety of white men about African American sexual power was harnessed politically not by any lurid account of inter-racial rape or marriage but by the appointment of two African American Readjusters to the Richmond school board. To understand how this could have happened, we must examine the way that the politics of patronage in the liberal state intersected with honor-based notions of masculine political and sex right.

In addition to rejecting their coalition partners' attempts to repeal the antimiscegenation laws, white Readjusters upheld the notion of social segregation between the races. Readjuster congressman John S. Wise, the son of the antebellum Virginia governor who hanged John Brown, made a point of explaining to white audiences that he always met with African American constituents on his back porch or in his kitchen.[57] But white coalition leaders backed black Readjuster demands for patronage distribution as a political necessity. Through an unlikely chain of events culminating in an alliance with the Republicans in the Senate, William Mahone captured Virginia's share of the federal patronage for the Readjusters.[58] Before passage of the Pendleton Act in 1883, which established a federal Civil Service Commission and instituted merit examinations for many former patronage positions, most government jobs were distributed through local partisan organizations as rewards to loyal party members. In return, federal and state appointees paid assessments on their wages to support electoral campaigns.[59] Thousands of jobs that paid cash wages on time were thus tied to partisan control of the federal government. Patronage power tied many men's political identities to their livelihood, and this politics of obligation bolstered the party that controlled the patronage and discouraged political experimentation among federal jobholders unhappy with local politics.

When combined with the attempts of the coalition to fashion for itself a color-blind identity as "Liberals," Readjuster patronage policy further encouraged the formation of a cohesive biracial political community with a common identity and goals. Responding to African American calls for increased state funding for black institutions, the Readjusters founded the Normal and Collegiate Institute for Negroes at Petersburg (now Virginia State College), established black hospitals and an insane asylum, and tripled the number of black teachers and principals. Black Readjusters occupied patronage appointments in Washington and in local communities. At the same time, black majority cities such as Petersburg and Danville elected African American men to municipal offices carrying both power and prestige. In 1882 Petersburg's new, Readjuster-dominated school board dismissed 25 percent of the city's white teachers and replaced them with African Americans. With black men serving as postmasters, city councilmen, school board members, justices of the peace, and policemen, it is no wonder that one young black Richmonder exulted that "[u]nder the Readjusters, now for the first time black men feel like men."[60] White Democrats saw things rather differently. When Daniel Norton, an influential African American Readjuster from Williamsburg, presided in the state Senate in the absence of the majority leader, the *Wytheville Enterprise* borrowed a page from the Readjusters' rhetorical playbook to note sourly, "It is the first time in the history of Virginia that a colored 'brother' has taken such high ground and it remained for the 'Liberal' party, so-called, to usher Sambo into such prominence."[61]

Of course, the redirection of patronage honor and benefit to black Virginians was not accomplished without a struggle. Despite official pronouncements directing the sharing of power along race lines, many white Readjusters hesitated to grant their black partners any real influence in party affairs. Whites frequently rigged the selection process for the local leadership committees to favor white Readjusters. Even so, by 1881 a good number of whites who had been with the movement since its inception in 1879 were being passed over for patronage positions in favor of black men in the interest of cementing the Republican-Readjuster alliance. More than one angry letter to Mahone complained about the favoring of these "side-door seekers."[62]

White opinion regarding black influence in the coalition spanned from the professions of complete equality among men that emanated from a few native white Republican Readjusters to the fear of "Negro domination" that prompted John Wise to reassure his party in 1882 that there was not "too much nigger in the Readjuster party."[63] More representative of the Readjusters' white rank and file was the opinion of "Old Commonwealth." Writing from Rockingham County, which was represented in Congress by the Readjuster John Paul, "Old Commonwealth" proclaimed that his district was "not ready for colored supremacy, although we do not deny to the colored brother any of his legal and constitutional rights."[64]

But where did legal rights end and colored supremacy begin? By supporting African American civil and political participation, including officeholding, and by distributing patronage power and rewards to black Readjusters, biracial coalition in Virginia challenged white social, political, and economic superiority. Allying politically with African Americans and distributing patronage to them, encouraging black men to climb "the ladder of authority," as Mahone put it,[65] opened the possibility of interpreting the Readjuster coalition as destabilizing social hierarchies based on race. Although nearly all white Virginians benefited by Readjuster rule— whether from lowered property taxes, from an economic upswing generated in part by resolution of the debt issue, or through the growth and prosperity of the public schools—the Democrats were increasingly able to capitalize on a nagging fear among whites that their possessive investment in whiteness was being devalued.[66] When black men supervised white postal workers or teachers, or meted justice from the magistrate's bench or the jury box, white Virginians worried about the distribution of authority in public life and any fraying of traditional links between authority, race, and manhood.

When white Virginians fretted about the authority of African American men in public, they spoke in the language of honor. As many anthropologists and historians have emphasized, honor may be partly understood as a language in which hierarchy is sexualized, in which masculinity and authority are conflated and venerated, and in which the feminine is seen both as a way of speaking about dishonor and the point at which honor is most at risk. Because of the explicit relations of honor and hierarchy visible in patronage—indeed, in its very etymology—patronage politics were especially liable to be analyzed using the vocabulary of honor, a vocabulary often couched in the idiom of sex.[67] To the astonishment of the Readjusters, who considered the antimiscegenation law a necessary but sufficient barrier to accusations of black social equality, white anxiety about the sexual power of black men could shift to a variety of other, seemingly nonsexual areas. To the extent that hierarchy was sexualized within the lexicon of honor, the authority of black men *anywhere* was capable of being sexualized. Although the Democrats ridiculed white Readjusters in general for their supposed "submission to the desires of the black man," they focused their complaints on a limited number of situations where black men exercised real or potential authority over white women. The most explosive of these places turned out to be the public schools. It was here that the debate about the relationship between black political and sexual rights reached its peak.

In the spring of 1883 Governor William E. Cameron replaced Richmond's Democratic and all-white school board with one dominated by Readjusters. Among the nine coalitionists Cameron chose were two African Americans, Richard Forrester and Robert A. Paul. Educated and propertied, Forrester and Paul were both respected and influential molders of black public opinion in Richmond. Each had held public office before his appointment to the school board.[68] Richmond's African American Readjusters were delighted at Forrester and Paul's elevation, and a mass meeting of Richmond blacks at First African Church celebrated the governor's action as proof that the Readjusters were truly "activated by the great principles of equal political and civil rights for all classes, irrespective of race and color."[69]

Richmond's Democratic leaders were outraged, but the city's leading Democratic newspaper drew some interesting distinctions. Although murmuring a protest against the increased African American influence over public institutions under the Readjusters, the *Richmond Dispatch* departed significantly from New South Democratic dogma by allowing that there was a sphere of legitimate black authority in public life. Regarding black men in public office, the *Dispatch* conceded that "there is no insuperable objection" to electing black men to the General Assembly, to city councils, or as magistrates and the like. The newspaper drew the line, however, at black influence over white schools, and expressed incredulity that "any white man should raise his voice in defense of such a wrong."[70]

That the leading Democratic newspaper in Virginia should acknowledge, however reluctantly, the right of black men to serve in local and state government is in itself reason for pause, and serves as a reminder of the political fluidity that enabled the sort of shifting allegiances represented by the Readjusters. But the logic of the *Dispatch* is not clear. If black men were acceptable as magistrates, then why not as members of local school boards?

The answer to this question has to do with the location of white women in postwar Virginia, and, more generally, with the articulation of the spheres themselves. In most societies in which the sexual purity of women is protected as the gate of entry to the caste, women lead highly restricted lives.[71] In the world according to Mahone, white women remained apart, sheltered from the rough-and-tumble public world in their private domestic oases. But the post-emancipation South did not resemble this world. The same unpredictable forces of emancipation, urbanization, and industrialization that mediated the entry of African American men into public space provided for a complementary expansion into the public sphere of black and white women. As women entered public space as workers, patrons, volunteers, and consumers, the definition of the private became less and less clear, and the places where women congregated became charged with sexual potential.[72] Within this context, the Readjusters' assertion of a racialized barrier between gendered public and private spheres left the coalition open to Democratic charges that black power over white schools was tantamount to black sexual power over white women teachers and students.

Public schools in the nineteenth-century South were a primary locus of patronage in the form of state employment.[73] Since the Civil War, those employees have been mainly women. Most children in Readjuster Virginia were taught by white women who were hired, promoted, and supervised by local boards of education.[74] Because of the role played by white women in schools, the Democrats' progression from black men's civil authority to black men's sexual authority was easier to make. The danger schools posed for the Readjusters could thus be constructed as different in degree, but not in kind, from that posed by the issue of intermarriage. By putting black men in positions of authority over white woman teachers, the integration of school boards threatened to expose the potential relationship between political and sex right that the Readjuster emphasis on the separation between public and private space was meant to suppress.

Capitalizing on the school issue, the Democrats made the conjunction of black male political and sexual power the main theme in the election of 1883. J. M. Gills, Amelia County's Readjuster chairman, wrote to Mahone after the election, saying "it surpassed anything ever before known for unfairness, misrepresentation and meanness. Bulldozing and intimidation was the order. Mixed Schools, Mixed Marriages, Social Equality and Negro rule and Negro supremacy was the cry of [Democratic] precinct leaders, used in the presence of women in every private family." Gills continued, "In my Precinct [Democratic] chairmen rode to the doors, called out the women and after going through the catalougue [sic] of ills that would follow if the Coalitionists succeed, would wind up by asking the women how they would like (calling a most objectionable Negro by name) to visit and examine their daughters."[75]

Throughout the fall of 1883, Democratic newspapers asserted that mixed school boards led to mixed schools, which led, inevitably, to miscegenation. The *Lynchburg News* insisted that a vote for the Readjusters was a vote for "mixed schools now and mixed marriages in the future."[76] Making the same argument in visual form in order to reach illiterate voters, the Democrats published a cartoon drawing depicting an African American male teacher about to spank a white girl. In the background of the drawing was a blackboard, on which was written the word "Coalition" next to a crude drawing of a mule's head, a traditional symbol of miscegenation. For its part, the *Richmond Dispatch* focused on fears of black male power over white woman teachers, straining at the boundaries of its own tortured logic to argue that two black men on a nine-member school board constituted a majority: "Of the nine new trustees, two are negroes; that is to say, as five members constitute a majority of the board, and can elect teachers, and three members constitute a majority of that majority, it may probably happen that the fifty or sixty young lady-teachers, as well as the principals and other schools officials, may have to depend upon the good will of these two negroes for their places." As if such reliance on black patronage power were not galling enough to whites, the *Dispatch* played up the sexual implications of black male school officials interrogating white woman teachers, and concluded the editorial with a statement resonating both of marriage and of rape, intoning, "The outrage has been consummated."[77]

The integration of the Richmond school board appears to have convinced a considerable number of white voters in Virginia that black male political and sexual power marched hand in hand.[78] That November the coalition lost control of the state in a close election that turned on the race question. White Readjusters who could support African American voters and jurors balked at the presence of black men in charge of white school-marms.[79] The Warren County Coalitionists, for example, passed a resolution favoring the civil and political rights of African Americans but opposed "social equality" and the appointment of Forrester and Paul to the Richmond school board.[80] Such an act points to both the relative success of the liberal rhetoric of separate spheres in masking the relationship between political right and sex right and to the Democratic success in merging the two in the school issue in 1883.

There is some irony in the fact that the schools proved more dangerous than intermarriage to Readjuster liberalism, for the latter has seemed the more fundamental issue to a number of nonsouthern, twentieth-century liberals. In her famous essay "Reflections on Little Rock," Hannah Arendt questioned the wisdom of launching the assault on fortress segregation through America's schools. Instead, Arendt argued, the fight against legalized racial discrimination should focus on voting rights and on "what the whole world knows to be the most outrageous piece of legislation in the whole western hemisphere": the antimiscegenation legislation that, in 1959, still disgraced the books of 29 of America's 49 states. In combination with the South's denial of African Americans' right of suffrage, these marriage laws, wrote Arendt, constituted "a much more flagrant breach of letter and spirit of the Constitution than segregation of schools." If the purpose of the Civil Rights movement was to abolish legal enforcement of social and political discrimination based on race, how could the Civil Rights Act of 1957 leave untouched "the most outrageous law of Southern states—the law which makes mixed marriages a criminal offense?" And why were American liberals so quick to dismiss the issue of black sexual rights, insisting, as Sidney Hook did in 1959, that African Americans were "profoundly uninterested" in the antimiscegenation laws?[81]

Despite Hannah Arendt's impression that American antimiscegenation laws were not under attack, most mid-twentieth-century Americans understood that in integrating the public schools the nation was implicitly addressing the question of intermarriage.[82] More clearly than Arendt, they saw that the schools had become the site upon which white anxiety about the relationship between political rights and sex rights had been displaced. This displacement was not some perversion of liberal ideology, but rather a consequence of its strategic deployment in a particular time and place. To insist, as Arendt did, that sex right and political right could meet only in the field of marriage was to ignore the many ways in which sexual boundaries had been displaced by those seeking to enlarge the political arena for African Americans as well as by those seeking to restrict it. She might have learned from the story of the Readjusters and their enemies what Governor George Wallace seems to have understood intuitively as he made his "stand in the schoolhouse door" in 1963: that (to quote Mary Douglas) "the homely experience of going through a door is able to express so many kinds of entrance."[83]

NOTES

1. Morton Sosna, *In Search of the Silent South: Southern Liberals and the Race Issue* (New York: Columbia University Press, 1977), 2.

2. On the ways in which liberalism was compatible with slavery, see James Oakes, *Slavery and Freedom, An Interpretation of the Old South* (New York: Knopf, 1990), 60, 72. Cf. *idem, The Ruling Race: A History of American Slaveholders* (Norton, 1982). On southern liberalism after the Civil War see Hugh C. Bailey, *Liberalism in the South: Southern Social Reformers and the Progressive Movement* (Coral Gables: University of Miami Press, 1969); Sosna, *In Search of the Silent South*; Joel Williamson, *The Crucible of Race: Black-White Relations in the American South Since Emancipation* (New York: Oxford University Press, 1984), ch. 3; George M. Fredrickson, *The Black Image in the White Mind: The Debate on Afro-American Character and Destiny, 1817–1914* (New York: Harper & Row, 1971), ch. 7; and Michael O'Brien, "C. Vann Woodward and the Burden of Southern Liberalism," *AHR* 78 (June 1973), 589–604. For a new work that includes a broad spectrum of black liberals, see Kevin K. Gaines, *Uplifting the Race: Black Leadership, Politics, and Culture in the Twentieth Century* (Chapel Hill: University of North Carolina Press, 1996). Recent work on liberalism in the South after emancipation takes a more economic and contractarian approach. See Amy Dru Stanley, "Beggars Can't Be Choosers: Compulsion and Contract in Postbellum America," *Journal of American History* 78, no. 4 (March 1992): 1265–92; Barbara Jeanne Fields, "The Advent of Capitalist Agriculture: The New South in a Bourgeois World," in Thavolia Glymph and John J. Kushma, eds., *Essays on the Postbellum Southern Economy* (College Station: Texas A&M Press, 1985), 73–94; Leslie A. Schwalm, *A Hard Fight for We: Women's Transition from Slavery to Freedom in South Carolina* (Urbana: University of Illinois Press, 1997), ch. 6 and p. 200, n. 49; and Laura F. Edwards, *Gendered Strife and Confusion: The Political Culture of Reconstruction* (Urbana: University of Illinois Press, 1997), chs. 1 and 2.

3. Definitions of liberalism offered for the nineteenth and twentieth centuries are notoriously inexact. Ronald Dworkin considers the difficulty of pinning down a concise definition of liberalism and then offers his own, one centered on the relationship between equality and a neutral state, in "Liberalism," in Stuart Hampshire, ed., *Public and Private Morality* (Cambridge: Cambridge University Press, 1978), 113–43.

4. Gunnar Myrdal, *An American Dilemma: The Negro Problem and Modern Democracy* (New York: Harper & Brothers, 1944), 466.

5. Virginia remained under military occupation until the state's readmission to the Union in 1870, thereby avoiding Reconstruction. On the Readjuster Movement see James Tice Moore, *Two Paths to the New South: The Virginia Debt Controversy, 1870–1883* (Lexington: University of Kentucky Press, 1974). See also Charles Chilton Pearson, *The Readjuster Movement in Virginia* (New Haven: Yale

University Press, 1917); Alrutheus Ambush Taylor, *The Negro in the Reconstruction of Virginia* (New York: Russell & Russell, 1926; rpt., 1969); James Hugo Johnson, "The Participation of Negroes in the Government of Virginia from 1877 to 1888," *Journal of Negro History* XIV (July 1929), 251–71; Nelson Morehouse Blake, *William Mahone of Virginia: Soldier and Political Insurgent* (Richmond: Garrett and Massie, 1935); Luther Porter Jackson, *Negro Office-Holders in Virginia, 1865–1895* (Norfolk, Va.: Guide Quality Press, 1945); Charles E. Wynes, *Race Relations in Virginia, 1870–1902* (Charlottesville: University of Virginia Press, 1961); Carl N. Degler, *The Other South: Southern Dissenters in the Nineteenth Century* (New York: Harper & Row, 1974); and Peter J. Rachleff, *Black Labor in Richmond, 1865–1890* (Urbana: University of Illinois Press, 1989), ch. 6.

6. For an introduction into the vast literature on the definition and analytical usefulness of the public and private spheres see the collections of essays edited by S. I. Benn and G. F. Gaus, *Public and Private in Social Life* (New York: St. Martin's Press, 1983); Craig Calhoun, ed., *Habermas and the Public Sphere* (Cambridge, Mass.: MIT Press, 1992); and Nancy Fraser, *Unruly Practices: Power, Discourse, and Gender in Contemporary Social Theory* (Minneapolis: University of Minnesota Press, 1993). The Ur text of discussions about the public and the private is Jürgen Habermas, *The Structural Transformation of the Public Sphere: An Inquiry into a Category of Bourgeois Society* (1965; Eng. trans. Cambridge, Mass.: MIT Press, 1989). On the gendered aspects of separate spheres see Nancy Cott, *The Bonds of Womanhood: "Woman's Sphere" in New England, 1780–1835* (New Haven: Yale University Press, 1977). For a broad introduction to the separate spheres ideology, the public/private dichotomy, and their influence on the writing of American history see Linda K. Kerber, "Separate Spheres, Female Worlds, Women's Place: The Rhetoric of Women's History," *JAH* 75 (June 1988), 9–39.

7. On the state of the public schools see William H. Ruffner, *Ninth Annual Report of the Superintendent of Public Instruction* (1879), v. On Reconstruction Virginia politics and the Conservative Party see Raymond H. Pulley, *Old Virginia Restored: An Interpretation of the Progressive Impulse, 1870–1930* (Charlottesville: University Press of Virginia, 1968), 1–92; Allen W. Moger, *Virginia: From Bourbonism to Byrd, 1870–1925* (Charlottesville: University Press of Virginia, 1968), 1–76; and Jack P. Maddex, Jr., *The Virginia Conservatives, 1867–1879: A Study in Reconstruction Politics* (Chapel Hill: University of North Carolina Press, 1970).

8. The 1880 election results for Virginia were: 96,449 for the Democrats; 84,020 for the Republicans; and 31,527 for the Readjusters. Despite the magnitude of their loss, the coalition nonetheless sent two Readjusters to Congress, both from the white farming counties of the western portion of the state. For election statistics see the *Richmond Whig*, 25 November and 2 December 1881.

9. Charles H. Causey to Mahone, 6 November 1880, box 23, Mahone Papers, Perkins Library, Duke University (hereafter abbreviated MP).

10. For concentrated evidence of the Readjusters' move towards liberalism, see the scrapbook entitled "The Liberal Movement," box 215, MP.

11. Mahone quoted in *New York Herald*; reprinted in *Staunton Spectator*, 26 April 1881.

12. As one Conservative lectured, "If a man will not pay one dollar a year towards the education of the children of his country [state], ought he be allowed to

vote?" *Staunton Spectator*, 4 January, 1 November, 1881. On the 1876 suffrage restriction see Maddex, *The Virginia Conservatives*, 197–98. Political nomenclature gets a bit confusing for Virginia during the Readjuster years. "Funders," "Conservatives," and "Democrats" may be read interchangeably. The "Straight-Outs" were Republicans who resisted alliance with the white former Democrats known as Readjusters after 1879. "Republicans" generally refers to Republican Readjusters, mainly African Americans.

13. Virginia historians disagree on the effect of the 1876 poll tax law. See the contrasting views of Pearson, *Readjuster Movement*, 49–50 and Wynes, *Race Relations*, 12–14, 135–36. Indirect evidence that suffrage restriction, rather than tax collection, was the Conservatives' aim in 1876 follows from the provision that separation of the tax from the ballot could be accomplished only by passage of popular referenda in two consecutive elections. Thus only a movement of the strength of the Readjusters could undo the Conservative restriction of the suffrage. However, because all three political parties in Virginia routinely paid the poll tax for their supporters, tax delinquency rates do not translate into disfranchisement rates. The necessity of paying the taxes of delinquent voters put a strain on the finances of all three parties. As one Readjuster directive on this subject instructed, "It would be well to keep from those who are able to pay the fact of our intention to finally pay their taxes." Flyer, J. A. Noon (Staunton) to precinct workers, 7 October 1882, box 58, MP.

14. Moore, *Two Paths*, 64. No one in Virginia advocated outright abolition of the capitation tax, as it funded the public schools.

15. Resolutions of the Rockingham Republicans, quoted in *Staunton Spectator*, 15 March 1881. See also "An Address to the Republicans of Virginia and our Sympathizers Beyond the Borders of This Commonwealth," March 1881, Mahone Scrapbooks, box 211, MP. Written by black Republican Readjusters, this address calls for an alliance with "that party which would be most liberal in securing to [black Virginians] the full and complete enjoyment of their political rights."

16. *Staunton Spectator*, 19 July 1881, quoting an interview with an Elizabeth City man in the Brooklyn, N.Y. *Eagle*. On sectional politics in antebellum Virginia see Charles Henry Ambler, *Sectionalism in Virginia from 1776 to 1861* (Chicago: University of Chicago Press, 1910); Alison Goodyear Freehling, *Drift Toward Dissolution: The Virginia Slavery Debate of 1831–1832* (Baton Rouge: Louisiana State University Press, 1982); John C. Inscoe, *Mountain Masters, Slavery, and the Sectional Crisis in Western North Carolina* (Knoxville: University of Tennessee Press, 1989), 125–54; Gordon B. McKinney, *Southern Mountain Republicans, 1865–1900: Politics and the Appalachian Community* (Chapel Hill: University of North Carolina Press, 1978); and Daniel W. Crofts, *Reluctant Confederates: Upper South Unionists in the Secession Crisis* (Chapel Hill: University of North Carolina Press, 1989).

17. *New York Times*, 20 June 1881.

18. Former President Grant, who opposed repudiation, endorsed the coalition in 1881 because of its stand on the suffrage issue. See Ulysses S. Grant to James D. Brady, 4 October 1881, Williams Papers, Alderman Library, University of Virginia. On the relationship of the national Republicans with the Readjusters see Vincent P. DeSantis, *Republicans Face the Southern Question: The New Departure Years, 1877–1897* (Baltimore: Johns Hopkins University Press, 1959), 141–60.

19. Broadside, "The Re-Adjuster Programme! An Address of the State Committee to the Readjuster Party of Virginia" (written by Mahone), 4 January 1881, Broadside Collection, Virginia Historical Society.

20. *Richmond Whig*, 24 June 1881. Quoted in Moore, *Two Paths to the New South*, 79.

21. *Richmond Whig*, 18 June 1881, quoting *New York Evening Post*, Mahone Scrapbooks, box 215, MP.

22. Letter from John R. Hathaway, editor of *Norfolk Day Book*, in *New York Times*, 17 June 1881, and *Times* editorial, that same day.

23. In 1878, local workingmen's parties organized nationally as the Independent or Greenbacker party and elected fifteen Greenbacker Congressmen and many local and state officials. Greenbackers attended the Readjusters' founding convention in 1879 and influenced the coalition's agenda as well as its organization. In Richmond, the Greenbackers served as a bridge to the Readjusters for the African American community. On black Greenbackers, see Rachleff, *Black Labor in Richmond*, 84. On the Greenbackers generally and independent politics in the period following the Great Railroad Strike of 1876, see Nell Irvin Painter, *Standing at Armageddon: The United States, 1877–1919* (New York: Norton, 1987), 27–30; Leon Fink, *Workingmen's Democracy: The Knights of Labor and American Politics* (Urbana: University of Illinois Press, 1983), esp. ch. 6; and Melton Alonza McLaurin, *The Knights of Labor in the South* (Westport, Conn.: Greenwood Press, 1978).

24. *Petersburg Index-Appeal*, 15 March 1881. The Petersburg delegates passed resolutions calling for freedom of the ballot, equality of all before the law, improved public education, tax reductions for working men, the appointment of blacks as jurors, and a more equitable system of state taxation.

25. The evolution of the Readjuster program can be most easily traced in their party platforms. See also Pearson, *Readjuster Movement*, 97–102 and Moore, *Two Paths*, 82.

26. *Staunton Spectator*, 26 April 1881; 10, 17 May 1881.

27. "An Appeal to the Voters of Lynchburg," n.d. (1881), box 200, MP.

28. *Staunton Spectator*, 5 April 1881, 4 October 1881, quoting Daniel.

29. *Marion Conservative Democrat*, 7 October 1881 (first quote); *Staunton Spectator*, 1 November 1881 (second quote).

30. After the Readjuster victory in 1881 the Democrats allied with the Straight-Out Republicans in an attempt to tap black Readjuster support. In 1882 this alliance ran black state senator Rev. John M. Dawson for Congress against Readjuster John S. Wise. African American Readjusters held firm in their opposition to what they perceived to be Democratic obfuscation of class issues through invocation of the color line.

31. Clipping, editorial (George S. Rouse), *Culpeper Times*, 2 December 1881, in Mahone Scrapbooks, box 215, MP.

32. *Florida Weekly Telegraph*, 3 December 1881, Mahone Scrapbooks, box 215, MP.

33. *Norfolk Review*, 25 May 1882, Mahone Scrapbooks, box 215, MP.

34. Clipping, n.p., Gouverneur, N.Y., 12 January 1882, Mahone Scrapbooks, box 215, MP.

35. The relationship of the Readjusters to liberalism conforms to what Ronald

Dworkin refers to as the "sceptical thesis" of liberalism that does not see it as an authentic and coherent political morality but rather as a "cluster of political positions" tied to a set of political and economic propositions (such as a free market economy and one man, one vote). See "Liberalism," 115–16.

36. R. R. Farr to Mahone, 5 November 1880, box 23, MP.

37. Nell Irvin Painter, "'Social Equality,' Miscegenation, Labor, and Power," in Numan V. Bartley, *The Evolution of Southern Culture* (Athens: University of Georgia Press, 1988), 47–67; Jim Cullen, "'I's a Man Now': Gender and African American Men," in Catherine Clinton and Nina Silber, eds., *Divided Houses: Gender and the Civil War* (New York: Oxford University Press, 1992), 76–96; Glenda Elizabeth Gilmore, *Gender and Jim Crow: Women and the Politics of White Supremacy in North Carolina, 1896–1920* (Chapel Hill: University of North Carolina Press, 1996), esp. ch. 3; Bryant Simon, "The Appeal of Cole Blease of South Carolina: Race, Class, and Sex in the New South," *Journal of Southern History* 62 (February 1996): 57–86; Edwards, *Gendered Strife and Confusion*.

38. Martha Hodes, "The Sexualization of Reconstruction Politics: White Women and Black Men in the South after the Civil War," *Journal of the History of Sexuality* (January 1993): 402–17, and *White Women, Black Men: Illicit Sex in the Nineteenth-Century South* (New Haven: Yale University Press, 1997), ch. 7. See also Peter Bardaglio, *Reconstructing the Household: Families, Sex, and the Law in the Nineteenth-Century South* (Chapel Hill: University of North Carolina Press, 1995), ch. 6.

39. *Congressional Journal*, 39th Cong., 1st sess., pt. 1, 10 January 1866, pp. 179–80.

40. Quoted in Steven A. Channing, *Crisis of Fear: Secession in South Carolina* (New York: Simon and Schuster, 1974), 287. This discourse was not limited to the South. In the postwar North, where black suffrage was combated fiercely, similar rhetorical and symbolic linking of black political and sexual rights was commonplace. In Ohio in 1867, to take one example, Democrats staged processions with floats on which young white women carried banners inscribed, "Fathers, save us from negro suffrage." Cited in David H. Fowler, *Northern Attitudes Towards Interracial Marriage: Legislation and Public Opinion in the Middle Atlantic and the States of the Old Northwest, 1780–1930* (New York: Garland, 1987), 231.

41. Alfred Avins, "antimiscegenation Laws and the Fourteenth Amendment: The Original Intent," *Virginia Law Review* 52: 1224 (1966); 1227.

42. Whereas the right to vote was deemed to belong to all citizens in the Fifteenth Amendment (1870), section two of the Fourteenth Amendment (1868) effectively limited the franchise to male citizens twenty-one years of age or older. Although some woman suffragists read the negative language of the Fifteenth Amendment ("the vote shall not be denied") as open to the possibility of female enfranchisement, the Supreme Court ultimately upheld the interpretation of Elizabeth Cady Stanton and Susan B. Anthony at the time: that the amendments had positively defined the franchise in masculine terms. On the passage of the suffrage amendments and the feminist response see William Gillette, *The Right to Vote: Politics and the Passage of the Fifteenth Amendment* (Baltimore: Johns Hopkins University Press, 1965) and Ellen Carol Du Bois, *Feminism and Suffrage: The Emergence of an Independent Women's Movement in America, 1848–1869* (Ithaca: Cornell Uni-

versity Press, 1978), ch. 6. Republican jurist Albion W. Tourgée put the matter well. In his words, the Reconstruction amendments defined the body politic as "the manhood of the nation" and "recognized and formulated the universality of manhood in governmental power." *A Fool's Errand, By One of the Fools* (1879; rpt., Cambridge, Mass.: Harvard University Press, 1961), 378.

43. Leonidas Bough to Mahone, 31 May 1881, box 30, MP.

44. *Richmond Whig*, 21 September 1883.

45. Joseph Porter, "A Card to the Voters," 29 October 1883, box 192, MP.

46. Michael Grossberg, "Guarding the Altar: Physiological Restrictions and the Rise of State Intervention in Matrimony," *The American Journal of Legal History* 26 (July 1982): 197–226; 204. See also Grossberg, *Governing the Hearth: Law and the Family in Nineteenth-Century America* (Chapel Hill: University of North Carolina Press, 1985), ch. 4; and Bardaglio, *Reconstructing the Household*, chs. 5 and 6. Nancy F. Cott notes that late-nineteenth-century American courts upheld a "double characterization of marriage (as private *and* public, contract *and* status)." See Cott, "Giving Character to Our Whole Civil Polity: Marriage and the Public Order in the Late Nineteenth Century," in Linda K. Kerber, Alice Kessler-Harris, and Kathryn Kish Sklar, eds., *U.S. History as Women's History: New Feminist Essays* (Chapel Hill: University of North Carolina Press, 1995): 107–21; 115.

47. For a similar argument for Reconstruction North Carolina see Laura F. Edwards, "'The Marriage Covenant is at the Foundation of all Our Rights': The Politics of Slave Marriages in North Carolina after Emancipation," *Law and History Review* 14 (spring 1996): 81–124.

48. John Mercer Langston, *Freedom and Citizenship: Selected Lectures and Addresses* (1883; Miami: Mnemosyne Publications, Inc., 1969), 158.

49. *Petersburg Lancet*, 15 July 1882. The *Philadelphia Evening Bulletin* of 9 November 1883, used precisely this language to explain the hatred of white Democrats for black Readjusters. Black Virginians had earned the wrath of the Bourbons there, it said, because "he who was a slave and a chattel is now a man and a voter."

50. Edwards, *Gendered Strife and Confusion*, 196.

51. Quoted in Eric Foner, *Reconstruction: America's Unfinished Revolution, 1863–1877* (New York: Harper & Row, 1988), 288.

52. Isabel V. Hull, *Sexuality, State and Civil Society in Germany, 1700–1815* (Ithaca: Cornell University Press, 1996), 288–89; 245–51.

53. This was true for African American women as well as men, although the meaning was not identical. See Edwards, *Gendered Strife and Confusion*, ch. 1.

54. Edmund Leach, "Characterization of Caste and Class Systems," in Anthony de Rueck and Julie Knight, eds., *Caste and Race: Comparative Approaches* (Boston: Little, Brown, 1967): 17–27, 19. On marriage as a marker of equality, see also Patricia Seed, *To Love, Honor, and Obey in Colonial Mexico: Conflicts over Marriage Choice, 1574–1821* (Stanford: Stanford University Press, 1988); Ramón Gutiérrez, *When Jesus Came, the Corn Mothers Went Away* (Stanford: Stanford University Press, 1991); and Verena Marinez-Alier, *Marriage, Class and Colour in Nineteenth-Century Cuba: A Study of Racial Attitudes and Sexual Values in a Slave Society* (Cambridge: Cambridge University Press, 1974).

55. *New York Times*, 20 May 1879 (first half of quote); 21 May 1879 (second half of quote). On the Kinney case see *ex parte Kinney*, 14 F. Cas. 602 (C.C.E.D. Va.

1879) (No. 7825). Edmund Kinney is identified as black and Mary Hall as white in the decision.

56. *Richmond State*, 8 March 1880; *Journal of the House of Delegates, 1881–1882*, 337. See also *Richmond Whig*, 13 May, 16 September 1881; 8 December 1882; 19 October 1883.

57. John S. Wise testimony, Senate Reports, 48th Cong., 1st sess., no. 579; U.S. Senate Committee on Privileges and Elections, Report on the Danville Riot (Serial 2178, Washington, 1884), 449.

58. William Mahone was elected by the General Assembly to the United States Senate in December 1879, but was not sworn in until March 1881. As it happened, the upper house of the 47th Congress was divided evenly between the two national parties, with two new senators, Mahone and David Davis of Illinois, to be seated. Davis had been elected as an Independent but had declared his intention to vote with the Democrats. Mahone's vote would therefore determine partisan control of the Senate, since Republican vice president Chester A. Arthur could break a tie. Mahone agreed to cooperate with the Republicans in exchange for assignments to four influential Senate committees and division of the federal patronage in Virginia between regular Republicans and Readjusters. On Mahone's decision see Blake, *William Mahone of Virginia*, 206, and the voluminous correspondence on this topic in the Mahone Papers, esp. boxes 23 and 25. On the relationship of the national Republicans to southern independent movements see De Santis, *Republicans Face the Southern Question*, 147–50, 182–227; and Stanley P. Hirshon, *Farewell to the Bloody Shirt: Northern Republicans and the Southern Negro, 1877–1893* (Bloomington: University of Indiana Press, 1962), 118–22, 138. On the political calculations of Republicans regarding Mahone's course in the Senate see David J. Rothman, *Politics and Power: The United States Senate, 1869–1901* (Cambridge, Mass.: Harvard University Press, 1966), 32–33.

59. Patronage assessments supported professional party workers, financed the printing of campaign materials, and in Virginia as elsewhere, paid the poll taxes of the indigent. On assessments see Stephen Skowronek, *Building a New American State: The Expansion of National Administrative Capacities, 1877–1920* (Cambridge: Cambridge University Press, 1982), 48, 53, 61, 65–66, 74–78. On civil service reform and the Pendleton Act see Ari Hoogenboom, *Outlawing the Spoils: A History of the Civil Service Reform Movement, 1865–1883* (Urbana: University of Illinois Press, 1968). Harold S. Forsythe points out that "the role of paid political workers, in addition to ordinary patronage, gave Virginia's machine politics . . . a distinctly northern cast." See " 'But My Friends are Poor': Ross Hamilton and Freedpeople's Politics in Mecklenburg County, Virginia, 1869–1901," *Virginia Magazine of History and Biography* 105 (autumn 1997): 409–38; 420.

60. Quoted in Rachleff, *Black Labor in Richmond*, 99.

61. Quoted in the *Staunton Spectator*, 25 April 1882.

62. Local party organizations were integrated in 1881. The party directive on this matter instructed that black and white Readjusters should meet "as one body," with the offices divided evenly between the races. On this see George Freeman Bragg, Jr., letter, 26 August 1926, to the *Journal of Negro History* (October 1926): 675. On the disinclination of white Readjusters to follow this directive, see W. J. S. Bowe to Mahone, 16 May 1881, box 30, MP (quote); Resolution, Head Quarters

[*sic*] Republican Readjuster State Executive Committee, Richmond, to Mahone, 16 May 1881, box 30, MP; and Sidney Mosby to Mahone, 12 April 1883, box 70, MP.

63. *Petersburg Index-Appeal*, 9 September, 2 November 1882.

64. Letter to the editor, *Staunton Spectator*, 13 September 1881.

65. Quote from Mahone's remarks on the Pendleton Bill (regulating federal patronage). Clipping, Mahone Scrapbooks, 1882–1883, box 206, MP.

66. The phrase "possessive investment in whiteness" comes from George Lipsitz, "The Possessive Investment in Whiteness: Racialized Social Democracy and the 'White' Problem in American Studies," *American Quarterly* 47 (September, 1995): 369–87. It refers to the psychological and material value of being identified as part of the dominant social group.

67. Many historians have interpreted the South as imbedded in a culture of honor, although—like the debate over southern liberalism—discussion of southern honor tends to end with emancipation. See, e.g., Clement Eaton, "The Role of Honor in Southern Society," *Southern Humanities Review* 10 (Special Bicentennial Issue, 1976): 47–58; Bertram Wyatt-Brown, *Southern Honor: Ethics and Behavior in the Old South* (New York: Oxford University Press, 1982); Edward L. Ayers, *Vengeance and Justice: Crime and Punishment in the 19th-Century American South* (New York: Oxford University Press 1984); Stowe, *Intimacy and Power*; and Kenneth S. Greenberg, *Honor and Slavery: Lies, Duels, Noses, Masks, Dressing as a Woman, Gifts, Strangers, Humanitarianism, Death, Slave Rebellions, The Proslavery Argument, Baseball, Hunting and Gambling in the Old South* (Princeton: Princeton University Press, 1996).

68. Richard Forrester was a dairy farmer and contractor in Richmond, wealthy enough to open bank accounts for each of his grandchildren as they were born. He had been a Republican since emancipation, and served as city councillor in Richmond from Jackson Ward. See Rachleff, *Black Labor in Richmond*, 19; Jackson, *Negro Office-Holders in Virginia*, 57. R. A. Paul was born a slave in Nelson County in 1846. After the war he accompanied his mother to Richmond, where he was employed as a waiter. Taught to read by his mother, Paul continued his education on his own, and eventually served on the board of stewards of the Third Street AME Church. He was, in addition, a member of numerous African American societies. He was elected captain of a local militia unit, and first became active politically in 1874, when he opposed ring rule in the Republican Party. In 1878 he switched to Greenbackerism, and later converted to the Readjusters on the strength of their legislative record. Under the Readjusters, Paul served as a bailiff, a U.S. Deputy Marshal, and a mailing clerk in the Richmond post office. In 1882 Paul was appointed personal doorkeeper to Governor Cameron. On Paul, see D. B. Williams, *A Sketch of the Life and Times of Capt. R. A. Paul* (Richmond: n.p., 1885), esp. 25–49.

69. Quote from Rachleff, *Black Labor in Richmond*, 104. This was not the first time that Cameron had replaced a school board. In 1882, propelled by Petersburg's large and active African American Readjuster community, Cameron removed a Democratic school board that refused to appoint black teachers in the city's black schools and replaced it with one dominated by Readjusters. Cameron's replacement of the Richmond board was upheld in a May Court of Appeals decision. In replacing the school board, the governor at once dealt a blow to Democratic power in Richmond and appropriated coveted patronage positions for Readjusters. Re:

the members of the school board and the Common Council, compare the membership information in the Record of the Richmond Common Council, vol. 21 (1 July 1878–18 December 1883), Richmond Public Library, with the listed school board members, *Richmond Dispatch*, 1 February 1883. On the judicial decision see the *Dispatch*, 12 May 1883.

70. *Richmond Dispatch*, 23 February 1883. Compare the *Dispatch*'s remarks to those of the *Norfolk Landmark* two years earlier. In May 1881, after reporting the election in Norfolk of several African American Readjusters as delegates to the forthcoming Readjuster state convention, where they would presumably influence Readjuster policy, the *Landmark* pronounced itself unequivocally opposed to black public power: "We declare that we are not willing to see Negroes, because they are black, and have certain vested political rights, made overseers of the roads, County Commissioners, members of juries, Magistrates, Councilmen, Mayors, or lawmakers, and so on, and so on." *Norfolk Landmark*, 3 May 1881.

71. Douglas, *Purity and Danger*, 144.

72. Historians tracing the evolution of Jim Crow segregation laws have pinpointed their genesis in centers of commensality and transportation, places where white women ventured forth into the world and were liable to come into close contact with men. As Edward L. Ayers has noted, "the more closely linked to sexuality, the more likely was a place to be segregated." *The Promise of the New South: Life After Reconstruction* (New York: Oxford University Press, 1992), 140. Barbara Y. Welke makes a similar argument in detail in "When All the Women Were White, and All the Blacks Were Men: Gender, Class, Race, and the Road to *Plessy*, 1855–1914," *Law and History Review* 13 (fall 1995): 261–316. The postwar southern expansion of women's sphere parallels that of the antebellum North, where the definition of the private sphere "became an expansive doctrine: home was anywhere women and children were." On the expansion and articulation of domesticity and the private sphere in the North see Paula Baker, "The Domestication of Politics: Women and American Political Society, 1780–1920," *American Historical Review* 89 (June 1984): 620–47, quote from 620; Nancy F. Cott, *The Bonds of Womanhood: "Woman's Sphere" in New England, 1780–1835* (New Haven: Yale University Press, 1977); and Mary P. Ryan, *Women in Public: Between Banners and Ballots, 1825–1880* (Baltimore: Johns Hopkins University Press, 1990).

73. Boxes 71, 72, and 73 of the Mahone Papers contain many letters from local Readjusters to Mahone asking to replace a Democratic teacher or school principal with a Readjuster. Leading white Republican Readjuster James D. Brady put the matter squarely in the spring of 1883 regarding the reluctance of Petersburg school superintendent Griffin Edwards to fire Democratic teachers in favor of Readjusters. "Cannot Mr. Griff Edwards, the Supt. be instructed that White Readjusters *must* teach the white schools, and colored Readjusters the colored schools? It is reported that he says 'Politics ought not to enter into these school matters.' How did he become Supt. if not *entirely* through a *mistaken* idea of *his* politics." Brady to Mahone, 7 May 1883, box 71, MP. Black Readjusters concurred. Richmond's colored schoolteachers met in May 1883 to demand that the city "put none but colored men to be princaple [*sic*] in colored schools wether [*sic*] the whites be good Readjusters or not." Lewis Lindsay to Mahone, 23 May 1883, box 72, MP.

74. The 1880 occupational census reports that roughly two-thirds of the

teachers in Virginia were women. Data from *Statistics of the Population of the United States at the Tenth Census* . . . Vol. I: *Population* (Washington, 1883), table 31, p. 742.

75. J. M. Gills to Mahone, 23 November 1883, box 82, MP. The reference to black men examining the daughters of white women could have referred either to the possibilities for black school superintendents or to the fact that in at least one city (Petersburg), the physician to the poor was an African American doctor.

76. *Lynchburg News*, 5 September 1883.

77. *Richmond Dispatch*, 12 May 1883.

78. See the many letters from May through November, 1883 in the Mahone Papers. E.g., in Lewis P. Nelson to Mahone, 31 October 1883, box 80, MP, he informs Mahone that Col. Gibson, who "is opposed to mixed schools, Negro Trustees or Negro managers where white children are going," will sweep the white vote in Culpeper County. One prominent Readjuster advised Mahone that the party's only chance to beat the Democrats in future elections was to "draw a *color line* under the name of *the white man's liberal Party of Virginia*." R[ichard] A. Wise to Mahone, 8 November 1883, box 81, MP.

79. "I fear many of our best white men have left us permanently as they object to the appointment of negroes on School Board in Richmond," one county leader warned Mahone. See Thomas H. Cross to Mahone, 26 May 1883, box 72, MP. Mahone was reported as having denounced Cameron for injuring both the party and the school interests by his actions in Richmond. See S. Bassett French to Mahone, 27 May 1883, box 72, MP.

80. *Staunton Spectator*, 4 September 1883.

81. Hannah Arendt, "Reflections on Little Rock," *Dissent* 6 (1959): 45–56 and "A Reply to Critics," 179–81; quotes from 56, 48, 181, 49, and 45. For a thoughtful reading of Arendt's purpose in the Little Rock essay see James Bohman, "The Moral Costs of Political Pluralism: The Dilemmas of Difference and Equality in Arendt's 'Reflections on Little Rock,'" in Larry May and Jerome Kohn, eds., *Hannah Arendt: Twenty Years Later* (Cambridge, Mass.: Harvard University Press, 1996), 53–80.

82. The Supreme Court saw the relationship clearly enough. Given the opportunity to rule on the constitutionality of antimiscegenation legislation in 1954, with the *Brown* decision still awaiting implementation, the Court declined to openly address the issue of marriage across the color line "while strident opposition is being voiced to less controversial desegregation because it allegedly leads to intermarriage." See Jack Greenberg, *Race Relations and American Law* (New York: Columbia University Press, 1959), 345. As Peter Wallenstein points out, the educated guesses of astute Court-watchers such as Greenberg regarding the relationship between the school desegregation cases and the antimiscegenation decisions were documented years later in the memoirs of the justices. See Peter Wallenstein, "Race, Marriage, and the Law of Freedom: Alabama and Virginia, 1860s–1960s," *Chicago Kent Law Review* 70 (1994): 371–437; 415–16.

83. Douglas, *Purity and Danger*, 114.

White Women and the Politics of Historical Memory in the New South, 1880–1920

"THERE IS NO true history of the South, novelist Thomas Nelson Page complained in 1894. Why, he lamented, were southerners so jealous of their reputation but "so indifferent to all transmission of their memorial?"[1] At first glance, Page's appeal to white southerners to defend themselves before the bar of history appears curious. His plea, after all, coincided with the flowering of the Confederate tradition and the glorification of the southern past. Yet Page's despair about "the want of a history of the southern people" was not groundless. During the first two decades after the Civil War white southerners, despite their purported obsession with their heritage, manifested little organized interest in their past and failed to agree upon its meaning. Although certain core ideas about the region's history emerged, they remained inchoate, even contradictory. So scattered were the organizations concerned with southern history and so small were their memberships that they could not realistically propagate an authoritative collective memory for white southerners.[2]

By the time of Page's death in 1922, a generation of elite white southerners had rallied to his call and compiled a heroic record of their past. This movement especially engrossed elite white women who donned the mantle of "guardians of the past" to a degree without precedence in the region's history. White women shaped the forms (both nonliterary and literary) and methods used to evoke the past, thereby establishing historical representations that endured long into the twentieth century.[3] By expanding the conception of voluntarism to include matters of history, a generation of white women acquired expertise in and influence through what is now called public history. Their legacy included the creation of an infrastructure for the dissemination of a collective historical memory at a time when few other groups were able to do so. These women architects of whites' historical memory, by both explaining and mystifying the historical roots of white supremacy and elite power in the South, performed a conspicuous civic function at a time of heightened concern about the perpetuation of social and political hierarchies. Although denied the franchise, organized white women nevertheless played a dominant role in crafting the historical memory that would inform and undergird southern politics and public life during the first half of the twentieth century. Their efforts, in short, assumed an importance considerably greater than mere antiquarianism.

White women looked to history as a means to shape the South. To give the white South a sense of its past was to define its aspirations for the future.[4] Like other crafters of historical memory, southern white women did not haphazardly inscribe meaning onto some preordained cultural tradition or representation of the past. Instead they devised ceremonies and formalized expressions, ranging from civic rituals and public monuments to fictional accounts, specific to their own times, needs, and possibilities.[5] In an age of marked elite interest in the past throughout the nation, southern white women understood how power can make some historical narratives possible but silence others. Not only did the collective memory promoted by the women incorporate claims to factual legitimacy but they also invoked and came to be viewed as authoritative traditions. And to the extent that the women's representations of history acquired cultural authority, they also became instruments of power.[6] That so much of the women's historical work took the form of discourse did not diminish its gravity. After all, "the stakes in debates over social memories," historian David Blight insists, "are quite real; material resources, political power, and life chances may all be at stake."[7]

The impulse that led white women to assume the role of guardians of the past may be traced to contentious contemporary debates over gender identities. Assumptions about race, class, and gender in the South, no less than elsewhere, were inherited, learned, borrowed, or informed by the common stock of social memory. So tightly bound together are collective memory and self-identification that memory is the thread of personal identity. When articulating a collective memory for the white South, white men and women necessarily defined themselves in relation to the region's historical hierarchies. Justifications of white power and male privilege were, like a mnemonic device that derives its efficacy from repetition, a recurring element in elite versions of the southern memory.

That the revision of gender identities would influence public memory and vice versa became apparent in the early attempts by white women to interpret the trauma of the Civil War. After Appomattox, women transformed their wartime soldier's aid societies into Confederate memorial associations charged with commemorating dead soldiers. Men often bankrolled these associations, but women assumed effective leadership. To do so was in keeping with the rituals of conspicuous mourning that Victorian convention assigned to women. Memorialization and mourning belonged to the realm of sentiment that white men deemed and white women accepted as "peculiarly fitting to women." Speaking at the 1875 unveiling of the Confederate monument in Augusta, Georgia, Reverend General C. A.

Evans explained, "it was not man's privilege but woman's to raise these monuments throughout the land."[8]

More than grief and conventions of mourning granted this task to white women. The historians LeeAnn Whites and Drew Gilpin Faust have argued persuasively that "the rehabilitation of southern white men became a central postwar responsibility for Confederate women." With the hierarchical order of the South shaken by war, many elite white women recoiled from the potential social chaos and committed themselves to reestablishing antebellum class and racial privileges. The commemoration of the Lost Cause celebrated traditional privileges of race, gender, and class while making them appear to be a natural and inviolable part of history. The participation of white women in the burgeoning Confederate celebration was a salve for their psychic wounds as well as those of Confederate veterans; women's memorial associations functioned as choruses that reassured white men of their manliness and authority, and of feminine deference.[9]

The struggle of elite women to assign meaning to the transformations unleashed by war explains much about the earliest efforts to sculpt a southern public memory. But the war alone did not precipitate the full array of historical activities undertaken by white women across the late nineteenth century. An explosion of organizations, clubs, and commemorative activities reflected the intensifying interest of white women in history during the 1890s and the early twentieth century. This turn-of-the-century preoccupation with matters past revealed concerns and motivations that were distinct from those of the war generation. The postwar activities of southern white women inspired later woman historical activists, but the civic rituals and public monuments at the century's end reflected new needs and possibilities.[10]

At the close of the nineteenth century much remained unresolved about the reconciliation of white women's agency with the ongoing effort to reestablish a patriarchal social order in the South. Disfranchisement, legal segregation, economic discrimination, and white violence all worked to bolster the power of white men in the region. Yet, a lingering mistrust of white men and an uneasiness with dependence on them encouraged white women to enhance their own power and sense of self. Even as many white women validated white male authority, they did so without renouncing their own claim to power—their role as partners in the millennial progress of the white race.[11]

When white women embraced civilization as the justification for their agency, they necessarily entered into the swirling debate about gender, race, civilization, and history. These four ideas were inseparable in the lexicon of the era. Civilization, the historian Gail Bederman explains, referred to a precisely calibrated stage of human development achieved when societies evolved beyond savagery and barbarism. Civilization itself was considered by many whites to be virtually a racial trait that only Anglo-Saxons and some other whites shared. Gender roles, Victorians believed, were one measure of civilization. The greater the gender differentiation in society, the reasoning went, the higher the civilization. Consequently, the elaborate code of conduct that divided the idealized lives of white men and women into distinct realms was intrinsic to advanced civilization. The perceived absence of such clearly defined gender roles among African Americans purportedly demonstrated their limited evolutionary progress.[12]

This significance attached to whiteness, masculinity, and civilization left ambiguous the role of white women as agents of civilization. The logic of some ideas of civilization suggested that it was intrinsically male. Anglo-Saxon men alone had the racial genius for self-government and the manly capacity of self-control that made the highest levels of social development possible. Accordingly, the story of human progress was a record of the power and beneficence of white men. What, if any, contribution white women had made to the advancement of civilization was open to debate. Merely vessels of civilization, women arguably furthered human evolution chiefly as wives and mothers. And even this contribution was possible only because of the support and protection provided by white men, a point underscored by the white-hot debate about lynching and the defense of southern white womanhood at the century's close.

This interpretation of civilization represented an implicit attack on female cultural authority. By no means was the "feminization of American culture" a fait accompli in the late nineteenth century, especially not in the South. Inherited ideals of "republican motherhood" and the cult of domesticity had long given women an important role in the transmission of culture within the home, and had even encouraged them to assume an ever-widening range of responsibilities. But not until long after the republican ideology had dissolved into mere slogans did white women begin to assume the acknowledged role of guardians of culture. Thus at the same time that women began to incorporate cultural custodianship into their domain, they confronted an ascendant, stridently masculine conception of civilization.[13]

Many white middle-class and elite women found in history an antidote to exaggerated assertions of men's roles in human progress. History for many white women became an instrument of self-definition. Of course, only certain readings of the southern past were conceivable in the late nineteenth and early twentieth centuries. Yet within the boundaries imposed by the prevailing beliefs of the era, the meaning of the history of the white South was open to multiple readings, which in turn allowed white women to use it for varied purposes. The historical activities of white women legitimated contradictory claims for power, some reactionary, others emancipatory. For many white women, their gendered identities could not be separated from their ties to the past—not just their personal, familial past, but also the collective "history" of the South. Beset by the transformations of the New South, elite white women found in history a resource with which to fashion new selves without sundering links to the old.

The essential point is that substantial numbers of white women refused to surrender either the field of history or the realm of public culture to men. They insisted that women of culture were integral to human progress. The field of history provided one opening through which white women could revise the link between manliness and civilization. By giving meaning to the past, women claimed for themselves the work of recording and narrating the progress of civilization. Through the crafting of historical memory, they laid claim to a new source of cultural authority.

Driven to "renovate" and "preserve" the past, elite white women looked to the women's organizations that proliferated across the New South as instruments with which to mold an authoritative historical memory for the region. By harnessing the energy and prestige of their members, even small groups exerted influence out of proportion to their size. The number of women's clubs devoted to filiopietism and history was staggering. For instance, two prominent but not atypical club women, Ida Caldwell McFadden of Texas and Mrs. Chalmers Meek Williamson of Mississippi, between the two of them, were members of the Association for the Preservation of Virginia Antiquities (APVA), United Daughters of the Confederacy (UDC), Daughters of the American Revolution (DAR), Daughters of the Pilgrims, Daughters of the War of 1812, Daughters of Colonial Governors, and Daughters of the Founders and Patriots of America, Scions of the Cavaliers, Order of the First Families of Virginia, Order of the Knights of the Golden Shoe Society, Order of the Crown of America, Descendants of the Barons of Runnemede, and Colonial Dames of America. The finely honed elitism of these societies is evident in their very names. Membership in them evinced an unmistakable claim by birthright to cultural dominion over the remembered past.[14]

The southern past was a focus, even preoccupation, of these and other white clubwomen in the New South. Given the overlapping memberships that were routine among women in hereditary, philanthropic, and civic associations, most women's voluntary associations inexorably became involved in historical matters. Women's clubs, ranging from the Every Saturday History Class in Atlanta to the Charleston Civic Club, maintained an active interest in local history, and virtually all state federations of women's clubs periodically took up historical issues. White women sometimes organized specifically to address historical concerns, as evidenced by the various women's organizations that pioneered historical preservation in the New South. So quickly did women's societies establish their expertise that, by the early twentieth century, state and local governments routinely deeded public property to women to operate for public edification.[15]

Clubwomen in Nashville, Tennessee, for instance, pioneered this new civic duty when they agitated for the preservation of the Hermitage, Andrew Jackson's home near Nashville. The State of Tennessee had purchased the home in 1856 with the intent of maintaining it as a shrine. But relatives of Jackson continued to occupy it until 1889 when a state senator proposed turning it into a home for Confederate veterans. A group of Nashville white women protested that the proposed facility threatened the integrity of the Hermitage as a shrine to Jackson. When polite supplication failed to sway the legislature, the women formed the Ladies' Hermitage Association. Their appeals, published in Nashville newspapers, aroused opposition to the plan and forced a compromise. In April 1889 the state conditionally conveyed the Hermitage to the association. In keeping with the prejudices of the day, male trustees oversaw the women. But as a practical matter the women's organization assumed responsibility for maintaining and operating the state's leading historic site. Similar preservation campaigns by women's associations took place in Charleston, South Carolina; Halifax, North Carolina; San Antonio, Texas; and Tampa, Florida; to name only a few examples.[16]

Organized white women in the South focused much of their attention on the proper use of public spaces. In an era when monuments and commemorative sites were typically sponsored by voluntary associations rather than by the state, women's groups often assumed the leadership in campaigns to transform public spaces into memory theaters where white southerners told their history to themselves and others. These women activists assumed that environment played a central role in promoting self-improvement, creating a well-ordered citizenry, and binding together communities. The construction of the Jefferson Davis monument in Richmond is but one illustration of this impulse. Calls for a memorial to the Confederate president rang out almost immediately after his death in 1889. In 1896 the United Confederate Veterans (UCV) launched a campaign to build an elaborate and costly marble shrine in the Confederate capitol. But as of 1899 they had raised only $20,000 of the $210,000 their plans required. With fund-raising stalled, the UCV grudgingly turned the project over to the UDC. During the following eight years the UDC revised the plans in favor of a more inexpensive and less grandiose monument and methodically raised money. Eventually they collected $70,000, a sum sufficient to complete the monument that now stands. The unveiling of the monument in 1907 was glaring testimony to the capabilities of the UDC and unintentional confirmation of the ineptitude of the UCV.[17]

White women fully appreciated the power of symbolic representations of the past located in public spaces. As Lizzie Pollard, president of the Southern Memorial Association in Fayetteville, Arkansas, explained in 1904, the Confederate monuments "we build will speak their message to unborn generations. . . . This is not alone a labor of love, it is a work of duty as well. We are correcting history."[18] As Pollard suggested, white women intended each Confederate and Revolutionary War monument they erected and each old building they preserved in the region as an antidote to the pejorative and dismissive portraits of the region and its past propagated by nonsoutherners. By "correcting history," organized white women assumed a crucial role in what historian Michel-Rolph Trouillot calls "the moment of retrospective significance": when a historical narrative is forged and meaning is assigned selectively to past events.[19]

White women also ascribed significance to the past by becoming at once the archivists and the narrators of southern history. The white women who organized the North Carolina exhibit at the 1907 Jamestown Exposition, for example, created one of the earliest public displays and de facto (if temporary) collections of North Carolina artifacts. The origins of the Exposition itself can be traced to white clubwomen in Williamsburg, Virginia, who were anxious to preserve the site of the Jamestown colony and who formed the Association for the Preservation of Virginia Antiquities (APVA) in 1889. Although not strictly a women's group, the APVA derived its energy and influence from the elite white women who comprised much of its membership. In 1900, the association proposed and secured support for an international fair to celebrate the tercentennial of the founding of Jamestown.[20]

The fair's boosters intended it to be the most important international celebration since the 1893 Chicago Exposition, and certainly the most important ever held in the South. The participation of southern states, however, was not assured. Southern states had a record of parsimonious appropriations for previous expositions. Several southern legislatures had allotted no funds for exhibits in Chicago and five southern states had no state buildings there. That Texas, Louisiana, and Arkansas had state buildings at all was, according to the official history of the fair, due to "the assistance rendered by women."[21]

By 1907, white clubwomen had acquired the organizational fortitude to insure that the South was represented to their satisfaction at Jamestown. Women's patriotic organizations were especially active in planning for the event. In North Carolina, three women organized and oversaw the installation of the state's historical exhibits. Mary Hilliard Hinton, a member of the North Carolina Daughters of the Revolution (DR) and an exhibit organizer, boasted, "As fashion and history repeat themselves, so again the daughters of Carolina have taken the lead and done their duty in placing her historically where she justly belongs—in the front rank."[22]

The North Carolina exhibit reflected the particular interests of the organizing committee. Various "relics" memorialized the "Edenton Tea Party," a 1774 protest meeting organized by women against British taxation, and celebrated its organizers, "the true, noble, refined women, who fulfilled the duty of home yet forgot not their country." Beyond highlighting the revolutionary contributions of these women, the exhibit also reminded—even politely tweaked—Virginians that the Roanoke settlement in North Carolina had preceded Jamestown. The "Lost Colony" of Roanoke, moreover, had been the birthplace of Virginia Dare, the first "infant child of pure Caucasian blood," a milestone which "proclaimed the birth of the white race in the Western Hemisphere." The North Carolina exhibitors staked out their state's claim to precedence in both the founding of white civilization in North America and the defense of fundamental liberties during the Revolution.[23]

To these historical activities of clubwomen may be added genealogical activities, public rituals such as Confederate Memorial Day, and campaigns to post roadside historical markers and build historic highways (such as the Natchez Trace and the Colonial Parkway linking Yorktown and Jamestown). White women also crusaded for the teaching of the "true history" of the South, especially with regard to slavery and the sectional strife of the nineteenth century, by censoring school texts, silencing college professors, and intimidating textbook publishers. Mrs. W. C. H. Merchant bragged to the 1904 meeting of the UDC that "owing to the efforts and influence of the United Daughters" every state of the former Confederacy had adopted texts sympathetic to the Lost Cause.[24] Likewise, women's organizations supplied classroom materials, conducted classes to "Americanize" immigrants, awarded cash prizes for student essays on topics dear to the organizations, and funded college scholarships. Finally, organized women lobbied for state archives and museums. White women of the New South, in sum, asserted a cultural authority over virtually all representations of the region's past.[25]

That voluntary and patriotic societies provided the means through which white women became architects of public memory is easier to explain than why southern white women between 1890 and 1920 assumed the leadership in preserving "links with the past." White men did not accede authority over public memory so much as white women grasped it. White women exhibited a keen appreciation of the place of history in public culture and demanded deference from men (as the example of the Ladies' Hermitage Association demonstrates). Many observers recognized that "step by step" women were "taking over the field of liberal culture."

But, as Earl Barnes explained in the *Atlantic Monthly* in 1912, "It is not through the generosity of men that liberal culture has come into the possession of women; they have carried it by storm and have compelled capitulation."[26] Men conceded that women had assumed responsibility for the past. After a Virginia woman publicly deplored the neglect of Jamestown, a male letter writer to the *New York Times* in 1902 asked, "Why is it we [men] are not more interested in the preservation of links with the past? If I am not mistaken, women are more inspired with this spirit than men. In fact, we are indebted to their noble work for most of what has been accomplished."[27]

The failure of men's voluntary associations to lead in the public interpretation of the past is puzzling. The United Confederate Veterans, of course, exerted considerable influence over white memory between 1890 and 1910. But the life span of the organization was only as long as that of its members and the Sons of the Confederacy, a spin-off organization, floundered. Likewise, the Sons of the American Revolution and similar groups nurtured the contemporary interest in matters past in the South, but they were, with few exceptions, junior partners to the women's organizations. The "capitulation" of men, to borrow Barnes's word, took place even though the late nineteenth century was a period of booming male fraternal societies. Indeed, one observer, writing in 1897, described the last third of the nineteenth century as the "Golden Age of Fraternity," a time when millions of men joined the Improved Order of Red Men, Knights of Pythias, and countless other orders. Yet male patriotic groups failed to appeal to large numbers of southern white men potentially eligible to join them. Southern men may have venerated the hallowed sacrifice of their ancestors, but they did so indolently. Perhaps because defeat loomed so large in the southern past, the sons of the Confederate generation looked elsewhere for less ambiguous sources of male power and status. Athletic, political, and financial exploits, not cultivation of the past, were the preferred means through which fin de siècle men defined themselves. Matters of history evidently did not coincide with the practical and social motivations that attracted white men to fraternal societies. Finally, white southern men almost certainly did not recognize fully the potential cultural power implicit in giving meaning to the past. That power became evident only over time through the energetic activism and cultural innovation of white women at the century's close.[28]

One group of southern white men, professional historians, did take an active interest in the southern past. Around the turn of the century a generation of academic "missionaries," trained at Johns Hopkins University and elsewhere, introduced to southern schools modern research methods, courses in southern history, and faculty and student associations dedicated to fostering a historical community committed to rigorous standards of scholarship. But the accomplishments of these historians should not be exaggerated. Trained historians in the South, however earnest they may have been, understood that the project of "renovating" the study of history demanded a rudimentary scholarly infrastructure that the New South lacked.[29] Resources for research and adequate avenues for publication were wholly lacking. Despite academic historians' efforts to revive the moribund historical societies scattered across the region, most existed in name only, some as vehicles for the enthusiasms of a few zealots and others as genteel social clubs that met sporadically without any discernable mission. Moreover, the professional historians seldom challenged the already prevailing opinion that slavery was a patriarchal, benevolent institution, the South's stand in the Civil War honorable, and Reconstruction a benighted experiment.[30]

Early academic historians in the South privately complained that amateur historians, and especially women, "wrote eulogy, but not history."[31] But pragmatic considerations tempered their contempt for women's historical activities. Professional historians and archivists recognized that women's organizations were a valuable constituency whose public support was often essential. Indeed, proposals for the creation of state archives and history museums in the South often implicitly solicited the support of women's patriotic and hereditary societies by pledging to provide public space in the facilities for their activities. In addition, academic historians and archivists hastened to the lecterns of virtually every women's patriotic, hereditary, and voluntary society in search of audiences. Thus, although male historians gained increasing prestige and influence over interpreting the southern past during the first two decades of the twentieth century, even they never underestimated the cultural authority wielded by organized white women.

Women active in historical matters, as the earlier quote from Mary Hilliard Hinton suggests, tirelessly reminded men of their jurisdiction over the past and diligently recorded men's praise of them. Even when compiling a historical narrative centered on white male exploits, which seemingly reaffirmed traditional definitions of masculine and feminine, white women forged a link between their gender, their race, and civilization. Few accounts of the continent's early settlement written by women failed to mention Virginia Dare's birth; likewise, few biographies of Revolutionary patriots ignored mention of the steadfast and essential support volunteered by the patriots' wives. Some women went further, insisting that white women played a role not only as recorders but also as unheralded agents of history. Only "sheer ignorance," in Hinton's words, prevented white women from assuming their proper place in the archives of history. One commonplace aim of white clubwomen was to record and emulate the heroic deeds of their forgotten predecessors. In 1896 DAR member Ellen

Douglas Baxter insisted that "While we recall with reverence, greater than pride, the deeds and character of our revolutionary forefathers, we must not forget that the women of this period . . . made them what they were . . . [and] made it possible for men to accomplish the grand results which history attributes to them alone."[32] Evelyn E. Moffitt, in a speech at the dedication of the Edenton Tea Party memorial in the North Carolina capitol in 1908, voiced similar frustration over the inattention to white women's historical contributions. "This daring and heroic stand, so interesting and ever so fascinating [—] the wonder is that it has not held a place on the page of every revolutionary history. But has not this been the case in America that the lives of the generality of women are not deemed to be important enough to trace along side the histories of their distinguished sons!"[33] White women even refused to concede the spotlight in the Confederate past entirely to men. Speaking for Confederate women before a 1900 Confederate reunion, Lizzie Pollard announced, "Many of us are veterans, veterans as much as the gray, battle scarred old soldiers, tho' we bided at home. Are we not veterans as well as they?"[34]

If southern women active in historical matters revised the gendered ideology of civilization, they still remained committed to it. When Ellen Douglas Baxter urged the women of the DAR to recall the deeds of revolutionary women, she did so in hopes that modern women would emulate their "same sense of duty," "quiet submission to the will of [their] husbands," and "long suffering, patience, and endurance."[35] According to Mrs. Patrick Matthew of the DR, Penelope Baker, the organizer of the Edenton Tea Party, represented "a leader and teacher of loyal womanhood, wife, mother, and with these elements of Christian love and obedience she became a jewel among her sex, a womanly woman of strength and vigor."[36]

This last phrase—"a womanly woman of strength and vigor"—reveals much about the civilizationist impulse of white clubwomen. Few white women looked to history to find inspiration for overturning the prevailing idea of civilization; instead their concern revolved around women's relation to it. Most clubwomen occupied a middle ground between feminists such as Charlotte Perkins Gilman who claimed that sex should not affect one's contribution to civilization, and antifeminists who countered that women could advance civilization only as wives and mothers. Instead, history seemed to offer a usable past in which white women had remained "womanly" even as they, in conjunction with white men, pulled civilization forward.

The usable history that white women fashioned acquired considerable cultural power because it addressed pressing social and political issues of the day in the New South. When white women collected, organized, and propagated a remembered past, they dictated the shape of contemporary public debates which were rooted in history, such as racial segregation, disfranchisement of black men, and inequitable funding for black and white education. Their activities created enduring obstacles to the production of alternative renderings of southern history and, by extension, alternative visions of the southern future. To collect relics, preserve sites, and build monuments was to establish the "facts" of southern history that subsequent narratives had to take into account.

The delineation and defense of social hierarchies was conspicuous in the history disseminated by white clubwomen. In the process of ordering the southern past, clubwomen inscribed inequalities into the history they composed. Ideas about the interrelationship of inherent racial attributes and civilization encouraged white women's clubs to indulge in Anglophilia, to venerate relics of Anglo-Saxon civilization in the South, to take an active interest in mountain whites of reputed pure Anglo-Saxon descent, and to memorialize the birth of Virginia Dare. These activities were entirely consonant with the women's beliefs about the indivisibility of race, gender, and civilization. Their elaborate vetting of ancestry (which also revealed the grip of notions about the link between blood, race, and civilization) and other rituals promoted a refined sense of status. The ever-popular Martha Washington tea parties and colonial balls, for instance, precisely apportioned roles among participants according to the standards of birth, wealth, and social station. Likewise, the organizations typically promoted stridently elitist narratives of history. Beyond preserving historic sites, the APVA, for instance, incorporated veneration of bloodlines and elite white culture into its mission. The Virginia past, when distilled by the APVA, sanctioned the continuing leadership of the state by a purportedly disinterested elite. Such invented traditions as the APVA-sponsored annual pilgrimages to Jamestown were intended to instill respect and awe for the state's dutiful white leaders who had founded the nation, established representative government, and purportedly provided disinterested public service. The unmistakable lessons of this past were deference to white social betters, reverence for established institutions, and fidelity to tradition.[37]

White women promoted a public memory that provided crucial ideological ballast for white supremacy by rooting the contemporary racial hierarchy in a historical narrative and in a manner that naturalized it. In autobiographies, essays on contemporary issues, nostalgic recollections published in the *Confederate Veteran*, and historical novels, white women contributed mightily to the moonlight-and-magnolia imagery of the Old South. Even before academic historians at Johns Hopkins, Columbia, and elsewhere produced their "pro-slavery" historiography, white women rendered idyllic the institution of slavery. Taken together, the writings and other representations of slavery and antebellum life achieved a kind of classic purity; the setting might vary from the Revolution to the Civil War, but women populated their accounts with idealized renderings of dashing and honorable white planters, beautiful and refined plantation mistresses, and content black mammies. The glorification of the loving and faithful black mammy was particularly conspicuous, reaching its zenith when the UDC proposed, and Congress considered, a national monument to black mammies on the Washington Mall. Behind this memory of domestic harmony and black subservience lurked anxieties about the brittle state of southern race relations, the domestic authority of white women, and traditions of interracial intimacy in an age of segregation. But the representations of black mammies and carefree slaves suppressed those concerns by extolling the memory of slavery as a golden age of race relations when love and "familial" duty bound the races together. By shaping the imagery of slavery and of black slaves white women also fixed the cultural legacy of slavery, virtually expurgating alternative representations of slavery as brutal or immoral. The implications for the present of this rendition of the past were explicit. Reconstruction, for example, was rendered as a bacchanalia of corruption and barbarism that ended only when the Ku Klux Klan and white vigilantism restored white rule and, by extension, civilization.[38]

Organized white women tirelessly disseminated this history by writing and censoring textbooks, by promoting rituals of "southern patriotism," by scrutinizing the contents of museums and archives, and later by monitoring the activities of professional historians and archivists. At a time when professional historians were few in number and southern cultural institutions and universities were acutely interested in garnering public support, white women in historical and hereditary societies exerted formidable influence.[39] The possible repercussions of alienating these groups were demonstrated in 1911, after Enoch M. Banks, a young history professor at the University of Florida, six years out of graduate school at Columbia, recklessly questioned the legitimacy of secession. Members of the UDC and UCV were unswayed by Banks's conclusions that "in the calm light of history" secession was contrary to the national interest and that "the North was relatively in the right while the South was relatively in the wrong."[40] They berated the University of Florida for employing an historian who was "not fitted to teach true and unprejudiced history." In little more than a month Banks resigned. Eager to appease the custodians of the Confederate tradition, both Governor Albert W. Gilchrist and University of Florida president Albert A. Murphree hailed the banishment of an historian with such "unsound views."[41] The lesson of the Banks affair and similar controversies was unmistakable: interpreters of the past risked the threat of swift and severe censure if they followed their research in new and controversial directions.

If the historical activities of white women affirmed hierarchies of class and race, they still did not constitute a seamless ideological hegemony.

Indeed, in important ways, their historical activities contributed to new fields of political and cultural struggle among whites. Appeals to the past legitimated contradictory claims, some emancipatory, some reactionary. For example, when white women in North Carolina commemorated the Edenton Tea Party in the state capitol, they challenged the notion that white women had no noteworthy role in the nation's founding. At the same time, the commemoration reaffirmed hierarchical power by focusing exclusively on the activities of elite white women. Organized white women in North Carolina and elsewhere in the South well understood the importance of the historical representations with which they filled public spaces; after all, their activities took place in an environment in which racial and gender distinctions had spatial dimensions. "An individual's sense of self, and the degree to which that self is at core male or female," historian Mary Ryan contends, "evolves through associations with place." Gilded Age men and women negotiated a complex geography of public spaces, virtually all of which was segregated according to race and part of which was explicitly segregated along gender lines. Historical sites, like all public places, had to be situated in the spatial grid of gender and race.[42]

White women active in commemorating the past created historic spaces that welcomed other white women. By doing so, they seemingly rendered ambiguous or contradictory the exact boundaries between the white male and female spheres in public spaces. The shift over time in the symbolic space occupied by monuments erected by women is revealing. They located the earliest Confederate memorials in cemeteries. By the end of the century, their preferred location for monuments was in conspicuous public spaces, especially courthouse squares. This migration of monuments symbolized the new authority that women's groups claimed to voice in public memory within the official, political landscape. In these and other instances, as, for example, when the North Carolina DR erected the commemorative marker to the heroines of the Edenton Tea Party in the North Carolina capitol, women intruded their presence into spaces previously associated solely with male power.[43]

Other sites established the historic domain of women—at least as understood at the time—as worthy of both historical recognition and preservation. When, for example, women shifted the focus on the Revolutionary era, in the words of Karal Ann Marling, "from swords and battles toward spinning wheels and balls," they incorporated feminine material culture into the recorded past.[44] Their fascination with the evolution of domestic spaces found expression in everything from the colonial revival to the mania for antiques, decorative arts, and historical kitsch of all kinds. By the turn of the century no historic home was complete without a colonial kitchen, spinning wheel, or other tropes of domesticity.[45]

The contradictory implications of white women's historical undertakings were equally evident in the women's debates over modernity and democracy. By invoking the past, different groups of white women sought to depict various visions of the region's future as disloyal to its heritage. Some white women cast the meaning of the southern past, for instance, in explicitly antimaterialist and antimodernist terms. Hostility to innovation was evident in those women's historical associations, reform groups, and literary societies that criticized fast-paced change, selfish individualism, and excessive materialism. In 1903, for example, President Belle Bryan of the APVA cautioned members not to be swayed from their "pure and lofty ideals" by the prevailing climate of "sordid aggrandizement and selfish pleasures."[46] Eight years later Mary Hilliard Hinton chided her contemporaries to whom monuments and tablets were "an utterly useless expenditure of money." To the contrary, she answered, reminders of the past safeguarded progress by "preventing the vandalic [sic] supremacy of materialism."[47]

Many white women who opposed woman suffrage also justified their stance by invoking tradition. Opponents to black woman suffrage in North Carolina appropriated the cultural power of the first Caucasian child born in North America when they beseeched "in the name of Virginia Dare, that North Carolina remain white" at the polls and that the innovation of woman suffrage be repudiated. Mary Hilliard Hinton, who assumed a prominent role in the antisuffrage movement in her native North Carolina, asserted that the historical record of women's participation in the colonial era demonstrated that women did not need the vote in order to exert public influence. Moreover, to heed "the song of the suffrage siren" would be to renounce the "cause bought by the blood of your fathers and tears of your mothers." She saw nothing incongruous in using the *Booklet*, a historical journal that she edited for two decades, both to eulogize Revolutionary Era women and to denounce woman suffrage. A delegate to the 1911 UDC national convention proclaimed that "no daughter will be a suffragette." Similarly, Mildred Rutherford, the historian of the UDC, invoked the Confederate tradition in her opposition to woman suffrage. She warned the Georgia legislature that "The women who are working for this measure are striking at a principle for which our fathers fought during the Civil War. Woman's suffrage comes from the north and the west and from women who do not believe in state rights and who wish to see the negro using the ballot."[48]

The civilizationist ideology and the historical memory that it informed, however, could also generate demands that defy any antimodernist (or even reactionary) label. Just as many women historical activists were prominent in the antisuffrage movement, so too were many conspicuous in the suffrage campaign. For some of the suffragists, their studies of history convinced them that granting the ballot to women would secure white political hegemony and elevate southern civilization. Rebecca Latimer Felton of Georgia, along with fellow suffragists Lila Meade Valentine of Virginia and Nellie Nugent Somerville of Mississippi, drew upon recollections of the Civil War and Reconstruction—when they believed "carpetbaggers" and black politicians tormented the South—to anchor their ideas about the need for woman suffrage.[49] Thus, Felton felt sanctioned by the past to arrange an exhibit of "real colored folks" in order "to show the ignorant contented darkey . . . [and] to illustrate the slave days" while serving on the board of the "Lady Managers" of the Chicago World's Fair in 1893, and also to repudiate Mildred Rutherford's claims that woman suffrage would blaspheme the "lost cause."[50]

But other white suffragists drew different inspiration from the past. They refused to allow southern traditions to be highjacked by the antisuffragists. Southern suffragists, Suzanne Lebsock has observed, as a rule did not invoke white supremacy as the principal justification for extending the right to vote to women. Instead they contended that the vote was a natural right, that it would make women both better mothers and more effective reformers.[51] Both the record of the past and the civilizationist ideology undergirded all of these claims. When Virginia suffragist leader Lucy Randolph Mason demanded the ballot as a natural right she skillfully affiliated her ancestors, including John Marshall and George Mason, with the cause. For her and other suffragists, their sense of themselves as prospective political participants to a considerable degree rested upon a cultural authority rooted in the southern past. The white-gloved respectability that these women derived from their ancestry and their membership in patriotic, hereditary, and historical societies countered antisuffragists' assertions that woman suffrage was both a foreign and radical abomination. Even while Susan Pringle Frost of South Carolina tirelessly promoted historical preservation in her hometown of Charleston, South Carolina, by appealing to sacred southern traditions, she was a dedicated suffragist and member of the National Woman's Party.[52] Bettie Ballinger reconciled her filiopietism for the founders of Texas, which led her to cofound the Daughters of the Republic of Texas, with her commitment to woman suffrage.[53] For Sallie Southall Cotten of North Carolina there was an intimate connection between her obsession with the saga of Virginia Dare and her lifelong commitment to organizing women into an effective movement.[54] And, finally, Jane Y. McCallum's zealous suffrage activism in Texas was matched only by her lifelong activism within the Colonial Dames. Her efforts to fashion a usable past relevant to women eventually led her to write *Women Pioneers*, a history of colonial America that stressed the contributions of women.[55] Suffrage, for these woman activists, was the historical culmination of the

4. James Fentress and Chris Wickham, *Social Memory* (London: Blackwell, 1992), 3.

5. The literature on collective memory is large. Works that analyze how memories reinforce collective identity include John Bodnar, *Remaking America: Public Memory, Commemoration, and Patriotism in the Twentieth Century* (Princeton, N.J.: Princeton University Press, 1992); Marie-Noelle Bourguet, Lucette Valensi, and Nathan Wachtel, *Between Memory and History* (New York: Harwood Academic Publishers, 1990); Maurice Halbwachs, *On Collective Memory*, trans. Francis J. Ditter, Jr., and Vida Yazdi Ditter (1950; reprint, New York: Harper & Row, 1980); Eric Hobsbawm and Terence Ranger, eds., *The Invention of Tradition* (Cambridge: Cambridge University Press, 1983); George Lipsitz, *Time Passages: Collective Memory and American Popular Culture* (Minneapolis: University of Minnesota Press, 1990); David Lowenthal, *The Past Is a Foreign Country* (Cambridge: Cambridge University Press, 1985); David Thelen, ed., "Introduction," *Memory and American History* (Bloomington: Indiana University Press, 1990), vii–xix; and Michel-Rolph Trouillot, *Silencing the Past: Power and the Production of History* (Boston: Beacon Press, 1995).

6. Michel Foucault, *Language, Counter-Memory, Practice: Selected Essays and Interviews*, Donald F. Bouchard, ed. (Ithaca: Cornell University Press, 1993), 150.

7. David W. Blight, "W. E. B. DuBois and the Struggle for American Historical Memory," in Geneviève Fabre and Robert O'Meally, eds., *History and Memory in African-American Culture* (New York: Oxford University Press, 1994), 68 n. 16.

8. *Ceremonies in Augusta, Georgia, Laying the Cornerstone of the Confederate Monument with an Oration by Clement A. Evans* (Augusta, Ga.: n.p., 1875), 9. On Victorian women and mourning, see Patricia R. Loughridge and Edward D. C. Campbell, Jr., *Women in Mourning* (Richmond: Museum of the Confederacy, 1985); Martha V. Pike and Janice Gray Armstrong, *A Time to Mourn: Expressions of Grief in Nineteenth Century America* (Stony Brook, N.Y.: The Museums at Stony Brook, 1980).

9. Drew Gilpin Faust, *Mothers of Invention: Women of the Slaveholding South in the American Civil War* (Chapel Hill: University of North Carolina Press, 1996), 252. On women, memorialization, and gender tensions, see Faust, *Mothers of Invention*, 234–54; Foster, *Ghosts of the Confederacy*, 36–46; and LeeAnn Whites, *The Civil War as a Crisis in Gender, Augusta, Georgia, 1860–1890* (Athens: University of Georgia Press, 1995), 160–224.

10. Faust, in contrast, stresses the continuity of the impulse behind the women's commemorative activities in the postwar years and at the turn of the century. See Faust, *Mothers of Invention*, 252–53.

11. Laura F. Edwards, *Gendered Strife and Confusion: The Political Culture of Reconstruction* (Urbana: University of Illinois Press, 1997), 107–44; Nancy MacLean, *Behind the Mask of Chivalry: The Making of the Second Ku Klux Klan* (New York: Oxford University Press, 1994); and LeeAnn Whites, "Rebecca Latimer Felton and the Problem of 'Protection' in the New South," in Nancy A. Hewitt and Suzanne Lebsock, eds., *Visible Women: New Essays in American Activism* (Urbana: University of Illinois Press, 1993), 41–61.

12. Gail Bederman, *Manliness & Civilization: A Cultural History of Gender and Race in the United States, 1880–1917* (Chicago: University of Chicago Press,

rich reform tradition of southern women, not a repudiation of regional heritage.

The historical memory promulgated by white women, then, influenced the public life of the New South in myriad ways. It shaped the civic spaces of the cities and towns of the New South, now increasingly important to southern life, as well as the lessons that those spaces taught. White women wrote themselves into the historical record of the white race both as participants in history and as narrators of the past. In the process, white women complicated the debate over women's roles in the public life in the New South. If the recalled past was not the decisive component of these debates over suffrage or race and public education, it nevertheless was assiduously invoked in them. Because competing interpretations of the past were central to the claims of white women and men to authority and privilege in the South, historical memory necessarily informed debates over urban design, education, and, of course, suffrage. Without a recognition of the sense of history that infused their campaigns, neither the self-assurance of the suffragists nor the tenacity of the antisuffragists can be understood fully. Having fashioned a usable past, white women in the New South appealed to it whether they pursued deeply conservative or avowedly innovative aims.

The influence that white women exerted over the public memory in the South eroded after World War I. The decline was especially symptomatic of the diminishing power of the Victorian concept of civilization. The historical connections that organized white women drew between race, gender, and "civilization" lost some of their persuasive power at a time when psychology, consumerism, and modernist culture eroded nineteenth-century ideals of masculine and feminine behavior. A growing enthusiasm for raw masculinity, which became increasingly evident in the popular culture of the 1910s and 1920s, rendered irrelevant older formulations of male power that rested on advanced civilization. Social scientists also challenged assumptions of innate racial attributes and cultural potentials. The exaggerated importance attached to ancestry, which flowed logically from the Victorian conflation of civilization with blood, now appeared hopelessly old-fashioned. As a result, the celebration of heroic Anglo-Saxon history lost the patina of modernity and urgency that it had once had.[56]

The transformation of women's public roles also had consequences for white women's historical activities. During the 1920s, the meaning of the past for women began to change. The extension of the right to vote to women and the new emphasis on "individualism and self-realization" threatened older norms of selfless service. "At the deepest level," explains Ellen DuBois, "the ratification of the Nineteenth Amendment undermined the consensus about what women's path through history signified."[57] Just when women called into question the purpose and structure of the organized women's movement, so too did some question the purpose of women's historical groups. The DAR, for instance, underwent a dramatic transformation during World War I, emerging as one of the shrillest voices of antiradical and anticommunist nationalism. The organization purged itself of members who were sympathetic to social reforms that previously had been tolerated, even endorsed. The scope and membership of other women's historical groups shrank as well. As Darlene Roth has demonstrated in her study of women's clubs in Atlanta, the members of women's clubs during the 1930s were less socially prominent, "less tightly knit," and less active in the full array of women's associations. By then, the UDC, DAR, Colonial Dames, and other historical associations were no longer at the center of the network of women's voluntary associations and no longer could yoke the energies of the largest portion of clubwomen to their causes.[58]

Finally, the activities of the state increasingly overshadowed the historical efforts of voluntary associations. Women's groups often had prodded southern states to assume some responsibility for representations of the past. The expansion of state authority was gradual, beginning with small steps such as the establishment of state archives. The opening of more and more publicly funded museums further extended state influence over collective memory. But along with the incorporation of history into the responsibilities of the state came professionalization. This professionalization and the expansion of academic historical scholarship in the South created a class of men anxious to wrest the cultural authority over the past from amateur woman historians. Professional historians advocated "objective" models of historical causation rather than the heroic narratives that patriotic societies championed. The activities of clubwomen became, at least in the eyes of academic historians, those of slapdash "antiquarians," a word that now acquired distinctly pejorative connotations. Women's organizations, shunted to the sidelines, became resources to be tapped during fund-raising campaigns but otherwise were worthy only of condescension.[59] Clubwomen still remained active; anyone who challenged "true" history still risked being pilloried; devotees of the Lost Cause still assiduously marked graves on Confederate Memorial Day. But the influence that white clubwomen once had over public memory in the South nonetheless waned.

The legacy of white women's turn-of-the-century historical activities for the public culture of the white South has been far-reaching. By crafting heroic narratives of southern history and by promoting the memorialization of that past, organized white women contributed mightily to justifications for white supremacy and elite rule in the region. They reconciled the

southern present with its past. In the process they helped mark the places for white and black southerners in the flow of history and public life of the South. White women created enduring "facts" of by "embalming the past in the amber of history," as Alabamian Id Sorsby so eloquently described the activists' accomplishment.[60] So ful were they at inscribing their narrative into the annals of the So silencing others that only a lengthy struggle by subsequent revision torians, ranging from W. E. B. DuBois to Kenneth Stampp, could d it (and then only incompletely). Finally, they created enduring insti which, despite waning influence over the transmission of historical ory, worked to perpetuate a white historical memory shaped by the rian ethos and its intertwined notions of race, gender, and civili Thus, even now, nearly a century removed from the tumultuous rac social struggles of the late nineteenth century, the southern landsc mains densely packed with monuments and relics that invoke th discredited world view.

Notes

1. Thomas Nelson Page, *The Old South: Essays Social and Political* (Ne Scribner's, 1894), 253, 256, 258.

2. See Gaines Foster, *Ghosts of the Confederacy: Defeat, the Lost Cause, Emergence of the New South, 1865 to 1913* (New York: Oxford University 1987), part 1. See also Susan S. Durant, "The Gently Furled Banner: Th velopment of the Myth of the Lost Cause, 1865–1900," (Ph.D. dissertation versity of North Carolina, 1972). For dissenting interpretations that stress coherent white historical memory, see Lloyd A. Hunter, "The Sacred South war Confederates and the Sacrilization of Southern Culture" (Ph.D. dissert St. Louis University, 1978), 63–64, 80–82; and Charles Reagan Wilson, *Bapt Blood: The Religion of the Lost Cause, 1865–1920* (Athens: University of G Press, 1980).

3. The focus of this essay is on organized, collective expressions of hist memory. Literary representations of the southern past by white women, comprised another important, but distinct, expression of white historical me are beyond the scope of this essay. For accounts that stress the enduring si cance of the activities of the UDC for southern racial politics, see Fred. A. B "The Textbooks of the 'Lost Cause': Censorship and the Creation of Sou State Histories," *Georgia Historical Quarterly* 75 (fall 1991): 507–33; idem, Speech and the 'Lost Cause' in Texas: A Study of Social Control in the South," *Southwestern Historical Quarterly* 97 (January 1994): 453–47; idem, dred Lewis Rutherford and the Patrician Cult of the Old South," *Georgia Hist Quarterly* 78 (fall 1994): 523–30; and Karen L. Cox, "Omen, the Lost Cause, the New South: The United Daughters of the Confederacy and the Transmis of Confederate Culture, 1894–1919" (Ph.D. dissertation, University of Soutl Mississippi, 1997).

1995), 1–44. See also Louise M. Newman, *White Women's Rights: Historical Origins of American Feminism, 1870–1930* (New York: Oxford University Press, 1998), chapter 1, 2.

13. Ann Douglas, *The Feminization of American Culture* (New York: Knopf, 1977). On women and "cultural custodianship," see Kathleen D. McCarthy, *Women's Culture: American Philanthropy and Art, 1830–1930* (Chicago: University of Chicago Press, 1991); and "Parallel Power Structures: Women and the Voluntary Sphere," in Kathleen D. McCarthy, ed., *Lady Bountiful Revisited: Women, Philanthropy, and Power* (New Brunswick, N.J.: Rutgers University Press, 1990), 1–31. For accounts that emphasize the enduring importance of "republican motherhood" ideology, see James M. Lindgren, *Preserving the Old Dominion: Historic Preservation and Virginia Traditionalism* (Charlottesville: University Press of Virginia, 1993), 58–74; and Anastatia Sims, *The Power of Femininity in the New South: Women's Organizations and Politics in North Carolina, 1880–1930* (Columbia: University of South Carolina Press, 1997), esp. 128–54.

14. See Peggy Anderson, *The Daughters: An Unconventional Look at America's Fan Club* (New York: St. Martin's Press, 1974); Cox, "Women, the Lost Cause, and the New South"; Wallace Evan Davies, *Patriotism on Parade: The Story of Veterans' and Hereditary Organizations in America, 1783–1900* (Cambridge: Harvard University Press, 1955); Margaret Gibbs, *The DAR* (New York: Holt, Rinehart, and Winston, 1969); Mrs. Joseph Rucker Lamar, *A History of the National Society of the Colonial Dames of America* (Atlanta: National Society of the Colonial Dames of America, 1934); Lucile E. Laganke, "The National Society of the Daughters of the American Revolution: Its History, Politics and Influence, 1890–1949," (Ph.D. dissertation, Case Western Reserve University, 1951); Stuart McConnell, "Reading the Flag: A Reconsideration of the Patriotic Cults of the 1890s," in John Bodnar, ed., *Bonds of Affection: Americans Define Their Patriotism* (Princeton, N.J.: Princeton University Press, 1996); and Francesca Morgan, "Home and Country: Women, Nation, and the Daughters of the American Revolution, 1890–1939" (Ph.D. dissertation, Columbia University, 1998), esp. 151–218.

15. Darlene R. Roth, *Matronage: Patterns of Women's Organizations, Atlanta, Georgia, 1890–1940* (Brooklyn, N.Y.: Carlson, 1994), 17–72; and Sims, *The Power of Femininity*, 128–54.

16. Mrs. Mary C. Dorris, *Preservation of the Hermitage, 1889–1915* (Nashville: Smith & Lamar, [1915?]); Charles B. Hosmer, Jr., *Presence of the Past: A History of the Preservation Movement in the United States Before Williamsburg* (New York: G. P. Putnam's, 1965), 69–72. See also Holly Beachley Brear, *Inherit the Alamo: Myth and Ritual at an American Shrine* (Austin: University of Texas Press, 1995); Lewis F. Fisher, *Saving San Antonio: The Precarious Preservation of a Heritage* (Lubbock: Texas Tech University Press, 1996); and Mollie Somerville, *Historic and Memorial Buildings of the Daughters of the American Revolution* (Washington: National Society, Daughters of the American Revolution, 1979), 190, 200. On women and historic preservation in general see Barbara J. Howe, "Women in Historic Preservation: The Legacy of Ann Pamela Cunningham," *Public Historian* 12 (winter 1990): 31–61.

17. Catherine Clinton, *Tara Revisited: Women, War & the Plantation Legend* (New York: Abbeville Press, 1995), 184–85; Angie Parrott, "Love Makes Memory

Eternal": The United Daughters of the Confederacy in Richmond, Virginia, 1897–1920," in Edward L. Ayers and John C. Willis, eds., *The Edge of the South: Life in Nineteenth-Century Virginia* (Charlottesville: University Press of Virginia, 1991), 219–20; and John H. Moore, "The Jefferson Davis Monument," *Virginia Cavalcade* 10 (spring 1961): 29–34.

18. Confederated Southern Memorial Association, *History of the Confederated Memorial Associations of the South* (New Orleans: Graham Press, 1904), 68. Similarly, Dolly Blount Lamar, president of the UDC, explained, "Memorials are the chief business of the United Daughters of the Confederacy, expressing as they do in permanent physical form the historical truth and spiritual and political ideals we would perpetuate." Lamar, *When All Is Said and Done* (Athens: University of Georgia Press, 1952), 135.

19. Trouillot, *Silencing the Past*, 26.

20. On women, the early APVA, and the origins of the Jamestown Exposition, see Lindgren, *Preserving the Old Dominion*, 42–75; and Robert T. Taylor, "The Jamestown Tercentennial Exposition of 1907," *Virginia Magazine of History and Biography* 65 (1957): 169–79.

21. Rossiter Johnson, ed., *A History of the World's Colombian Exposition* (New York: Appleton, 1898): III, 433, 478. Even Virginia's reproduction of Mount Vernon, which was one of the exposition's centerpieces, was almost entirely funded through the efforts of Virginia clubwomen.

22. Mary Hilliard Hinton, "North Carolina's Historical Exhibit at Jamestown Exposition," *North Carolina Booklet* 7 (October 1907): 138.

23. Ibid., 138–44.

24. Mrs. W. C. H. Merchant, "Report of the Historical Committees, UDC," *Confederate Veteran* 12 (February 1904): 64.

25. See the histories of the various women's historical organizations in Bailey, "The Textbooks of the 'Lost Cause'"; and "Free Speech and the 'Lost Cause' in Texas"; Cox, "Women, the Lost Cause, and the New South," passim; Foster, *Ghosts of the Confederacy*, 163–79; and Sims, *Power of Femininity*, chapter 6.

26. Earl Barnes, "The Feminizing of Culture," *Atlantic Monthly* 109 (June 1912): 770.

27. "Critic," Letter to the Editor, *New York Times* 2 March 1902. See also Michael Kammen, *Mystic Chords of Memory: The Transformation of Tradition in American Culture* (New York: Knopf, 1991), 266–69.

28. C. Lance Brockman, ed., *Theatre of Fraternity: Staging the Ritual Space of the Scottish Rite of Freemasonry, 1896–1929* (Jackson: University Press of Mississippi, 1996); Mark C. Carnes, *Secret Ritual and Manhood in Victorian America* (New Haven: Yale University Press, 1989); Mary Ann Clawson, *Constructing Brotherhood: Class, Gender and Fraternalism* (Princeton: Princeton University Press, 1989); and Lynn Dumenil, *Freemasonry and American Culture* (Princeton: Princeton University Press, 1984). On the Sons of the Confederacy, see Foster, *Ghosts of the Confederacy*, 178–79.

29. Franklin L. Riley to Thomas M. Owen, 15 August, 10 November 1898, Thomas M. Owen Papers, Alabama Department of Archives and History.

30. A fusion of the theory of evolution and Anglo-Saxonism enabled Herbert Baxter Adams to trace the origins of New England towns to Teutonic antecedents

in German forests. David D. Van Tassel, "From Learned Society to Professional Organization: The American Historical Association," *American Historical Review* 89 (October 1984): 944. On racism in early American historical scholarship, see Bruce Clayton, *The Savage Ideal: Intolerance and Intellectual Leadership in the South, 1890–1914* (Baltimore: Johns Hopkins University Press, 1972), esp. chapter 8; John David Smith, *An Old Creed for the New South: Proslavery Ideology and Historiography, 1865–1918* (Athens: University of Georgia Press, 1991), esp. 103–284.

31. R. D. W. Connor to Captain Ashe, 5 February 1909. Series 1, Box 1, Folder 68, R. D. W. Connor Papers. Series 1, Box 1, Folder 68, Southern Historical Collection, University of North Carolina Library, Chapel Hill. See also Connor to C. Alphonso Smith, 3 February 1909.

32. Ellen Douglas Baxter, "A Lesson from the Lives of the Women of the Revolution," *American Monthly Magazine* 7 (January 1896): 28.

33. "The Unveiling and Dedication of the Edenton Tea Party and Memorial Tablet," *North Carolina Booklet* 8 (April 1909): 282.

34. *Confederate Veteran* 8 (May 1900): 252.

35. Baxter, "A Lesson from the Lives of the Women of the Revolution," 32.

36. Mrs. Patrick Matthew, "Penelope Barker," *North Carolina Booklet* 8 (April 1909): 277.

37. Catherine W. Bishir, "Landmarks of Power: Building a Southern Past, 1855–1915," *Southern Cultures* 1 (1993): 5–46; Davies, *Patriotism on Parade*, 44–73; Karal Ann Marling, *George Washington Slept Here: Colonial Revivals and American Culture, 1876–1986* (Cambridge: Harvard University Press, 1988), 85–114; Morgan, "Home and Country," 28–83, 151–218; Kammen, *Mystic Chords of Memory*, 194–253.

38. Bailey, "Mildred Lewis Rutherford and the Patrician Cult of the Old South"; Clinton, *Tara Revisited*, 191–204; Grace Elizabeth Hale, *Making Whiteness: The Culture of Segregation in the South, 1890–1940* (New York: Pantheon, 1998); Jessie W. Parkhurst, "The Role of the Black Mammy in the Plantation Household," *Journal of Negro History* 23 (July 1938): 349–50; Kirk Savage, *Standing Soldiers, Kneeling Slaves: Race, War, and Monument in Nineteenth-Century America* (Princeton: Princeton University Press, 1997), 155–61; and Cheryl Thurber, "The Development of the Mammy Image and Mythology," in Virginia Bernhard et al., eds., *Southern Women: Histories and Identities* (Columbia: University of Missouri Press, 1992), 87–108.

39. For one statement of the need to "maintain friendly relations" with women's groups, based on years of experience, see William D. McCain, "The Public Relations of Archival Depositories," *American Archivist* 3 (October 1940): 235–44.

40. Enoch Marvin Banks, "A Semi-Centennial View of Secession," *Independent* 70 (February 9, 1911): 302–3.

41. The Banks case is ably chronicled in Fred Arthur Bailey, "Free Speech at the University of Florida: The Enoch Marvin Banks Case," *Florida Historical Quarterly* 71 (July 1992): 1–17. For similar efforts in other southern states, see Bailey, "Textbooks of the 'Lost Cause'" and "Free Speech and the 'Lost Cause' in Texas." (See note 3.)

42. Mary Ryan, *Women in Public: Between Banners and Ballots, 1825–1880* (Baltimore: Johns Hopkins University Press, 1990): 59.

43. Foster, *Ghosts of the Confederacy*, 128–31; H. E. Gulley, "Women and the Lost Cause: Preserving a Confederate Identity in the American Deep South," *Journal of Historical Geography* 19 (1993): 125–41; Morgan, "Home and Country," 151–218; Whites, *Civil War as a Crisis in Gender*, 160–98; and Joel J. Winberry, "'Lest We forget': The Confederate Monument and the Southern Townscape," *Southeastern Geographer* 23 (November 1983): 107–21.

44. Marling, *George Washington Slept Here*, 97. For discussions of the colonial revival and domesticity, see Alan Axelrod, *The Colonial Revival in America* (New York: Henry Francis du Pont Winterthur Museum, 1985); and Jay Cohn, *The Palace or the Poorhouse: The American House as a Cultural Symbol* (East Lansing: Michigan State University Press, 1979), 193–212.

45. The Daughters of the American Revolution even adopted the spinning wheel as its icon.

46. Isobel Bryan, "Report of the President for 1903," *Yearbook of the Association for the Preservation of Virginia Antiquities, 1901–1904* (Richmond: William Ellis Jones, 1905), 7.

47. "Marking the Site of the Old Town of Bloomsbury," *North Carolina Booklet* 11 (July 1911): 51.

48. Elna Green, "Those Opposed: The Antisuffragists in North Carolina, 1900–1920," *North Carolina Historical Review* 67 (July 1990): 318, 320; Janet G. Stone-Erdman, A Challenge to Southern Politics: The Woman Suffrage Movement in North Carolina, 1913–1920" (M.A. thesis, North Carolina State University, 1986), 83–89; UDC delegate quoted in Lloyd C. Taylor, "Lila Meade Valentine: The FFV as Reformer," *Virginia Magazine of History and Biography* 70 (October 1962): 482; *Georgia House Journal*, 1914, 287. Rutherford made similar arguments before the legislature three years later. See Atlanta *Journal*, 20 July 1917. On Rutherford, see Grace Elizabeth Hale, "'Some Women Have Never Been Reconstructed': Mildred Lewis Rutherford, Lucy M. Stanton, and the Racial Politics of Southern White Womanhood, 1900–1930," in John Inscoe, ed., *Georgia in Black and White: Explorations in the Race Relations of a Southern State, 1865–1950* (Athens: University of Georgia Press, 1994), 173–201.

49. Marjorie Spruill Wheeler, *New Women of the New South: The Leaders of the Woman Suffrage Movement in the Southern States* (New York: Oxford University Press, 1993), 41–42.

50. Rebecca Latimer Felton to William H. Felton, 15 March 1893. Felton Papers, University of Georgia. See also A. Elizabeth Taylor, "The Last Phase of the Woman Suffrage Movement in Georgia," *Georgia Historical Quarterly* 43 (March 1959): 11–28.

51. Suzanne Lebsock, "Woman Suffrage and White Supremacy: A Virginia Case Study," in Hewitt and Lebsock, *Visible Women*, 62–100.

52. Sydney R. Bland, *Preserving Charleston's Past, Shaping its Future: the Life and Times of Susan Pringle Frost* (Westport, Conn.: Greenwood Press, 1994), esp. 47–108.

53. Elizabeth Hayes Turner, "'White Gloved Ladies' and 'New Women' in the Texas Woman Suffrage Movement," in Bernhard et al., eds., *Southern Women*, 129–56; Elizabeth Hayes Turner, *Women, Culture, and Community: Religion and*

Reform in Galveston, 1880–1920 (New York: Oxford University Press, 1997), 261–86.

54. Cotten wrote an epic poem about Virginia Dare and also tried to interest various publishers in a play about her. See William Stephenson, *Sallie Southall Cotten: A Woman's Life in North Carolina* (Greenville, N.C.: Pamlico Press, 1987), esp. 89–128.

55. Janet G. Humphrey, *A Texas Suffragist: Diaries and Writings of Jane Y. Mc-Callum* (Austin: Ellen C. Temple, 1988).

56. Bederman, *Manliness & Civilization*, 232–39. (See note 12.)

57. Ellen Carol DuBois, "Making Women's History: Activist Historians of Women's Rights, 1880–1940," *Radical History Review* 49 (winter 1991): 66.

58. Roth, *Matronage*, 90–98; Morgan, "Home and Country," 400–479; Patricia C. Walls, "Defending Their Liberties: Women's Organizations During the McCarthy Era," (Ph.D. dissertation, University of Maryland, 1994), 22–55.

59. The marginalization of women historians is only incompletely charted to date. See Anne Firor Scott, *Unheard Voices: The First Historians of Southern Women* (Charlottesville: University of Virginia Press, 1993), Part 1; Kathryn Kish Sklar, "American Female Historians in Context, 1770–1930," *Feminist Studies* 3 (1975): 171–84. For one compelling illustration of men elbowing aside woman history activists, see Grace Elizabeth Hale, "Granite Stopped Time: The Stone Mountain Memorial and the Representation of Southern Identity," *Georgia Historical Quarterly* 82 (spring 1998): 25–38; Robert W. Harllee, "Custodians of Imperishable Glory: The Stone Mountain Memorial Controversy," (M.A. thesis, Emory University, 1980).

60. Mrs. Idyl King Sorsby, "Relics and Antiquities," *Transactions of the Alabama Historical Society, 1898–1899* (1904), III: 56.

William J. Northen's Public and Personal Struggles against Lynching

BETWEEN 1906 AND 1907, William J. Northen, an ex-governor of Georgia and Confederate veteran, undertook an unprecedented campaign against white racial hatred and violence in his state by attempting to establish a network of antilynching leagues. During a ten-month period, Northen visited approximately ninety counties in the state, where he pushed his program of interracial cooperation before audiences of black and white men. In February 1907 he attended the Georgia Equal Rights Convention, an organization of elite African Americans who had sworn a year earlier "to agitate, complain, protest, and keep protesting against the invasion of our manhood rights."[1] Henry Hugh Proctor, the African American minister of First Congregational Church in Atlanta, later recalled a private meeting with Northen. "With tears streaming down his cheeks," Northen told the black leader that he "would be willing to die, if need be, if he thought that thereby he could bring the races together in harmony and good-will."[2]

Northen could hardly have chosen a less promising time or place for his movement. Since the 1890s, southern state and local governments had passed a flurry of restrictive laws, segregating African Americans into separate schools and other unequal public accommodations. The dramatic rise in white racist violence during the late nineteenth century was proving particularly destructive in Georgia, where mobs lynched at least 441 black victims between 1880 and 1930. In August 1906, white Georgians had overwhelmingly endorsed gubernatorial candidate Hoke Smith, a politician who had enthusiastically supported the adoption of a state amendment disfranchising African Americans. When Northen began his campaign, blacks had been almost completely abandoned by their former white allies, including the national Republican Party and the tattered remnants of the Populist Party. They now struggled almost completely alone against this vicious new strain of white racism.[3]

Though deeply committed to antilynching reform, Northen disregarded African American appeals for racial equality and integration. Instead, he measured the early-twentieth-century South against his idyllic memories of a hierarchical antebellum social order that established impenetrable racial distinctions between white masters and black slaves and clear class distinctions between a slaveholding elite and its non-slaveholding white counterpart. Associating emancipation with social decay, Northen viewed Georgia as dangerously close to descending into "anarchy and governmental hell," as the result of the growing threats posed by black crime, violent white retribution, and miscegenation. Northen's antilynching movement sought to augment the power and authority of an elite group of "sun-crowned, God-given" white businessmen, planters, and ministers who would protect the sexual purity of white women from black rapists and the integrity of "civilization" from white mob participants. White politicians and white newspaper editors overwhelmingly rejected Northen's challenge to chivalric notions that had heretofore promised all white men a shared role as guardians of white women's virtue and upholders of white supremacy. While elite black Georgians welcomed Northen's stand against lynching and his respect for "law-abiding" African Americans; they were troubled by the ex-governor's commitment to white racial dominance, his fears of black resistance, and his use of violent and racist imagery. Despite early opposition to his movement, the ex-governor remained hopeful that he and the "first class" whites whom he so exalted had the willpower and resolve necessary to stand between their state's "purity" and the destructive passions of white "savages" and black "fiends from hell."[4]

At seventy-one, his once auburn beard now gray, Northen traced his lineage to pre-Revolutionary America and proudly embodied the genteel traditions of Georgia's landed elite. Throughout his life, he fondly recalled his close ties with African Americans before the Civil War. As he remembered, "An old negro Mammy nursed me in my babyhood; I grew up with negro slaves in the fields; negroes in the home and negroes all about me. In the community in which I was reared there were thousands of slaves on plantations" as large as six thousand acres in area.[5] At nineteen, Northen devoted his life to God, and he remained active in the church for the rest of his life, ultimately serving as president of the Georgia Baptist Convention and the Southern Baptist Convention. After serving in the Confederate army for a short period and working as an attendant in Confederate hospitals during the Civil War, Northen returned to his position as headmaster of the Mount Zion Academy in Hancock County. In 1873 worsening health problems forced Northen into retirement on a small farm. Though he frequently complained of continued physical weakness over the course of his life, Northen's condition gradually improved and his farming operations grew to comprise more than eight hundred acres. His service as a state representative and president of the State Agricultural Society helped ensure his election as governor in 1890 with the support of the Farmers' Alliance.[6]

After his election, Northen became a sworn enemy of many of his erstwhile Alliance friends when they bolted the Democratic Party to become

Populists. Overheard calling for the murder of congressional candidate Tom Watson in 1892, Northen flatly rejected Populists' attempts at pulling black and white voters together around their shared interests as farmers. Nevertheless, he won reelection in 1892 with the backing of many black ministers and Republicans who were impressed with the governor's support for black education and antilynching legislation.[7] His loss in the 1894 general assembly election, however, embittered Northen forever against the masses of black voters. Blaming his defeat on their defection, the ex-governor concluded that the typical black voter became "a Republican, an Independent, or a what-not," not to pursue his own interests but "just so he may oppose and fight against anything he believes the white man wants." His memories of slavery and his subsequent political experiences strengthened Northen's longstanding determination that "the South is a white man's country, and it will never be delivered over to negroes, whatever the power and influence brought to bear to force this fearful end." Throughout his later life, however, Northen believed that this white domination imposed a "greater obligation upon the stronger element . . . to be righteous, just and fair to the weaker and the more ignorant element."[8]

Despite his growing distrust of black political participation, Northen continued to speak out against mob violence and advocate cooperation between the "the better part of the negroes" and white people for "better conditions."[9] At the turn of the century, however, these antilynching sentiments were overshadowed by Northen's fears of black crime, his acute sensitivity to the criticisms of outsiders, and his goal of attracting northerners and Europeans into his state as president of the Georgia Investment and Immigration Bureau. In 1899, he repudiated attacks against mob violence issued by African Americans and northern whites as "incendiary in the extreme," only encouraging black men to rape white women. He also frequently expressed concerns that sensational accounts of southern lynchings might frighten away potential white settlers. In a 1904 interview, Northen, clearly worried about Georgia's international image, looked back on his state's worst decade of racial violence only to conclude that relations were "far more cooperative" between the races than at any time since the outbreak of the Civil War.[10]

Northen's wistful nostalgia for the antebellum Georgia of his youth, however, suggests that he had private misgivings about the rapid social changes and dislocations that were occurring in his state. Since the Civil War, his once prosperous native cotton belt had stagnated economically. In the early 1900s, the previously intimate ties between white landlords and black tenants were increasingly being dissolved as growing numbers of both groups abandoned the region's plantations for the greater opportunities available in the state's burgeoning towns and cities. In these unsettled times, white absentee landlords had little contact with their black laborers, and whites feared the "strange" poor blacks who frequently traveled by foot through the countryside. Many of these black and white migrants made their way to Atlanta, whose population increased more than fourfold between 1890 and 1910 to nearly 155,000 residents. The sea of strange black and white faces that he now regularly encountered as a resident of Atlanta must have disturbed Northen, who had spent much of his life in Greene and Hancock Counties, where an individual's character could quickly be determined by reputation or last name. Events in Atlanta in 1906 convinced the ex-governor that these transformations might herald a race war culminating in nothing less than the "disintegration and death of our civilization." Fearing this stark threat, Northen was now willing to focus his energies exclusively on easing Georgia's racial tensions even at the risk of tarnishing his state's reputation.[11]

In September of that year, Hoke Smith's racist gubernatorial campaign rhetoric and a series of grossly exaggerated white newspaper accounts of an alleged wave of sexual assaults against white women by blacks helped to trigger the Atlanta race riot. On September 22, thousands of white men shot, stabbed, and tortured innocent African Americans in the center of downtown Atlanta. Throughout the night, white mobs repeatedly clashed with police attempting to protect white businesses from looting and sacking, and they openly defied the orders of public officials to cease their attacks. Although the state militia had reestablished order by morning, whites raided black neighborhoods over the next two days. At the riot's conclusion, at least twenty-five African Americans had been murdered. Hundreds more were permanently injured, and thousands left Atlanta, never to return. Far from serving as an unequivocal display of white dominance, however, the riot also demonstrated the cohesiveness of Atlanta's black community and African American determination to resist white violence at any cost. Blacks dramatically turned back armed white mobs at least twice—first in the city center, and then in a settlement just south of the city. The exaggerated newspaper stories preceding the riot revived Northen's fears that black crime and disorder were escalating out of control. Once more, the deep racial antagonisms manifested in the riot's violence led Northen to conclude that similar scenes "can be repeated in almost any section of Georgia, where there are large numbers of people like those who made the mobs in this city."[12]

Casting about for a solution to what appeared to be an impending racial crisis, Northen was deeply influenced by a series of editorials and letters published in the *Atlanta Constitution* that August. The first, written by "Mrs. M. L. H." from Bibb County, placed part of the blame for black sexual assaults on "the white race" for failing "to continue in its relation of mentor, adviser and friend to a people wholly simple, half-civilized" as had been the case during slavery. The solution to the present period of strife, the writer argued, was "religious and moral suasion exercised, primarily by the white race, secondarily by leaders of the negro race." Praising M. L. H.'s letter, the *Constitution* challenged local white Christian religious leaders to accept as their "mission" the elimination of "the depraved, criminal germ in this half-civilized race." In reading the series of responses to these editorials subsequently published in the *Constitution* over the two-week period, Northen found that Atlanta's white Protestant ministry had endorsed "with remarkable unanimity" the views of the woman writer and the newspaper's editors.[13] These letters and editorials, stressing the potential role of Christianity in alleviating Georgia's racial problems, struck a deep chord in Northen, who had formed the Businessmen's Gospel Union two years earlier in hopes that Christian laymen using "business-like efforts" could help summon "the kingdom of God on earth." While Northen acknowledged the potential tensions between businessmen's concerns with their "social position" and Christ's emphasis on charity and selfless service, his organization succeeded in enlisting a number of Atlanta's leading businessmen, including Coca-Cola magnate Asa G. Candler and millionaire industrialist John Eagan.[14]

With these newspaper editorials in mind, Northen began his antilynching efforts by working closely with white businessmen in Atlanta who were promoting limited interracial cooperation with black ministers and professionals immediately after the riot. In the short term, these white civic leaders viewed their efforts as a means of preventing continued racial violence and encouraging business owners to reopen their stores and factories. In the long term, these whites hoped that their law-and-order movement would answer the criticisms of northern writers who described Atlanta "as one of the worst of American cities" and compared its population to "the adventurous riff-raff" that once inhabited "the mining towns of the West."[15] In November and December, Northen used his contacts among businessmen and ministers to help organize "Law and Order Sunday." That day, over one hundred ministers around the city delivered sermons on the Christian's duty to obey the laws of the state. That evening, hundreds of white and black Atlantans crowded into First Congregational Church to hear Booker T. Washington speak on the twin evils of black crime and white mob justice.[16]

The white businessmen's interracial campaign had limited and self-serving goals. They refused to address long-standing black grievances against the police, streetcar companies, and local courts. At the same time, the businessmen's desire for favorable publicity led them to issue threats against their black critics and even abandon their reform activities once they had won the praise of northern journalists. Northen ultimately sought to expand the businessmen's movement, not only by extending it beyond Atlanta but also by transforming it into a permanent movement based on "the principles and the preaching of the gospels." Northen decided to begin by concentrating his efforts on developing law-and-order organizations in Georgia. If that succeeded, the ex-governor, weakened by age and poor health, hoped to "take the entire South," even if doing so meant "nearing the end of my life."[17]

In its early stages, Northen's movement garnered the enthusiastic support of Atlanta's business community. White businessmen appear to have originally viewed Northen's movement as supporting their own long-term goals of promoting the stability and racial harmony necessary for Georgia's continued economic development. Perhaps more important, the favorable attention the ex-governor received in the northern press advanced a vision of Atlanta and Georgia as progressive, stable, and forward looking—the very images that white Atlantans had long promoted as a means of luring outside investment into their state. In January of 1907, the *Atlanta Georgian* praised Northen's movement for establishing "in the minds of our neighbors to the North of us a confidence and respect which are not to be despised" and rendering "more stable and secure the foundations of our civilization."[18] Throughout his campaign, this newspaper (which became the *Atlanta Georgian and News* in early February after purchasing a rival) joined the *Constitution* in faithfully publishing Northen's dispatches and writing editorials praising his efforts.

Between December 1906 and April 1907, Northen conducted a whirlwind tour of his state, speaking in more than ninety counties and successfully establishing law-and-order organizations in almost every county he visited. Before his arrival in a particular county, the ex-governor would contact a public official, a pastor, or a prominent planter with whom he was familiar. According to Northen, each contact would "invite a limited number of conservative, law-abiding, good citizens to meet me at some convenient place for a conference on lawlessness, crime and violence, with the view to such organized action as these men may think would be wise and helpful." Viewing religious leaders, businessmen, and civic leaders as his natural allies, Northen depicted the ideal leaders of his movement as "calm, conservative . . . sun-crowned, God-given men." Though attendance at some meetings approached fifty, Northen described as typical a meeting in Colquitt County that drew only ten—the president of a bank and a cotton mill, a mayor, four merchants, a newspaper editor, a county school commissioner, and two bank cashiers.[19]

Admitting to saying "quite a lot of things not clean enough for the public ear," the ex-governor opened each meeting by asking, "What can we do to save the fair women of Georgia from outrage and shame brought upon them by fiends from hell?" Frequently narrating "a thrilling story from real life about a strange or tramp negro who came dangerously nigh [to] making an assault," Northen reminded audiences that similar assaults took place "almost every day" in the state. Northen's fascination with black assaults was intensified by his growing conviction that the masses of post-emancipation blacks, undisciplined by white supervision, were retrogressing, morally and physically. In 1911 he would quote a doctor from Macon, who described the "appalling" nature of the black male's "degeneration, physically, mentally, and morally," as well as his "almost universal infection from venereal diseases." Although Northen openly acknowledged that a woman's letter had inspired his movement, he refused to invite women to his meetings. Just as Northen's paternalism attempted to shield white women from black sexual assaults, it also attempted to "protect" them from the rough-and-tumble public realm of civic debate, especially explicit discussions of rape and interracial sex.[20]

Like other white southern men of his generation, Northen viewed the sexual violation of a man's female relatives as a challenge against his masculine authority and his claims to political and social power. If this threat were not avenged, a man risked utter humiliation and social ostracism.[21] Metaphorically linking Georgia's social order with a woman's body, Northen modeled his vision of elite leadership on the patriarch's role as the guardian of his wife's and daughters' sexual purity. Just as an individual man protected the bodies of his dependent women from outside pollution, "first-class whites" were to defend "the purity of our state" from the crime of black rapists, whose violation of white women, Northen clearly believed, imperiled the authority and racial dominance of the state's white male elite.[22]

In addition, these "first-class whites" were charged with protecting the purity of Georgia's social order from a second threat—that posed by white men "easily savage enough to lynch and burn human beings." Like Northen, white male Georgians of all social classes embraced their self-appointed roles as the "protectors of women." In contrast to Northen's faith in the leadership of a small elite, the communal nature of mob violence minimized social distinctions among white men even when businessmen and landholders participated in or inspired the violence, as they often did. Lynching did not simply establish clear gender boundaries between white male guardians and the women they protected. Its practice also established clear racial boundaries between white enforcers of order and the degraded bodies of alleged black violators.[23] As Northen also understood, extralegal violence challenged the authority and legitimacy of the state's legal system, which was controlled by the very landowning and commercial elite whom he exalted as Georgia's natural leaders. Large armed mobs initially organized to threaten African Americans might also destroy private property and use violence to wrest power from civic authorities. "Once [we] give the mob the right-of-way for any offense whatever," Northen warned, "and the way will be open, wide open, for all defiance of the law," perhaps ultimately leading to a bloody battle between the members of mobs and the upholders of law for control of the state.[24] Apparently unsure of the outcome of this violent male contest, Northen sought to bolster the authority of elite whites. He justified the elite's increased powers on the basis of their unique masculine role in shielding an otherwise defenseless state from the ravages of this "law-abiding" element's polar opposites: the savagely violent white mob participants and the physically diseased, wholly undisciplined black "tramp" rapists.

Northen's fascination with safeguarding white women from the "outrages" of black criminals prevented him from questioning the dominant myth that lynchings were overwhelmingly a response to black assaults. In reality, only a minority of lynchings involved even accusations of rape or attempted rape; far fewer still, the actual commission of these crimes. In addition to its symbolic function in reaffirming the power and dominance of white men, mob violence played a powerful role in intimidating blacks, controlling black behavior, discouraging open black resistance against racial injustice, and preventing black economic competition. At the same time the incidence of lynching and its dominant social functions varied markedly by region even within individual states—ranging from a tool of labor control in the cotton belt to a means of reestablishing black deference and servility in the less lynching-prone upper Piedmont cities of Atlanta and Rome.[25] Instead of challenging the false myths that legitimized lynching and inflamed the members of mobs, Northen sought to redefine dominant chivalric notions that sanctioned white mob violence as a fitting response to black crime. The members of Northen's "legions of honor" vowed not only to protect white women from black assaults, but they also promised to defend the state from white mobs.[26]

Northen's legions of honor also sought to enroll and empower a select group of "law-abiding negro ministers and negro laymen" who are "fully and heartily ready and anxious to help solve the awful conditions which confront us." Northen called on whites to follow his example of not hesitating to "salute" a "law-abiding" African American and "tell him I am his friend and will be his staunch friend as long as he behaves himself as a member of the community." This recognition, Northen suggested, "helps the negro to make himself a man." Working together, the white and black "first classes" would classify the populations of each county so that they could know, "definitely and fully, the character of all the people among whom we live." Only "law-abiding" blacks had access to the information necessary to make a complete and accurate list of the "vicious and villain-ous negroes," who "lounge around dives and dens and clubs during the day and commit burglaries and assaults at night."[27]

At the same time that Northen sought to elevate "first-class" blacks to positions of partial authority in his organizations, the ex-governor also sought to provide black women with some of the same sexual protections previously limited to white women. "Law-abiding" black men had a special assignment in helping to unearth "a large body of low down, filthy, morally corrupt and physically rotten white men who have negro concubines." Once brought out into the open, every "last one of such white men" was to be sent to the state penitentiary for twenty-five years. Punishing these men was absolutely vital, Northen stressed. According to him, "We can never settle the problem of the races as long as we allow corrupt white men to ruin the homes of negroes and make for them a lot of strumpets and wenches instead of pure, clean women." Although Northen's choice of "strumpets" and "wenches" drew on a traditional, racist vocabulary, he hoped to offer black women and black men legal recourse against white sexual violence at a time when none existed. Northen did not just seek to save white men from corruption, he clearly empathized with the victims of this "gross and cruel" abuse. At the same time, however, he was also a determined opponent of miscegenation. Northen associated racial inter-mixture with the blurring of racial lines, which, he believed, violated God's law and would result in racial equality and a weakening of the social fabric. The very tools designed to protect black women from sexual exploitation would also prevent consensual interracial relationships. By suggesting that these "third-class" white mob participants were themselves guilty of mis-cegenation and sexual abuse, Northen was making arguments strikingly similar to those previously developed during the 1890s by Ida B. Wells, one of the most eloquent black critics of mob violence. Wells, like Northen, used the crimes of lynching and licentiousness to discredit the "manly" claims of white mob participants to social and political authority. Unlike the ex-governor, however, she implicated a wide range of white southerners, including members of the elite classes, in the commission of these crimes.[28]

To support the efforts of his local organizations, Northen hoped to ap-point a twenty-lawyer commission that would suggest the passage of new statutes allowing committees to "handle properly and as they deserve, the vicious elements of our communities both white and black." Because Northen associated black and white "idleness" with rapists and mobs, he wanted legislation defining vagrancy with wide latitude so that white leaders might send individual blacks and whites to "the work house for fifteen years, or as long as may be necessary to get them in the habit of perspiring a little under moderate exercise." By reforming the characters of "strange," "idle" blacks, Northen hoped to prevent assaults from occurring in the first place. In case crimes were committed, however, local committees needed legislation that would reduce the opportunities for suspected rapists to escape the death penalty through "delays in the courts" and "trifling technicalities," to avoid the opportunity for lynching. The black criminal was best handled "discreetly" by the state and by "first class whites," Northen argued, who would punish him by "breaking his neck by law and not by murderous mobs." Reflecting a concern with the forms of trial by jury rather than substantive justice, Northen's desire to "patch up" Georgia's notoriously punitive and racially biased criminal justice system risked further eroding criminal suspects' thin rights and encouraging executions that were little more than legal lynchings.[29]

Northen also feared a "second class" within the white and black communities that threatened the state's social order by encouraging the criminal activities of these "third-class" lawbreakers. Among blacks, this group consisted of "preachers and a good lot of so-called Christian laymen and quite a number of newspaper editors" who never actually committed assaults or robberies, but who nevertheless "hold secret meetings and plot and plan" or who "swear they will not work for white people, except upon very limited conditions." The second class among whites included a few editors, some ministers, and "a very large number of politicians" who never joined mobs themselves but who publicly supported extralegal violence and stirred racial strife through their intemperate utterances. While Northen consciously highlighted the similarities between each corresponding class of blacks and whites, he emphasized that "only the first class of white people" would direct the committees and only they would be allowed "to pursue and capture and bring to trial and conviction the alleged criminal."[30]

Using evangelical proselytization as a model, Northen's campaign and the new legal compulsions that he envisioned sought to transform public sentiment on black crime and white mob violence "by converting the wicked and savage people of both races that they may be brought to be clothed and settled in their right mind." Once their classifications were complete, the committees would assemble their surrounding populations at least once a month to hear speeches on law and order from a prominent "first-class" white businessman, judge, or other civic leader. Northen hoped that these rallies would marshal public sentiment against extralegal vengeance and place pressure on local officials to enforce an existing antilynching law adopted by the general assembly during his governorship. This law required sheriffs to organize posses to prevent potential lynchings and made mob members criminally liable for injury or death of their victims. As with similar legislation passed in several other southern states, however, the measure proved unenforceable. In the spring of 1907, the ex-governor sent out a series of circulars requesting sheriffs to enforce these laws and support the efforts of the local law-and-order leagues.[31]

More than any other group, elite blacks throughout Georgia and the South welcomed Northen's movement. The accommodationist Booker T. Washington made a one-hundred-dollar donation to fund the ex-governor's travels. W. E. B. DuBois, an Atlanta resident and Washington's radical critic, applauded Northen's sincerity and "good work," even while criticizing the law-and-order efforts of the city's businessmen as a mere "advertising" campaign. First and foremost, elite blacks recognized Northen's possible role in undermining the acceptability of a chivalric ideal that glorified white participation in lynchings and condoned the brutal sexual abuse of black women. Just as Northen envisioned a special role for "first-class" blacks in promoting law and order among "third-class" African Americans and whites, many elite blacks had long assumed the duties of providing moral guidance for the black masses and protecting black women from the sexual depredations of white men.[32] Black Georgians were also aware of the implicit threats underlying the cooperation Northen proffered. According to Northen's logic, black *critics* automatically became members of a "second" or "third" class of blacks whose characters needed to be restored through persuasion or compulsion.

As much as anyone else, William Jefferson White recognized the benevolent possibilities of Northen's movement and the potential pitfalls of refusing to cooperate with the ex-governor. Born in 1831 to a white planter and a mother of black and Indian descent, White rose to prominence during Reconstruction as a Baptist leader and helped found Augusta Institute, which was moved to Atlanta and eventually renamed Morehouse College.[33] Throughout his life, W. J. White remembered the comments of a white minister that the young black man's conversion to Christianity at age twenty-four was "one of the most remarkable evidences of the power of God[']s grace he had ever witnessed."[34] Whereas many black Baptists responded to escalating white violence during the 1890s by embracing separatism, White continued to argue that "progressive colored people of the south must put themselves in close touch with the same class of white people" so that "these two working in harmony and true friendship will be able to remove the things that make trouble on either side of the race line."[35] Throughout the 1890s, White promoted cooperation between black Baptists and white members of both the Southern Baptist Convention and the American Baptist Home Mission Society as a way of securing financial contributions for the establishment of black denominational schools and missionary schools. In the wake of growing racial tensions, however, these tentative steps toward interracial cooperation withered. Radical black separatists repeatedly accused White and his allies of being "hired" by "white folks" because of their willingness to accept financial contributions from whites and employ white teachers in their schools. Meanwhile, mainstream black Baptists praised his unwavering commitment to black control over the administration of schools and churches.[36]

William Jefferson White's vocal criticisms against white racial injustice as editor of the *Georgia Baptist* resulted in repeated threats against his life by white mobs. In February of 1906, he organized the Georgia Equal Rights Convention in reaction to Jim Crow laws and growing calls for black disfranchisement. That September, a white mob threatened White's life, and he fled his home in Augusta. Returning after his most recent brush with racial violence, White commended Northen's antilynching efforts and his attempts to promote interracial cooperation. "With each race the true friend of the other," the black editor agreed, "the white and colored people of Georgia can by themselves, develop Georgia in all of her various resources as the state has never yet been developed." But White also included a caveat: "To do this, there must be mutual confidence and mutual friendship. Neighborhood friendship is essential to the peace and safety in every community. This friendship must not be racial but mutual between all races composing the community."[37]

White invited the ex-governor to Macon to attend the second annual meeting of the Georgia Equal Rights Convention in February. During the three-day session, Northen was joined by a handful of other whites who shared his opposition to lynching. Northen's attendance at the convention provided him an opportunity to counsel blacks to speak out against crime in their community. Explicitly acknowledging Northen's efforts, convention members endorsed a series of pledges promising to "join hands with all races and plead for majesty of law" and support the "strict enforcement" of laws, "whether affecting whites or blacks." Declaring that "peaceful relations now exist between the races," the convention argued "that negroes do not encourage crime nor harbor criminals of the race" and "that whites and blacks should dwell together in peace and harmony, mutually dependent on one another."[38]

Although White and other participants supported Northen's stand against lynching, they, unlike Northen, viewed its eradication and the moral progress of black men as precursors to achieving their "manhood rights" of full citizenship and equality. "For forty long years," White had argued earlier in 1906, "we have struggled and toiled, trying to make it manifest to the world that our enslavement was not of God and that as free men we are worthy to stand side by side with the freeman of other races."[39] Despite their willingness to cooperate with Northen and other whites in 1907, convention participants demanded "better educational facilities" for African Americans. They argued that voting was the "safest guaranty of all the rights of citizenship." Finally, they described the Jim Crow railroad car and streetcar as "degrading and unjust" as well as "revolting to one's sense of justice."⁴⁰ Later that summer, suggesting that the advocates of disfranchisement were besmirching their own "honor" as whites, Henry Hugh Proctor and other black ministers in Atlanta publicly attacked such legislation on the grounds that it threatened to "retard the cooperative movements for law and order" organized by Northen and the members of Atlanta's white business community.⁴¹ These and other black religious leaders were attempting to stretch the boundaries of the limited power promised by Northen's movement to guarantee their rights to full political participation and equality.

In contrast to the qualified support he received among African Americans, Northen was shocked by the "scores and hundreds" of white men who rejected his antilynching movement outright and openly asserted instead that the African American was nothing but "a brute, without responsibility to God, and his slaughter nothing more than the killing of a dog." In March, Northen admitted that most white newspapers outside of Atlanta refused to publish letters announcing his aims, and many of his "old-time friends" were purposefully avoiding his meetings. Northen noted that his movement was finding its coldest reception among "prominent politicians," nearly every one of whom "expects to be governor some day and . . . wants to be careful with his record."⁴² These politicians recognized the potential unpopularity of Northen's criticism of a chivalric code that elevated all white men to a privileged position of guardianship over white women and dominance over African Americans. Larry Gauth of Artiens, Georgia, joined other white critics in repudiating the ex-governor's attempts to appropriate a special authority and status for the small clique of elite whites who would organize each county's law-and-order leagues and discipline potential white lawbreakers. Emphasizing that "our white people do not need missionaries," Gauth argued that Northen should focus his attention solely on convincing blacks to turn over their own criminals rather than "trying to direct the intelligent white men of our state." Gauth dismissed as "rot" all that was spoken by White and others about "elevating the colored race" at the meeting of the Equal Rights Convention. Rather than identifying a "law-abiding" element among blacks, Gauth portrayed *all* black men as potential rapists and linked the commission of this crime to integration and black advancement. As a consequence, Gauth rejected Northen's antilynching movement with its attempts to promote the moral attainments of some African Americans. According to him, "When the blacks hear a leading white man counseling and pleading with his own people to bear with these black-hearter [*sic*] criminals, and see then societies organizing in the towns to apprehend and punish white men who take vengeance in their own hands, it simply puts the devil in the heads of those negroes . . . and makes mob violence only the more necessary."⁴³

Though shocked at such extremism, Northen had anticipated these criticisms against his movement, especially among the "second" and "third" classes of whites he so distrusted. The ex-governor was unprepared, however, for the defection of the very elite whites in whom he initially expressed so much faith. In linking black assaults to idleness and "the strange negro," Northen spoke to the longstanding fears shared by many white planters, especially those in the Cotton Belt, the large swath of territory in central Georgia where Northen focused his early energies. Viewing slavery as their lodestar, these landowners were constantly frustrated by the relative independence of black tenants determined to wring the best possible deal out of difficult circumstances. Like Northen, white planters associated "strange and tramp negroes" with labor agitation and resistance to white directives. The morning after a speech in Hawkinsville, J. Pope Brown, one of the state's wealthiest planters and chairman of the local law-and-order committee, advised Northen: "Everywhere you go, press the danger to come from the strange or tramp negro. I never allow one to stop on my place."[44] White planters in the Cotton Belt had long embraced lynching as their ultimate weapon in a varied arsenal of corporal punishments aimed at controlling black workers and preventing black protests. Because Brown and other whites shared Northen's suspicions that some black ministers and other black civic leaders encouraged labor resistance and shielded recalcitrant blacks from white authorities, African American schools and churches in the region were often the targets of white violence. In the early 1900s, state legislators from the region secured passage of a series of loosely worded vagrancy measures and contract labor laws that compelled black laborers to remain on plantations, especially during the harvest season. Given their fears of black resistance and potential labor disruptions, many planters were comforted by Northen's avowed goal of reestablishing the mythically humane and trouble-free white dominance that they associated with slavery. Urging his committees "to restore, as far as possible, the relations broken forty years ago between the races," Northen remembered that "then, we never dreamed of the things that now alarm us by night and disturb and trouble us all through the sunlight of the day."[45] Nevertheless, as Northen came to understand all too well, most whites in the region remained unwilling to part with their most powerful tool of labor control: physical coercion through violence and lynching.

White businessmen came to have their own reservations with Northen's movement, despite their early cooperation with the ex-governor. Deep tensions existed between Northen's fears of an impending race war and a growing confidence among commercial leaders that "a new birth of Southern prosperity would cause the race problem to vanish."[46] Northen continued to argue that Georgia was facing a profound racial crisis long after

Atlanta's business community bathed in praise from the northern press for restoring order in its city and for addressing the very problems responsible for the riot. In small cities outside Atlanta, white businessmen struggling to promote industrial growth also spoke out against Northen's movement, arguing that a visit by the ex-governor might lead outsiders to associate their communities with racial strife and instability. In response to a letter from Northen requesting the privilege to speak in their county, the editors of a newspaper in Dalton acknowledged their desire for "the good will of all sections and peoples" but questioned the necessity of a visit. "The absence of rape cases together with the absence of mobs," they argued, "cause[d] the gentlemen making up the city council to decide that it was better to leave well enough alone and not invite Mr. Northen to come, for by his coming, he might stir up a feeling of antagonism between the races that doesn't now exist." In the early twentieth century, civic leaders in Dalton and other Georgia mill towns sought economic development through an aggressive boosterism, promoting their towns' positive characteristics and minimizing potential liabilities. As in Atlanta, Dalton's business elite carefully guarded its city's local and national reputations, dependent as its economy was on outsiders, especially Northerners, who provided vital investment capital as well as crucial access to national markets. Although Northen eventually visited Dalton, city fathers remained cool to his movement and feared any public criticism of their city or any potential disturbance within it. In late March and early April, the city's *North Georgia Citizen* published a series of editorials warning that "the more you stir a hornet's nest the worse you will get stung." The *Manufacturers' Record*, published in Baltimore by New South apostle Richard Edmonds, voiced similar criticisms and called upon newspapers to suppress the "agitation" of Northen and other racial reformers by refusing to publish their "discussions of the negro problem."[47]

In March and April, the *Atlanta Journal* drew on these growing criticisms against Northen's movement in a series of blistering editorials. During the 1906 election, the newspaper had served as Hoke Smith's campaign organ; in promoting Smith's gubernatorial campaign, its editor, James Gray, had repeatedly trumpeted the cause of disfranchisement. Although Northen purposefully distanced himself from the controversies surrounding black voting rights, Gray suspected that Northen's movement was drawing Georgians' attentions away from this issue. Like Gray, a growing number of white reformers—including the influential Populist Tom Watson—argued that the passage of disfranchisement legislation might finally allow white Georgians to move beyond racial issues and "proceed to the settlement of other vital questions with which they are concerned."[48] On March 17, the *Journal* criticized Northen's movement as elitist and antidemocratic and accused the ex-governor of attempting to "defeat the will of the people" through advocacy of his own solution to the state's racial problems. A week later, Gray broadened his attack, playing on the fears of white businessmen with a reminder that the *American Magazine*, "a periodical of wide circulation," had recently published a quote from Northen declaring that "'Georgia's injustice to the negro' lies at the foundation of this question." Warning that a national audience would read Northen's statement, the *Journal* argued, "Therein we find an exact illustration of the harm which comes of this agitation."[49]

Although Northen defended himself from the *Journal's* attacks, he never regained his earlier optimism that white businessmen and religious leaders might bring salvation to his state. By June, he had resigned as president of the Businessmen's Gospel Union after discovering that some of the businessmen on his committee were not only "not in sympathy with my work, but were in sympathy with the attack made on me by the Atlanta Journal."[50] Similarly, at the April meeting of the Evangelical Ministers' Association, Atlanta's white ministry dismissed Northen's reform plans as "extravagant." As white ministers readied themselves for a coming struggle over the passage of a state prohibition law, his movement appeared potentially divisive and distracting. On April 11, temperance leader J. C. Solomon published in the *Golden Age* an editorial praising his friend Northen as "loving and brave, kind and true, good and great." Nevertheless, Solomon criticized Northen's movement for having "missed the mark" by ignoring the "liquor question." "If Georgia would lift this midnight shadow which hangs as a horrible nightmare over our fair but almost defenceless women—if she would stop the hellish crime," he emphasized, "then destroy the saloon."[51]

Although Northen continued seeking donations for his movement as late as June, he had quit visiting counties by the beginning of April. In 1911, two years before his death, Northen looked back on his battle against mob violence and black crime in a letter responding to an invitation from the editorial secretary of the Southern Baptist Convention to contribute articles on race relations. Recalling the abuse heaped on him by whites ever since he had first spoken out against lynching in the 1890s, Northen vowed to avoid public discussions of the race issue. Writing of his "sensitive" nature and the "burdens" he had carried for so many years during his solitary efforts, he felt that he had done his "duty" and argued that his conscience was clear.[52]

In announcing his retirement aims, Northen sought release from his disappointments with Georgia's white male population, which had repeatedly proved unwilling to follow his "righteous effort to recover the civilization" for which Confederate soldiers "so gladly gave their lives, their treasure and their blood."[53] In his 1911 letter, Northen remembered his shock at the shamelessness of lynching advocates, some of whom had sent him photographs of dismembered black victims during his tenure as governor. During his 1906–1907 movement, white Georgians had rejected Northen's attempts to empower a small group of elite whites in hopes of eradicating a practice that symbolically reaffirmed the shared status of all white men. At the same time, he was disappointed by the ultimate refusal of elite whites to fulfill their destinies as leaders of his campaign. The threat that the Atlanta race riot posed to the city's social stability and its commercial livelihood had stirred local businessmen to restore order in its aftermath. But it was their very fear of negative publicity and potentially disruptive social change that ultimately alienated white businessmen from Northen's movement and prevented them from seeking their own permanent solution to the problem of white mob violence. White planters overwhelmingly shared Northen's concerns with black labor resistance but ultimately proved unwilling to abandon a powerful tool of labor control. Similarly, white religious leaders came to advocate temperance reform as the most effective weapon against disorder after originally sharing Northen's view that Christianity had a special role to play in resolving their region's vexing racial problems.

Northen linked his public battle against lynching with his personal struggle "to make my life, by the grace of God, pure and simple and good."[54] His anxieties regarding the declining masculine authority of elite whites mirrored his own personal uncertainties as to whether or not he could muster the resolve necessary to complete his campaign despite his declining health. Northen's insistence in 1911 that his "skirts were clear" from any personal responsibility for his failure to solve Georgia's racial problems suggests that he may have suffered grave self-doubts in the aftermath of his campaign.[55] No matter how strenuously he attempted to distance his own soul from the sins of white mobs and black rapists, no matter how much he struggled to sacrifice his own concerns with "social position" in the service of God, Northen could scarcely contain his own passions and rage as he attempted to defend his honor from the fierce attacks his movement endured. Confident in his righteousness and moral superiority, Northen maligned critics and denounced the enemies of good order with a viciousness that revealed his own fascination with vengeance and violent domination. In an early dispatch, the ex-governor publicly advocated the hanging of lawyers who helped guilty criminals escape punishment. After the *Atlanta Journal's* attacks against his movement, he threatened to lead another statewide campaign, at the end of which "an outraged people" would "rise up and crush the Journal into eternal forgetfulness." Black audiences must have especially bristled at Northen's appropriation of imagery associated with lynching in phrases that spoke of "breaking the criminal's neck" or encouraged "the use of bloodhounds" to track down criminals.[56]

Rather than completely rejecting Northen's solitary efforts, black Georgians grasped at the unique opportunities for racial progress embedded in a movement otherwise saturated with racist imagery and a desire to bolster white racial dominance. After listening to Northen's address at the 1907 Equal Rights Convention, W. J. White wrote a newspaper article noting the distinct limits of the ex-governor's goals, especially his refusal to support "the political equality of white and colored Georgians." Despite this criticism, however, the black journalist was careful to avoid discrediting Northen's movement or alienating him. White concluded, "The colored Georgian must hold himself ready to cooperate with the white Georgian for law and order and if there is a failure in the movement let the failure be wholly at the door of the whites."[57] African Americans endorsed Northen's denunciations of lynching and his goal of protecting black women from white sexual exploitation. As these elite blacks understood all too well, the failure of Northen's campaign would mean the continued murder, abuse, and intimidation of untold numbers of African Americans. Despite their mutual opposition to lynching and their mutual desire for interracial cooperation, White and Northen remained deeply divided. Whereas Northen sought to recover the lost antebellum world of his youth, White and other elite black males hoped to create a new racial order—one that would nurture their goals of self-determination and full equality. Though Northen expressed a willingness to sacrifice his life in pursuit of his antilynching program, his vision for Georgia's future never transcended his memories of its past.

NOTES

Research for this essay was supported in part by an Andrew W. Mellon Postdoctoral Teaching Fellowship in Southern Studies at Emory University. I was introduced to Northen's antilynching efforts by Joel Williamson's *The Crucible of Race: Black-White Relations in the American South since Emancipation* (New York: Oxford University Press, 1984), 288–91. Gregory Lamont Mixon also discusses Northen's early efforts in "The Atlanta Riot of 1906" (Ph.D. dissertation, University of Cincinnati, 1989), 693–706. This essay supports Williamson's portrayal of Northen as a paternalistic "Conservative" on the race issue, heavily influenced by his memories of slavery and a distrust of the white masses. It, however, expands upon Williamson's research by detailing the evolution of Northen's movement and placing it within Georgia's larger social and cultural contexts.

This essay was also influenced by Nancy MacLean's *Behind the Mask of Chivalry: The Making of the Second Ku Klux Klan* (New York: Oxford University Press, 1994) and Gail Bederman's *Manliness and Civilization: A Cultural History of Gender and Race in the United States, 1880–1917* (Chicago: University of Chicago Press, 1995), 46–53. Like MacLean's Klan, Northen's fears of disorder and social change were expressed in metaphors of pollution and sexual impurity. In contrast to the Klan's support of vigilantism and a "reactionary populism," however, Northen rejected mob violence and attempted to augment the power of a small white elite. As suggested by Bederman's research, Northen legitimized the authority of this elite on the basis of the restrained "white manliness" that he believed distinguished them from the "savagery" of black rapists and white mob participants. Northen's representation of lynching as "unmanly" and his desires of providing elite "law-abiding" black men with positions of partial authority in his antilynching leagues set the ex-governor apart from virtually all white southerners of his era and even most white northerners.

1. "Georgia Equal Rights Convention," 13, 14 February 1906, W. E. B. DuBois Papers, reel 1, University of Massachusetts, Amherst, 16.

2. Rev. H. H. Proctor, "A Southerner of the New School: William J. Northen," *Southern Workman* 42 (July 1913): 406.

3. C. Vann Woodward, *The Strange Career of Jim Crow*, 3rd ed., rev. (New York: Oxford University Press, 1974), 83–102; W. Fitzhugh Brundage, *Lynching in the New South: Georgia and Virginia, 1880–1930* (Urbana: University of Illinois Press, 1993), 262; John Dittmer, *Black Georgia in the Progressive Era, 1900–1920* (Urbana: University of Illinois Press, 1977), 97–101; Williamson, *Crucible of Race*, 341–55.

4. *Atlanta Georgian and News*, 13, 28 March 1907.

5. W. J. Northen, "Christianity and the Negro Problem in Georgia: Address Delivered before the Evangelical Ministers' Association of Atlanta," 4 September 1911, box 3, Gov. William J. Northen Papers, Georgia Department of Archives and History, Atlanta, 11–12; this passage was brought to my attention by Williamson's *Crucible of Race*, 288.

6. *Atlanta Constitution*, 26 March 1913; James Calvin Bonner, "The Gubernatorial Career of W. J. Northen" (Master's thesis, University of Georgia, 1936), 15–17; Barton C. Shaw, *The Wool-Hat Boys: Georgia's Populist Party* (Baton Rouge: Louisiana State University Press, 1984), 22–29; Williamson, *Crucible of Race*, 288.

7. Edward L. Ayers, *The Promise of the New South: Life after Reconstruction* (New York: Oxford University Press, 1992), 274; C. Vann Woodward, *Tom Watson: Agrarian Rebel* (New York: MacMillan, 1938; New York: Oxford University Press, Galaxy Books, 1963), 239; Bonner, "Gubernatorial Career of W. J. Northen," 47–71; Shaw, *Wool-Hat Boys*, 78–83.

8. W. J. Northen, "The Negro at the South," 22 May 1899, box 3, Northen Papers, 7, 15 (first two quotes); Northen, "Christianity and the Negro Problem in Georgia," 15 (third quote).

9. Northen, "Negro at the South," 16.

10. Ibid., 13, (first quote); W. J. Northen, "Races in Harmony; South Safe As Home," in *The Possibilities of the Negro in Symposium* (Atlanta: Franklin Printing and Publishing Co., 1904), 80 (second quote); *Atlanta Constitution*, 26 March 1913; Bederman, *Manliness and Civilization*, 68; Williamson, *Crucible of Race*, 288.

11. *Atlanta Georgian*, 18 January 1907 (quote); *Atlanta Georgian and News*, 28 March 1907; on Georgia's social transformations and these new fears, see this volume: Nancy MacLean, "The Leo Frank Case Reconsidered: Gender and Sexual

Politics in the Making of Reactionary Populism," from *Journal of American History* 78 (December 1991): 921; Steven Wayne Wrigley, "The Triumph of Provincialism: Public Life in Georgia, 1898–1917" (Ph.D. dissertation, Northwestern University, 1986), 30–41; Ray Stannard Baker, *Following the Color Line: An Account of Negro Citizenship in the American Democracy* (New York: Doubleday, Page and Company, 1908), 69–70. Lawrence M. Friedman, *Crime and Punishment in American History* (New York: Basic Books, 1993), 193–97; Ayers, *Promise of the New South*, 157.

12. *Atlanta Georgian and News*, 28 March 1907 (quote); Charles Crowe, "Racial Massacre in Atlanta, September 22, 1906," *Journal of Negro History* 54 (April 1969): 150–73; David F. Godshalk, "In the Wake of Riot: Atlanta's Struggle for Order, 1899–1919" (Ph.D. dissertation, Yale University, 1992), 8–77.

13. *Atlanta Constitution*, 3 October 1906 (quotes from M. L. H.'s letter); W. J. Northen, "An Illustrated Lecture: the Atlanta Riot and the Minister's View-Point," box 3, Northen Papers, 2 (subsequent quotes).

14. *Atlanta Evening News*, 22 November 1906; clipping, 15 December 1904, Scrapbooks, vol. 5, box 6, Northen Papers, 110 (quotes).

15. "Facts about the Atlanta Murders," *World's Work* 13 (November 1906): 8147 (quote); Godshalk, "In the Wake of Riot," 120–89; Brundage, *Lynching in the New South*, 211–15.

16. *Atlanta Evening News*, 22 November 1906; *Atlanta Constitution*, 1, 9 December 1906.

17. *Atlanta Constitution*, 23 December 1906; *Atlanta Georgian*, 3, 18 January 1907; *Atlanta Georgian and News*, 20, 28 March 1907.

18. *Atlanta Georgian*, 30 January 1907.

19. *Atlanta Georgian*, 18 January 1907; *Atlanta Georgian and News*, 13, 28 March 1907.

20. *Atlanta Georgian and News*, 28 March 1907 (first quote); Northen, "Christianity and the Negro Problem in Georgia," 13 (second quote).

21. Bertram Wyatt-Brown, *Southern Honor: Ethics and Behavior in the Old South* (New York: Oxford University Press, 1982), 53.

22. *Atlanta Georgian and News*, 28 March 1907.

23. *Atlanta Georgian and News*, 28 March 1907 (quote); Jacquelyn Dowd Hall, *Revolt Against Chivalry: Jessie Daniel Ames and the Women's Campaign Against Lynching*, rev. ed. (New York: Columbia University Press, 1993), 149–57; MacLean, *Behind the Mask of Chivalry*, 162–65; Stewart E. Tolnay and E. M. Beck, *A Festival of Violence: An Analysis of Southern Lynchings, 1882–1930* (Urbana: University of Illinois Press, 1995), 76–77.

24. "The Evolution of LAWLESSNESS and Unchallenged CRIME," n.d., box 3, Northen Papers, 4–5.

25. Hall, *Revolt Against Chivalry*, 130–45; Brundage, *Lynching in the New South*, 103–39; Tolnay and Beck, *A Festival of Violence*, 69–75.

26. *Atlanta Georgian and News*, 28 March 1907; "Lawlessness, Crime and Violence," 1 January 1907, box 3, Northen Papers, 3.

27. *Atlanta Georgian and News*, 28 March 1907.

28. *Atlanta Georgian and News*, 28 March 1907 (quotes); Northen, "Negro at the South," 2; Bederman, *Manliness and Civilization*, 57–67.

"For Colored" and "For White": Segregating Consumption in the South

> As the advertising industry, which is dedicated to the creation of masks, makes clear, that which cannot gain authority from tradition may borrow it with a mask. Masking is a play upon possibility and ours is a society in which possibilities are many. . . . Said a very dark Southern friend of mine to a white businessman who complained of his recalcitrance in a bargaining situation, "I know, you thought I was colored, didn't you." . . . the "darky" act makes brothers of us all.
>
> —Ralph Ellison

IN THE TURN-OF-THE-CENTURY South, the small-town train station often sat apart.[1] Whereas the courthouse stood tall in the sky and central, fixing a town like an axle pierces a wheel, the train station hung low, attempting dignity while hugging the ground. Courthouses flaunted their authority, but as structures, southern train stations wore disguises. Their architecture often hid the importance of the transactions they sheltered, their location at the juncture of regional and national economies, their seeming stasis even as they monitored the movement between local and larger worlds.[2]

By the late nineteenth century, train stations and the trains that ran between them had become the first important sites of a new kind of struggle. African Americans resisted the creation of a new segregated social order not just at the courthouse and polling places where they fought with registrars and election officials to maintain an integrated franchise. They also tested each restriction of their rights in the expanding commercial spaces of the modernizing economy. On trains as early as the 1880s and later in the new commercial spaces of growing southern towns and cities, the few black southerners with the money to make purchases pushed at multiplying local and state laws and conventions. White southerners in turn elaborated more intricate regulations and put up more segregation signs. As white southerner Edgar Gardner Murphy wrote, "ours is a world of inexorable divisions. . . . Segregation has made of our eating and drinking, our buying and selling, our labor and housing, our rents, our railroads . . . our recreations . . . a problem of race as well as of maintenance." As African Americans lost the right to vote across the region and the Supreme Court in 1896 in *Plessy v. Ferguson* declared separate but equal constitutional, a new politics of consumption became more important, not as a substitute for electoral politics but as a manner of testing, a ground where segregation remained vulnerable. The marketplace, southern blacks asserted, would not join the ballot box as an arena of racial exclusion.[3]

This new politics of consumption became possible in large part because the expansive nature of America's increasingly consumer-oriented economy continually generated both new products and new places to purchase them. While certainly the South did not lead this economic transformation of the country, the movement off the farm and the plantation, away from subsistence agriculture, and into sharecropping and mill work generated a demand for consumer goods among black and white southerners of all classes. Train stations were not public facilities like courthouses. While certainly sites of congregation, they were places where people purchased an item, transportation, rather than asserted a right, citizenship. Many new types of commercial spaces and practices would follow—stores run on cash instead of credit, mail order shopping, modern advertising, small-town shopping districts, and chain stores. The dynamic and changing nature of consumer culture in turn posed a protracted and never quite solvable problem for southern whites attempting to segregate their world. Few African Americans may have retained the vote, but many had something whites wanted, at least a few dollars to spend. Between the end of the nineteenth century and the middle of the twentieth, whites' efforts to enforce black inferiority in these new spaces met African American resistance and insistence on their right to make purchases. The boycotts and sit-ins of the Civil Rights movement would complete this transformation of consumption itself into a politicized right.

TRAINING THE GROUND OF DIFFERENCE

In 1884 at the age of twenty-two, the ex-slave Ida B. Wells boarded a train in Memphis. Her future as a well-known journalist and antilynching activist ahead of her, Wells was traveling out to the Shelby, Tennessee, school where, as the oldest daughter, she taught to support her recently orphaned siblings. Sitting in the "ladies' coach" as usual, Wells was surprised when the white conductor announced he could not take her ticket there. When he later returned and demanded that she move to the other second-class car, Wells refused. The other car, she insisted, was a smoker. Annoyed at her refusal, the conductor grabbed her arm and tried to drag her from her seat. Wells fought back, biting the back of his hand. Nursing his injury, the conductor hurried to find reinforcements. Three white men then forced Wells from her seat as white passengers stood on the cushions and cheered. Wells announced to the white mob that she would get off the train at the very next stop rather than allow them to drag her into the dirty and crowded smoker. Though her linen duster hung in tatters, Wells had managed to hold onto her ticket. When she finally got back to Memphis, she hired a lawyer. Ida B. Wells had decided to sue.[4]

Wells' persistence in filing a lawsuit—she won locally but then lost on appeal—might have been more rare, but her struggle on the train was not unusual in the 1880s. After the United States Supreme Court repealed the Civil Rights Act in 1883, whites across the South attempted to draw the color line on southern streetcars and railroads. The companies that owned these transportation routes often resisted, wary of the effort and expense involved in providing separate cars and policing racial separation. Like Wells, many southern African Americans resisted segregation in individual ways that sometimes ended in violence. Young middle-class blacks became increasingly assertive. One Georgia newspaper rallied black resistance: "When a conductor orders a colored passenger from the first class car it's a bluff, and if the passenger goes to the forward or smoking car, that ends it; should he refuse, it ends it also, for the trainman will reflect seriously before he lays on violent hands, for he knows that such a rash proceeding makes him amenable to the law." Ida B. Wells had not been so lucky, but other southern blacks testified to how they had called the trainmen's "bluff" and argued repeatedly that they simply wanted the first-class accommodations to which the tickets they had purchased entitled them. Southern transportation routes were often spaces of racial conflict.[5]

When middle-class blacks entered the commercial and yet public spaces of railroads, they placed their better attire and manners in direct juxtaposition with whites' own class signifiers. Because many whites found it difficult to imagine African Americans as anything other than poor and uneducated, finely dressed blacks riding in first-class cars attracted their particular ire. A white conductor told the middle-class sixteen-year-old Mary Church who, like Wells, would become an activist and a writer, "this is first class enough for you." Out in public, many whites looked considerably worse than better-off blacks. Slavery had made black identity the mudsill of antebellum social hierarchies. But in the aftermath of Reconstruction, despite pervasive discrimination and violent oppression, some African Americans managed to obtain the education, financial resources, and respectability that signified middle-class status. Class and race, then, became more visibly unhinged as railroads disrupted local isolation, and the possibility grew that whites might make a mistake in identifying strangers. Confusion reigned. In an increasingly anonymous world where class status depended upon appearances, this uncertainty endangered the very meaning of white racial identity.[6]

Railroads became the focus of late-nineteenth-century racial conflict because their connecting lines broke down local southern racial settlements often violently pieced together in the years during and after Reconstruction. Trains moved beyond the reach of personalized local relations of class and racial authority. Most often, travelers found themselves in close proximity to people they did not know, from fellow passengers to line employees, moving through places with which they were not familiar. Visible cues became increasingly important as markers of identity, as ways to categorize others as railroads spread traveling pockets of anonymous social relations, more akin to the nation's largest urban centers, across the most isolated areas of the region. The problem of black middle-class riders in first-class cars, then, was less any white fear of racial interaction than that the visible dress and deportment of these travelers belied any notion of southern blacks' racial inferiority.[7]

White southerners devised what Katharine Lumpkin, an interracial activist and herself a white southerner, would later call those "deadly serious . . . signs and separations," then, to reproduce a white supremacy that had become detached from the personalized relations of local power. Segregation tried to make racial identity visible in a rational and systematic way, despite the anonymity of social relations within train cars. Racialized spaces could counter the confusion of appearances created by the increased visibility of a well-dressed, well-spoken black middle class. An African American became, as W. E. B. DuBois described, someone who "must ride Jim Crow in Georgia." The individual's appearance then little mattered. "Colored" inferior cars meant "colored" inferior people. Systemized spatial relations replaced the need to know others personally in order to categorize them.[8]

Yet no matter what they tried, whites could never achieve the tight and absolute racial ordering of these expanding spaces of transportation despite their desire. As Ray Stannard Baker followed the newly erected "color line" through the spaces of southern transportation in 1906 and 1907, the white midwestern journalist found the streetcar "an excellent place for observing the points of human contact between the races." "In almost no other relationship," he added, "do the races come together, physically, on anything like a common footing. In their homes and in ordinary employment, they meet as master and servant; but in the street cars they touch as free citizens, each paying for the right to ride, the white not in a place of command, the Negro without an obligation of servitude." Baker observed an ambiguity there that surprised him. The sign in the Atlanta cars read, "White people will seat from the front of the car toward the back and colored people from the rear toward the front." Yet no boundary existed, and the cars marked no imaginary race line with colored curtains or signs. Baker saw "this very absence of a clear demarcation" in many cross-racial interactions within the region: "The color line is drawn, but neither race knows just where it is. Indeed, it can hardly be definitely drawn in many relationships, because it is constantly changing. This uncertainty is a fertile source of friction and bitterness." Despite the new laws and the new signs, Baker found the streetcars—and he implied, most southern spaces—places of racial uncertainty.[9]

On a childhood visit to Columbia, South Carolina, in 1892, the white southerner John Andrew Rice recalled his first sighting of the new racial order: "the main entrance to the town was the depot, and here was something new, something that marked the town as different from the country and the country depots . . . : two doors to two waiting rooms and on these two doors arresting signs, 'White' and 'Colored.'" A decade later, as a result of state laws the "town" signs had spread across the countryside, and segregation became, again in Katharine Lumpkin's words, "all so plainly marked." The railroads, as the historian Edward Ayers has recently claimed, "took a piece of the city with them wherever they went." Whites spread segregation to try to contain the confusion of appearances generated by a modernizing, increasingly consumption-oriented world.[10]

A PREHISTORY OF SATURDAYS IN TOWN

The railroads transported urban life in more material ways as well, in the forms of the new consumer products of an industrializing economy and the pictures and stories, the new medium of advertising, that made them known. Nationally, beginning in the mid-nineteenth century, a modernizing advertising industry borrowed minstrel-type representations to appeal to Americans across lines of class, gender, region, and religion. In the minstrel show, a form of comic theater, "blacked-up" white men—their faces darkened first with burnt cork and later cosmetics—"played" black men and women. From its pre–Civil War origins, minstrelsy had evolved by the post–Civil War period into a broadly produced, commercially successful entertainment form, recognizable by most Americans. Minstrel acts, touring alone or as part of larger vaudeville shows, had performed across the country. Through newspaper accounts and the illustrations of broadside notices tacked up everywhere to announce the shows, even Americans white and black alike who did not attend performances would have been familiar with their depictions of "darky" types, white caricatures of African American identities. Advertisers—technological advances made the reproduction of visual images more affordable just as manufacturers attempted to enlarge the markets for their goods—borrowed this instantly recognizable iconography.[11]

Aunt Jemima is well known even today. But modern American advertising began with the standardized "uncles," "mammies," "dandies," "savages," and "pickaninnies" of minstrelsy hawking a vast array of products. Trade cards, an early form of advertising distributed at stores, often used racialized images. A card for Mitchell's Kidney Plasters, a patent medicine, featured a "dandy," an outlandishly dressed black man, attempting to use the telephone. A mule stood at the end of a second phone as the man, looking perplexed, shouted "Bless my stars! He must be a foreigner and can't understand." White consumers, of course, saw which figure was the real ass. A trade card for a group of tailors combined the characteristics of "dandies" and "savages." It presented a group of garishly dressed blacks, their checkered and striped pants above their ankles, having their picture taken in a lush tropical setting graced with a sharecropper's cabin, its chimney smoking somewhere between Dixie and Africa. African Americans, early ads implied, were not a part of the modern American world.[12]

As advertising became a more sophisticated and professionalized industry in the late nineteenth century and early twentieth century, advertisers developed trade cards in which the racial imagery related directly to the ad copy and the product. Early versions simply depicted blacks holding or embodying the product. A trade card for Purina Mills of St. Louis combined the connection to product with the African scene, signified by almost naked black men and spindly palms. In this advertisement a foregrounded "African" boy wore the Purina Breakfast box like a suit and with Western spoon and dish in hand, proclaimed "I Like the Best!" Purina almost made him civilized.[13] Other advertisers chose brand names that signified blackness and allowed for an easy incorporation of racial imagery within product pitches. From 1905 through the 1920s, "Nigger Head" and "Niggerhead" became common product names, used for canned fruits and vegetables, stove polish, teas, tobacco, oysters, and clams. "Niggerhair Chewing Tobacco," for example, claimed to be as thick and tightly packed as its namesake. "Korn Kinks" breakfast cereal was only slightly more subtle, promoting its "delicious malted flakes" with dialect tales of little "Kornelia Kinks" and her mop-headed adventures.[14]

Images of black figures serving whites, from minstrel characters' provision of entertainment to Aunt Jemima's smiling supply of pancakes, permeated an expansive advertising industry's increasingly sophisticated and subtle productions as well. Trade cards peaked in the 1880s, although more local merchants and manufacturers continued to use them through the first two decades of the twentieth century. Larger concerns shifted much of their promotion into the new mass-circulation magazines. In many early ads, racial representations transferred their most visible racial marker, their color and the permanence of this difference, to brand-name products that also often had racial names. A card for Coates Black Thread offered not just an image but a story as a white woman supervised her servant: "Come in Topsey out of the rain. You'll get wet—Oh! It Won't hurt me Missy. I'm like Coates Black Thread. Da Color won't come off by wetting." An 1895 "Onyx" Black Hosiery ad again in the *Ladies' Home*

Journal depicted a crowd of "pickaninnies" with the caption "Onyx Blacks—We never change color."[15]

Soap advertisements in particular used whites' conceptions of blacks' racial characteristics to explain their products. In the late nineteenth century Kirkman's Wonder Soap began featuring a mammy complete with head rag standing over a washtub, one hand upon a naked black boy getting in the water on the right while her other hand held the white bar soap above a naked white boy getting out on the left. Only Kirkman soap, of course, could turn "pickaninnies" into white boys: "Sweet and clean her sons became—It's true, as I'm a workman—And both are now completely white. Washed by this soap of Kirkman." Common were these pitches that praised products as almost able to perform the impossible, such as Henry's Carbolic Salve, which "would almost make a nigger white."

By the twentieth century, advertisers had developed individualized black characters within evolving narratives. "Spokeservants" included the Gold Dust Twins, Aunt Jemima, and the Cream of Wheat Uncle. The Gold Dust advertisements, for example, moved beyond the common image of the working black servant and subtly merged the service of the product with the service of the black figures promoting it. A doubling and magnification of a racially figured subservience occurred in these ads as the twins worked for the washing powder, both as trademarks and as representations of servant labor, and the washing powder then worked for the consumer. A 1902 ad captioned "the Passing of the Washboard" emphasized these translations as shirts cleaned white danced between the black twins and the soap which had done the work. Use Gold Dust, the ad proclaimed, and "Let the Gold Dust twins do your work."[16] As the Gold Dust twins cleaned into the twentieth century, their image gradually changed from a blackface-influenced caricature to a more sentimental racist cuteness to a final cartoonish simplicity of form. Yet their message remained the same: "if you have not yet availed yourself of our services, lose no time, but summon us through your nearest grocer and 'let us do your work.' Your servants, the Gold Dust Twins."[17]

The spokeservant ads, like the long line of representations of blacks that had preceded them, implied a particular type of consumer. The person who would find humor in the visual and verbal puns and garbled speech, who would feel flattered by this blacked-up service, was not particularly northern or southern, a Catholic or a Protestant, a city dweller or a farmer, or even at times a man or a woman. The implied audience, the consumer, was, however, always white. Advertisers fused the myriad nameless men and women across the country into a national mass market in large part by figuring the consumer as white. They made whiteness by defining blackness. African Americans, whether symbolically or materially, worked for the white folks. Being white, being a consumer, being a modern American, meant having some kind of black help.

Across the turn-of-the-century South, country and general stores exposed even the most rural southerners to the new verbal and visual language of advertising. But general stores like train stations wore disguises. Often staked by northern manufacturers and distributors who lent money to promising young white men who had located the right railroad stop or crossroads, country stores masqueraded as indigenous southern economic development. At the center of life in the turn-of-the-century South, general stores were more than places for picking up local gossip, kerosene, and lard, or for chewing tobacco and local color around spattered stoves. With all their folksy charm, in the years immediately after the Civil War and especially by the 1890s, country stores were the entry points into the region for an expansive consumer culture with its new ways of buying and selling, the stage upon which many southerners first encountered the new branded items with their colorful packaging, collectible trade cards, and eye-catching outdoor signs. These southern consumers, however, despite the implications of national advertising, were not just white.[18]

For white and black southerners alike the store embodied abundance—the sights, smells, and imagined tastes of the shelves piled high and the floor overrun with bright and shiny and pungent goods. But from the Reconstruction Era through the Great Depression, money was scarce. The country store became the central economic institution across the region, at the turn of the century and in the most rural areas even as late as the 1950s, by inventing a way for people to shop locally without money. Country merchants were able to sell the new products because they supplied credit along with sardines, soap, and tobacco. Southern storekeepers were both bankers and merchants.

Yet despite the northern manufacturers and distributors' motto of "a store within reach of every cabin in the South," there was little chance of burying the region in a hedonistic wash of buying run amuck. Before the 1920s, many white and black southerners could purchase on their general store accounts only what the storekeeper approved. For many African American and white tenants and sharecroppers, consumption was doubly mediated. Not only the storekeepers but the owners of the farms where they worked controlled their buying. In many localities, the same white man in fact often served as storekeeper, creditor, and landowner. Tenants and croppers always needed the boss's approval and often his literacy abilities to write up store orders the merchants would accept. Successful storekeepers, depending not just on current sales but also upon future payment, managed the encounter between scarcity and abundance, need and desire, with a delicate and practiced hand. Though many storekeepers had not been planters, through the general store a new way of business reinforced an older localized white-male authority. At least through the early twentieth century, trains broke down some local southern social relations even as they supplied the goods that helped merchants reconstitute others.[19]

General stores also solved locally the problem of inscribing racial difference within consumption. The symbolic subversions of white supremacy, possible in a new world of appearances and first seen in white anxiety over the figure of the mixed race, middle-class black riding first class on the train, contradicted whites' new segregated order. Storekeepers, by combining the old racial inferiority of plantations and paternalism with the new consuming world, mediated the symbolic dangers through their individual power over their actual customers. They controlled what African American southerners bought with their limited credit and rarer cash. African American storekeepers were rare, and even in predominately black areas white men often tended the stores. These white merchants, in conjunction with the white landholders who wrote up store orders for their tenants, marked the color line in poor-quality goods. A black man who needed clothing received a shirt "good enough for a darky to wear" while a black family low on provisions could have only the lowest grade of flour. Storekeepers also controlled the rituals of deference through which blacks were forced to make their purchases. African Americans often had to wait until all whites were served to take whatever grade of cornmeal, molasses, or sidemeat storekeepers or their clerks would give them.

The pioneering African American economist Paul K. Edwards suggested in 1932 that African Americans often demanded brand-name products in order to acquire quality goods. Even so, country stores were places of racial mixing, and southern African Americans faced less discrimination there than at the courthouse or polling place. In many parts of the rural South, the fact that whites and blacks purchased many of the same items in the same stores subverted an ideology of absolute racial difference. The personal authority of the storekeeper, then, eased these contradictions through exerting a great degree of control over both his white and black customers' buying.[20]

Mail order catalogues offered the only late-nineteenth-century challenge to the rural monopoly of the country store, but this shopping alternative was available only to those whites and blacks with the cash to make the purchases. Called the "Farmer's Friend," "the Nation's largest supply house," "a Consumer Guide," "a city shopping district at your fingertips," and the "world's largest country store," by the late nineteenth century the catalogs of the Chicago-based Montgomery Ward and Sears and Roebuck made their way into many southern homes. A white Georgia farm woman mentioned its presence in her 1906 rural home with little fanfare, noting in her diary that she had used her telephone to place an order for her white neighbor. The thick books' beguiling pictures and clear descriptions made one thousand general-store inventories readily available. Customers could thumb through, gawk, and stare at the offerings at will, unconstrained by the country store's complicated social geographies and crowded interior and the observations of merchants, clerks, and friends. Mail order catalogs multiplied consuming possibilities for southerners and, along with the U.S. Post Office's 1898 institution of rural free delivery, or RFD, made shopping a more private affair.[21]

Some storekeepers gave in and contented themselves with the profit made by lending customers money at interest to make mail order purchases. Other southern merchants, along with their midwestern colleagues, resorted to more desperate measures like sponsoring bonfires and handing out prizes to those who turned in the catalogs for burning. Local storekeepers circulated rumors that Sears and Ward were blacks and that they sold by mail because "these fellows could not afford to show their faces as retailers." Sears published photographs to prove the whiteness of its founders while Ward countered with reward offers for the name of the person who had started the rumor that he was a mulatto. Although local southern merchants' actions had little effect on catalog sales, they did reveal the racial anxieties that permeated the continuing expansion of consumption. Catalogs placed the consuming practices of blacks beyond local white knowledge and control. Although few southern African Americans had the means to buy much from catalogs, the possibility that some distant merchant might make money out of local blacks, or that an African American might try to be "uppity" by purchasing products similar to or better than the things owned by his white neighbors excited white fears and sometimes white violence. Money and white supremacy were both at stake. Outside of the localized geography of shopping at the general store, southern whites found the potential racial contradictions of consumption much more difficult to control.[22]

Shopping between the Signs

By 1910, between an often railroad-spurred urban growth and the migration of white and black southerners away from rural areas, over seven million people lived in the region's cities and towns. A white southerner recounted the attractions of town life to a national industrial commission investigating agriculture: "cheap coal, cheap lights, convenient water supply offer inducements; society and amusements draw the young; the chance to speculate, to make a sudden rise in fortunes, to get into the swim attracts others. . . . All these things, and many more of the same sort have acted and reacted between the town and the country, and the country has become permeated with tendencies to town life and efforts to imitate."

These new, increasingly less rural, more closely settled places, then, asserted an influence far beyond even the growing proportion of the southern population leaving the farms. New towns and expanding cities, much like trains, spread anonymous social relations. Cross-race interactions there had not had time to groove paths that whites could use and blacks could abide. Families were not entangled. People were not known.[23]

In memoirs, diaries, and autobiographies, as well as southern fiction describing the 1930s and 1940s, both black and white southerners recounted the ritual of Saturdays spent shopping in town. White accounts—often from a middle-class perspective—sometimes stressed that whites left Saturdays in town to blacks. The white sociologist John Dollard, investigating a black belt Mississippi town in 1935 and 1936, described this shopping and socializing: "Saturday is by all odds the big day of the week. In the summer the stores are open all afternoon and evening. . . . The country Negroes mill through the streets and talk excitedly, buying and enjoying the stimulation of the town crowds. The country whites are paler and less vivacious [than the town whites]; there are not so many of them, but still a considerable number." The African American sociologist Charles S. Johnson discovered in the late 1930s a similar mixing of blacks and whites in southern cities and towns. In his 1931 novel *Sanctuary*, William Faulkner added rich detail to these academic accounts, describing the magical process by which the countryside seemed to empty out into the towns: "it was Saturday. . . . To the left [the street] went on into the square, the opening between two buildings black with a slow, continuous throng, like two streams of ants. . . . The adjacent alleys were choked with tethered wagons. . . . The square was line[d] two-deep with ranked cars, while the owners of them and of the wagons thronged in slow overalls and khaki, in mail-order scarves and parasols, in and out of stores." By the 1930s, going to town had become routinized for most southerners of both races, and the new racial order of segregation had expanded as whites attempted to order systematically the spaces of consumption, which had outgrown the limits of personal authority and local customs.[24]

The commercial geography of 1930s southern towns, the business districts that served many white and black southerners, closely matched in content if not exact layout the "Southerntown" Dollard had described: "A square block of buildings and the four streets around it make up the business district." Businesses there included department stores and drugstores where white customers could "receive courteous curb service . . . and the cold shock of a 'coke' in the throat" without leaving the car. Other enterprises included white law offices serving both white and black patrons and a small hotel and restaurant. Stores serving only African Americans but rarely owned by them lined another street. Somewhat isolated from the other commerce, "a small industrial section devoted to ginning cotton and pressing cotton seed," sat at the edge of the commercial district. A movie theater, "white downstairs and colored in the gallery, with separate entrances," completed the town.[25]

But while the white northerner Dollard stressed the separations, the African American Johnson emphasized the racial mixing. "Negroes," he claimed, were "served in all the business establishments of the towns visited for this study, except in cafés, barbershops, beauty parlors, and some amusement places. Grocery and dry-goods stores depend as much on the Negro buying public as on the white." Despite northern manufacturers' and advertisers' conception of the abstract consumer as white, then, southern consumers came in a multitude of hues. The elaboration of state laws and codes that began with the late-nineteenth-century battles over railroads, Johnson found, had created "no uniform pattern of segregation and discrimination" in "private commercial establishments." "Legal codes," he observed, "do not deny Negroes access to such establishments except where eating is involved, nor guarantee him the privileges usually accorded the white public. . . . The policies of stores vary widely, as do the relations between [white] clerks and Negro patrons. One generalization can be made: In the interracial situation in trade relations there is constant uncertainty." Commerce proceeded, then, upon a great deal of white denial over the contradiction between market incentives and segregation's promise of racial separation and certainty. Making race and making money did not always coincide.[26]

Farm Security Administration photographs captured this tension between segregation's claims of absolute racial ordering and the racial messiness of consumer culture in places that depended upon both white and black customers. In the late 1930s after the director Roy Stryker shifted the project's focus to southern town life, photographers took hundreds of pictures of the shopping districts of small towns and small cities across the region. Marion Post Wolcott's 1939 photographs of Saturday afternoons in Clarkesdale and Belzoni, Mississippi; Greensboro, Georgia; and Starke, Florida, for example, depict integrated crowds. In Clarkesdale a heterogenous group of black and white men, women, and children mixed under store awnings and seeped out onto the sidewalk at a downtown street corner. In Belzoni, across from the A&P and in front of Turner's Rexall Drugs, a crowd of blacks sat, stood, and visited, backed by a small knot of young white men, while three white women leaned on the window front to the right. In a Wolcott photograph of a Saturday afternoon in Greensboro, a white woman with her child encountered two young black women as all three shopped at a grocery store for their weekly provisions. And white men, women, and children mixed with African American men, women, and children under the awning of the "Home-Owned" Western Auto Associate Store in Starke, Florida, in a December 1940 Wolcott photograph.

Racial separation was difficult to maintain on the crowded sidewalks and squares and under store porches during these ritualistic Saturday afternoon trips to town.[27]

Yet FSA photographs also provided evidence of the proliferation of segregation signs making assertions of racial order. Signs blared "For Colored" and "For White" about the very streets in which blacks and whites mingled. The intimacy of touching lips to water, for example, attracted the particular attention of white southerners. In a 1938 photograph by John Vachon, a black boy finishes his drink at a fountain on the side lawn of the Halifax, North Carolina, courthouse as the huge sign affixed to an adjacent tree proclaims his race. At a Lumberton, North Carolina, tobacco warehouse the fountains and the racial signs stand side by side, and the black man and the white boy drinking indicate their racial identities even as they refresh their thirsts. Of course, no sales were at stake here—water was free. Public restrooms, too, sold nothing and offered a space for performing the most private activities. Their signs, the condition of their facilities, and the convenience of access shouted out the racial worth of their users. At a bus station in Durham, North Carolina, the "White Ladies Only" restroom faced out on a busy commercial street, its sign signifying not only race but the associated difference whites asserted within womanhood. "Colored Women," no doubt, had to hunt down an alleyway or behind the station.[28]

Consuming food combined a similar touching of the product to lips and the intimate routines of human maintenance. Because they made public the decidedly home-centered rituals of eating, cafés, restaurants, and diners usually served only one race. Jack Delano took a May 1940 photograph of an exception, "A cafe near the tobacco market" in Durham, North Carolina, where even the separate doors through which customers moved to the clearly marked white and colored tables inside were racially marked. More typical was "Bryant's Place" for "Hot Fish" in Memphis, Tennessee. A 1937 Dorothea Lange photograph captured its window advertising "for colored." But there were exceptions. The Belle Glade, Florida, "Choke 'Em Down Lunch Room," built quickly on pilings over a marsh, had a sign advertising hot and cold lunches, cold drinks, and "whites and colored served" in a 1939 Wolcott image.[29]

Watching movies, like eating, involved a close and sedentary social experience, and theaters were carefully ordered with whites downstairs and African Americans in the "too hot or too cold" balcony. Like the café in Durham, theaters also had separate entrances, a well-lighted and inviting front door for whites, a side alley and often dark doorway for blacks. Delano shot the white front and black side entrances of a theater in Greensboro, Georgia, whereas Marion Post Wolcott captured the colored entrance to the theater in 1939 Belzoni. In some places, however, whites designated only part of the balcony, always the worst seats, for "colored." Always, black southerners had to share their space, as on trains, with whites who wanted to act outside the boundaries of acceptable white-middle-class behavior. A Marked Tree, Arkansas, domestic interviewed by Charles Johnson complained, "when they fill up the downstairs some of the white fellows come up and set [sic] with the colored. . . . Sometimes they come up with their girlfriends. It's just like it is always—the white can come on your side, but you don't go on theirs." Blacks could watch the same movie and drink the same soda as whites as long as they declared their race and, by white implication as well as the shabby surroundings, their inferiority as they enjoyed their purchases.[30]

But perhaps whites were so intent on racially ordering the relatively sedentary experiences like eating and watching movies because they understood just how resistant to racial segregation the new commercial spaces of consumption would prove to be. Segregating shopping proved more difficult than racially ordering trains, streetcars, buses, cafés, and theaters. Inside shops racial identity could not be secured with segregation signs which allowed for customers of both races while literally grounding black inferiority in inferior spaces. Certainly whites' desire for absolute racial difference could have been met by excluding African Americans from white stores—a solution practiced by most restaurants and often required by law—and by limiting black purchases of consumer items considered too fine for "colored" consumers. To some degree these policies were pursued, but many white southern businesses could not afford to exclude paying customers no matter their color, especially when the next store down the street would probably make the sale anyway. Within this most intimate geography of southern white consumption, then, the collective white need for superiority clashed headlong with white individuals' desire for greater income, and money often won.[31]

What occurred within the interiors of southern stores revealed even more clearly the racial contradictions of integrated shopping within a regional culture of segregation and a national culture of white consumption. The testimonies collected in the 1920s and 1930s by African American sociologists working alone or in conjunction with white sociologists give a rare glimpse of the interactions of whites and blacks inside stores. Whites expected certain deference in public encounters, an interaction "on terms of superior and inferior" that became a general code of black shopping behavior. "In places of business," a white scholar of racial "etiquette" observed, "the Negro should stand back and wait until the white has been served before receiving any attention and in entering or leaving he should not precede a white but should stand back and hold the door for him. On the streets and sidewalks the Negro should 'give way' to the white person." Yet because few southern communities created complete segregation, southern shopping proved resistant to whites' attempts at racial ordering. Store clerks in businesses with large numbers of black customers often served shoppers in turn, sometimes making whites wait until African Americans had been served. And sites of shopping—the buildings that housed dry goods, drugstores, clothing and shoe stores, and five and dimes—almost never wore segregation signs.[32]

Fierce price competition between grocery stores enabled many African Americans not dependent on landowner store orders to find better treatment in these sites of consumption. Johnson found that African Americans in the town of Cleveland, Mississippi, preferred to shop at stores owned and operated by Chinese, instead of the grocery chains, enjoying there greater "freedom" and escape from "traditional observances." These stores, he implied, had replaced country stores as centers of socializing as well: "On Saturday migrant farmers may be seen loitering . . . sitting around on the counters and benches enjoying unrestrained conversation. They wait on themselves even to the extent of going behind the counters for articles. There is no particular racial etiquette to observe."

In southern cities, however, Johnson found that many African Americans with the resources made the opposite choice, preferring chain stores where clerks were "most likely to place all relations on an economic basis and extend all services to all customers regardless of race." An African American porter at a chain grocery in Houston, Texas, put the situation bluntly: "We carry packages for everybody, whether they are colored or white. We take them as they come." Chain stores, African Americans insisted, did not resort to the galling practice of selling black customers inferior quality foodstuffs, often especially set aside for this purpose. A black professional from Richmond summed up the economic incentives that blurred the color line within Southern grocery stores: "Of course none of them want to give you the same service they give white people, but competition for Negro trade is so keen that every store has to make some pretense of fair play."[33]

The most contradictory places among Southern sites of consumption were clothing and department stores. Foodstuffs, medicines, sodas, and ice cream were quickly consumed, and their purchases did not so readily mark the bodies of consumers. Clothing, more than other types of consumption, conveyed a lasting meaning and incited white fears of upwardly mobile African Americans and the unhinging of class and racial identities that such "New Negroes" signified. After all, at the turn of the century many whites had found the most galling aspect of African Americans' presence in first-class railroad cars to be their fine and fashionable dress. Early advertisers had clothed their black figures in mismatched and gaudy attire that caught white consumers' attention while confirming their superiority. But in southern apparel stores whites' conceptions of blacks ran headlong into

African Americans' own consuming desires. A white mailman's wife expressed the persistence of white anxiety over black dress into the 1930s. Spying the child of an African American professional entering a store, she exclaimed within earshot of a white sociologist, "it's a shame how these nigguhs can dress their children up. They fix them up better than we can afford to fix ours!"[34]

Having little control over what types of clothing African Americans with the means could purchase, white merchants and clerks attempted to assert racial difference at least within the shopping ritual itself. Blacks often could not try on clothing, hats, gloves, or even shoes. At best, some establishments permitted African Americans to examine hats only with a cloth over their heads, and dresses, skirts, shirts, and pants over other clothing. Some shoe stores allowed blacks to try on shoes but would not provide assistance. Other businesses insisted that they discriminated equally, denying unclean whites as well as African Americans—who were of course all assumed to be unclean—the right to try on clothing items.

But blacks again used their value as paying customers to seek less racially discriminating service. Many walked out of shops, often after expressing anger at poor service, and sought needed items in stores with less discrimination. Clothing had a way of moving beyond whatever racial conventions southern white merchants and clerks strung feebly in place. In Natchez, Mississippi, a white sociologist overheard white salespeople admitting unwittingly that clothing could cross the color line. A black customer had attempted to return a coat. After one white clerk refused to accept the now tainted item, a white assistant manager intervened. The first clerk then said to the other white saleslady, "this is perfectly terrible; I think it is awful. We can't put this coat back in stock." The second clerk replied, "I know it. Who wants a nigger coat? . . . Some little white girl will probably come in and buy it and not know it is a nigger coat." Segregation signs could not racially divide clothing. Whites lived with the contradictions that, in an age of mass production and widespread consumption, identical hats, shoes, dresses, and pants implied.[35]

Because white southern store owners needed African American customers, many southern commercial districts remained racially integrated despite the labels for colored and for white. The signs of segregation were as much admissions of weakness as labels of power. African American southerners could not vote, but despite white efforts to keep them down, they could spend. Neither the new marketplaces nor the new products provided liberation, but whites and African Americans consumed the same products and often shopped for the same goods in the same places. Even if the level of service offered was markedly different, white salespeople often had to serve black customers. These very public contradictions subverted whites' dependence on segregation as the signifier of absolute racial difference. African American consumers could and did play on the contradictions between making race and making money. The difficulty lay in transforming these private, individualized concessions into publicly visible, collective recognition of the importance of African American consumption to white profits. Claiming a right rather than seeking a privilege meant challenging whites directly, meant making a movement. And in the late 1950s and 1960s, through boycotts, sit-ins, and picket lines, southern blacks would win some of their most important early victories in those spaces of consumption, in the commercial districts of southern towns and cities.

NOTES

1. This paper draws from and summarizes the arguments more fully made and documented in chapter 4 of Grace Elizabeth Hale, *Making Whiteness: The Culture of Segregation in the South, 1890–1940* (New York: Pantheon, 1998), 121–98. Ralph Ellison, "Change the Joke and Slip the Yoke," *Partisan Review* (spring 1958), reprinted in *Shadow and Act* (1964; rpt., New York: Vintage International, 1995), 54–55.

2. On southern train stations, see *Railroad Magazine* and the photographs and drawings of southern stations in the Division of Transportation of the National Museum of American History, Smithsonian Institution (hereafter NMAH).

3. Edgar Gardner Murphy, *The Basis of Ascendancy* (New York: Longmans, 1909), 122, 138. Edward L. Ayers, *The Promise of the New South: Life After Reconstruction* (New York: Oxford University Press, 1992), 3–33, 132–59.

4. Ida B. Wells, *Crusade for Justice: The Autobiography of Ida B. Wells* (Chicago: University of Chicago Press, 1970), 18–20.

5. *Savannah Tribune*, 7 May 1887, in Horace Calvin Wingo, "Race Relations in Georgia, 1872–1908" (Ph.D. dissertation, University of Georgia, 1969), 130. C. Vann Woodward, *The Strange Career of Jim Crow* (1955; rpt., New York: Oxford University Press), 23–24, 27–28, 38–40, 97, 140, 169; Ayers, *Promise*, 16–20, 136–46; August Meir and Elliot Rudwick, "The Boycott Movement against Jim Crow Streetcars in the South, 1900–1906," in *Along the Color Line: Explorations in the Black Experience*, edited by Meir and Rudwick (Urbana: University of Illinois Press, 1977), 267–89; and Robin D. G. Kelley, *Race Rebels: Culture, Politics, and the Black Working Class* (New York: Free Press, 1994), 55–76.

6. Mary Church Terrell, *A Colored Woman in a White World* (1940; rpt., New York: Arno Press, 1980), 296–98. Stereotypes of poorly dressed and poorly spoken African Americans were key figures in the development of an increasingly national and commercial popular culture. On the national context of whites' imagination of the black other, see Ellison, "Change the Joke"; Eric Lott, *Love and Theft: Blackface Minstrelsy and the American Working Class* (New York: Oxford University Press, 1993); David Roediger, *The Wages of Whiteness: Race and the Making of the American Working Class* (New York: Verso, 1991); Alexander Saxton, *The Rise and Fall of the White Republic: Class Politics and Mass Culture in Nineteenth Century America* (New

York: Verso, 1990); David Nasaw, *Going Out: The Rise and Fall of Public Amusements* (New York: Basic Books, 1993); Robert W. Rydell, *All the World's a Fair: Visions of Empire at America's International Expositions, 1876–1916* (Chicago: University of Chicago Press, 1984); and Michael Rogin, "'The Sword Became a Flashing Vision': D. W. Griffith's *Birth of a Nation*," in *Ronald Reagan, the Movie and Other Episodes in Political Demonology* (Berkeley: University of California Press, 1987), 190–235.

7. Ayers, *Promise*, 136–46. On the importance of the visual in middle-class identity of the late nineteenth century, see Karen Halttunen, *Confidence Men and Painted Women: A Study of Middle Class Culture in Victorian America, 1830–1870* (New Haven: Yale University Press, 1982); and T. J. Jackson Lears, *No Place of Grace: Antimodernism and the Transformation of American Culture, 1880–1920* (New York: Pantheon, 1981), 1–47.

8. Katharine Du Pre Lumpkin, *The Making of a Southerner* (1946; rpt., Athens: University of Georgia Press, 1991), 215; W. E. B. DuBois, "Dusk of Dawn: An Essay Toward an Autobiography of a Race Concept" (1940), in *W. E. B. DuBois Writings* (New York: Library of America, 1986), 666.

9. Ray Stannard Baker, *Following the Color Line: American Negro Citizenship in the Progressive Era* (1908; rpt., New York: Harper and Row, 1964), 30, 31.

10. John Andrew Rice, *I Came Out of the Eighteenth Century* (New York: Harper and Brothers, 1942), 41–42; Katharine Du Pre Lumpkin, *The Making of a Southerner* (1946; rpt., Athens: University of Georgia Press, 1991), 133; Ayers, *Promise*, 145, 136–46; and John W. Cell, *The Highest Stage of White Supremacy: The Origins of Segregation in South Africa and the American South* (New York: Cambridge University Press, 1982).

11. Lott, *Love and Theft* (see note 6); and Jackson Lears, *Fables of Abundance: A Cultural History of Advertising in America* (New York: Basic Books, 1994). For the pervasiveness and variety of racial imagery in general and minstrel-type imagery in particular in advertising from the late nineteenth century onward, see the Warshaw Collection of Business Americana (hereafter Warshaw), NMAH. For minstrel show materials—scripts, songs, and images of characters—see the Sam De Vincent Illustrated Sheet Music Collection, NMAH.

12. Mitchell's Kidney Plasters trade card, Afro-Americana, Box 4; Harrington and Company Merchants Tailors trade card, Dry Goods, Box D.66; in Warshaw, NMAH. For more examples of the types of advertising imagery cited throughout this essay, see Hale, *Making Whiteness*, 151–68. (See note 1.)

13. "I Likes the Best!" Purina Mills, Food Stuffs, Box 4, Warshaw, NMAH.

14. "Nigger Head Tobacco," William S. Kimball and Co., Tobacco, Box H-M; and "Korn Kinks," H. O. Company, Cereal, Box C.41, both in Warshaw, NMAH; and Kenneth Goings, *Mammy and Uncle Mose: Black Collectibles and American Stereotyping* (Bloomington: Indiana University Press, 1994), 20, 79. Darkie Toothpaste by Hawley and Hazel was still being sold in the 1970s.

15. "Onyx" Black Hosiery ad in the *Ladies' Home Journal* (April 1895): 30, Afro-Americana, Box 4, Warshaw, NMAH. The J and P Coates Black Thread trade card is from Goings, *Black Collectibles*, plate 2.

16. See the Fairbank's Soaps and their later specialized Gold Dust Washing Powder trade cards in Soap, Box 2, Warshaw, NMAH. Advertisements that stress

the service of the product and black twins include a December 1899 ad, "Scrubbing Floors," in an unidentified magazine; "The Passing of the Washboard," *The Delineator* (November 1902): 829; and "Three times a day, 1095 times a year," *The Delineator* (December 1901): no page number; all in Soap, Box 2, Warshaw, NMAH. Examples of trade cards with servant themes include Libby, McNeill, and Libby Meats' "Dinah keeps the children quiet"; Imperial Shirts' "Topsy's Delight"; Eureka Poisoned Fly Plate's "Golly, I wish missus would get . . . "; Rising Sun Stove Polish's "A Tale . . . "; and D. White and Sons's "What Brush You Usin Sae?"; all in Afro-Americana, Box 4, Warshaw, NMAH. I have drawn from Patricia Morton, *Disfigured Images: The Historical Assault on Afro-American Women* (Westport, Conn.: Greenwood, 1991).

17. Coates Thread trade card in Goings, *Black Collectibles*, plate 2; Universal Clothes Wringer Trade Card, Afro-Americana, Box 3; Armour "Star" Hams and Bacon advertisement, "The Why of 'The Ham What Am!'" Afro-Americana, Box 3; in Warshaw, NMAH. Other trade cards using spokeservants include E. R. Durkee and Company trade card "De Kurn'l done give me a bottle dis yere Durkee's salad Dressin'," Afro-Americana, Box 3, Fleischmann's Yeast trade card "I can make anything in de bakin line wif. . . ," Afro-Americana, Box 4; in Warshaw, NMAH. For the letter from the twins, see the Gold Dust Twins pamphlet: N. K. Fairbank Company, "Who Are We?" (Chicago: N. K. Fairbank Company, no date), in Soap, Box 2, Warshaw, NMAH.

18. Susan Atherton Hanson, "Home Sweet Home: Industrialization's Impact on Rural Households, 1865–1925" (Ph.D. dissertation, University of Maryland, 1986); Thomas D. Clark, *Pills, Petticoats, and Plows: The Southern Country Store* (1944; rpt., Norman: University of Oklahoma Press, 1989); Edward L. Ayers, *Promise*, 13–19, 81–103; Thomas J. Schlereth, "Country Stores, County Fairs, and Mail Order Catalogues: Consumption in Rural America," in Simon J. Bronner, *Consuming Visions: Accumulation and Display of Goods in America, 1880–1920* (New York: W. W. Norton, 1989), 339; and Gerald Carson, *The Old Country Store* (New York: E. P. Dutton and Co., 1965).

19. Clarke, *Southern Country Store*, 34, 55–59, 76; Ayers, *Promise*, 13–19, 81–103; Hanson, "Home Sweet Home," 7–8, 54–56; and Melton A. McLaurin, *Separate Pasts: Growing Up White in the Segregated South* (Athens: University of Georgia Press, 1987).

20. Clarke, *Southern Country Store*, 9–10, 35, 55–57; Paul K. Edwards, *The Southern Urban Negro as a Consumer* (1932; rpt., New York: Negro Universities Press, 1955), 159; Charles S. Johnson, *Patterns of Negro Segregation* (New York: Harper and Row, 1943), 63–65. Photographs of southern country stores taken by the FSA in the late 1930s often depicted integrated shopping or socializing. See Russell Lee, "A Negro woman trading a sack of pecans for groceries," LC-USF34-31759-D, and "A Negro woman waiting for groceries in a general store," LC-USF34-31757-D, Jarreau, La., October 1938; Jack Delano, "On the porch of a general store," LC-USF33-20816-M3, Hinesville, Ga., April 1941; Dorothea Lange, "A country store located on a dirt road, on a Sunday afternoon," LC-USF34-19911-E, Gordonton, N.C., July 1939; Jack Delano, "A general store . . . " LC-USF34-43438-D, Manchester (vicinity), N.C., April 1941; and Marion

Post Wolcott, "A part of the interior," LC-USF34-52678-D, "The front of the general store," LC-USF34-52655-D, and "The front of the Whitley general store," LC-USF34-52677-D, Wendell, N.C., November 1939; all in the Prints and Photographs Division, Library of Congress (hereafter PLOC). Some African Americans also ran general stores, although they too were rare. See Davis, *Deep South*, 258, for an account of poor whites' deferential treatment of an African American store owner from whom they hoped to get credit. See Maya Angelou, *I Know Why the Caged Bird Sings* (New York: Random House, 1969) for a discussion of her grandparents' store in the 1930s.

21. Charles A. Le Guin, ed., *A Home-Concealed Woman: The Diaries of Magnolia Wynn Le Guin, 1901–1913* (Athens: University of Georgia Press, 1990), 196; Stuart and Elizabeth Ewen, *Channels of Desire: Mass Images and the Shaping of American Consciousness* (New York: McGraw-Hill, 1982), 63–68; Schlereth, "Consumption in Rural America," 364–72. On Montgomery Ward and Sears, see Frank B. Latham, *A Century of Serving Customers: The Story of Montgomery Ward* (Chicago: Montgomery Ward Co., 1971); and Gordon L. Weil, *Sears, Roebuck, U.S.A.: The Great American Catalog Store and How It Grew* (New York: Stein and Day, 1977).

22. Ewens, *Channels of Desire*, 67–68; See John Dollard, *Caste and Class in a Southern Town* (1937; rpt., New York: Doubleday Anchor, 1957), 48–49, for a description of a white northerner living in Mississippi who hated southern whites so much that he made all his purchases from the Sears, Roebuck catalog.

23. Harry Hammond, *Report of the Industrial Commission on Agriculture and Agricultural Labor*, vol. 10 (Washington, D.C.: Government Printing Office, 1901), 820; and Ayers, *Promise*, 9, 3–20, 25.

24. Dollard, *Caste and Class*, 4–5; Johnson, *Negro Segregation*, 63–77; William Faulkner, *Sanctuary* (1931; New York: Vintage International, 1993), 111; Jack Temple Kirby, "Black and White in the Rural South, 1915–1954," *Agricultural History* (July 1984): 420–21.

25. Dollard, *Caste and Class*, 4.

26. Johnson, *Negro Segregation*, 63.

27. Marion Post Wolcott, "Saturday afternoon in the Delta area," LC-USF33-30640-M5, Clarksdale, Miss., October 1939; "On the main street," LC-USF34-51879-D and LC-USF34-51878-D, Greensboro, Ga., spring 1939; "Grocery store on a Saturday afternoon," LC-USF33-30409-M5, Greensboro, Ga., June 1939; "Main street on Saturday afternoon," LC-USF33-30592-M1, Belzoni, Miss., October 1939; and "A street corner," LC-USF34-56719-D, Starke, Fla., December 1940; all in PLOC.

28. John Vachon, "A drinking fountain on the county courthouse lawn," LC-USF33-1112-M1, Halifax, N.C., April 1938; Arthur Siegel, "A drinking fountain," LC-USW3-26442-D, Bethlehem-Fairfield shipyards, Baltimore, Md., May 1943; and Esther Bubley, "Tobacco sales. Drinking fountains at a Lumberton warehouse," Milton Meltzer Collection, Schomberg Center for the Study of Black Culture, New York Public Library; Jack Delano, "A street scene near the bus station," LC-USF33-20522-M5; Russell Lee, "Man drinking at a water cooler in the street car terminal," LC-USF33-12327-M5, Oklahoma City, Okla., July 1939; John Vachon, "A railroad station," LC-USF33-1172-M4, Manchester, Ga., May 1938; and

Esther Bubley, "A rest stop for Greyhound bus passengers on the way from Louisville, KY, to Nashville, TN, with separate accommodations for colored passengers," LC-USW3-37919-E, September 1943; all in PLOC except as noted.

29. Jack Delano, "A cafe near the tobacco market," Durham, N.C., May 1940, LC-USF33-20513-M2; Dorothea Lange, "A fish restaurant for Negroes in the section of the city where cotton hoers are recruited," LC-USF34-17593-E, Memphis, Tenn., June 1937; Marion Post Wolcott, "A lunch room," LC-USF34-50500-D, Belle Glade, Fla., January 1939; all in PLOC; Johnson, *Negro Segregation*, 59; and Bertram Wilber Doyle, *The Etiquette of Race Relations in the South: A Study in Social Control* (1937; rpt., New York: Schocken Books, 1971), 146–47.

30. Dollard, *Caste and Class*, 4; Johnson, *Negro Segregation*, 72–74, quote, 73; Jack Delano, "The movie house," LC-USF33-20963-M4 and "The new moving picture theater," LC-USF33-20956-M4, Greensboro, Ga., May 1941; Marion Post Wolcott, "The Rex theater for Negro people," LC-USF34-52508-D, Leland, Miss., November 1939; Dorothea Lange, "The Rex theater for colored people," LC-USF34-17417-E, Leland, Miss., June 1937; and Marion Post Wolcott, "Negro man entering movie," LC-USF33-30577-M2, Belzoni, Miss., October 1939; all in PLOC.

31. Gunnar Myrdal, *An American Dilemma: The Negro Problem and Modern Democracy* (1944; rpt., New York: Harper and Row, 1962), 627–39; Baker, *Following the Color Line*, 34–35 (see note 9); Johnson, *Negro Segregation*, 56–77. (See note 20.)

32. Jack Delano, "The 'gossip corner,'" LC-USF33-20540-M1, Stem, N.C., May 1940; and John Collier, "A drugstore," LC-USF34-80516-D, LC-USF34-80523-D; and LC-USF34-80540-D, Haymarket, Va., August, 1941. Doyle, *Etiquette of Race Relations*, 146–59, quote, 143; Davis, *Deep South*, 15–24, quote, 22–23.

33. Johnson, *Negro Segregation*, 63–65; Myrdal, *Dilemma*, 627–39.

34. Davis, *Deep South*, 272; Johnson, *Negro Segregation*, 65–70; Myrdal, *Dilemma*, 637–38.

35. Davis, *Deep South*, 16; Johnson, *Negro Segregation*, 65–70, 296–97; Dollard, *Caste and Class*, 127; Myrdal, *Dilemma*, 636–39.

The Leo Frank Case Reconsidered: Gender and Sexual Politics in the Making of Reactionary Populism

THE TRIAL and lynching of Leo Frank have long fascinated historians and popular audiences alike. A Jewish, northern-bred factory supervisor, Frank was accused in 1913 of the murder of Mary Phagan, a thirteen-year-old local white worker in his employ in Atlanta. The killing was grisly; the morning after, Phagan's corpse was found in the factory's basement mangled and caked with blood and grime. Within days, police had arrested Frank, and the lead prosecutor, Hugh Manson Dorsey, soon affirmed his belief in Frank's guilt. Dorsey's certainty persisted throughout the subsequent two years of the case, despite other evidence pointing to the factory's janitor, Jim Conley. A black man with a prior record of arrests for theft and disorderly conduct, Conley might seem the logical target in a society committed to white supremacy and willing to lynch African Americans on the slimmest pretext. Yet, for reasons that will become clearer in the course of this essay, a curious reversal of standard southern practice occurred. The prosecutor, the jury, and much of the public not only absolved a black suspect but in fact relied on his testimony to condemn a wealthy white man. As Phagan's minister, who at first believed Frank guilty but changed his mind after the verdict, mused in hindsight, it was as if the death of a black man "would be poor atonement for the life of this innocent little girl." But in Frank, "a Yankee Jew . . . here would be a victim worthy to pay for the crime."[1]

Fostered by sensational press accounts, the case engaged popular interest from the outset. Some ten thousand people turned out to pay homage to Phagan as her body lay in state. Frank's trial, which consumed four months and culminated in a conviction and death sentence, absorbed more attention than any other in the state's history. Over the next year and a half, his attorneys appealed the case all the way through the United States Supreme Court, to no avail. When the last rejection was handed down in April of 1915, they shifted to a new strategy: a campaign for executive clemency. This effort inaugurated an impassioned battle—involving hundreds of thousands of people from the state and the nation—over whether the Georgia Prison Commission or the governor, John Marshall Slaton, should commute Frank's death sentence. Ultimately, his supporters won.

Citing evidence unavailable to the jurors, Slaton commuted the sentence to life imprisonment shortly before Frank was to hang. This act won the governor accolades from some quarters but produced in others a fury so intense that—as armed masses of people surrounded his home pledging revenge—he became the first state executive in United States history to declare martial law for his own protection. Two months later, on August 16, 1915, an assembly of prominent male citizens from Mary Phagan's hometown kidnapped Frank from the state prison farm, drove him across the state to the county of her birth, and there carried out the jury's sentence. Their act drew widespread popular acclaim.[2]

That the Frank case aroused such interest among both contemporaries and later scholars is understandable, for in it the central conflicts of early-twentieth-century southern history erupted. Some historians, for example, have pointed out that the system of white supremacy and the prevalence of lynching in the New South encouraged the mobs who threatened the governor and murdered Frank. Others have emphasized the anti-Semitism directed against Frank, which made this "an American Dreyfus case." They have argued that this break in the general pattern of lynching—the murder not of a rural African American, but of a prominent, metropolitan white—can be explained only in light of the social tensions unleashed by the growth of industry and cities in the turn-of-the-century South. These circumstances made a Jewish employer a more fitting scapegoat for disgruntled whites than the other leading suspect in the case, a black worker. Moreover, in pitting the old Populist leader Tom Watson against the rising urban Progressives who rallied to Frank's defense, the case provided dramatic personae for deep-rooted political conflicts.[3]

Yet one aspect of the Frank case has never received sustained attention: gender. Deepening the conflicts other historians have described, gender and sexual themes saturated the outcry against Frank. Although he stood trial on the charge of murder alone, the allegation that he had raped Mary Phagan became the centerpiece of the case against him. As we will see, however, the facts were ambiguous. Clear evidence of rape never emerged—but there were indications that Phagan may have been sexually active. Whatever the facts of her death, the striking point for our purposes was the determined refusal of wide sections of the state's nonelite adult white population to countenance the latter possibility. Their staunch insistence that Phagan died to preserve her chastity evinced profound concern about changing relations between the sexes and generations and about shifting sexual mores among wage-earning women.[4] The outcry against commutation for Frank can only be understood in light of these contested relations. But these, too, must be viewed in a wider context, for the furor over gender relations and sexuality fueled class hostilities and anti-Semitism.

Indeed, the patterns revealed here have a larger significance. The case constitutes a spectacular instance of a pattern of political mobilization best described as reactionary populism. At first sight, the term appears an oxymoron. Most American historians, after all, associate populism with grassroots democratic mobilizations, reaction with the elite opponents of such initiatives. In most instances, such associations work—but not in all. My purpose is to draw attention to such exceptions: to moments and movements in which the antielitism characteristic of populism coexists with, actually garners mass support for, a political agenda that enforces the subordination of whole groups of people. The mobilization against Leo Frank illustrated this dynamic, but it was hardly alone in American history. The Frank case directly stimulated the establishment of the second Ku Klux Klan, perhaps the quintessential example of this phenomenon. Shortly after Frank's lynching, Watson advised that "another Ku Klux Klan may be organized to restore HOME RULE." It was. William J. Simmons unveiled the new order two months later at a ceremony that purportedly involved many lynchers of Leo Frank. From its base in Atlanta, the second Klan soon spread to all sections of the nation, with Watson's blessing. The reactionary populism promoted by the leaders of the second Klan, as by their predecessors in the Frank case, included hostility toward *both* big capital *and* working-class radicalism; extreme racism, nationalism, and religion as alternatives to class explanations and strategies; and—the primary focus of this essay—militant sexual conservatism. My contention is that since changing gender and generational relations contributed so much to the appeal of reactionary populism, sexual conservatism, like class grievances and racial antipathies, should be seen as one of its defining elements.[5]

The concept of reactionary populism also helps make sense of the particular features of the Leo Frank case. First, it highlights the distinction between the elite following of conventional conservatism and the popular basis of the opposition to Frank, which included farmers, small-town merchants and professionals, urban workers, and others who harbored well-founded resentments against large capital and its political representatives, whether liberal or conservative. Second, the depiction evokes both the self-representation of Frank's opponents—who resisted class politics and gathered instead under the mantle of "the people"—and the defensive, restorationist character of their protest. In the end, they sought solutions not in radical change nor even substantive reform, but rather in anti-Semitism and murder. After describing the context of Mary Phagan's murder, this essay briefly delineates the responses of different groups to the trial and to the subsequent struggle over commutation. It then examines the gender themes of the opposition to Frank and how these contributed to the dynamic of reactionary populism, which would shape Georgia politics for years after the murders of Mary Phagan and Leo Frank.

Gender analysis thus opens a new window on the Frank case and the social order that produced it. Through this window, we see more clearly how change and contestation, not stasis and consensus, constituted the very essence of early-twentieth-century southern history. Economic development acted as a solvent on older relations of power and authority— between men and women and between parents and children as well as between workers and employers and blacks and whites. The dissolution of the older sexual order produced losses as well as gains. The popular anxieties and resentments thereby created proved multivalent; they made class hostilities at once more volatile and more amenable to reactionary resolution. To observe these operations in the Frank case is to gain insight into the processes by which protean concerns about the family and sexuality may help tame and redirect popular opposition to a dominant social order. The inclusion of gender as a category of analysis is thus not an optional flourish, but a vital tool to uncover elements upon which both mobilization and outcome hinged.

The setting for the case was, appropriately enough, Atlanta, the showcase city of the New South. Virtually destroyed during Gen. William T. Sherman's march to the sea in 1864, by the turn of the century Atlanta had resurged as a modern metropolis. From 1880 to 1910, the number of the city's residents more than quadrupled to almost 155,000. Atlanta's booming and relatively diversified economy fueled this growth. The value of its manufacturing grew by almost ninefold over these years, while the city's position as a major rail center linking the Southeast with the North enhanced its leading role in trade, distribution, insurance, and banking. By 1910, approximately 28 percent of Atlanta's labor force was engaged in manufacturing and mechanical pursuits, 26 percent in commercial activity.[6]

Young women such as Mary Phagan played an important role in this expanding economy, which led the region in the extent and variety of women's labor force participation. The number of female workers aged sixteen and over in the city's manufacturing industries doubled between 1900 and 1919 to more than four thousand, while thousands of others staffed its burgeoning white-collar and service sectors. Atlanta offered only the most accelerated example of developments taking place as legions of young women entered the region's workforce. More than seven in ten of the South's female industrial workers were under the age of nineteen, according to a 1907 United States Senate study of working women. Of the southern families included in this study, 94.5 percent of those with daughters aged sixteen or older had at least one in the labor force. That the earnings of daughters made up from one-quarter to two-fifths of total household income indicates the extent of their families' reliance on their contributions. The spread of youthful female wage-earning broadened the ranks of those who might find personal meaning in Phagan's fate.[7]

The release of daughters from the confining household economy of the rural South signified a wider transformation. The relative decline of the agrarian economy threw older relations of power open to question and stimulated organizing by diverse groups with rival visions for the state's future. In the years after its establishment in 1891, for example, the Atlanta Federation of Trades assumed an active role in city and state politics, backing labor candidates for office and proposing legislation to limit exploitation, promote the health and welfare of working people, and enhance popular control over public institutions.[8] Such efforts unnerved Atlanta's rising urban business elite, who after 1901 sought to centralize power and to impose their own concepts of order on the tumultuous, expanding city. Their efforts to supplant elective municipal offices with appointive boards in 1911 and again in 1913 met with stiff opposition from trade unionists and working-class voters, forcing compromises that satisfied no one. Such conflicts influenced both groups' perceptions of the Frank case: workers viewed the mobilization to overthrow his conviction as yet more evidence of the ruling class's contempt for democracy; elites read the clamor for his execution as confirmation of the unruliness of the lower classes and of the need to control them with a firm hand.[9]

In addition to class divisions inside Atlanta, tensions between its elite and the agrarian forces that had once dominated the state also shaped responses to the case. Although three quarters of Georgia's population was still rural in 1910, that margin slipped rapidly as the state's urban population grew by 400 percent from 1880 to 1920. Atlanta's numerical growth augmented the power of its business and civic elite, whose Progressive vision of an active, development-promoting central state was anathema to the landed classes. Indeed, in the years preceding Phagan's death, Georgia's town and country interests had clashed repeatedly over such issues as the regional apportionment of taxes and legislative representation. In 1908, for example, farm representatives Tom Watson and Joseph Mackey Brown attacked the Progressive governor Hoke Smith for his efforts to overturn an archaic county-unit voting system that favored rural areas. The two later vilified Governor Slaton for his role in the enactment in 1913 of a rural-urban tax equalization measure perceived as a "deliberate attack on landowners." These prior disputes fed into the Frank case, as Watson and Brown assumed leadership of the anti-Frank forces while Smith and Slaton came to advocate commutation.[10]

In this highly contentious milieu, Mary Phagan became a symbol capable of unifying groups with a wide variety of grievances. In many ways she was perfect for the role in which Frank's opponents cast her. Just approaching her fourteenth birthday when she was murdered, Phagan was described by her mother as "very pretty" with "dimples in her cheeks."[11] And indeed, her widely publicized picture depicted an attractive, engaging young woman, whose appearance contrasted so starkly with her brutal fate that people were moved to outrage. "The killing of Mary Phagan was *horrible*," one Athens, Georgia, woman declared to her brother. "I hope the right man will be found and *not* hung or killed but *tortured to death*."[12]

Whereas Phagan's death produced almost universal horror, different details of her short life appealed to different audiences. The descendant of an established Piedmont farm family that had lost its land and been reduced first to tenancy and then to wage labor, she emblemized the plight of rural Georgians.[13] Having started factory work at a very young age to help support her widowed mother and five siblings, Phagan also personified the bitter dilemma of the region's emerging industrial proletariat, forced to rely on children's wages to make ends meet. Her reported membership in the First Christian Bible School and her destination the day of the murder, the annual Confederate Memorial Day parade, endeared her as well to rural conservatives usually unsympathetic to landless farmers or organized labor. Indeed, farm owners vexed over the flight of their tenants might find in Phagan's fate ammunition for efforts to dissuade would-be migrants to the city.[14] Yet, not everyone rallied around Phagan. Blacks, Jews, and the urban, white, gentile elite reacted to other aspects of the case of more direct concern to them. For blacks that aspect was racism, for Jews anti-Semitism, and for the urban white elite potential threats to their class power.

The position of African Americans in relation to the case was difficult. Although the black press later condemned Frank's lynching as it did all lynching, the evolution of the case led many in the black community to the side of Frank's accusers. Several black observers voiced resentment at the outpouring of sympathy for him, in sharp contrast with ongoing white indifference to the outrages suffered routinely by African Americans. What proved most decisive in shaping blacks' attitudes toward the case was the strategy of Frank's defense: a virulent racist offense against the only other suspect, the janitor Jim Conley. Many elite supporters of commutation for Frank expressed outrage that a white employer was indicted, rather than a black worker with a criminal record, and shock that their appeals to white supremacy failed to rally the jury or the public. When Frank's attorneys based their case on the most vicious antiblack stereotypes of the day and on outspoken appeals to white solidarity, blacks rallied around Conley for the same reasons that Jews rallied around Frank. Thus, whereas gentile whites split on class lines in the case, blacks and Jews responded in a cross-class manner to perceived cross-class threats.[15]

It was not only Jews who supported Leo Frank, however. Both in Georgia and nationwide, the gentile urban elite in general and its Progressive wing in particular espoused clemency for Frank. The support he garnered from leading Georgia Progressives is the more notable since some had earlier campaigned against child labor. That they came to the aid of one of its beneficiaries reflects in part the elitist, social-control impulse some historians have described as characteristic of southern Progressivism.[16] In fact, the concern of elites about the Frank case reflected profound fears about the stability of the social order over which they presided. Time and again, they complained about the spread of "anarchy" and "mob rule" as revealed in the case. "Class hatred was played on" by the prosecutors, Frank's attorney complained in court. "They played on the enmity the poor feel against the wealthy" and encouraged "discontent." A prominent Progressive supporter of Frank, the Reverend C. B. Wilmer, observed that "class prejudice . . . was perfectly obvious" at every stage in the case and warned of the dangers of pandering to it.[17]

Wilmer's fear reflected his constituency's own class prejudice, which became more candid as the case progressed. In true patrician style, Frank's supporters repeatedly asserted that "the best people" were on his side. Often their elitism was less subtle. Frank's attorney Reuben Arnold, for example, described those who believed his client guilty as "ignorant people," referred to the courtroom audience as "that gang of wolves" and "a vicious mob," and characterized a white worker who had testified against Frank as "the ugliest, dirtiest reptile . . . [whose] habitat was in the filth." So oblivious were Frank's backers to the sentiments of those beneath them in the social order that they hired William J. Burns, the most notorious union-busting private detective in the country, to discredit the case against their client. Burns barely escaped alive from his inquiries in Phagan's hometown of Marietta.[18]

That debacle was but one indicator of how actions by representatives of the employing class in the case escalated working people's hostility.[19] Among Georgia trade unionists, the murder had heightened the sense of urgency about ending child labor. They expressed revulsion at the way the city's mainstream press sensationalized the dead girl's miserable fate while ignoring the political economy that sent her, like thousands of other youths, out to work in the first place. "Mary Phagan," proclaimed the *Atlanta Journal of Labor*, was "a martyr to the greed for gain" in American society, "which sees in girls and children merely a source of exploitation in the shape of cheap labor that more money may be made or the product may be disposed at a cheaper price." The unionists' anger was understandable. For almost two decades, the Atlanta Federation of Trades and the Georgia Federation of Labor had made abolition of child labor their preeminent political demand. Yet, with the state's planters and industrialists solidly arrayed against them and with scarcely any support from other quarters, they could not secure even the miserable standards achieved in other southern textile states. Indeed, at the time of Mary Phagan's death, Georgia alone among the states allowed factory owners to hire ten-year-old children—and to work them for eleven-hour days.[20]

If other elements of the Frank case determined the reactions of African Americans and the urban elite, its gender themes appealed to an audience much wider than the ranks of wage earners, a class still in the process of formation and deeply tied to the countryside. Indeed, although most historians of the case have assumed that urban workers constituted most of the opposition to Frank, research on those who signed petitions against commutation reveals a diverse coalition. Opposition came from all areas of the state, rural black belt as well as industrial Piedmont. Of the 36 percent of signers whose occupations could be determined, the overwhelming majority were landholding farmers, followed by renting farmers, merchants, and lower-level white-collar workers. The data no doubt understate industrial workers and landless farmers, who were more likely to be mobile or uncounted in the census. Nevertheless, they show that the case had meaning not only, perhaps not even primarily, for the dispossessed but also, perhaps especially, for people of small property. And whether they were farmers, shopkeepers, clerks, or wage earners, those most concerned with the gender and sexual issues of the Frank case were gentile whites who had, or could anticipate having, family ties to female workers. Since relatively few immigrants had settled in the South, the families of such working women made up an unusually homogeneous group. Most were native southerners, and if they did not work the land, their parents or grandparents had. Through their letters about the Frank case to the governor, the Georgia Prison Commission, and the press; their testimony in court; and their collective public actions, these people left a record of their perceptions of gender, class, and state power. The concerns revealed therein were distinct from those of either blacks, Jews, or the white elite.[21]

First, there were the "working girls" themselves. We can sense the vulnerability they felt—and perhaps their anger, too—in the fear and nervousness over Phagan's murder that so disrupted the factory that it had to be shut down for the week. In the trial, a few female employees took the unpopular step of vouching for Frank's character from the stand. But a score of their peers used the trial as an opportunity to vent grievances and settle old scores by testifying against their former manager.[22] Some women and children, presumably from the working and lower middle classes, participated in the demonstrations against commutation, which pitted them against the prominent women who came to Frank's defense. By and large, however, women's voices were few in the public chorus raised against

Frank. Perhaps hesitant to make demands on the state in their own right, they wrote only a handful of the myriad letters against him and rarely signed the many petitions.[23]

The relative silence of women, particularly the young women presumably most directly touched by Phagan's murder, provides a clue to the nature of the uproar over the case. The compelling issues at stake involved not simply female victimization in a static sense, but shifts in the power different groups of men wielded over young women in the new circumstances created by their employment. Among older male opponents of Frank, there was, mingled with evident love and concern for their daughters' welfare, real anger at having lost control of them. In his agitation against Frank, Tom Watson spoke of female employees as being in the "possession" of their bosses, implicitly equating access to women's labor with ownership of their persons. Some male peers of working women were likewise inclined to view them as property, albeit of a different kind. This sense of proprietorship was apparent in the common ritual among young men in southern factory neighborhoods of "rocking" or beating up wealthier outsiders who came to poach "their" women. Antipathy toward Frank thus fed on earlier rivalries among men of different classes over access to working-class women.[24]

Indeed, paternalistic outlooks dominated the campaign against Frank. The circular for a mass meeting to oppose commutation billed the event as "a citizen's meeting in the interest of our mothers, sisters, and daughters," presuming an audience of outraged men. One man who warned the governor not to commute the sentence invoked "the citizens of Ga. who have girls" as a distinct political constituency, announcing that "the parents of girls are provoked."[25] These people identified with the victim's family. They implored Slaton, as one forty-nine-year-old farm father put it, to "think of Mary Phagan and her people." "Suppose you had a little girl murdered by such a fiend," another man demanded. He urged the governor to prove himself "a friend and protector to the little girls of Georgia" by refusing to "let money or anything offered defeat Justice." These men begged the governor to let the sentence stand, since, according to one, "our wives and daughter[s] are at stake."[26]

Some spoke as parents who had entrusted their children to employers' custody in exchange for the wages that their labor could bring. They now felt furious at Frank's alleged betrayal of that trust. "A little girl of tender years," fumed Churchill P. Goree, "attacked and murdered by the man to whom she had a perfect right to look for protection." Whereas these fathers saw their own paternalism as benevolent and protective, they saw that of their daughters' employers as exploitative and deeply resented it. Indeed, their inability to protect their daughters signaled their own loss of power, authority, and status in the New South, since dominion over one's dependents was the most basic prerequisite of male independence and honor in the yeoman world from which their culture derived.[27]

Frank's alleged use of his class power to gain sexual access to women in his employ further infuriated them. It added humiliation and guilt to their loss of power. Fathers familiar with factories must have known that male supervisory employees could use their control of job assignments to pressure female subordinates into dates and sexual favors. "The factory was a great place for a man with lust and without conscience," one of the prosecuting attorneys reminded the jury. Few needed to be told. One female petitioner for Frank, however, who had taught among mill workers for eighteen years, turned this common sense to unorthodox ends. She urged the governor to commute Frank's sentence—reasoning that if he *had* assaulted Mary, "the mill boys would have known it to a man, and lynched him before he reached jail." "They have strong class feeling," she explained, "and I know the bitter resentment they feel towards the 'super' who abuses his position in regard to the mill woman." Indeed, in the view of one enraged writer, Frank was a "low skunk white livered hell hound defiler and murderer of infants."[28]

Such anxieties about the sexual prerogatives of class power were rife, in the courtroom and out. Mary Phagan "died," the lead prosecutor told the jury, "because she wouldn't yield her virtue to the demands of her superintendent." Another man later drew out the logic of this allegation. Commutation of Frank's sentence, he maintained, would send the "brutes . . . who commit rape on poor girls" the message "that money can do anything." Sexual control of men over women and of parents over daughters thus became the object of class conflict in the case, as nonelite white men acted out their anger at their inability to safeguard the women of their families and class from the predations of the richer and more powerful.[29]

The extraordinary depth of that anger may reflect the fact that the Frank case came on the heels of a massive evangelical campaign against "white slavery." Conducted by the Men and Religion Forward movement, the campaign aimed to abolish the city's protected vice district. One of the leaders of the crusade was Mary Phagan's own minister, the Reverend L. O. Bricker. In mass meetings, public visits to the brothel district by ministers and their parishioners, and a dramatic series of more than two hundred newspaper advertisements that ran regularly between 1912 and 1915, the campaign drove home the message that Atlanta's widespread child prostitution industry was the awful fruit of the low wages paid working girls. Promoting an image of prostitutes as naive victims of cunning men, the reformers implored adults to act on behalf of "the fallen girls in their virtual slavery."[30]

The trial itself aggravated concerns about female industrial employment. Testimony about working conditions in the National Pencil Factory—the workplace of Frank and Phagan and the site of the crime—revealed pitifully low pay and precarious employment. More striking, though, were the casual but repeated references to the factory's excruciating filth. Witness after witness described floors that had gone unwashed for years, now steeped not only in oil and dirt but also in blood from the accidents that took place "almost every two weeks," as when the "girls . . . mash their fingers on the machines" or when a machinist "had his head bursted open."[31] Few could remain dispassionate while imagining their own children in this environment.

Other testimony revealed working conditions that degraded women specifically. Operatives described other, numerous blood stains near the dressing rooms from "girls whose sickness was upon them." Management assertions that such stains were common "in establishments where a large number of ladies work" no doubt inflamed the anger they sought to allay. Witnesses also reported that only a makeshift divider separated the women's dressing room from the men's. Such conditions outraged those schooled in the myth that southern gender conventions applied to all white women. Even more appalling to them was supervisors' practice of peeking into the women's dressing room to see if any of the women were shirking work.[32]

Frank's alleged involvement in such snooping contributed materially to his downfall. It gave force to the charge of "perversion" that ensured his conviction. It was a key piece of circumstantial evidence buttressing the prosecution's case that the murder was an attempt to cover up a premeditated attempted rape.[33] Other such evidence included operatives' testimony that Leo Frank had a "lascivious" character, as well as innuendos about other sexual improprieties: clandestine trysts with prostitutes, homosexual liaisons, and even the bizarre anti-Semitic fantasy that Frank engaged in sexual acts with his nose. The prosecution and press discussed these accusations in titillating detail, producing a "folk pornography" that aggravated the popular outrage the testimony itself elicited.[34] In a society in which such "unnatural acts" as sodomy and cunnilingus were capital crimes, those who gave credence to the charges saw Frank as a moral pariah.[35]

The allegations of perversion carried weight because the concerns they evoked were so tangible and the symbols they deployed so potent among those with ties to female workers. The language of sexuality also offered compelling metaphors for nonsexual aspects of the case, for it best expressed the speakers' feelings of loss of control and impending chaos in their world. References to "the rape of justice" and the "prostitution of the courts" abounded, signifying the sense of intimate, personal violation that changing power relations in society aroused among the losers.[36]

The charge of perversion did not resonate with Frank's opponents as simply a metaphor for social disorder. It also encapsulated class and gender conflicts over the very definition of propriety in the new circumstances of female employment. These conflicts surfaced in the testimony of women workers about perceived sexual harassment by Frank. Their reports that he touched them, called them by first names, spied on them, and met with them behind closed doors constituted ample proof of his dishonorable character in the view of ordinary working people. Frank's defenders, on the other hand, who shared his notions of employers' prerogatives and who did not have to endure the unwanted familiarity that communicated inferior status and powerlessness, seemed unable to comprehend the girls' interpretation, much less to counter it convincingly. The closing speech to the jury by Frank's attorney, Reuben Arnold, was a model of this insensitivity. He expressed astonishment at the charges of sexual misconduct made by the prosecution and annoyance at their "prudish" failure to catch up with the times and be more "broad-minded" about practices like an employer putting his hand on a female employee's shoulder. He also made a rhetorical effort to belittle the complaints that Frank violated the privacy of the women's dressing room: "Surely a woman isn't so absolutely sacred that you can't ask her to perform her contract . . . and if she isn't doing it, ask her why, and find out why."[37] Arnold's incredulity was the measure of the vast social distance separating him from Leo Frank's opponents.

Yet the gender meanings of the case involved far more than a conflict among men over control of women. In addition to stirring up resentment about the potential sexual power of employers, the case also dramatized common adult concerns about the implications of employment for young women's *own* behavior and sexual activity. Among Frank's opponents, the intense, nearly universal insistence that Mary Phagan died "in defense of her virtue" barely camouflaged their anxiety about young women's— perhaps increasingly—active sexual agency. Then as now, it was frequently difficult to separate agency from victimization since women often experienced men's disproportionate social power most painfully and intimately in sexual relations.[38] This was particularly the case for dependent adolescents such as Mary Phagan, not yet fourteen at the time of her death. Their vulnerability notwithstanding, there was nevertheless a liberating potential for these young women in paid labor outside the home, and the sparse evidence available indicates that they themselves perceived and acted upon it, much as their parents feared it.

Unfortunately, historians have been slow to recognize that potential in the South; as a result, our knowledge of its manifestations is limited. The northern bias of women's history and labor history and the male, agrarian bias of southern history have produced—through neglect—the impression of static gender and generational relations in the South. An impressive body of literature now documents the ways young working women transformed gender roles and claimed once-taboo pleasures for themselves in the North and Midwest in the early twentieth century. "But these 'modern' workers, pioneers of a new heterosocial subculture," as Jacquelyn Hall has astutely observed, "disappear when historians take up the subject of the 20th-century South. Below the Mason-Dixon line, historians find no Sister Carries, no 'charity girls,' no 'women adrift,' only the timeless figures of the promiscuous black woman and the passionless white." Hall's pioneering studies show, however, that relations between women and men in southern cities and small towns were indeed changing in those years, due in good part to the spread of female wage earning. This background can help account for the conflicts within and between classes over sexual behavior that surged into view when women workers went out on strike.[39]

Indeed, while the *form* of women's labor force participation and responses to it may have been different in the South, there seems to be no reason to doubt that the basic processes were analogous to those in the North. Certainly contemporary southern observers recognized that a transformation was afoot. "The business girl," wrote William J. Robertson in his 1927 survey of the changes that had swept the South since 1900, "is almost as prevalent in the South as she is in the North." Robertson's remark was as much a lament as an observation, for he attributed to "the women themselves," no longer sheltered by "their fathers and brothers," a veritable revolution in relations between the sexes among the younger generation. Female modesty and male chivalry were giving way to a new "frankness and lack of convention," Victorian morality to widely practiced casual sex. Whether or not they sympathized with the developments they witnessed, informed commentators at the time believed that young working women throughout the country were claiming new independence and employing it in pursuit of male companionship and sexual adventure. Evangelist Billy Sunday delivered the same sermons on the sexual transgressions of "working girls" to audiences north and south in the 1910s, confident that Atlantans committed the same sins as Yankees.[40]

So the issue of young women's labor was not specific to the Frank controversy. On the contrary, the responses of participants echoed earlier reactions toward female labor voiced by middle-class reformers and male craft unionists. As early as 1891, in a sensational and widely debated article, the journalist Clare de Graffenried portrayed southern mill communities as places that turned the natural order upside down: idle fathers lost their manhood, as wives and daughters, their modesty and chastity gone, toiled in the mills. It was not until the turn of the century, however, as the

campaign against child labor gained momentum, that contention over gender roles began in earnest. Fear that an enforced early adulthood, freedom
from parental supervision, and close association with the opposite sex were
leading young women astray pervaded the discourse over youthful female
labor in the North and South, particularly after the massive 1907 Senate
investigation of female wage earning reported that it did indeed contribute
to "immorality" among young working women. In 1910 the Georgia Federation of Labor urged women to stay out of industry; their proper place
was in the home and not competing with male breadwinners. At the same
time, however, the federation endorsed woman suffrage and equal pay and
the *Atlanta Journal of Labor* published regular columns by Ola D. Smith, a
labor organizer and working-class feminist who insisted on women's right
to labor and to participate in public life.[41]

These varied, often ambivalent, reactions suggest that female employment acutely tested earlier patterns of paternal authority. Even if she continued to live with her family, a daughter going out to work had opportunities to assert her own autonomy and to make choices about her relations
with men that would have been difficult for her grandmother to imagine.
By keeping all or part of her wages, by courting or marrying against her
parents' wishes, she might not only defy her father's sense of his own prerogatives but also endanger his strategy for family survival. In the classes
from which Frank's opponents came, paternal authority was integral to
organizing a household's subsistence. Farmers, tenants, wage earners, and
small-business people alike had a material stake in control of their children's behavior. Youths made vital contributions to their households'
maintenance, whether plowing the family's land, tending its store or garden, supervising younger children while parents worked, or bringing in
cash from mill or factory work. Moreover, in the absence of elementary
social security provisions from the state, parents had to look to their children for support in old age. Wage-earning daughters threatened not only
to affront the cultural values of their parents but also to disrupt patterns of
household economy. Such practical concerns informed fathers' desires to
regulate their children's behavior.[42] In these new circumstances, the
boundaries of male dominance and the methods of its enforcement became
open to renegotiation. The Leo Frank case was an episode in that process.

The testimony of women workers during the trial gave cause for parental alarm in this regard. Several witnesses, for example, told of "girls" in the
factory "flirting" with male passersby out the dressing room window. Despite orders from management to stop and efforts by disapproving older
female employees to prevent the practice, the girls persisted. Reports of
the flirtations led at least one father to make his daughter quit the job
against her will. Other testimony showed that by bringing young women
and men together in daily interaction, the National Pencil Factory, like

other factories in the South, became a site of courtship as well as production. Indeed, reports indicated that a few of Mary Phagan's male co-workers had taken a shine to her themselves and that their antipathy to Frank flowed in part from jealousy. Evidence of unwed motherhood and prostitution among some former employees of the National Pencil Factory also came to light. Some young women workers evidently engaged in forms of self-assertion and interaction with men that threatened prevailing gender codes. Revelations of their activities during the trial confirmed common adult fears about the implications of wage labor for the sexual purity of Atlanta's "working girls."[43]

This context helps make sense of an otherwise mysterious aspect of the case: Although the sexual accusations leveled against Frank were widely accepted by those who believed him guilty, they lacked foundation. Medical examiners, for example, never found clear evidence of rape. The case initially made by Frank's defense—that Conley had killed Phagan in an attempt to rob her—was as plausible as the prosecution's case; indeed, her handbag was never found. By the time of Frank's commutation, moreover, some of the testimony against him had been discredited, while new evidence pointed toward Conley. Nevertheless, the popular desire to believe the rape charge was so great that even Frank's own attorneys ultimately altered their strategy and argued as if a rape had accompanied the robbery they initially alleged was the motive for the crime. For the historian, the question is *why* the charge of rape won so much credence.[44]

The answer reflects the central role of sexual conservatism in this instance of reactionary populism. The belief that Mary Phagan was raped by Leo Frank rather than robbed by Jim Conley can be read in part as a massive exercise in denial on the part of people unwilling to acknowledge youthful female sexual agency. For although there was no compelling evidence of recent or forcible intercourse, there were physical signs that Phagan may not have been a virgin.[45] Once her body had been found and examined, there were two choices: to believe that she had been murdered to cover up a perverse sexual assault that failed to leave the normal evidence, or to admit that perhaps she had been sexually active before the day she was murdered and to come to terms with the new social reality this scenario represented. Frank's opponents refused to do the latter; their gender code did not allow for such ambiguities. Either a woman was chaste and worthy of protection or she shamed herself and her people, thereby relinquishing her claim to protection.

The mere innuendo that Phagan was unchaste drew howls from Frank's opponents. "Shame upon those white men who desecrate the murdered child's grave, *and who add to the torture of the mother who lost her,*" bellowed Tom Watson, "by saying Mary was an unclean little wanton." Another man condemned Frank's supporters for what he described as their efforts "to portray her character as a strumpet." For all the speakers' sympathy for Mary Phagan as a young virgin struggling against an employer's lust, they would have nothing but contempt for a sexually active Mary Phagan, even as the victim of brutal robbery and murder. Like the scores of young women workers who became unwed mothers or prostitutes, without the halo of innocence and purity Phagan could not have served their purposes.[46]

Frank's accusers' response to the case reflected a longing to ward off the change in sexual behavior that a nonvirgin Mary would have represented. They actively promoted a mythology of Phagan as a sexual innocent who died in a noble effort to defend her "virtue."[47] This mythology registered grievances about contemporary class relations while it harkened back to an ideology of gender relations developed in an agrarian household economy. As a graphic morality play, it offered a way of coping with social change that avoided the complex reality of women's sexual initiative. And in so doing, it helped old gender and class ideology survive in a new age.

For in death, Phagan became a role model for her peers in a moral tale of epic proportions. She became, in the words of a resolution by an Atlanta union, an example of the girl who, despite her poverty, "yet holds pure the priceless jewel of virtue and surrenders her life rather than yield to the demands of lustful force." The editor of the city's labor paper applauded the union's call for a "shrine of a martyr to virtue's protection." A local minister made even more explicit the instructive power her example was to have. He solicited contributions for a monument depicting "the little factory girl who recently laid down her life for her honor" shown "in the agonies of death." He wanted the statue to stand "on the State Capitol grounds . . . as a lesson to the working womanhood of Georgia who are having to battle their way alone." It was left to the United Confederate Veterans of her hometown, however, with the support of the United Daughters of the Confederacy to build such a monument as "a symbol of the purity of the little virgin." They hoped that in rewarding Phagan, "who surrendered her sweet young life to save her honor," they would teach others high esteem for chastity, "that Christian attribute—the crown, glory and honor of true womanhood."[48]

That two organizations devoted to the glorification of the Old South, with its roots in slavery and racist, patrician values, should rally against a white employer rather than a black worker indicates the complexity of the conflicts in the case. And, in fact, although the case raised issues concerning the susceptibility of working-class women to economic and sexual exploitation that a radical labor or women's movement might address, these issues were resolved in a thoroughly reactionary way. Not only did the leaders of the agitation against Frank make a fetish of virginity and deny women's sexual agency; they also demanded "protection" of women by men rather than measures that might enable young women to protect themselves, thus reinforcing the paternalism of male supremacy.[49] The most graphic illustration of this was the lynching of Frank by twenty-five men calling themselves "the Knights of Mary Phagan." The name was an obvious appeal to the chivalric tradition that the lynching acted out, a tradition in which, as Jacquelyn Hall put it, "the right of the Southern lady to protection presupposed her obligation to obey." The mob that killed Frank included leading citizens of Phagan's hometown, who had pledged themselves at the time of the commutation to avenge her family's honor. Their act evoked plaudits from many quarters; "no finer piece of Ku-Kluxing was ever known in Georgia," the official state historian later exulted.[50] Most telling was the behavior of the crowd that gathered around Frank's suspended body. One reporter described the scene as being "like some religious rite"; the participants exhibited a "curiously reverent manner" and an air of "grave satisfaction." Phagan's family also endorsed the paternalistic settlement. Indeed, her mother's first public statement after the lynching was that "she was satisfied with the manner of ending the case." Popular sanction for the lynching was further evident in the way it became enshrined in the folk culture of the South. The "Ballad of Mary Phagan," composed during the trial and performed for anticommutation crowds by the popular musician Fiddlin' John Carson, was later updated to glorify her avengers. It was sung for decades afterward in mill communities throughout the region. Frank's lynching thus scored a symbolic triumph for Old South gender ideology, as represented by the Knights of Mary Phagan, over the emerging power of industrial capitalism, as represented by Frank, while the way of life associated with that earlier culture was rapidly losing ground.[51]

In the end, this "chivalrous" resolution of the gender concerns not only expressed the popular malaise that the case revealed. It also helped submerge the radical potential in the popular mood. The paternalistic reaction to the gender issues constituted an integral element of a more general reactionary populist response. The conservative dynamics of this populism were most obvious in the way class antagonisms ultimately were channeled into anti-Semitism, and in the way the lynching assuaged popular hostility to the state. But in each case, the power of gender issues contributed to the outcome.

That the Frank case served as a forum for the expression of class enmity has already been demonstrated. Yet as the commutation struggle unfolded, the hostilities of the popular classes toward large capital and its representatives more and more took on an anti-Semitic cast. "Our country has been battered to the shylocks of high finance," declared one pro-Watson editor, for example, while other Frank opponents denounced "Dirty Jews with thir Dirty Dollars" and "big Hebrew money."[52] If not all of Frank's opponents shared this approach, none condemned anti-Semitism in forthright terms. As a result, through the active efforts of some and the passive default of others, Jews became the foil for all capitalism's evils, whereas Georgia's and the nation's most powerful capitalists escaped notice or blame.[53]

To view the anti-Semitic trajectory of the case as a conscious, cynical sleight of hand on the part of leading Frank opponents would be simplistic. Politicians such as Tom Watson and Joseph Mackey Brown, themselves men of substantial property who stood to lose should a genuinely anticapitalist labor movement develop, *did* energetically promote anti-Semitic interpretations of class hostilities. Yet their inclination to view the case in this way came from the petty producer-based political culture they shared with their followers. Indeed, given the antipathy of Populism and producerist ideology more generally to "unproductive" finance capital, with which Jews were particularly associated in the minds of many contemporaries, the potential for anti-Semitic responses to the case existed without the machinations of men like Watson and Brown.[54]

What is most interesting for our purposes here, however, is not the source of this potential but the role gender issues played in its realization. Just as sexual anxieties infused prejudices against African Americans in southern society, so fears about changing gender roles and sexual jealousies combined with class hostilities in the anti-Semitism of the Frank case. Popular associations of Jews with the vice trade and stereotypes about the alleged lust of Jewish men for gentile women made Frank vulnerable as a suspect in the first place.[55] One opponent of commutation for Frank informed the Georgia Prison Commission that "there is two things most of them [Jews] will do. One is they will steal or make or have money [and] the other is this[:] do every thing possible [*sic*] all through life to seduce our Gentile Girls and Women." Tom Watson, who had recently added anti-Catholicism to his arsenal, implied that Jewish employers had a penchant for taking sexual advantage of women akin to that he alleged against papal priests. He described the factory as "a Jewish convent as lascivious as a Catholic monastery," a belief some of his readers endorsed. Years later a Ku Klux Klan writer, complaining of supposed "outrages inflicted upon innocent girls by Hebrew libertines," referred back to the Frank case as evidence. Anti-Semitism thus provided simple answers for the complicated questions of changing patterns of class power and female sexuality. Capitalism was a good social system, unless manipulated and deformed by Jews; young women were pure, asexual beings, unless lured into depravity by treacherous racial others.[56]

Whereas anti-Semitism deflected economic class hostilities, the lynching itself defused political class hostilities. Popular distrust of the state apparatus and suspicion that it was becoming a tool of the wealthy emerged early in the controversy over commutation. Over and over again, Frank's opponents decried the elite's control of political affairs and denounced class injustice in the court system. Governor Slaton's commutation of Frank's sentence confirmed these beliefs. "As usual," one writer put it, "the rich have triumphed over the poor, the strong over the weak, those who neither toil or spin over the working people. . . . God help the poor; the rich take care of themselves."[57] And Frank's opponents were right that immense amounts of money and power, resources to which Mary Phagan's people had no access, were marshaled on his behalf, and the governor did yield to this power and override the authority of a duly constituted jury. Georgians could readily interpret Slaton's disregard for the decisions of the jury and the appeals judges as reflecting a larger pattern in which the state of Georgia by the early twentieth century served capital, usually to the detriment of other classes. Not only did the government exclude all women, most blacks, and many poor whites from the electorate and deny them all but rudimentary education and welfare. It also bolstered the power of wealth through violent opposition to strikes, through class and race privilege in the court system, and through vagrancy, contract, and lien laws that limited workers, and tenants' freedom of movement.[58]

Yet rather than proposing substantive measures to redress class injustice, Frank's opponents instead sought solutions in a political ideology developed under conditions that no longer existed. They directed their hopes toward the restoration of a now-mythical republican state, in which "the people"—white, male heads of household in the producing classes—controlled a government of limited powers. The rationale for the lynching expressed this reactionary populist ideology. Frank's opponents viewed vigilante activity as a legitimate exercise of popular sovereignty when state policy no longer reflected the citizenry's will. They equated the killing of Frank with a tradition of popular mobilization against the powerful in the service of "justice." The Knights of Mary Phagan were but the latest in a line that included Christ driving the money changers from the temple, Martin Luther and the early Protestants, the *sans culottes* of the French Revolution, and the patriots of the Boston Tea Party. "*All power is in the people*," explained Watson in a paean to the "righteous wrath" of the "Vigilance Committee" that murdered Frank. "When the constituted authorities are unable, or unwilling to protect life, liberty, and property," he averred, "*the People must assert their right to do so.*"[59] Many Frank opponents defended the lynching on the grounds that by "rob[bing] the law of part of its terror," as one petition put it, the commutation of his sentence encouraged disrespect for the law and promoted "anarchy" and "mob rule." In other words, the act of the mob, in administering the stern punishment prescribed by the courts, would achieve the *conservative* goal of preserving fear of the law. Taking Frank's life would ensure order, stability, and respect for property.[60]

Here again, though, conceptions of gender contributed to the motives and the rationale. They influenced the sanction given to the lynching and to the model of state power it represented. Punishment for alleged rape served as the ultimate justification for lynchings in southern society. "Any man," explained one after the commutation, "who has very much family pride in their hearts, would be in favor of mob law, under the circumstances."[61] Defending the Knights of Mary Phagan, James G. Woodward, the labor-backed mayor of Atlanta, voiced the inaccurate but eminently useful white apologia for lynching: "when it comes to a woman's honor, there is no limit we will not go to avenge and protect it." This culture of "honor" had material roots in the historical role of patriarchal authority in the household economies of plantation slavery and yeoman farming in the preindustrial South. It drew its emotional power from the intersection of white supremacy and female subordination. It was a profoundly reactionary creed, in that it aimed to buttress both hierarchies against the leveling potential of social change. Through the lynching of Frank, it scored a symbolic triumph over the emerging culture of "Mammon" associated with industrial capitalism, by meting out honor's "ultimate punishment" (death) for honor's "ultimate offense" (rape).[62]

The reactionary populist resolution of the case also had a more tangible impact on the state's public life, sparking turmoil reminiscent of the 1890s. Criticism of Frank's lynching led one country editor to explode that "the common people" were "tired of having orders dished out to them by a bunch of kid glove politicians and city editors." The editor denounced Frank's supporters as "the same gang that has practiced gag-rule for so long . . . that has ridden roughshod over the people . . . that stole the election from Watson" in 1894 and crushed the Populist movement for which he then campaigned. The scale of such rage, which involved not merely polemical attacks but also crowds threatening Jewish businesses and burning the governor in effigy, terrified elite Georgians. "You can have no conception of the situation [here]," Frank's attorney Luther Z. Rosser informed an associate after the lynching. "Public opinion has never been so wild, so unreasonable, and so savage . . . the hatred and bitterness here now is inconceivable." The unrest unleashed by the commutation and the lynching upset the state's economy and endangered its prospects for outside investment. It also delivered a severe blow to the ambitions of the urban political elite with which Rosser, like Slaton, was associated. This group had no doubt about the cause of their predicament. "The real cause of all the present trouble is Tom Watson," as Rosser summed up the consensus. The conclusion appeared simple: "Georgia [has] to put her foot down on Watson . . . [to] crush him as a political power for all time in this state."[63]

The state's leaders failed utterly in this endeavor, their inability to reestablish hegemony a measure of the potency of the conflicts unleashed by the Frank case. Rather than destroying Watson, they themselves suffered stinging reverses. Slaton's commutation of Frank's sentence proved the end of a once-promising political career. Watson's candidate for governor, Leo Frank's prosecutor Hugh Manson Dorsey, swept the polls in the primaries after Frank was lynched, trouncing his establishment-backed rivals in one of the largest electoral victories in Georgia's history. Although the results stunned elite observers, no one had any doubt that the Frank case had made Dorsey governor. Rebuffed at the polls, Watson's opponents fell back on more circuitous strategies to undermine his influence, including having him prosecuted by the federal government on charges of obscenity for his political journalism and trying to expel him from the state Democratic Party. These behind-the-scenes efforts, too, yielded only humiliating defeats for their orchestrators, as Watson tapped an undreamed-of reservoir of popular support that shielded him from their power and within a few years catapulted him to a seat in the United States Senate. From this august post, he would defend the second Ku Klux Klan from its critics. This organization, whose might by the mid-1920s surpassed that of any other right-wing movement in American history, gained direct impetus from Watson's agitation in the Frank case. In short, although the victory proved pyrrhic—in the long run quite tragic—for many of their supporters, the forces of reactionary populism had scored a significant triumph over their establishment adversaries, the consequences of which would resound for years.[64]

There were many reasons why the potent conflicts involved in the Frank case took the direction they ultimately did. Cases of female sexual victimization, in part because of the reality of women's vulnerability in our society, may be particularly prone to conservative manipulation and repressive panaceas. Then, too, other features of contemporary southern life made a reactionary outcome more likely: the region's repressive political economy, the racial divisions that undermined coherent class loyalties, the hold of petty-producer political and cultural traditions on the industrial labor force then in the process of formation, and not least, the sway of the demagogic politicians that the one-party South produced in abundance, who used populist rhetoric to gain support but opposed genuine working-class politics and political radicalism. The key point for this essay, however, is that the Frank case could never have incited the passions it did without changes in female behavior and family relations as the context, and without the charged issues of sexuality and power between the sexes and generations as the trigger.[65]

That being the case, the hypotheses confirmed here could be applied to other, analogous movements and episodes. Certainly the Frank case, like any significant historical event, was in some respects singular. Yet if the context and form were distinct, the prominence of gender and sexual themes was by no means unique. One of the most hotly contested issues in American politics north and south in these years was Prohibition, a movement suffused with such themes. Nor was Tom Watson the only politician to harness the emotions revealed in the Frank case toward racist, restorationist ends; many of his contemporaries proved equally adept. Similarly, the Ku Klux Klan of the 1920s blended populist appeals, vitriolic racism, and militant sexual conservatism. For their part, the white Citizens' Councils later organized to combat the civil rights movement found the specter of "social equality" and racial "amalgamation" their most effective rallying cry. In our own time, the New Right has transformed the terms of debate in United States politics by using a populistic, familial idiom to incite opposition to abortion rights, affirmative action, and the welfare state. Without discounting the important differences between these phenomena, one may yet note suggestive parallels with the pattern of reactionary populism here described. In each case, gender and sexual themes played a critical role in mobilizing a mass following for a reactionary political agenda put forward in the name of "the people."[66]

Others have rightfully drawn attention to the class and race dynamics of such movements. The Frank case, however, shows that to fully comprehend them, we must also consider changing relations between men and women and parents and children as vital components of the perceived social crises to which those movements respond. And to explain their powerful appeal, we must examine the role of gender and sexuality in their ideologies. "The public and the private worlds are inseparably connected," Virginia Woolf long ago pointed out; "the tyrannies and servilities of the one are the tyrannies and servilities of the other." It is time to bridge the artificial barriers between women's history and labor history, between family history and political history, so that we may grasp the systematic links between them.[67] In the writing of history, as in politics, we ignore the connections at our peril.

Notes

Many people have offered helpful comments on various versions of this article. Without implicating them in the result, I would like to thank Edward Ayers, Leonard Dinnerstein, Maureen Fitzgerald, Joyce Follett, Jacquelyn Hall, Wally

Hettle, Jackson Lears, Gerda Lerner, Alan Maass, Leisa Meyer, and David Thelen. I owe special gratitude to Linda Gordon for her careful readings, astute advice, and unflagging encouragement.

1. L. O. Bricker, "A Great American Tragedy," *Shane Quarterly* 4 (April 1943), 90. In this rare instance, racist beliefs helped persuade whites that the black suspect was innocent. Convinced that an illiterate African American could neither construct such elaborate accounts, nor adhere to them in the face of grueling cross-examination, nor employ the linguistic forms used in the murder notes found by Mary Phagan's body, many whites accepted his testimony as to Frank's guilt. See Leonard Dinnerstein, *The Leo Frank Case* (New York, 1968), 45–46, 53.

2. For details of the case, see Dinnerstein, *Leo Frank Case*; and Clement Charlton Moseley, "The Case of Leo M. Frank, 1913–1915," *Georgia Historical Quarterly* 51 (March 1967), 42–62.

3. On the episode's anti-Semitic content, against the backdrop of the industrialization of the South, see Dinnerstein, *Leo Frank Case*; and Steven Hertzberg, *Strangers within the Gate City: The Jews of Atlanta, 1843–1915* (Philadelphia, 1978), 202–15. On its connection to the defeated Populist movement of the 1890s, see C. Vann Woodward, *Tom Watson: Agrarian Rebel* (New York, 1938). On the response of blacks, see Eugene Levy, " 'Is the Jew a White Man?': Press Reaction to the Leo Frank Case, 1913–1915," *Phylon* 35 (June 1974), 212–22. For popular treatments, see Harry Lewis Golden, *A Little Girl Is Dead* (New York, 1965); and Charles Samuels and Louise Samuels, *Night Fell on Georgia* (New York, 1956).

4. I describe Phagan and her peers as "women" in defiance of their contemporaries' habit of depicting such female wage earners as "working girls" and referring to them by their given names. These diminutive labels resisted acknowledging the social adulthood thrust upon such young women, even as they remained dependent on their parents. However much the labelers may have wished that Phagan and her peers enjoyed the sheltered naiveté evoked by the term *girl*, their employment and consequent exposure to a working-class sexual culture suggested otherwise. I hope the language employed here will foster respectful, rather than sentimental, approaches to historical understanding of Phagan and her peers.

5. Tom Watson's *Jeffersonian*, Sept. 2, 1915, quoted in Woodward, *Tom Watson*, 446. See also Dinnerstein, *Leo Frank Case*, 149–50. On the second Klan's ideology and practice, see Nancy MacLean, "Behind the Mask of Chivalry: Gender, Race, and Class in the Making of the Ku Klux Klan of the 1920s in Georgia" (Ph.D. diss., University of Wisconsin, Madison, 1989). On the Boston antibusing movement as a case of "reactionary populism," see Ronald P. Formisano, *Boston against Busing: Race, Class, and Ethnicity in the 1960s and 1970s* (Chapel Hill, 1991), esp. 172–202. Formisano notes that among the opponents of busing, "the alienated right most complained of was . . . the right of parental control over their own children," a pattern consistent with the argument advanced here. Ibid., 171. Such an analysis might prove fruitful for some of the paradoxical movements of the intervening years. See Alan Brinkley, *Voices of Protest: Huey Long, Father Coughlin, and the Great Depression* (New York, 1983); and Leo P. Ribuffo, *The Old Christian Right: The Protestant Far Right from the Great Depression to the Cold War* (Philadelphia, 1983).

6. Hertzberg, *Strangers within the Gate City*, 28, 98; Blaine A. Brownell, *The Urban Ethos in the South, 1920–1930* (Baton Rouge, 1975), 5, 11–17; Kenneth Coleman, ed., *A History of Georgia* (Athens, 1977), 233; Thomas M. Deaton, "Atlanta during the Progressive Era" (Ph.D. diss., University of Georgia, 1969), 1–2, 15–18.

7. Julia Kirk Blackwelder, "Mop and Typewriter: Women's Work in Early Twentieth-Century Atlanta," *Atlanta Historical Journal* 27 (fall 1983), 21; U.S. Department of Commerce, Bureau of the Census, *Fourteenth Census of the United States Taken in the Year 1920*, vol. 9: *Manufactures, 1919: Reports for States* (Washington, 1923), 268–69; U.S. Department of Labor, Bureau of Labor Statistics, Bulletin 175, *Summary of Report on Condition of Woman and Child Wage Earners in the United States* (Washington, 1916), 16–17, 19–20.

8. For an outstanding perception of the transformation of the region, see William J. Robertson, *The Changing South* (New York, 1927). For such perceptions in Georgia, see Steven Wayne Wrigley, "The Triumph of Provincialism: Public Life in Georgia, 1898–1917" (Ph.D diss., Northwestern University, 1986), esp. 30–40. On labor response to the change, see Mercer Griffin Evans, "The History of Organized Labor in Georgia" (Ph.D. diss., University of Chicago, 1929).

9. Deaton, "Atlanta during the Progressive Era," 386, 399; Franklin M. Garrett, *Atlanta and Environs: A Chronicle of Its People and Events* (3 vols., New York, 1954), II, 602, 611; Eugene J. Watts, *The Social Bases of City Politics: Atlanta, 1865–1903* (Westport, 1978), 21; Evans, "History of Organized Labor in Georgia," 276. On the coming of age of Atlanta's "commercial-civic elite" and their efforts to tame the disruptive forces of metropolitan life, see Brownell, *Urban Ethos in the South*.

10. Wrigley, "Triumph of Provincialism," 31, 40 (on population), 230. See also ibid., 107, 122, 178, 212–17, 232–35, 250.

11. Brief of Evidence at 1, *Leo M. Frank v. State of Georgia*, Fulton County Superior Court at the July Term, 1913. Atlanta Miscellany (Special Collections Department, Robert W. Woodruff Library, Emory University, Atlanta, Ga.). The original trial transcript has not survived, but both the prosecution and the defense accepted the Brief of Evidence as a correct account and relied on it in subsequent appeals, beginning with the Supreme Court of Georgia, Fall Term, 1913. See Dinnerstein, *Leo Frank Case*, 222–23.

12. Helen Newton to Edwin D. Newton, May 2, 1913, folder 2, box 5, Carlton-Newton-Mell Collection (Special Collections Department, University of Georgia Libraries, Athens).

13. Mary Phagan's family's roots in Cobb County were emphasized in a petition against commutation from a mass meeting there to the governor. See "Hearing before Gov. John M. Slaton re: Commutation of the Death Sentence of Leo Frank, Atlanta, Ga., June 12–16, 1915," p. 41, Atlanta Miscellany. See also Moultrie M. Sessions to J. H. Hurford, May 17, 1915, folder 22, box 35, John Marshall Slaton Collection (Manuscripts Section, Georgia Department of Archives and History, Atlanta). In 1910, rural Georgians' per capita wealth of $195 was less than half that of urban Georgians. Wrigley, "Triumph of Provincialism," 39–40.

14. Thomas E. Watson, "The Official Record in the Case of Leo Frank, a Jew Pervert," *Watson's Magazine* 21 (Sept. 1915), 256. For farmers' complaints about the rural labor shortage, see Wrigley, "Triumph of Provincialism," 128–30, 249–51.

15. On blacks and the Frank case, see Eugene Levy, "'Is the Jew a White Man?'" See also Hertzberg, *Stranges within the Gate City*, 207–8. For examples of the racism of Frank's defense, see Reuben Arnold, *The Trial of Leo Frank: Reuben Arnold's Address to the Court on His Behalf*, ed. Alvin V. Sellers (Baxley, 1915), 51–52, 64, 67; "Hearing before Gov. John M. Slaton," 141–43; C. P. Connolly, *The Truth about the Frank Case* (New York, 1915), 88, 93; *The Frank Case: Inside Story of Georgia's Greatest Murder Mystery* (Atlanta, 1913), 132. Frank's opponents also exhibited racism against blacks, but it played a role subordinate to the other issues they raised. The response of Jews to the anti-Semitism directed against Frank has been analyzed well by others, including Dinnerstein, *Leo Frank Case*; Golden, *A Little Girl Is Dead*; and Hertzberg, *Strangers within the Gate City*.

16. Gentile urban support was evidenced by public statements and editorials in the leading dailies and periodicals of Georgia and the nation and by myriad letters and petitions from prominent citizens in support of commutation. For a list of Frank supporters in Georgia, see "Georgia Letters and Petitions for Commutation of Sentence for Leo M. Frank to Life Imprisonment," folder 6, box 5, Slaton Collection. On the conservatism, racism, and elitism of southern Progressivism, see J. Morgan Kousser, *The Shaping of Southern Politics: Suffrage Restriction and the Establishment of the One-Party South, 1880–1910* (New Haven, 1974); and John Dittmer, *Black Georgia in the Progressive Era* (Urbana, 1977). The hallmarks of this ambivalent tradition often appeared in the Frank case, as when *Augusta Chronicle* editor Thomas Loyless, praised by liberals for denouncing the lynching of Frank, used race-baiting to browbeat Frank's opponents. See, for example, *Augusta Chronicle*, Sept. 27, 1915, 4. For a more sympathetic appraisal, see Dewey W. Grantham, *Southern Progressivism: The Reconciliation of Progress and Tradition* (Knoxville, 1983).

17. Arnold, *Trial of Leo Frank*, ed. Sellers, 35. Similarly, he charged the state with using as witnesses, "the discharged employee, the men and women who hated wealth and was willing to defeat it in the spirit of the anarchist." *Atlanta Constitution*, Oct. 26, 1913, reel 2822, Leo Frank Collection (American Jewish Archives, Cincinnati, Ohio). There were also private warnings that Frank's execution "through mob demand" would create uncertainty in the popular mind about the judicial process. A. D. Lasker to Jacob Billikopf, Dec. 28, 1914, reel 1069, ibid. See also Louis Marshall to Herbert Haas, Dec. 24, 1914, ibid. For C. B. Wilmer's statement, see "Hearing before Gov. John Slaton," 75. The alarm of elites became most prominent after the near riots that followed Slaton's commutation of Frank's sentence and after the lynching, as hundreds of letters in the summer and fall of 1915 to the *Augusta Chronicle* commending its stand against "Watsonism" show. The pattern parallels that found by David L. Carlton: town elites' concerns about lynching "generally had less to do with a concern for social justice than with fears for social stability." David L. Carlton, *Mill and Town in South Carolina, 1880–1920* (Baton Rouge, 1982), 246.

18. For a reference to the "best people," see *Forsyth Advertiser*, July 9, 1915, reel 2824, Frank Collection. For a listing of Frank's supporters headed "Names That Count for Much," see *Augusta Chronicle*, Dec. 18, 1915, supplement, pp. 29–30. Arnold, *Trial of Leo Frank*, ed. Sellers, 12, 21, 30, 42–43. See also the slurs in Connolly, *Truth about the Frank Case*, 18, 22, 23, 30. The prosecutor had a field day with this elitism, which enabled him to pose as the defender of the witnesses'

reputations, "though they may be working girls." *Argument of Hugh M. Dorsey, Solicitor-General, at the Trial of Leo M. Frank* (Macon, 1914), 21–22. On the episode of William J. Burns, see Dinnerstein, *Leo Frank Case*, 100–101; Jacquelyn D. Hall, "Secrets: Reading the Fulton Bag and Cotton Mill Spy Reports," 12, paper delivered at the Seminar on Race, Class, and Gender in Southern History, University of California, San Diego, June 22–24, 1989 (in Nancy MacLean's possession).

19. In July 1913 one of the most active union locals in Atlanta resolved that the coverage of the case in the Atlanta press had led its members to "look with suspicion . . . upon so-called journalism . . . wherever the lives, liberty, property or interests of industrial workers are involved." *Atlanta Journal of Labor*, Aug. 1, 1913, p. 6. A northern correspondent later attributed Frank's lynching in part to the resentment against class bias in the court system that surfaced early in the case "among the working classes." *New York Times*, Aug. 20, 1915, p. 5.

20. *Atlanta Journal of Labor*, May 2, 1913, p. 4; Evans, "History of Organized Labor in Georgia," 229; Elizabeth H. Davidson, *Child Labor Legislation in the Southern Textile States* (Chapel Hill, 1939), 69–88, 194–214; A. J. McKelway, "Child Labor in Georgia," *Child Labor Bulletin* 2 (Aug. 1913), 54–55.

21. For a portrayal of Frank's opponents as ignorant and fanatical workers, see Dinnerstein, *Leo Frank Case*; and Leonard Dinnerstein, "Atlanta in the Progressive Era: A Dreyfus Affair in Georgia," in *The Age of Industrialism in America*, ed. Frederic Cople Jaher (New York, 1968), 127–59. The generalization in the text is based on information in the 1910 manuscript census population schedules about signers of petitions against commutation (now in the Slaton Collection) from the following Georgia counties: Cherokee, Emanuel, Franklin, Paulding, Polk, Worth. Manuscript Census Records, Georgia, Thirteenth Census of the United States, 1910, Records of the Bureau of the Census, RG29, microfilm T624, reels 179, 186, 189, 206–7, 207–8, 219. Of the 206 of 566 signers whose occupations could be determined, the breakdown was: landowning farmers or laborers on family-owned farms (74); merchants (38); tenant farmers (30); lower-level white-collar workers (20); skilled workers (14); unskilled workers (12); professionals (8); high white-collar workers (2). Incomplete samples produced roughly similar profiles in DeKalb, Douglas, Lincoln, Oglethorpe, and Tift counties. Ibid., reels 184, 183, 199, 206, 216. By 1910 only 2 percent of the population in the eleven former Confederate states was foreign-born, a smaller proportion than in 1865. Rowland T. Berthoff, "Southern Attitudes toward Immigration, 1865–1914," *Journal of Southern History* 17 (Feb. 1951), 342.

22. "Everybody was excited that morning after Mary Phagan was killed," one of the factory's managers testified. "Looked like everybody was worried. . . . The whole factory was wrought up. I couldn't hardly keep anybody at work . . . for I couldn't get any work out of them." Brief Evidence at 39, *Leo M. Frank v. State of Georgia*. Frank's attorney maintained that the "little girls" who testified that Frank had gone into the dressing room with a female supervisor, presumably for immoral purposes, had done so out of spite because the woman had fired them. Arnold, *Trial of Leo Frank*, ed. Sellers, 35.

23. For glimpses of women's participation on both sides, see *Augusta Chronicle*, June 23, 1915, p. 1; *American Israelite*, March 26, 1914, reel 2822, Frank Collection; Nathaniel E. Harris, *Autobiography* (Macon, 1925), 361. Almost all the women who wrote letters against commutation did so as mothers of female workers. See

Mrs. Henry L. Ozburn to John M. Slaton, June 22, [1915], reel 2, Leo Frank Correspondence (Special Collections, Brandeis University Library, Waltham, Mass.); "A Mother" to Mr. Davidson, n.d., folder 2, box 35, Slaton Collection; "A Mother" to Slaton, Nov. 23, 1914, folder 1, box 35, ibid. Likewise, Esther Gerald implored Slaton to judge Frank "as if it was one of your own Daughters." Esther Gerald to Slaton, May 26, 1915, folder 10, box 45, ibid. A rare exception to the public silence of young female workers described herself as "a poor working girl" when she wrote to condemn the commutation. "A Friend of the Just," to Slaton, June 22, 1915, reel 2, Frank Correspondence.

24. Watson, "Official Record," 284. See Dolores Janiewski, *Sisterhood Denied: Race, Gender, and Class in a New South Community* (Philadelphia, 1985), 128; Jacquelyn Dowd Hall, James Leloudis, Robert Korstad, Mary Murphy, Lu Ann Jones, and Christopher B. Daly, *Like a Family: The Making of a Southern Cotton Mill World* (Chapel Hill, 1987), 223–24. On class rivalries among southern men over women, see also Victoria Byerly, *Hard Times Cotton Mill Girls: Personal Histories of Womanhood and Poverty in the South* (Ithaca, 1986), 114; and the richly evocative short story "The Old Forest," in Peter Taylor, *The Old Forest and Other Stories* (Garden City, 1985).

25. On the circular, see *Augusta Chronicle*, June 11, 1915, p. 1. A. J. Cash to Slaton, June 14, 1915, folder 4, box 45, Slaton Collection. For explicit appeals to readers' concerns for their daughters' sexual vulnerability, see also Thomas E. Watson, "The Celebrated Case of the State of Georgia vs. Leo Frank," *Watson's Magazine* 21 (Aug. 1915), 196, 230. One of the original jurors in the case maintained that Slaton's decision to commute had imperiled the "daughters, wives, sisters and mothers" of Georgia. *New York Times*, June 25, 1915, reel 2822, Frank Collection.

26. See, for example, W. S. Lancaster to Slaton, Dec. 29, 1914, folder 10, box 45, Slaton Collection; T. B. Hogan to Slaton, folder 1, box 35, ibid.; R. J. Smith to "Prison commissioners," April 29, 1915, folder 1, box 35, ibid.; W. L. Dubberly to Slaton, folder 1, box 35, ibid.; Cash to Slaton, June 14, 1915, folder 4, box 45, ibid.; J. G. Scoggins to Slaton, June 5, 1915, folder 10, box 45, ibid.; J. D. Long to Slaton, May 31, 1915, folder 10, box 45, ibid.; J. D. Chason to Slaton, May 31, 1915, folder 10, box 45, ibid.; J. E. Stembridge to Slaton, June 21, 1915, folder 4, box 45, ibid.; Thomas N. Smoke to Slaton, folder 1, box 35, ibid.; Donald Clark to Slaton, May 25, 1915, folder 10, box 45, ibid.; Good Hope Local Union 593 to Slaton, folder 1, box 35, ibid.; J. H. Baxer to Slaton, May 18, 1915, folder 10, box 45, ibid.; Petition from Omega, Georgia, to Slaton, n.d., folder 1, box 35, ibid.; Petition from Garfield, Georgia, to Slaton, May 28, 1915, folder 10, box 45, ibid. See also Jno. H. Wellington to Slaton, June 24, 1915, reel 2, Frank Correspondence; W. T Parrott to Slaton, n.d., reel 2, ibid.; "A Georgian" to Slaton, June 23, 1915, reel 2, ibid.

27. Churchill P. Goree to Slaton, June 1, 1915, folder 10, box 45, Slaton Collection. See also "A mother" to Mr. Davidson, n.d., folder 2, box 35, ibid.; Mrs. H. Bolton to Prison Commissioners, May 31, 1915, folder 10, box 45, ibid. For a pathbreaking study of the gender inequality at the heart of the household economy and political culture of the antebellum yeomanry, see Stephanie McCurry, "Defense of Their World: Gender, Class, and the Yeomanry of the South Carolina Low Country, 1820–1860" (Ph.D. diss., State University of New York,

Binghamton, 1988). Other suggestive accounts include Steven Hahn, "Honor and Patriarchy in the Old South," *American Quarterly* 36 (spring 1984), 145–53; and Edward L. Ayers, *Vengeance and Justice: Crime and Punishment in the Nineteenth-Century American South* (New York, 1984), 10–29, 274–75.

28. Frank A. Hooper, quoted in *Frank Case*, 109. On sexual harassment in the mills, see Byerly, *Hard Times Cotton Mill Girls*, 121; and Hall et al., *Like a Family*, 253, 314–15. Louise A. Lane to Slaton, May 15, 1915, folder 8, box 35, Slaton Collection. This teacher was one of the few procommutation writers who empathized with the workers. "A Georgian" to Slaton, June 23, 1915, reel 2, Frank Correspondence.

29. *Argument of Hugh M. Dorsey*, 145. See also Minnie Weldon to editor, *Watson's Magazine* 21 (Dec. 1915), 108–9. W. R. Pearson to Slaton, May 27, 1915, folder 10, box 45, Slaton Collection.

30. "An Advertising Campaign against Segregated Vice," *American City* 9 (July 1913), 4; "How Atlanta Cleaned Up," *Literary Digest*, May 3, 1913, pp. 1012–13. On the role of L. O. Bricker and the campaign, see Harry G. Lefever, "Prostitution, Politics, and Religion: The Crusade against Vice in Atlanta in 1912," *Atlanta Historical Journal* 24 (spring 1980), 7–29. Bricker's relationship to Phagan appears in Bricker, "Great American Tragedy." The Atlanta campaign coincided with the peak of nationwide agitation over "white slavery." On the wider panic's roots in concerns about changing gender roles among female wage earners, see Joanne Meyerowitz, *Women Adrift: Independent Wage-Earners in Chicago, 1880–1930* (Chicago, 1988), esp. 61, 64. See also Egal Feldman, "Prostitution, the Alien Woman, and the Progressive Imagination, 1900–1915," *American Quarterly* 19 (summer 1967), 192–206.

31. Brief of Evidence at 16, 30, 77, 80, 105–7, 119, 131, *Leo M. Frank v. State of Georgia*. Of southern working women over the age of sixteen, 68 percent earned under six dollars a week in 1907, 92.5 percent under eight dollars. Younger workers, such as Phagan, earned considerably less. U.S. Dept. of Labor, *Summary of the Report*, 22; Deaton, "Atlanta during the Progressive Era," 154.

32. Brief of Evidence at 15–16, 30, 35, 119, 172–73, 222, *Leo M. Frank v. State of Georgia*. Other female industrial workers in the South shared the grievance of violated privacy. "Most galling of all" the management practices applied to women workers involved in a strike in Elizabethton, Tennessee, "was company surveillance of the washroom." See Jacquelyn Dowd Hall, "Disorderly Women: Gender and Labor Militancy in the Appalachian South," *Journal of American History* 73 (Sept. 1986), 364.

33. See *Argument of Hugh M. Dorsey*, 25–27, 139; and "Hearing before Gov. John M. Slaton," 87–89. Watson also put great emphasis on this testimony and on Frank's failure to cross-examine these female employees. See Thomas E. Watson, "A Full Review of the Leo Frank Case," *Watson's Magazine* 21 (March 1915), 238–40; Watson, "Celebrated Case," 184–85. For the consensus that the perversion charge lay behind Frank's conviction, see, for example, Lucian Lamar Knight, *A Standard History of Georgia and Georgians* (2 vols., Chicago, 1917), II, 121–22; Harris, *Autobiography*, 350; and Dinnerstein, *Leo Frank Case*, 19. Frank asked rhetorically in a public statement: "Is there a man in Atlanta who would deny that the charge of perversion was the chief cause of my conviction, or deny that the case,

without that charge, would be an entirely different question?" ibid., 102. For a similar suggestion from one of Frank's lawyers, see "Hearing before Gov. John M. Slaton," 185–86, 189–90.

34. The charges can be found in Brief of Evidence at 50–51, 55–62, 165, 222–23, *Leo M. Frank v. State of Georgia*; "Hearing before Gov. John M. Slaton," 146, 148, 187–91; W. E. Thompson, *A Short Review of the Frank Case* (Atlanta, 1914), 24–25. Some employees testified to Frank's good conduct and character, but they apparently were not as persuasive as those who impugned him. See Brief of Evidence at 120–21, *Leo M. Frank v. State of Georgia*. On reports of rapes and lynchings serving as "folk pornography," see Jacquelyn Dowd Hall, *Revolt against Chivalry: Jessie Daniel Ames and the Women's Campaign against Lynching* (New York, 1979), 150–51. For the indulgence of Frank's leading opponent in such "folk pornography," see, for example, Watson, "Official Record," 271–73. Watson was later tried for obscenity for his writings on Catholics, which a grand jury found "obscene, lewd, lascivious, and filthy." *Augusta Chronicle*, Nov. 30, 1915, pp. 1, 4.

35. Golden, *A Little Girl Is Dead*, 133.

36. See, for example, Watson, "Official Record," 267, 268, 293.

37. *Atlanta Journal*, Aug. 21, 1913, pp. 1, 7, 9, 11, reel 2822, Frank Collection. See also Arnold, *Trial of Leo Frank*, ed. Sellers, 36.

38. On the ambiguity and the reality of female sexual agency in the period covered by this essay, see Ellen Carol DuBois and Linda Gordon, "Seeking Ecstasy on the Battlefield: Danger and Pleasure in Nineteenth-Century Feminist Thought," *Feminist Studies* 9 (spring 1983), 7–25.

39. Hall "Secrets," 28. For developments in the North and Midwest, see Meyerowitz, *Women Adrift*; Kathy Peiss, *Cheap Amusements: Working Women and Leisure in Turn-of-the-Century New York* (Philadelphia, 1986); and Elizabeth Ewen, *Immigrant Women in the Land of Dollars: Life and Culture on the Lower East Side, 1890–1925* (New York, 1985). On the interlacing of gender and class conflicts during a strike in Atlanta while Frank's case was on appeal, see Hall, "Secrets." See also Hall, "Disorderly Women"; and Hall et al., *Like a Family*, 184–236. The only overview of southern women's history in this period remains the classic by Anne Firor Scott, *The Southern Lady: From Pedestal to Politics, 1830–1930* (Chicago, 1970). It highlights postbellum changes in women's roles but focuses on middle-class women.

40. Robertson, *Changing South*, 126–29. A study of youthful female workers in the South in the 1920s found "a desire for financial freedom" and "a general desire for independence" among their motives. Further attesting to their agency, most of those surveyed felt confident that they *had* improved their lives and achieved their goals by getting work in cities. Orie Latham Hatcher, *Rural Girls in the City for Work* (Richmond, 1930), 41, 83–84. On the nationwide similarity of young working women, see, for example, Robert A. Woods and Albert J. Kennedy, eds. *Young Working Girls: A Summary of Evidence from Two Thousand Social Workers* (Boston, 1913) esp. 1, 7–8; and Ben B. Lindsey and Wainright Evans, *The Revolt of Modern Youth* (New York, 1925). The Frank case occurred on the cusp of a shift that Joanne J. Meyerowitz notes in the 1910s—from a sentimental, Victorian view of working women as passive victims to a more modern recognition of them as agents and sexual actors. See Meyerowitz, *Women Adrift*, esp. 119. Mark K. Bauman,

"Hitting the Sawdust Trail: Billy Sunday's Atlanta Campaign of 1917," *Southern Studies* 19 (winter 1980), 385–99; William G. McLoughlin, "Billy Sunday and the Working Girl of 1915," *Journal of Presbyterian History* 54 (fall 1976).

41. Clare de Graffenried, "The Georgia Cracker in the Cotton Mills," *Century Magazine* 51 (Feb. 1891), 483–98. On the ensuing debate, see LeeAnn Whites, "The De Graffenried Controversy: Class, Race, and Gender in the New South," *Journal of Southern History* 54 (Aug. 1983), 454n. For contemporary perceptions of young working women's immorality, see U.S. Dept. of Labor, *Summary of the Report*, 273–74, 380–82; Fred S. Hall, "Child Labor and Delinquency," *Child Labor Bulletin* 3 (Nov. 1914), 37–51; and Felix Adler, "Child Labor in the United States and Its Great Attendant Evils," in National Child Labor Committee, *Child Labor* (New York, 1905), 15. See also Meyerowitz, *Women Adrift*, esp. 48. For an example of how such concerns infused discussion of the Frank case, see, "The Mary Phagan Side of It," *Columbia [South Carolina] Record*, undated clipping, [c. April 1915], reel 2824, Frank Collection. Evans, "History of Organized Labor in Georgia," 253, 212, 249; Hall, "Secrets," 35–38. On southern craft unionists' uneasiness with unskilled women workers' failure to conform to their notions of sexual respectability, see ibid.; and Hall, "Disorderly Women." For the Atlanta labor movement's positions on issues involving working women, see *Atlanta Journal of Labor*, July 5, 1912, p. 1; ibid, Feb. 7, 1913, p. 4; and ibid, Aug. 15. 1913, p. 4.

42. On southerners' reliance on the labor and services of family members, see, for example, Margaret Jarman Hagood, *Mothers of the South: Portraiture of the White Tenant Farm Woman* (1939; reprint, New York, 1977); Allison Davis, Burleigh Gardner, and Mary B. Gardner, *Deep South: A Social Anthropological Study of Caste and Class* (Chicago, 1914), esp. 327–28, 409–10, 413; Herbert G. Gutman, *The Black Family in Slavery and Freedom, 1750–1925* (New York, 1976); John Kenneth Morland, *Millways of Kent* (Chapel Hill, 1958), esp. 84, 95; Lois MacDonald, *Southern Mill Hills: A Study of Social and Economic Forces in Certain Mill Villages* (New York, 1928), esp. 131; and Jennings J. Rhyne, *Some Southern Cotton Mill Workers and Their Villages* (Chapel Hill, 1930). On the way gender and generational hierarchy undergirded the household economy of antebellum yeomen, see McCurry, "Defense of Their World."

43. Brief of Evidence at 20, 23, 135, 173–74, 223–24, *Leo M. Frank v. State of Georgia*; Watson, "Celebrated Case," 200; "Hearing before Gov. John M. Slaton," 94. On workplace-based courting elsewhere in the South, see Byerly, *Hard Times Cotton Mill Girls*, 131, 156; Janiewski, *Sisterhood Denied*, 98; and Hall et al., *Like a Family*, 86, 140–41. Concerns about the effects of wage labor on working women's sexual behavior appeared dramatically in the responses of middle-class reformers, labor spies, and craft unionists to the Fulton Bag and Cotton Mills strike in Atlanta during the years of the Frank case. See Hall, "Secrets."

44. Brief of Evidence at 45–50, 159, 161–64, *Leo M. Frank v. State of Georgia*; "Hearing before Gov. John M. Slaton," 11–12. For the change in the case made by Frank's lawyers, see "Hearing before Gov. John M. Slaton," 10–13.

45. See, for example, Brief of Evidence at 15–16, 46–50, *Leo M. Frank v. State of Georgia*.

46. Watson, "Full Review," 266. See also Watson, "Official Record," 190. J. D. Chason, M.D., to Slaton, May 31, 1915, folder 10, box 45, Slaton Collection. A

former Augusta resident pointed out that the red-light districts there were "filled with mill girls"; prostitution was "organized and wide open" with "not the smallest protest on the part of anybody there." "The trouble with Georgia," he concluded, "is that she thinks too little of Mary Phagan alive and too much of Mary Phagan dead." Edwin W. Walker to editor, *New York Sun*, Sept. 10, 1915, reel 221, Lynching File, 1899–1919, Tuskegee Institute News Clippings File (Hollis Burke Frissell Library, Tuskegee Institute, Tuskegee, Ala.).

47. This is not to deny that Phagan may have been a virgin, but to underscore the intensity of the will to *believe* that she was among Frank's opponents and their agency in constructing the meaning of her death. Nor am I using the word "mythology" loosely: as icon, Mary became an important part of the folk culture of the South and of mill workers in particular. Her ordeal was recounted in the "Ballad of Mary Phagan," which in several versions circulated through the mill regions of the South in ensuing decades. See Gene Wiggins, "The Socio-Political Works of Fiddlin' John and Moonshine Kate," *Southern Folklore Quarterly* 41 (1977), esp. 100–104; Stephen R. Wiley, "Songs of the Gastonia Textile Strike of 1929: Models of and for Southern Working-Class Women's Militancy," *North Carolina Folklore Journal* 30 (fall-winter 1982), 94–95.

48. *Atlanta Journal of Labor*, Sept. 12, 1913, p. 4; J. C. Parrott to editor, ibid., Sept. 15, 1913, p. 4. For other homilies on Mary in the same vein, see Watson, "Official Record," 275, 279, 280; Watson, "Full Review," 257, 266; and *Argument of Hugh M. Dorsey*, 76, Marietta Journal and Courier, July 16, 1915, pp. 1, 6.

49. Dr. Anna Howard Shaw made this point nicely, retorting to the incoming governor's claim that Georgians believed the commutation of Frank's sentence had allowed money to triumph over women's "honor." "Perhaps if Georgia were more ready to protect by law the honor of young girls," she stated, "and to better the working conditions that menace it, lynch law might not so often be invoked to mend morals by murder." *De Kalb [Illinois] Chronicle*, Aug. 26, 1915, reel 2822, Frank Collection.

50. Hall, *Revolt against Chivalry*, 151; Knight, *Standard History of Georgia and Georgians*, II, 1182–96. On popular support for the lynching, see Dinnerstein, *Leo Frank Case*, 139–46; Harris, *Autobiography*, 368, 371; and L. Z. Rosser to Slaton, Sept. 1, 1915, folder 3, box 49, Slaton Collection. Although the identity of the lynchers was said to be known to many, they were never indicted, much less prosecuted or convicted.

51. *Atlanta Georgian*, Aug. 17, 1915, reel 2824, Frank Collection; *Newnan [Georgia] Herald*, Aug. 20, 1915, p. 2. "Mary Phagan's folks," said the owner of the tree from which Frank was hanged, "hugged and patted that old tree and then they stood still and looked upward for a long time. I think they must have been praying." *Atlanta Constitution*, Aug. 21, 1915, p. 2. Wiggins, "Socio-Political Works of Fiddlin' John"; Wiley, "Songs of the Gastonia Textile Strike of 1929," 94–95; Olive W. Burt, ed., *American Murder Ballads and Their Stories* (New York, 1958), 61–64.

52. *La Grange [Georgia] Graphic*, Feb. 14, 1916, folder 12, box 45, Slaton Collection; J. M. Gassaway to Slaton, June 6, 1915, folder 10, box 45, ibid.; H. O. Durham to R. E. Davison, June 1, 1915, folder 1, box 35, ibid. For other examples of economic and class grievances expressed in anti-Semitic form, see J. R. and

T. Bunn to Prison Commissioners, May 24, 1915, folder 1, box 35, ibid.; R. W. Daniel to Prison Commissioners, May 22, 1915, folder 2, box 35, ibid.; E. F. Dumas to Slaton, May 27, 1915, folder 1, box 35, ibid.; C. A. Jackson to Slaton, folder 1, box 35, ibid.; H. J. Sandlin to Prison Commissioners, June 2, 1915, folder 14, box 35, ibid.; J. P. Berrong to Slaton, May 15, 1915, folder 10, box 45, ibid. Virtually all of the crowd actions (boycotts, warnings out of town, arson, etc.) after Frank's commutation not aimed at the governor were aimed at Jewish merchants or employers. See the leaflet *Carry Me in Your Purse* ([Marietta], c. late June 1915) and accompanying letter "To the Citizens of Marietta," reel 2825, Frank Collection; *New Orleans American*, June 23, 1915, pp. 1, 9, reel 2825, ibid.; *Augusta Chronicle*, Aug. 29, 1915, p. 7; *Athens [Georgia] Daily Herald*, Oct. 20, 1915, p. 1; Hertzberg, *Strangers within the Gate City*, 213; and B. H. Meadows to Nathaniel E. Harris, July 1, 1915, July 7, 1915, folder 1, box 228, Nathaniel E. Harris Papers, Executive Department Correspondence (Georgia Department of Archives and History).

53. See Watson, "Full Review," 242; Watson, "Official Record," 262, 267, 292–97; Watson, "Celebrated Case," 222. One editor advised anyone who doubted that prejudice against Jews existed to "board an Atlanta street car filled with home-going working people." *Southern Ruralist*, March 15, 1914, reel 2822, Frank Collection. On anti-Semitism as a diversionary surrogate for anticapitalist sentiments, serving profoundly antiradical ends, see Carey McWilliams, *A Mask for Privilege: Anti-Semitism in America* (Boston, 1948); and the more theoretically inclined analysis of European anti-Semitism, Abram Leon, *The Jewish Question: A Marxist Interpretation* (Mexico City, 1950).

54. In a political culture extolling the "producing classes," Jews often occupied unpopular positions as rural peddlers, country merchants, and urban merchants and businessmen. The economic interests of many Atlanta Jews, moreover, had led them in the 1890s to oppose the popular demand of Georgia Populists for free silver, creating lasting resentments; see Hertzberg, *Strangers within the Gate City*, 184, 152–53, 163. See also Thomas D. Clark, "The Post–Civil War Economy in the South," in *Jews in the South*, ed. Leonard Dinnerstein and Mary Dale Palsson (Baton Rouge, 1973), 160–67. For a more general discussion, see John Higham, "American Anti-Semitism Historically Reconsidered," in *Jews in the Mind of America*, ed. Charles H. Stember et al. (New York, 1966), 237–58.

55. In Atlanta, for example, in the decade before the Frank case, Prohibitionists had accused Jews of promoting vice and encouraging black men to take liberties with white women. Hertzberg, *Strangers within the Gate City*, 161–62, 186–87, 214. In the national campaign against "white slavery" that fed into the Frank case, foreign men, in particular Russian Jews, were blamed for the prostitution industry. Feldman, "Prostitution, the Alien Woman, and the Progressive Imagination," 192–206. Many writers have noted the importance of sexual themes and anxieties in the most extreme forms of racism, including Lillian Smith, *Killers of the Dream* (New York, 1948), 27–28, 83–84, 111, 121–22, 124; Hall, *Revolt against Chivalry*, 145; Davis, Gardner, and Gardner, *Deep South*, 24–25; James Weldon Johnson, *Along this Way* (New York, 1968), 170, 311–13, 391; and Charles Herbert Stember, *Sexual Racism* (New York, 1976).

56. M. M. Parker to Prison Commissioners, May 31, 1915, folder 2, box 35, Slaton Collection. See also G. M. Wilson to Prison Commissioners, n.d., folder 10,

box 45, ibid.; Jno. H. Wellington to Slaton, June 24, 1915, reel 2, Frank Correspondence. For Watson's statement, see Golden, *A Little Girl Is Dead*, 23. For the backing of a former Populist and later Klan supporter, see Robert L. Rodgers to Thomas E. Watson, Sept. 9, 1915, folder 41, box 5, Robert L. Rodgers Papers (Manuscripts Section, Georgia Department of Archives and History), Blaine Mast, *K.K.K., Friend or Foe: Which?* (n.p., 1924), 22, 19. For examples in later Ku Klux Klan literature of the claim that Jewish men sought to take advantage of Protestant girls in general, and female employees in particular, see *Imperial Night-Hawk*, April 30, 1924, p. 6; Alma White, *The Ku Klux Klan in Prophecy* (Zarepath, N.J., 1925), 53–54; and Alma White, *Heroes of the Fiery Cross* (Zarepath, N.J., 1928), 10, 34–36.

57. [Name illegible] to Watson, June 25, 1915, reel 2, Frank Correspondence. See also "A Friend of the Just" to Slaton, June 22, 1915, ibid.; H. L. Williamson to Slaton, June 21, 1915, ibid.; H. G. Williams to Slaton, June 24, [1915], ibid.; B. H. Hatfield to Slaton, May 11, 1915, folder 10, box 45, Slaton Collection; Claud Mahaffey to Slaton, June 21, 1915, folder 4, box 45, ibid.; John Brack to Slaton, June 15, 1915, folder 4, box 45, ibid.; F. J. Bivirrs to Slaton, n.d., folder 1, box 35, ibid.; W. S. Landrim to Slaton, June 14, 1915, folder 4, box 45, ibid.; William H. Crouse to Prison Commissioners, May 14, 1915, folder 1, box 35, ibid.; "A Committee" to Slaton, n.d., folder 4, box 45, ibid.; W. W. Poole to Slaton, June 21, 1915, folder 7, box 50a, ibid.; A. J. Oiler to Slaton, June 21, 1915, folder 4, box 45, ibid.; L. F. Roberts to Prison Commissioners, May 28, 1915, folder 15, box 35, ibid.; A. Purvis to Harris, June 28, 1915, folder 2, box 229, Harris Papers.

58. On the lobbying effort for Frank, see Dinnerstein, *Leo Frank Case*, 117–35; and the more revealing correspondence between A. D. Lasker, Julius Rosenwald, and Jacob Billikopf, reel 1069, Frank Collection. Numerous people protested Slaton's usurpation of the jury's role in deciding Frank's guilt. See, for example, "General Public" to Slaton, June 22, 1915, reel 2, Frank Correspondence; W. L. Sikes to Slaton, June 24, 1915, ibid; I. A. Christian to Slaton, n.d., ibid.; "The Life Takers" to Slaton, June 24, 1915, ibid.; petition from citizens of Franklin County to Slaton, June 23, 1915, ibid. Scores of other letters and petitions simply asked Slaton not to "interfere" with the courts' decisions, and to "let the law take its course." On the class role of the state in southern society before World War I, see Kousser, *Shaping of Southern Politics*; and Jonathan M. Wiener, "Class Structure and Economic Development in the American South, 1865–1955," *American Historical Review* 84 (Oct. 1979), 970–92.

59. Watson, "Official Record," 254, 290–91. For other defenses of the lynching couched in a restorationist, populist idiom, see A. Morgan to editor, *North American Review*, Sept. 1, 1915, reel 2824, Frank Collection; *Marietta Journal and Courier*, Aug. 20, 1915, p. 6; *Madisonian*, July 16, 1915, p. 4; ibid., Aug. 20, 1915, p. 4. The *Newnan Herald* sympathetically quoted editorials approving of or apologizing for Frank's lynching from nine small-town Georgia papers. *Newnan Herald*, Aug. 27, 1915, p. 1. See also P. A. Blanchard to Slaton, n.d., folder 10, box 45, Slaton Collection: "*delays* and *miscarriages* of justice IS THE CAUSE of nearly every occurance of mob violence. . . . Lawyers, technicalities of the law, Newspapers for hire, officers for sale: these are the withering curse of our land." Another anticommutation writer asserted: "The majority of the citizens of Georgia are worn threadbare over the way this case his been handled, and if . . . we are allowed to be run over[,]

mistreated and trampled under foot by the moneyed Brutes of this country[,] then it is time to Shoulder Arms and demand [justice] at the muzzle of our Guns." Smoke to Slaton, May 29, 1915, folder I , box 35, ibid.

60. Omega, Georgia, petition, n.d., folder 1, box 35, Slaton Collection. Other petitioners maintained that the commutation had "set a dangerous precedent which will tend to promote anarchy and increase mob law." "Citizens of Troup County" to Slaton, telegram, June 24, 1915, reel 2, Frank Correspondence. The clearest statement of the dangers of commutation argued that when juries could be overridden and class justice enthroned, "the bedrock principles of good government is destroyed and obedience to law and good morals can no longer be fostered. . . . the strong arm of the law . . . is our only protection and hope for society in the future." J. D. Chason to Slaton, May 31, 1915, folder 10, box 45, Slaton Collection. Another stated that commutation would "thwart the . . . Courts, to which alone we can look for protection." L. D. McGregor to R. E. Davison, June 1, 1915, folder 5, box 49, ibid. "I am fearful," wrote another, "that we are now bordering on anarchy." J. E. Stembridge to Slaton, June 21, 1915, folder 4, box 45, ibid. Another explained that having the courts "sustained . . . is our only hope in the future." A. B. Cooke to Mrs. John M. Slaton, June 3, 1915, folder 4, box 45, ibid. The frequent use of phrases such as "our only hope" to appeal for stern justice underscores the writers' perception that their society was undergoing a transition, whose outcome appeared as uncertain as it was ominous to those who felt they had something to lose. For defenses of the lynching in these terms, see Sessions to A. W. Knapp, Aug. 27, 1915, folder 22, box 35, ibid.; W. E. Millican to Slaton, Aug. 19, 1915, reel 2, Frank Correspondence.

61. T. B. Hogan to editor, *Augusta Chronicle*, July 28, 1915, p. 4. Another wrote that if Frank's sentence were commuted, "if there shall be left in Georgia, men who love their wives, their daughters, and their state, they will wipe out, with gunpowder and leaden bull, the stain on Georgia's name, that she didn't have men enough to protect her courts and her women." Donald Clark to Slaton, May 25, 1915, folder 10, box 45, Slaton Collection. The editor of one country paper, a reactionary populist, insisted that only fear of lynching kept would-be rapists at bay. *Madisonian*, Sept. 13, 1915, p. 4. Contemporary antilynching activists and historians have noted that despite evidence that only a fraction of lynchings involved allegations of rape, the apologia that lynching was in retribution for rape endured. See Ida B. Wells-Barnett, *On Lynchings* (New York, 1969), 87–88; Walter White, *Rope and Faggot: A Biography of Judge Lynch* (New York, 1929), 16–17, 54–55, 65–66, 82; Arthur F. Raper, *The Tragedy of Lynching* (Chapel Hill, 1933), 9, 20, 50; Johnson, *Along this Way*, 329–30, 365–66; Hall, *Revolt against Chivalry*, 146–49; George M. Fredrickson, *The Black Image in the White Mind: The Debate on Afro-American Character and Destiny, 1817–1914* (New York, 1971), 274, 282; Ayers, *Vengeance and Justice*, 237.

62. For James G. Woodward's remark, see *Atlanta Constitution*, Aug. 19, 1915, reel 2824, Frank Collection. Cf. the incoming governor of Georgia, Nathaniel Harris, on Frank's lynching: "there is something that unbalances men here in the South where women are concerned . . . that destroys men's ability and even willingness to do cold and exact justice." *New York Times*, Aug. 20, 1915, p. 4, reel 2825, ibid. Cf. D. M. Parker, of Baxley, Georgia, to editor, *New Republic*, Aug. 7, 1915,

p. 23. See also Harris, *Autobiography*, 363. Several anti-Frank writers, notably Watson, posed the conflict over commutation in terms of "money" versus "manhood" or "honor." For other examples, see H. J. Sandlin to Prison Commissioners, June 2, 1915, folder 14, box 35, Slaton Collection; J. P. Berrong to Slaton, May 15, 1915, folder 10, box 45, ibid.; C. E. Parker to Slaton, June 21, 1915, folder 4, ibid. Perhaps the intense concern with the loss or "sale" of honor and the frequent use of the metaphor of prostitution among Frank opponents reflected anxiety over their loss of independence and control as a result of the increasing domination of the market over their lives.

63. *La Grange [Georgia] Graphic*, Feb. 24, 1916, folder 14, box 45, Slaton Collection; Rosser to B. Z. Phillips, Aug. 21, Aug. 25, 1915, folder 3, box 49, ibid.; *Augusta Chronicle*, Sept. 30, 1915, p. 7; ibid., June 22, 1915, p. 1; Harris, *Autobiography*, 356–61; Dinnerstein, *Leo Frank Case*, 131–33; Rosser to Slaton, Sept. 1, 1915, folder 3, box 49, Slaton Collection; Rosser to Phillips, Sept. 15, 1915, ibid. See also Editor to Joseph M. Brown, Aug. 4, 1915, folder 11, box 35, ibid. Thomas Loyless, the editor of the *Augusta Chronicle*, drew the same conclusions and editorialized against Watson single-mindedly in ensuing months; the battle won him myriad letters of hearty support from elite Georgians—and of irate disdain from more ordinary residents.

64. *Augusta Chronicle*, Oct. 3, 1915, sec. C, p. 6; ibid., Sept. 14, 1916, p. 1; ibid., Sept. 16, 1916, p. 4. See also Phillips to Jacob Schiff, May 17, 1916, folder 3, box 49, Slaton Collection; E. F. Dumas to Brown, May 4, 1914, folder 2, box 3, Joseph Mackey Brown Papers (Atlanta Historical Society, Atlanta, Ga.); Dinnerstein, *Leo Frank Case*, 159. For examples of the efforts against Tom Watson and his support, see *Augusta Chronicle*, Feb. 4, 1916, p. 5; ibid., Feb. 6, 1916, sec. C, p. 4; ibid., Feb. 13, 1916, p. 5; ibid., Feb. 18, 1916, p. 1; ibid., Feb. 21, 1916, p. 4; Rosser to Slaton, Sept. 1, 1915, folder 3, box 49, Slaton Collection; *La Grange [Georgia] Graphic*, Feb. 14, 1916, folder 12, box 45, ibid.; *Talbotten [Georgia] New Era*, folder 14, ibid. The obscenity prosecution is described in Fred D. Ragan, "Obscenity or Politics? Tom Watson, Anti-Catholicism, and the Department of Justice," *Georgia Historical Quarterly* 70 (spring 1986), 17–46. On Watson's campaign and conduct in the Senate, see Woodward, *Tom Watson*, 451–86. On the Klan's gains from the Frank case, see ibid., 446; and Dinnerstein, *Leo Frank Case*, 149–50.

65. On the availability of cases of women's sexual victimization for conservative manipulation, see Judith R. Walkowitz, *Prostitution and Victorian Society: Women, Class and the State* (Cambridge, Eng., 1980); and Judith R. Walkowitz, "Jack the Ripper and the Myth of Male Violence," *Feminist Studies* 8 (fall 1982), 543–76. See also DuBois and Gordon, "Seeking Ectasy on the Battlefield." On southern politicians' use of populist rhetoric, see Kousser, *Shaping of Southern Politics*, 80, 233–37. For populist rhetoric used toward explicitly procapitalist, antiradical ends, see Tom Watson, *Socialists and Socialism* (Thomson, Ga., 1910). For the antiradical, anti-working class positions of leading Watson allies in the Frank case, see the campaign brochure by Hugh M. Dorsey, *The Record: Upon Which Governor Hugh M. Dorsey Asks Your Support for U.S. Senator* (Atlanta, 1920), esp. 8–9, Hugh Manson Dorsey folder, File II, Names Section (General Library, Georgia Department of Archives and History); and the scores of diatribes against organized labor, couched in racist, populist terms, by Joseph Mackey Brown, Brown Papers.

66. On the role of concerns about family life and gender in the agitation against liquor, see Norman H. Clark, *Deliver Us from Evil: An Interpretation of American Prohibition* (New York, 1976); and Barbara Leslie Epstein, *The Politics of Domesticity: Women, Evangelism, and Temperance in Nineteenth-Century America* (Middletown, 1981). V. O. Key, Jr., with Alexander Heard, *Southern Politics in State and Nation* (New York, 1949); Joel Williamson, *The Crucible of Race: Black/White Relations in the American South since Emancipation* (New York, 1984). For the interplay of populism, racism, and sexual conservatism in the second Klan, see MacLean, "Behind the Mask of Chivalry"; and Charles Alexander, *The Ku Klux Klan in the Southwest* ([Lexington, Ky.], 1965). "Whenever, wherever, race relations are discussed," as Lillian Smith put it, "sex moves arm in arm with the concept of segregation." Smith, *Killers of the Dream*, 124. On the councils, see Neil R. McMillen, *The Citizens' Councils: Organized Resistance to the Second Reconstruction, 1954–64* (Urbana, 1971). For perceptive early interpretations of the New Right, see Linda Gordon and Allen Hunter, "Sex, Family and the New Right: Anti-Feminism as a Political Force," *Radical America* 11–12 (Nov. 1977–Feb. 1978), 9–25; and Rosalind Pollack Petchesky, "Antiabortion, Antifeminism, and The Rise of the New Right," *Feminist Studies* 7 (summer 1981), 206–46.

67. Virginia Woolf, *Three Guineas* (1938; reprint, New York, 1966). See also Joan Kelly, "The Doubled Vision of Feminist Theory: A Postscript to the 'Women and Power' Conference," *Feminist Studies* 5 (spring 1979), 222–23.

False Friends and Avowed Enemies: Southern African Americans and Party Allegiances in the 1920s

IN THE LATE twentieth century, historians, political scientists, and journalists ponder the unstable political allegiances of our time. The New Deal coalition, an uneasy bargain between African Americans, white southerners, northern urbanites, Old Progressives, and labor, has frayed on all sides. In the past decade, most observers—some reluctantly, some with alacrity—have accepted the fact that there has been a realignment among the constituencies of the Republican and Democratic parties, even if they cannot agree on the elements of that realignment or whether it might spawn more Ross Perots. Looking to history to understand the factors that produce realignment is vital to the current discussion; how do voters decide to change parties?[1]

To answer that question, historians turn to critical elections: moments when large numbers of voters transfer party allegiance for presidential candidates in what seems to be a lasting shift. The 1936 presidential election serves as a model. In that election huge numbers of African Americans abandoned the Republican Party for the Democratic Party. Because the movement was so dramatic, it serves as a test case for the factors that produce changes in voting behavior. The leading historian of the 1936 realignment, Nancy Weiss, argues for proximate causes: "Most blacks who voted in 1932 were loyal to the Republicans as the party of emancipation. But by 1936, blacks had moved overwhelmingly into the Democratic column. In four years, Roosevelt and the New Deal changed the political habits of black Americans in ways that have lasted to our own time."[2] Moreover, Weiss continues, African Americans moved from the Republican to the Democratic column because of "Franklin Roosevelt's ability to provide jobs, not his embrace of Civil Rights."[3] Indeed, she argues, "the race issue never became part of the New Deal."[4] Thus, 1936 seems to be the clearest possible twentieth-century example of realignment, from one presidential election to the next.

This essay offers a caution to such explanations of political behavior that focus on a single election and argues instead for the importance of much longer histories of voting behavior when accounting for dramatic realignments, particularly when studying oppressed voting constituencies.[5]

Changes in political ideology may be harder to track for groups that have limited alternatives in the political process. The incremental changes in hearts and minds that occur when voters have no means to express their political desires—in other words, when they are disfranchised or when they perceive no viable political alternative at the ballot box—are key to subsequent voting behavior.

The "push" factors, those that drive people from parties, are harder to measure than the "pull" factors. Simply stated, the reasons African Americans decided to leave the Republican Party are just as important as the reasons they decided to join the Democratic Party. Race, gender, and region played key roles in the famed realignment of 1936, roles that cannot be taken into account unless one takes a long view of voting behavior. To understand African Americans' move from the Republican to the Democratic Party in 1936, one must look to the racialist policies of Lily White Republicanism during the 1920s; to the importance of woman suffrage in southern political culture; to the leadership of a quasi-political party, the National Association for the Advancement of Colored People (NAACP); and to the importance of southern experience of migrants to the North in reconfiguring voting constituencies.

Both political parties, indeed virtually all white Americans, were racist in 1932. African Americans had learned to accept racism as a given and to maneuver in a complicated political surround, sniffing out the main chance, winning partial victories, and settling for incremental recognition in the democratic process. They learned to broker hope and its glimmers. Killing hope often takes longer than offering a glimpse of it. The Republicans spent the period 1920 through 1932 snuffing out African Americans' political aspirations. The Democratic promise of jobs in the First New Deal rekindled those aspirations. An analysis of realignment must include both.[6] When the actual life experiences of voting African Americans are taken into account, their 1936 *Farewell to the Party of Lincoln* was the bitter end of a long goodbye, not a sudden and dramatic voting change based simply on economic interests.[7]

Three historians have suggested that realignment in the 1930s went back to the 1920s. David Burner finds that whereas only 3 percent of Harlem blacks voted Democratic in 1920, 28 percent were Democrats in the next election. Chicago parallels Harlem four years later; in 1924, 5 percent of Chicago's blacks voted Democratic, but in 1928 that percentage increased to 29 percent.[8] In his work on national Republican leaders' reaction to African Americans during the period, Richard B. Sherman points to a rise in black protests to national leaders during the 1920s, but his valuable study by definition is unlocated and does not focus on African American agency.[9] Kenneth Goings has raised the lone voice pointing to earlier—and southern—origins for black voters' abandonment of the Republican Party.[10] As southern African Americans poured into Harlem and Chicago in the Great Migration of the 1920s, some found their first opportunity to vote. Others discovered that their votes would count for the first time. Large numbers disavowed the Republican Party at once.

Many of those Harlem voters had abandoned North Carolina as well, as they followed the East Coast migrant stream to New York. An examination of the racial politics in North Carolina from 1919 to 1929 demonstrates how African Americans attempted to bring pressure on the Republican Party and how woman suffrage increased that pressure. The passage of the Nineteenth Amendment and its political wake represented a critical impetus in the political realignment of black voters from the Republican to the Democratic Party. Woman suffrage opened the way back to the polls for disfranchised black voters and changed the climate of the polling place from one of danger to relative safety. When the NAACP subsequently attacked white Republicans who had failed to stand up for black women's voting registration, they called into question of the party's right to represent African Americans. As woman suffrage created a new political culture that brought blacks in urban, upper South states back to the polls, Republican abandonment of African Americans became crystal clear to them.[11]

As he traveled around North Carolina in the fall of 1920, John Parker, the Republican candidate for governor, felt pretty good about his chances. He had long supported the Nineteenth Amendment mandating woman suffrage; on the other hand, his opponent, the Democrat Cameron Morrison, had opposed it vociferously in the Democratic primary the previous spring. In August woman suffrage became law, and now white women were registering in astonishing numbers. If Parker could persuade enough women to register Republican, he could capitalize on the history of relatively close elections in North Carolina.

Twenty years earlier, in 1900, most black North Carolinians lost the right to vote when the Democrats disfranchised black men two years after a violent racial massacre in Wilmington following the 1898 election. Subsequent racial massacres were not necessary; just one executed promise to kill black voters had produced a chilling effect. Thus, even though one half of North Carolina's black men were literate and qualified to vote, the threat of violence worked with the law to keep them away from the polls.[12] Yet, Democratic politicians continued to shake the specter of black suffrage at white voters twenty years later. During the Democratic primary, which he ultimately won, Morrison had vilified the proposed federal amendment to grant woman suffrage as a racially risky proposition. He had campaigned against his opponent, a man who supported woman suffrage, by arguing that the amendment would bring "the Negro" back into politics by prompting federal enforcement of the Fifteenth Amendment and by inviting black women to the polls. Morrison won the Democratic nomination for governor. After the passage of the Nineteenth Amendment granting woman suffrage ten weeks before the general election, Democratic campaign bosses muzzled Morrison and sent out speakers who had been pro-suffrage to convince white women to register Democratic.[13]

Thus, Parker, the Republican candidate, had every reason to expect that calm assurances to white women would win their votes, since the Democrat Morrison had been such a mortal enemy of woman suffrage. But Parker had to answer Morrison's argument by guaranteeing that his party would neither seek federal intervention at the polls nor welcome black women into the party. To entice white women to register as Republicans, Parker had to promise them that they were not joining a "Negro" party. Parker put it succinctly on the stump: "The negro as a class does not desire to enter politics. The Republican party of North Carolina does not desire him to do so." More crudely, Parker underscored his statement by reading the sarcastic poem, "How Could We Do Without You, Mr. Nigger?"[14] The Republicans, he boasted, could do very well without "*Mr.* Nigger," but he failed to consider black women.

Frederick Douglass once said, "The Republican Party is the deck, all else is the sea."[15] But Douglass had been dead a long time in 1920. For twenty years, since disfranchisement, the Republican Party in the South floundered as it dealt with its black constituents. Some state committees remained black and white or all black, despite the fact that black men had a difficult time exercising the franchise in those states. Other states, such as North Carolina, had excluded African Americans from lily-white conventions and had failed to protect them at the polls. Nonetheless, North Carolina Republicans never disavowed black voters as completely and as finally as they did in the 1920 race. African Americans had clung to the Republican Party as to a leaky lifeboat. All the while the Republicans argued that they could best represent African American voters in national politics and federal appointments. But in 1920, to appeal to a huge pool of new voters—white women—Republican rhetoric for the first time promised that there would be no black Republicans: now or ever. With those statements, they finally pulled the plug on the lifeboat and prepared to watch their black constituents sink.

From 1900 until 1920, the Republican Party's hold on southern African Americans depended on several variables, not the least of which was simply that the party seemed the only alternative. Rather than challenge the violence that accompanied Democratic disfranchisement at the turn of the century and the shadow it cast over the polls in the first twenty years of the century, the national Republican Party urged southern blacks to avoid active participation in politics and to trust white Republicans to look after their best interests. After the Democrats gained the presidency in 1912, Republicans could blame violations of black civil rights on the Democratic administration and claim to be helpless to enforce the Constitution. Until the passage of the Nineteenth Amendment, southern blacks spent twenty years without recourse to challenge this logic at the polls, even if they questioned the motives and tactics of the Republican Party in the interim.

After disfranchisement in 1900 and their subsequent expulsion from the Republican state organization in 1902, a few black men in North Carolina attempted to keep a hand in politics by forming parallel Republican state executive committees and holding black Republican statewide conventions.[16] Foreshadowing the tactic used by the Mississippi Freedom Democratic Party at Atlantic City in 1964, two hundred black Republicans met in North Carolina in May 1908 and elected fifty delegates to the Republican National Convention. The assembly adopted a resolution that condemned the "body of [white] men recently assembled . . . in debarring every negro Republican of wealth, intelligence and character, . . . can no more represent the Republican party . . . than the devil can represent the principles and teachings of our Holy Savior and Redeemer." The black delegates deplored white Republicans who "after receiving negro votes . . . [made] the negro stepping stones into high positions of honor and trust, . . . and kicked him out of the primaries, conventions, and party councils, [and] endorsed the revised Southern Constitutions and Jim Crowism."[17] Although the 1908 national convention rejected the black delegates, North Carolina's black Republicans repeated the same futile exercise in 1912.[18]

In the 1916 presidential election, North Carolina's African Americans assembled in yet another "Mass Convention of all true Republicans . . . of whatever race or color or previous condition." The purpose of the convention was to formulate strategy to take back the party organization and to stop "bosses and designing politicians" from using African American voters as a "football."[19] The mass meeting again elected black delegates from each congressional district to challenge the North Carolina Lily Whites at the Republican National Convention.

In 1916, however, having tried this strategy twice to no avail, a group of interested black men met in Raleigh to form the "Twentieth Century Voters Club," a conspicuously non-partisan appellation.[20] Thus, in the four national elections between black disfranchisement and woman suffrage, North Carolina's dispossessed Republican African Americans tried a variety of strategies to regain a political toehold. Now they finally hinted at abandoning the Republican Party altogether. With this move, they borrowed a tactic that W. E. B. DuBois had been advocating since 1908 when he endorsed the Democrat William Jennings Bryan for the presidency with the words: "An avowed enemy is better than [a] false friend."[21]

When they learned about the Twentieth Century Voters Club, some whites calmly predicted political realignment. The return of black voters to the ballot box was inevitable, they argued. Moreover, African Americans in the Twentieth Century Voters Club knew their appearance would hurt the Republicans in November, a consequence about which they cared as much as they would "about a possum up a tree!"—in other words, not at all. These white pundits observed that the Lily White Republicans and disfranchisement had put black men in a "disinterested political [humor] and in an interested civic humor," a condition that would encourage a black man to "vote as a citizen, without partisan bias." Neither party would "dare an appeal" now to the black voter, but there was "no reason why the literate negro should refrain from exercising what is his undoubted right." Who could blame him, they asked, if he held "a perfectly human tinge of malice" toward the Republicans at the polls?[22] Some whites, within the parameters of the literacy test, were beginning to try to disarm the most powerful weapon of southern politics: fear of the black man at the polls.[23]

Blocked from participation in the Republican Party at every turn, after 1915 southern African Americans began to look toward the NAACP as a way to express political opinions.[24] Deeply committed to woman suffrage in principle and as a strategy to regain full civil rights, in the years prior to 1920 the NAACP worked as sort of a secret agent among southern African Americans. Southern white people seemed confused at first about what its goals might be. In 1916, when W. E. B. DuBois and Joel E. Spingarn visited Durham to address a conference on the future of black higher education, they shared the stage with leading racial accommodationists and whites who were determined to limit blacks to industrial education.[25] By 1918, Du Bois himself was the newsworthy event. When he visited North Carolina to preach a dual message of patriotism and black civil rights, seven NAACP branches flourished in the state.[26]

The 1920 passage of the Nineteenth Amendment is important to black realignment for three reasons. First, historians have tended to forget that black women's voting allegiance to the party of Lincoln had roots far more shallow than those that black men planted in emancipation. While southern black women had been active in Republican Party political culture for decades, their formative experience as party members had come when the Republicans failed to defend their right to vote as they attempted to register across the South in 1920.[27] Second, black women's voting in the upper South found a fault line in the edifice of white supremacy. Their organized South-wide campaign to register black women to vote represented the first time that black voters had approached registrars en masse since the violence that had driven blacks from the polls and the state laws that had officially disfranchised them at the turn of the century. Simply by exercising their new right under the Nineteenth Amendment, black women registrants and voters dared whites to use violence against them.[28] Since disfranchisement, the Republican Party in the South had counseled black Republicans that it was too dangerous for them to vote. Black women's attempts to vote exposed the fact that the Republicans were loath to support a return of African Americans to the polls, even in a safer voting environment. Finally, the Nineteenth Amendment produced the most vocal and straightforward Lily White utterances to date from Republican politicians, as they attempted to gain white women's votes by disavowing black women's votes.[29] Ironically then, woman suffrage heralded both the brighter day Republicans had long promised to African Americans and the beginning of the eclipse of the party's African American support.[30]

By 1920, a strong organizational structure helped the NAACP and the state federation of colored women's clubs mount a campaign to register black women, even though the Republican Party did not want their votes. That year, Charles H. Moore of Greensboro, an Amherst-educated African American, served as secretary of the black state Republican committee; Moore worked closely with the NAACP and the clubs to register black women. In this endeavor, however, Moore followed rather than led. He looked to the NAACP for guidance as he deplored the "unrepublican treatment of our colored citizens (male and female) by the 'lily-white' managers of the Republican organization in this state."[31]

"Unrepublican treatment" it certainly was. Since 1900, Republican showings in North Carolina elections had remained strong, primarily because of the party's strength among white voters in western counties. North Carolina's Republican officials and candidates strategized that any white women they could recruit from Democratic families might provide the balance of power in the fall of 1920. Democratic U.S. senators Furnifold Simmons and Lee Overman had stood with gubernatorial candidate Cameron Morrison in opposition to woman suffrage. Whereas Simmons backed down at the eleventh hour on the grounds of expediency, not conviction, Overman remained opposed.[32] When the Democrats floated a forged letter falsely attributed to the Republicans urging black women to register and vote, Frank A. Linney, state chairman of the [white] Republican State Executive Committee, set out to disavow the letter and with it the Negro race.

Linney pledged to the states' white women "if we carry the state in this election, you will have a strictly white government . . . and . . . the Republican Party's policy will be to let the negro stay out of politics." Moreover, Linney challenged the Democrats to "meet us half way . . . to eliminate any possibility of the negro question in this or any subsequent campaign."[33] It was then that Republican gubernatorial candidate Parker made his statement, "The negro as a class does not desire to enter politics. The Republican Party of North Carolina does not desire him to do so."[34]

It was clear, white Democrats observed, that the campaign of 1920 represented the Republican Party's attempt to "establish a 'white' Republican party in North Carolina."[35] Democrats chortled: "The average North

Carolina negro . . . has too much self-respect to take part in a campaign from which he has been ordered to keep away by the Republican candidate for governor."[36] Enduring similar experiences on the national scene in 1920, Walter White, assistant secretary of the NAACP, said with exasperation of the Republican Party: "Negative goodness will not suffice. Positive action correcting the evils of America is the only thing that can appease colored voters and enlist their support at the polls next November."[37]

By 1920 African Americans in the South began to have confidence in the NAACP's ability to act as a national political force. Just before the November election, someone sent a newspaper account of the Linney and Parker disavowals to the national NAACP office, where it lay yellowing until Herbert Hoover nominated Parker to the Supreme Court in 1930.[38] That someone may have been Charles Moore. Moore responded to Linney's exclusion of black voters in a letter in his hometown white newspaper. To warn Frank Linney that his rejection of black Republicans would return to haunt him, Moore quoted Disraeli: "'You will not hear me now, but the time is coming when you will hear me.' Likewise do we say to Mr. Linney and his kind that the time is coming, in fact is already near at hand."[39]

Moore was right; the times were changing. Successful disfranchisement depended upon an intensely localistic political style, one based on personal violence or its threat. There were always literate African Americans in the South, and in North Carolina, where elections remained close between Republicans and Democrats, sixty thousand literate black men could represent the balance of power in an election. Moreover, black women had a higher literacy rate than black men.[40] To make disfranchisement work, whites had to frighten literate African Americans from the polls, since continuation of "legal" electoral principles depended upon illegal practices.

To argue for the blow to violence at the polls that woman suffrage landed, it is helpful to look at the campaign of 1920 after the passage of the Nineteenth Amendment in August. Democratic handlers kept gubernatorial candidate Cameron Morrison away from women, sending instead other white men who had supported woman suffrage to boldly go where no man had ever gone before: into ladies' parlors and behind woman's clubs' podiums to convince white women to register Democratic. That white women would register Democratic seems a foregone conclusion to us today, but Democrat Aubrey Brooks thought he faced a difficult task as he set out on a speaking tour to women audiences. At that moment he did not know, of course, what historians have argued since about women's voting behavior. He did not know that he would find the new world he was poised to enter not alien, but familiar. He did not know that its inhabitants would act as his own people did. Brooks and his fellow Democrats could not know then that women voters would most often adopt the party affiliation of their male family members.

The old guard Democratic machine opposing woman suffrage had argued that it acted in the best interest of women for two reasons. First, woman suffrage would bring African Americans into politics, endangering white women's virtue, and, second, politics as practiced in the South was a filthy and violent pursuit, no place for a lady. Brooks's task was to reverse this reasoning, to argue that the polls were just the place for white ladies, and that voting was every white woman's duty, and if ladies encountered African Americans at the polls, they would remain above them. In short, he had to overcome his own party's culture, and he began by removing the threat of "Negro domination" from politics. Brooks's newspaper buddy and fellow pro-suffragist Tom Bost served notice to the state that Brooks would "not holler nigger, nor will he glorify red shirts. He is more interested in shirtwaists."[41]

Women's entrance into political space dramatically changed the culture of the polling place from violence to vigilance. In an effort to attract women voters, leaders in both parties fell over themselves to make the polls safe places for white "ladies," as the dominant Democratic press consistently referred to the white women they hoped to encourage to register. To turn women out, white male and female Democrats spoke as if registration was a duty; "nothing [was] to be gained by assuming a superior, condescending attitude toward 'politics,'" one woman warned. "Politics . . . is good or bad just as we make it. And the ballot is the key that opens for us the doors of citizenship in the greatest republic the world has ever known."[42] Such language elevated the act of registering and casting a vote to an action fit for the highest-minded woman. Moreover, white women could not let black women surpass them: "it is entirely proper for colored women who are qualified to register and vote; and they are registering."[43]

Thus, with the entrance of women into electoral politics the white Democratic press and politicians promised safety and acknowledged black civil rights. Woe to the man who got up to old tricks at the polls, warned none other than H. E. C. Bryant, a North Carolina reporter who had built his reputation upon his favorable coverage of the 1898 election violence. "Junketing through the south," Bryant reported, "I have found beyond a reasonable doubt that men—politicians—do not want to monkey with the women at the ballot box. . . . In many instances [throughout the South] democratic registrars have resigned their long-time jobs rather than register women." Southern white politicians were "confused and embarrassed" by woman suffrage, but they could find no way around it. Now they were "registering their wives, sisters, and daughters."[44]

Everything about press coverage of women's registration sounded just the right note to ensure white women that they could venture into public space without losing caste. For example, a press report commenting on the large number "of Charlotte ladies [who] had their names placed upon the registration books during the past few weeks" evokes an image of aristocratic females ordering registrars to execute their wishes. But in the same story, when African Americans do the same thing, the tone changes: "in several precincts of the city a number of negro women registered."[45] Ladies have their names placed; women register. The nouns and verbs, unrelated elsewhere to color, here serve it very well.

What we have here is a contemporaneous carving out of segregation in a new space: the polls. For all of segregation that was real—separate water fountains, waiting rooms, and train cars—there was plenty that depended upon imaginary lines, tacitly agreed upon.[46] With this sort of language, we are hearing the creation of a new imaginary hierarchical space in which white and black women move about together—as they already did in kitchens and on sidewalks—but where, in the same space, the positions of the races are unequal. One race of ladies orders actions to be performed; another race of women aggressively pushes its way onto the voting registers. In other words, Democrats scrambled to place a rhetorical overlay of hierarchy on a space supposedly equal under law.

The point is that when the Democrats needed to deploy it, the inviolability of white womanhood could instantly cloak the polls with an aura of respectability and safety. The electoral arena became yet another place in which white women could assume their superiority even as the evidence of their equality with black women stared them in the face. The lie thickened.

After the election, whites marveled at the change white women's presence had made. Polling places were literally transformed from sites of "politics" to sites of civic industry. "The women of Charlotte . . . were desperately in earnest. There was no frivolity. It was a unique situation: a peculiar experience. . . . The day marks an epoch in America." "Aged" women had appeared and voted with "sober intensity." "Patience, characteristic of women," served them well. It had been a "sweep of [the] 'fair'" at the polls.[47] The day after the election, one white man, tongue in cheek, longed for a return to the day before yesterday, when his lazybones registrar occasionally stirred himself to register a white man, gazed at a floor "spattered with juice and littered with paper," and breathed an air "foul with tobacco smoke." In those sweet bygone days, "a fight or two would enliven the proceedings." Now, all was lost as "women at the tables handed out tickets" while others screeched up in automobiles piled high with more female voters. Alas, "men kept on their hats," fondled their cigars unlit, and "as a body and as individuals were silent. It was the women who were doing the talking and the joking." "The old-time ward-heeler was forced into realization, regretfully perhaps, that his occupation is gone."[48] Henceforth, "the new order of things" would require a male candidate to "stand for something in his community other than mere politics."[49] Lest the white men forget their promises of safety, their admonitions to duty, and their grudging acknowledgments that black men and women had—in theory at least—the right to vote, the white League of Women Voters would oversee elections in the future, providing female registrars to replace those men who did not want to "monkey" with women at the polls. Voter turnout doubled from that of 1916, and the Democrat Cameron Morrison polled 308,000 votes to the Republican Parker's 230,000.[50]

Just as the woman suffrage campaign subjected local polling places to national standards, southern African Americans attempted to hold federal Republican nominees to a similar standard. "The time is coming when you will hear me," Charles Moore had warned, and that time came sooner than Frank Linney ever dreamed. In May 1921, President Warren G. Harding nominated Frank Linney to be United States district attorney for the western district of North Carolina, subject to confirmation by the Senate. Black North Carolinians sprang into action, challenging Linney to repeat his disavowal of black voters before the confirmation committee by sending a telegram to the chairperson about the 1920 election.[51] Linney had no choice but to "stand pat" on his lily white policy on the national stage, and in early June, a group of more than twenty leading black men rushed to Washington to testify before the committee. Charles Moore was among them, as was an NAACP member from Greensboro, Dr. A. M. Rivera. Linney, they argued, "was not a proper man for district attorney . . . he was ready to enter into a combination to shut the negro out from his rights at the ballot box." They accused him of "collusion" with the Democrats "to nullify one of the great principles of our government."[52] The committee's decision would be an "acid test of Americanism." The NAACP mounted a vigorous campaign as well to block Linney.[53]

Once again the Republicans failed North Carolina's African Americans, and Frank Linney gained confirmation as U.S. district attorney over their objections. But the protest against Linney served as a stalking horse for the one the NAACP would mount against Herbert Hoover's 1930 nomination of John J. Parker to the U.S. Supreme Court. Apparently unaware that they had newspaper articles on Parker in their own files, in 1930 the NAACP contacted members of the group who had gone to Washington to testify against Linney. A. M. Rivera had saved a clipping describing Parker's racist speeches, which he sent straight away to Walter White.[54] Linney did not live to see his friend Parker lose the 1930 nomination in consequence of the collective sins they committed in the 1920 woman suffrage campaign; he died of a heart attack on election day in 1928 at four o'clock in the morning while listening to the Democratic convention on the radio. Linney never heard Charles Moore's warning. But the time came when Parker did.[55]

The NAACP did not just help to defeat John Parker; it believed that it helped defeat two Republican senators who had voted to confirm Parker's nomination as well. Thus, six years before the realignment, the leading national African American organization had publicly turned against the Republican Party in consequence for its deeds in the South in the 1920 election.[56] Yet, while the NAACP cut many ties in the Republican Party with their opposition of John Parker, they knew their welcome among the Democrats in 1930 would be limited as well. Just after the Parker defeat an outbreak of lynching occurred across the South, and most attributed it to economic hard times. But Walter White wrote to James Weldon Johnson, secretary of the NAACP, that lynchings were a sign that the "Bourbon South"—white Democrats—held African Americans accountable for the Parker defeat.[57]

Nevertheless, on tour in 1930 in North Carolina, Johnson urged southern African Americans to "participate in the Democratic primaries at least temporarily." "I think that the first step to be taken by the Negro toward political freedom is a declaration of political independence," Johnson argued. "The time has arrived when he should decline to wear the brand of any particular party."[58] In part, Johnson urged southern African Americans to register Democratic since the winners of the Democratic primaries were almost always guaranteed election. A major southern African American newspaper seconded Johnson's recommendation: "All thoughtful Negroes are in hearty agreement with him."[59] The year before Johnson's advice to vote Democratic, the NAACP began backing a lawsuit against the whites-only primary in Texas.[60] In 1931, anticipating the 1932 election, Johnson stepped up his campaign, reminding black voters: "Abraham Lincoln is not a candidate."[61]

Although the GOP lost the North Carolina governor's race in 1920, they won the presidency. With their victory and the comparative safety the onslaught of women brought to the polls, Republicans could no longer hide behind a racist Democratic national administration or the threat of Democratic election violence to camouflage their own reluctance to support black voting rights. Moreover, Republicans now bore the responsibility to enforce federal election laws and to redress their abuse. Southern black Republicans and the NAACP attempted to judge federal appointees on their commitment to the civil rights guaranteed by the U.S. Constitution. When their party failed to judge its own nominees in the same way, support for Republicans ebbed even further.

There had been rumors during the 1920 registration period that black women were registering as Democrats, a charge the Democrats denied by arguing that "it is as natural for a negro—either man or woman—to vote the republican ticket as it is for a 'duck to take to water.'"[62] But was it more natural for the drakes than for the ducks? Did the black women who registered in October 1920 register as Republicans? The answer seems to be that they did. But there is a larger question: would they stay Republicans?

The answer seems to be no, a factor that has been mostly overlooked in the literature on political realignment in the 1930s.[63]

The voting registers that exist today in North Carolina are sparse and scattered, but the few surviving books reveal a growing number of black voters in the state's urban areas after 1920.[64] One set, in Charlotte, makes clear that in 1928, some African Americans registered as Democrats. One African American woman, who had been an avid suffragist, "realigned" herself and registered Democratic.[65] This fledgling southern black Democrat had tested the party of her fathers and found it lacking. She must have held out a slim hope that the Democratic Party would accept her or that she could tip any balance of power. The Democratic Party had abused African Americans as a matter of course, but the hurt was fresher with the Republicans. The year 1920 had provided an "acid test of Americanism," and the Republicans failed miserably. Black Democratic registration was an anti-Republican act, a harbinger of the massive exodus to come in 1936.

The passage of the Nineteenth Amendment created political problems for the Republican Party that it failed to solve in the Republican administrations that ruled the country in the 1920s. Why have these problems been discounted by those who study the realignment of the 1930s? Those who studied the realignment rarely looked to the southern context of their (newly) northern African American voters, and they rarely took into account the difference that having black *women* voters made to party politics. Scholars of southern politics counted out African Americans as political actors after disfranchisement and then saw woman suffrage as an issue peripheral to racial and party politics. Moreover, they saw white Democrats as monolithically opposed to black civil rights. Students of woman suffrage in the South have asked what difference the amendment made in women's politics, but few have asked what difference the amendment made in men's politics. An exception has been historian Sarah Wilkerson-Freeman, who, in her study of North Carolina, has argued that women "transformed American politics." Black women's brave attempts to register and the NAACP's use of those attempts as political weapons on the national level represent an important part of that transformation.[66]

Perhaps the primary reason that woman suffrage and the realignment of the 1930s have not been linked more closely is that the Nineteenth Amendment and its wake in the 1920s produced the change of heart among southern African Americans that precedes a change in behavior. Empirical data can exist only for behavioral changes. Southern African Americans could not vote as they pleased because whites circumscribed their choices and their actions in ways that kept them from recording their politics. When studying subordinate groups, it misleads to seek causality only concurrently with measurable changes. The massive empirical evidence for the realignment of African Americans from the Republican to the Democratic Party came only after migration and only after the Democratic Party offered an economic reason for switching. During the decade of the 1920s southern African Americans made up their minds to seize the first opportunity to abandon the Republican Party, even if they had no tangible way to register their decisions. By 1930, it was clear that the Republican Party, long a false friend, had become an avowed enemy.

NOTES

1. For a long view of realignment that takes into account immigrant ideology and generational change but neglects African Americans, see Kristi Anderson, *The Creation of a Democratic Majority* (Chicago: University of Chicago Press, 1979). On realignment, see V. O. Key, "A Theory of Critical Elections," *Journal of Politics* 17 (February 1955): 4; James L. Sundquist, *Dynamics of the Party System* (Washington: Brookings Institution, 1973); Walter Dean Burnham, *Critical Elections and the Mainsprings of American Politics* (New York: W. W. Norton, 1970); Allan J. Lichtman, "Critical Election Theory and the Reality of American Presidential Politics, 1916–1940," *American Historical Review* 81 (April 1976): 342; Everett Carll Ladd, Jr., with Charles D. Hadley, *Transformations of the American Party System: Political Coalitions from the New Deal to the 1970s* (New York: Norton, 1975); Arthur M. Schlesinger, Jr., *The Politics of Upheaval* (Boston: Houghton Mifflin, 1960); Doug McAdams, *Political Process and the Development of Black Insurgency, 1930–1970* (Chapel Hill: University of North Carolina Press, 1982).

2. Nancy J. Weiss, *Farewell to the Party of Lincoln: Black Politics in the Age of F. D. R.* (Princeton: Princeton University Press, 1983), xiii. Weiss presents much evidence to refute her own conclusion. For example, she discusses black leaders' disenchantment with the Republican Party in the 1928 election, but she fails to count history as a harbinger of action. Historians have accepted Weiss's argument over Samuel Lubell's, which is that the realignment started in 1928. See Lubell, *The Future of American Politics*, 2d ed. (New York: Doubleday and Co., 1956).

3. Weiss, *Farewell to the Party of Lincoln*, 209–20. For a more general history of the experience, see Harvard Sitkoff, *A New Deal for Blacks: The Emergence of Civil Rights as a National Issue*, vol. 1: *The Depression Decade* (New York: Oxford University Press, 1978); for detailed local studies, see Weiss, xiv, n. 3.

4. Weiss, *Farewell to the Party of Lincoln*, xvi.

5. Duncan MacRae, Jr., and James A. Meldrum, *The American Political Science Review* 54 (September 1960): 669–83.

6. Recent work argues that Franklin Roosevelt and the First New Deal did more than simply offer jobs for African Americans. The Democrats offered hope for other political changes and represented a tangible departure from racism as usual in politics. See Patricia Sullivan, *Days of Hope: Race and Democracy in the New Deal Era* (Chapel Hill: University of North Carolina Press, 1996). Weiss nods in the direction of hope, yet it does not alter her monocausal conclusion. Weiss, 210–11.

7. Weiss uses anecdotal evidence to argue for continued loyalty among southern blacks to the Republican Party. Robert Church's Republicanism and the black

Republicans of Memphis are important examples. Church, however, was at odds with the NAACP and other southern African Americans when he championed the Republican Party. See Walter White to the Editor, *Chicago Defender*, 2 February 1932; *Chicago Defender*, 30 January 1932, clippings, both in folder 541, box 24, James Weldon Johnson Manuscripts, James Weldon Johnson Collection, Beinecke Library, Yale University, New Haven, Conn. White denied that Church's resignation from the board of the NAACP had anything to do with the NAACP's opposition to Republican John Parker's nomination to the Supreme Court. White's denial is most likely for public consumption.

8. Burner's work is significant for the case at hand because the North Carolina and the Virginia migrant streams led straight to New York. From David Fulton to the Delaneys to Edward Johnson, Harlem's earliest black politicians were veterans of post-disfranchisement upper-South politics. See David Burner, *The Politics of Provincialism: The Democratic Party in Transition, 1918–1932*, reprint (Westport, Conn.: Greenwood Press, 1981), 238–39, 241.

9. Richard B. Sherman, *The Republican Party and Black America from McKinley to Hoover, 1896–1933* (Charlottesville: University Press of Virginia, 1973), 140–43. There is no reference to woman suffrage in the passage that covers the election of 1920, nor in the index.

10. Kenneth W. Goings, *"The NAACP Comes of Age": The Defeat of Judge John J. Parker* (Bloomington: Indiana University Press, 1990), 22–24 and *passim*.

11. Evelyn Brooks Higginbotham, working from the northern perspective at the end of the decade, deplores the lack of attention to the difference that black women might have made in party politics. See Higginbotham, "In Politics to Stay: Black Women Leaders and Party Politics in the 1920s," in *Women, Politics, and Change*, Louise A. Tilly and Patricia Gurin, eds. (New York: Russell Sage Foundation, 1990): 199–220. The debate of the difference that black voting made in the upper South urban areas is unresolved. In *Gender and Jim Crow*, I argue that 1920 marked an important moment in black registration, and the scattered voter registration books I found in North Carolina demonstrate that registration of black voters became much more frequent after 1920. See Gilmore, *Gender and Jim Crow: Women and the Politics of White Supremacy in North Carolina* (Chapel Hill: University of North Carolina Press, 1996). The best information for North Carolina is a survey of black voting conducted in urban areas in 1932 that counts several thousand black voters in North Carolina. It should be emphasized that this is a small percentage of blacks statewide. See Paul Lewinson, *Race, Class, and Party: A History of Negro Suffrage and White Politics in the South* (New York: Grosset and Dunlap, 1959).

12. Gilmore, *Gender and Jim Crow*, 110, 130.

13. For more detail, see ibid., 207–8.

14. "The Republicans and the Negro," *Charlotte Observer*, 24 October 1920; *Charlotte Observer*, 11 October 1987, 4C; *Winston-Salem Journal*, 20 October 1920, 2; *Winston-Salem Journal*, 31 October 1920, 1; "Heartily Favors Woman's Suffrage," *Everywoman's Magazine*, July–August 1920: 3, in Gertrude Weil Papers, North Carolina Division of Archives and History, Raleigh, NC.

15. Frederick Douglass, quoted in Sherman, *The Republican Party and Black America*, front material.

16. For the expulsion of black Republicans from the state convention in 1902, see Gilmore, *Gender and Jim Crow*, 129–30; Sherman, *The Republican Party and Black America*, 29–36; David C. Roller, "The Republican Party of North Carolina, 1900–1916," (Ph.D. dissertation, Duke University, 1965), 100–110; Eric Anderson, *Race and Politics in North Carolina, 1872–1901: The Black Second* (Baton Rouge: Louisiana State University Press, 1981), 250.

17. Clipping from the *Raleigh News and Observer*, 13 May 1908, in file 1908–1914, box 14, scrapbooks, Charles N. Hunter Collection, Manuscript Department, Perkins Library, Duke University. They took hope from the compromise on the separate black and white delegations from Louisiana in 1904, when the Cohen delegation (the black delegation) obtained some seats, according to Sherman, *The Republican Party and Black America*, 47–48. Sherman does not mention the rejection of black delegates at the 1908 convention (79–80).

18. Clipping from the *Raleigh News and Observer*, 26 March 1912, file 1908–1914, box 14, scrapbooks, Hunter Collection. Booker T. Washington claimed that blacks were excluded from southern party councils in Virginia, North Carolina, and Texas, but participated elsewhere. But this is scarcely a consolation, since only in those three states was there a chance for the two-party politics that were so completely out of the question in South Carolina, Georgia, Alabama, or Louisiana. See Sherman, *The Republican Party and Black America*, 102, 104. These black delegations were often at cross-purposes with convention floor managers for particular candidates. For a discussion of this in 1912, see Norman M. Wilensky, *Conservatives in the Progressive Era: The Taft Republicans of 1912* (Gainesville: University of Florida Monographs, *Social Sciences* 25 [Winter 1965]): 29–30.

19. Broadside, "Headquarters of the North Carolina Republican Executive Committee (Colored)," 11 March 1916, in file 1887–1899 (misfiled), box 13; "The Negro and Politics," *Raleigh Times*, 20 March 1916, reprinted from *Charlotte Observer*, file 1915–1918, box 15, scrapbooks, both in the Hunter Collection.

20. "Negroes of City Have Organized Political Clubs," *Raleigh News and Observer*, 3 November 1916, clipping in file 1915–1918, box 15, scrapbooks, Hunter Collection.

21. As quoted in Sherman, *The Republican Party and Black America*, 77.

22. "Negro in the Plot," *Raleigh Times*, 4 November 1916, clipping in file 1915–1918, box 15, scrapbooks, Hunter Collection.

23. Other articles in the *Raleigh Times* seem to adopt a matter-of-fact tone about black people in public life. The *Times* was an afternoon paper, competing against the much more widely read and powerful *News and Observer*, which built its reputation on generating scares of "Negro domination" in politics. Earlier in the year, in "That 'Colored' Convention," 18 March 1916, the *Times* argued that the black Republican state convention amounted to nothing, and one should not "begrudge" African Americans their four-year ritual. At the same time, the editor argued, if African Americans tried to reenter state politics as a partisan (i.e., Republican) force, the state would have ways of stopping them. It seems that some whites wanted to put the issue of race to the side in politics and were exploring acceptable ways to do that.

24. For information on the rise of the NAACP, see Eugene Levy, *James Weldon Johnson: Black Leader, Black Voice* (Chicago: University of Chicago Press, 1973);

B. Joyce Ross, *J. E. Spingarn and the Rise of the NAACP, 1911–1939* (New York: Antheneum, 1972); Goings, *"The NAACP Comes of Age."*

25. DuBois's first widely publicized visit to the state was in November 1916, when he gave the opening address at an educational conference with leading local whites who supported industrial education. The white press seemed a bit vague about who he was. See "Educators Meet at Durham, N.C.," n.p., [November] 1916; "Conference on Education," n.p., [November] 1916; "Big Conference on Education," n.p., November 1916; "Negro Educators in Meeting at Durham," *Atlanta Journal*, 23 November 1916; "Federal Aid for White and Negro Rural Schools Is Urged," *Wilmington Star*, 23 November 1916; "Negro Educators Meet," *Nashville American*, 25 November 1916, all on microfiche 103, Hampton University Clipping Files on Microfilm. By 1918, it is DuBois himself who is the news lead. He toured the state, sponsored by NAACP branches in some places, by social service agencies in others.

26. "Negro Leader Is Speaker Here," *News and Observer*, 11 May 1918, file 1915–1918, box 15, scrapbooks 1915–1932, Hunter Collection; NAACP to Governor Bickett [North Carolina], telegram 9 November 1918, file "Lynching—Winston-Salem, N.C., 1918–1926," C363, NAACP Papers, Manuscript Division, Library of Congress, Washington, D.C.

27. Elsa Barkley Brown, "Negotiating and Transforming the Public Sphere: African American Political Life in the Transition from Slavery to Freedom," *Public Culture* 7 (1994): 107–46.

28. Gilmore, *Gender and Jim Crow*, 224.

29. Contrary to the argument here, historians have written that woman suffrage mattered little to political parties, since women voted as their male relatives did. This criticism began early with articles such as Malcolm M. Willey and Stuart D. Rice, "American Women's Ineffective Use of the Vote," *Current History*, 20 July 1924: 641–47. See also William L. O'Neill, *Everyone Was Brave: A History of Feminism in America* (Chicago: University of Chicago Press, 1971); Joel H. Goldstein, *The Effects of the Adoption of Woman Suffrage: Sex Differences in Voting Behavior—Illinois, 1914–1921* (New York: Praeger, 1984). For an early revision of women's activism in the 1920s, see J. Stanley Lemons, *The Woman Citizen: Social Feminism in the Late 1920s* (Urbana: University of Illinois Press, 1973). For new work that argues for the power of women's politics and centers that argument in North Carolina, see Sarah Wilkerson-Freeman, "Women and the Transformation of American Politics: North Carolina, 1898–1940" (Ph.D. dissertation, University of North Carolina at Chapel Hill, 1995).

30. For discussion of the difference suffrage made in setting political agendas, see Susan Lebsock, "Woman Suffrage and White Supremacy: A Virginia Case Study," in *Visible Women: New Essays in American Activism*, Nancy A. Hewitt and Suzanne Lebsock, eds. (Urbana: University of Illinois Press, 1993), 62–100; William Chafe, "Women's History and Political History: Some Thoughts on Progressivism and the New Deal," in *Visible Women*, 101–18; Nancy Cott, "Across the Great Divide: Women in Politics before and after 1920," in *Women, Politics, and Change*: 153–86; Cott, *The Grounding of Modern Feminism* (New Haven: Yale University Press, 1987), 85–114; Lebsock, "Women and American Politics, 1880–1920," in *Women, Politics, and Change*, 177–98; Marjorie Spruill Wheeler, *New*

Women of the New South: The Leaders of the Woman Suffrage Movement in the Southern States (New York: Oxford University Press, 1993); William A. Link, *The Paradox of Southern Progressivism, 1880–1930* (Chapel Hill: University of North Carolina Press, 1992); Wilkerson-Freeman, "Women and the Transformation of American Politics."

31. For more on the registration campaign, see Gilmore, *Gender and Jim Crow*, 211–24. Charles H. Moore had been a professor of Latin and Greek at Bennett College and at North Carolina Agricultural and Mechanical College for Negroes and broke with his former boss, James Dudley, on the suffrage issue. See *Africo-American Presbyterian*, 20 August 1898, 1; "Still Urging Negro Women to Vote," *Greensboro Patriot*, 19 October 1920; Charles H. Moore to James Weldon Johnson, 15 November 1920, file General Correspondence 11/15–30, 1920, container 6, May–December 1920, Series C, NAACP Papers; "Former Slave Made Mark in Greensboro," Ben L. Smith, *Greensboro Daily News*, 17 February 1960, Charles Henry Moore, clipping in the North Carolina Collection Clipping File through 1975: Biography, reel 26, p. 532, North Carolina Collection, Wilson Library, University of North Carolina at Chapel Hill.

32. Clara Booth Byrd, "North Carolina," in *The History of Woman Suffrage*, vol. 6, ed. Ida Husted Harper (New York: National American Woman Suffrage Association, 1922), 490–500.

33. "Republican State Executive Committee," Frank A. Linney to "The Women of North Carolina," [October 1920], broadside in the North Carolina Collection.

34. "The Republicans and the Negro," *Charlotte Observer*, 24 October 1920; *Charlotte Observer*, 11 October 1987, 4C; *Winston-Salem Journal*, 20 October 1920, 2; *Winston-Salem Journal*, 31 October 1920, 1; "Heartily Favors Woman's Suffrage," *Everywoman's Magazine*, July–August 1920: 3, in Weil Papers.

35. *Charlotte Observer*, 24 October 1920, 6.

36. "The Negro Out of Politics," *Charlotte Observer*, 6 October 1920.

37. White quoted in Sherman, *The Republican Party and Black America*, 134.

38. "Declares the Republican Party in North Carolina Does Not Want the Negro," file Voting, 21–31 October 1920, C 284, NAACP Papers. Goings, *"The NAACP Comes of Age,"* 24.

39. "Letter to the Editor," *Greensboro Daily News*, 24 October 1920.

40. The NAACP pointed out that the South's argument for temporary expedience in using a literacy test to disfranchise black men was inapplicable to the situation in 1920 for two reasons. First, literacy had grown quickly among blacks from 1900–1920. Second, black women were more literate than black men, and whites feared them for that reason. See *The Crisis* 21 (November 1920): 7–8.

41. *Greensboro Daily News*, 14 September 1920, 1. The red-shirts were members of North Carolina's White Government Leagues, founded in the 1898 election. These men adopted the red shirt from South Carolina's Ben Tillman, who led mobs of white men against black voters.

42. "Women Should Register and Vote," Louise Alexander, *Greensboro Patriot*, 23 September 1920, 1; "Woman's Duty to Vote," *Asheville Citizen*, 17 October 1920; "Woman's Duty to Vote," *News and Observer*, 24 October 1920, 9: "Mary

Hilliard Hinton Will Register and Vote," *News and Observer*, 8 October 1920, 1; *Greensboro Daily News*, 27 September 1920, 1.

43. "Woman's Duty to Vote," *News and Observer*, 24 October 1920, 9, reprinted from the *Asheville Citizen*.

44. "No Prospect of South Voting G.O.P. Ticket," *Charlotte Observer*, 6 October 1920, 1. Whereas whites whipped their women forward, some black men worried that black women could not be protected at the polls and opposed their registration out of fears for their safety. See *Gender and Jim Crow*, 212–13; "Why Cannot the Negro be Let Alone?" *Durham Morning Herald*, 24 October 1920, 4.

45. *Charlotte Observer*, 24 October 1920.

46. For an explanation of this process, see Grace Elizabeth Hale, *Making Whiteness: The Culture of Segregation in the South, 1890–1940* (New York: Pantheon Books, 1998), esp. chapters 3 and 4.

47. "Women Vote in Large Numbers," *Charlotte News*, 3 November 1920, 10.

48. "While the Voting Was Going On," *Charlotte Observer*, 3 November 1920, 6.

49. "Women in Local Elections," *Charlotte Observer*, 5 November 1920, 6.

50. *Greensboro Daily News*, 7 October 1920, 8; n.p., n.d., the first program of the Charlotte League of Women Voters, Charlotte Woman's Club Papers, Special Collections, Atkins Library, University of North Carolina at Charlotte; Kathryn L. Nasstrom, "'More Was Expected of Us': The North Carolina League of Women Voters and the Feminist Movement in the 1920s," *North Carolina Historical Review* (July 1991): 307–19; Wilkerson-Freeman, "Women and the Transformation of American Politics," 371–76.

51. *News and Observer*, 21 May 1921, clipping in file 1919–1922, box 15, scrapbooks 1915–1932, Hunter Collection.

52. *News and Observer*, 11 June 1921, file 1919–1922, box 15, scrapbooks 1915–1932, Hunter Collection; Charlotte Hawkins Brown to James Weldon Johnson, 25 May 1931, folder 64, box 4, Johnson Mss.

53. W. C. Craver to the Editor, *Greensboro Daily News*, 16 June 1921, clipping in file 1919–1922, box 15, scrapbooks 1915–1932, Hunter Collection; Sherman, *The Republican Party and Black America*, 1948, 154–55.

54. Rivera is listed as "Dr. A.M. Rivers" in a story about the Linney protest in the *News and Observer*, 9 June 1921, clipping in file 1919–1922, scrapbooks, 1915–1932, Hunter Collection; Goings, *"The NAACP Comes of Age,"* 24. See also Richard L. Watson, Jr., "The Defeat of Judge Parker: A Study in Pressure Groups and Politics," *Mississippi Valley Historical Review* (September 1963): 213–34; Weiss, *Farewell to the Party of Lincoln*, 17; Sherman, *The Republican Party and Black America*, 239–45.

55. "Frank A. Linney Dies at His Home in Boone after Heart Attack," *Greensboro Daily News*, 30 June 1928, Biographical Clipping File through 1975, vol. 89, 166, North Carolina Collection.

56. "Wagner Hits 1930 Lynching Record," *New York Amsterdam News*, 7 January 1931, clipping in scrapbook "James Weldon Johnson, 1931," Johnson Mss.

57. Walter White to James Weldon Johnson, 22 August 1930, folder 540, box 24, Johnson Mss.

58. "Negroes Told to Go Into Politics," *Carolina Tribune*; "Some Sour Advice to Negroes at Shaw's Founders' Meeting," *Raleigh Times*, n.d.; clippings in scrapbook "James Weldon Johnson 1931," Johnson Mss.

59. *Norfolk Journal and Guide*, 13 January 1930, clipping in scrapbook "James Weldon Johnson 1931," Johnson Mss.

60. "Court Bars Negro in Texas Primary," *New York Times*, 25 July 1928, clipping in scrapbook "Political Campaign, 1928," Johnson Mss.

61. "A Negro Looks at Politics," offprint from the *American Mercury*, n.d. [1931], scrapbook "James Weldon Johnson, 1931," Johnson Mss.

62. "Deny Registrars Are Failing to Put Test," *Asheville Citizen*, 22 October 1920, 14.

63. On new voting groups and party identification, see Philip E. Converse, "Of Time and Partisan Stability," *Comparative Political Studies* 2, 139–71. Lewinson, *Race, Class, and Party, passim*.

64. There are scattered books in Boards of Elections offices and warehouses. The Salisbury books are in the Edith M. Clark History and Genealogical Room, Rowan County Public Library, Salisbury, N.C. The most extensive evidence is in Lewinson, *Race, Class, and Party*.

65. Mary McCrorey registration, Ward 2 Register, 1918, and various registers from the 1920s, Board of Elections, Charlotte, N.C.

66. Wilkerson-Freeman, "Women and the Transformation of American Politics."

Chapter 10 BRYANT SIMON

Race Reactions: African American Organizing, Liberalism, and White Working-Class Politics in Postwar South Carolina

> One of these days I'm gonna get tired
> Of ridin' the back end of the street cars.
> I'm gonna get tired of goin' down side alleys
> To a picture show.
> Yes, and I'm gonna get damn tired
> Of sitting "up front" on a passenger train;
> One of these days I'm gonna get mad;
> And all the hurts heaped up inside of me—
> Hurts I've taken and swallowed from years back,
> They gonna burst like a big stick of dynamite,
> And everybody's gonna hear that blast
> 'Cause [it's] gonna go off with a loud boom.
> —Frenise Logan, "Dixie Hospitality," 1942[1]

IN 1938, South Carolina textile workers snubbed the state's political establishment. Incumbent senator "Cotton Ed" Smith warned millhands that carpetbaggers and scalawags were on their way back to the South. Their return to the region, he predicted, would bring back the tragic days of Reconstruction: wanton corruption and vice, the usurpation of state's rights, and the weakening of white supremacy. Worst of all, nefarious Yankees and their sympathizers would end the privileges of race. They would place black men in hot steamy textile mills right next to innocent young white women. At the poll stations, blacks would jostle with whites. But Smith's backers offered workers one last chance to stop the evil advance of New Deal liberalism by sending the longtime lawmaker back to Washington to do battle with President Roosevelt and his cronies.

In mill precincts across the state in 1938, textile workers turned their backs on Smith in favor of the candidacy of Olin Johnston. A former millhand, Johnston appealed to textile workers' class identities. He campaigned on a sturdy New Deal platform of higher wages, shorter hours, support for the Congress of Industrial Organizations (CIO), and "100 percent" loyalty to the "reforms and policies of President Roosevelt."[2] This message played well on the mill hills, but not in many other places. Smith won only a smattering of votes in the state's textile districts, but still scored a decisive victory over Johnston.[3]

Looking back, "Cotton Ed" Smith's defeat of Olin Johnston marked a transition in the politics of South Carolina's white textile workers. It was the end of millhands' faith in the New Deal and federal intervention; it was the last time that these laborers stressed their economic interests ahead of their concerns for white supremacy. Slowly, unevenly, in the wake of the 1938 election, race moved to the center of their political debate. Since the days of the demagogue Cole Blease, working-class whites had taken white supremacy for granted. The best jobs were reserved for whites only and voting was for whites only. As long as blacks were barred from politics and kept out of the factories, white workers felt free to disagree with other whites on a wide range of issues. Throughout the 1920s and 1930s, South Carolina voters repeatedly split along class lines without bringing up the matter of race. Before 1938, it was possible, as Olin Johnston and other candidates demonstrated, for a South Carolina politician to avoid the question of race, to refrain from talking about it, to consider it a given. Afterwards this was impossible. Admission into the political game required that politicians announce at the outset their staunch and unyielding support for white supremacy. That was the first order of business, much like during the Depression, when candidates started their campaign speeches by spelling out their positions on labor and capital, and went on from there. After 1938, politics revolved around who was the most determined to keep African Americans down and the federal government and courts at bay.

Before 1938, white workers occupied the liberal edge of South Carolina politics. They were FDR's most fervent supporters. The president could do no wrong in their eyes. Workers backed government action and the expansion of federal power and they were the leading critics of corporate wealth and private property. Responding to shifts in national politics and African American attempts to gain a political voice, white workers emerged as a reactionary political force during the war years and after.

Black men and women had never accepted the South's repressive racial order or willingly worn its ugly brand of inferiority, but they often hid their pain behind many masks of getting along. Whites read African American gestures as clear windows into their collective psyche. They believed all of the mumbled "yes sirs," tipped hats, and moving off of wooden sidewalks. They convinced themselves that African Americans accepted, even liked, segregation, Jim Crow, and disfranchisement. Beginning in the late 1930s, this fantasy became harder than ever to believe.

Sometime between the last days of the New Deal and first moments of World War II, a gear in the machine shifted and the world moved a little. Nothing would ever be the same.[4] In hundreds of quiet and dramatic ways,

African Americans broadcast that they would no longer endure the humiliations of discrimination and second-class citizenship in silence. They announced that they intended to grab hold and not let go of long-denied freedoms. Tens of thousands protested with their feet. Cramming what they could into cardboard suitcases and flimsy trunks, black women and men from towns, cities, and farms crowded onto trains headed to the promised lands of Chicago, Detroit, Atlantic City, New York, and Hartford. Most African Americans, however, stayed behind in the land of their parents. More than half of the nation's black community remained in Dixie in 1945. Even here in the heart of the old Confederacy, African Americans had freedom on their minds, and whites could not help but notice.

In a place like prewar South Carolina, joining the NAACP represented a brave act of a defiance, a clear vote by the disfranchised against Jim Crow. In 1938, fewer than twelve hundred African Americans in eight different Palmetto communities belonged to the NAACP. The next year, Levi Byrd, a plumber's helper from Cheraw, brought these separate groups together to form the State Conference of Branches of the NAACP. From then on, the organization's membership rolls grew. By 1945, as many as thirty thousand, although the number was probably closer to thirteen thousand, African Americans belonged to one of South Carolina's forty branches of the NAACP.[5]

Throughout the 1940s, the South Carolina NAACP represented, in the words of one historian, "the vanguard of the African American struggle for freedom in the South."[6] "To meet the challenge of the times" and "let the world know that democracy . . . is an actuality, rather than a far fetched ideal," during the war, the statewide organization pressed for "Double V"—"Democracy in America, Democracy Abroad." "JOIN the NAACP," read a 1942 flier, "Stay on Guard Against" educational inequalities, police brutality, unfair treatment in the courts, and discrimination in parks and playgrounds. Above all, NAACP activists demanded the badge of citizenship—the right to vote—which, they trusted, was the key to democracy in America and in South Carolina.[7]

The South Carolina story was a familiar Deep South story. In 1940, African Americans made up 43 percent of the state's population. Only Mississippi had a larger percentage of black residents. In almost half of the state's forty-six counties, African Americans outnumbered whites. Yet the poll tax, fraud, easy to manipulate registration rules, and raw racism kept all but a few black Republicans away from the polls. In Beaufort, South Carolina, African Americans composed more than two thirds of the population, but not a single black resident could vote. More than thirty thousand black men and women lived in Greenville County, but only thirty-five were listed on the voting rolls, and they could vote only in the rather meaningless general election, not the decisive Democratic primary.[8]

Beginning in the late 1930s, a few African Americans tried to shoulder their way into power, and into the Democratic Party.

The schoolteacher Lottie P. Gaffney led one charge in upcountry Cherokee County. On the first Tuesday of August 1940, Gaffney along with four other women and a couple of ministers went at the designated time to the designated place to register to vote. They rapped hard on the door. The registrar looked out and could not believe it. "Darkies," he said to Gaffney, more shocked than mad, "have never registered in the South and especially in Cherokee County." Then he slammed the door in their faces. They kept knocking all afternoon, but the registrar would not answer. African Americans in Columbia, Greenville, Charleston, Cheraw, and Spartanburg followed in Gaffney's footsteps and tried to register to vote. Very few people were to gain their rights. Most were treated like a Spartanburg man who was told that if he continued to ask to have his name placed on the voting roll his house would be torched and he would be "scalped."[9]

Shifting currents in political thought during the war years and after promoted the grassroots efforts of African Americans in South Carolina. Outside the South, tolerance for white supremacy withered as the nation geared up for battle against racist, fascist foes. At the same time, race became more central to liberalism. Throughout his first six years in office, Franklin Roosevelt, fearful of alienating southern congressional conservatives, refrained from talking about the nation's tortured race relations, concentrating his recovery efforts instead on economic issues. Yet as the New Deal lost steam after the setbacks of 1937–1938, a new version of liberalism started to take shape. "This new liberalism," writes historian Alan Brinkley, "has focused less on the broad needs of the nation and the modern economy than on increasing the rights and freedoms of individuals and social groups."[10]

Changes in liberal priorities altered the staging of politics. Typically, politics are cast as morality plays and filled with stock characters. In the dramas fashioned by the newer liberals, the fat, bloated southern Bourbon replaced the fat, bloated "economic royalist" as the nation's leading bad guy. Long-victimized African Americans replaced brawny industrial laborers as the driving force to a fairer, more just society. Liberals now envisioned reshaping America, starting with the South first. They pointed to Dixie conservatives as the major block to reform and considered extending the vote to African Americans as an essential step in remaking the nation. With blacks participating in elections and backing liberals, the Bourbons would be doomed. With these conservatives out of the way, liberals could begin to reform American democracy. In the end, then, it was not that the new liberals did not care about economic issues or the distribution of wealth, it was that these issues, central to the political debate during the first days of the New Deal, now took a backseat to the quest for racial equality.[11]

Developments in Washington and elsewhere during the war years encouraged the new brand of liberalism. Activists applauded when President Roosevelt, prodded by A. Phillip Randolph and his March on Washington Movement, signed Executive Order 8802, outlawing racial discrimination in hiring on war-related projects and establishing the Fair Employment Practices Committee (FEPC) to investigate violations. Up the hill, liberal lawmakers did battle with southern Democrats over voting rights, winning some fights and losing others. In 1942 Congress passed the Soldiers Vote bill, making it easier for servicemen, including African Americans from southern states, to cast absentee ballots in federal elections. Liberals also came close to getting rid of the dreaded poll tax. An anti–poll tax measure passed in the House in 1942, only to be filibustered to death by southern conservatives in the Senate.[12] Then in the spring of 1944 came the Supreme Court's *Smith v. Allwright* decision.

Throughout the South, cunning Democrats had kept African Americans out of the party by claiming that it was a private club, which could set its own rules and requirements for membership. Undercutting this pillar of white supremacy, the justices ruled in *Smith* that political parties were not private clubs, but agents of the government. As an arm of the state, the Democratic Party, they maintained, could not bar African Americans from participating in primaries—the real elections in the south—without violating the Fifteenth Amendment.

Led by the increasingly combative NAACP, African Americans in South Carolina jumped at the opportunity created by the *Smith* ruling. Neatly dressed ministers, teachers, undertakers, and plumbers, in cities and small towns, lined up outside registrars' offices in the spring of 1944, demanding a voice in the Democratic Party. Predictably, party regulars tried to keep them out, but these black citizens would not go away easily or quietly. That summer, a group of African American, pro-Roosevelt Democrats along with a few whites, organized under the banner of the Progressive Democratic Party, traveled to Chicago to the national party convention. They petitioned delegates to seat them in place of the state's all-white, largely anti–New Deal contingent. Treating the insurgents as something of a nuisance, party leaders sent them back to South Carolina with vague promises of an investigation and future consideration. The Progressive Democrats had lost, but at the same time, they had delivered a clear message to white South Carolinians that they intended to be heard in the political arena.[13]

African American teachers banging on the door of the registrar's office, black activists publicly challenging the leaders of the state Democratic Party, African American men in crisply pressed uniforms with rifles slung over their right shoulders, the Supreme Court toying with primary laws, Soldiers Vote bills, and federal sanctions against job discrimination—these developments were too much for many white South Carolinians to take. In schools, at home, and the media, they had been taught that suffrage was a racial privilege, not a generic democratic right. Now African Americans laid claim to the franchise in the most aggressive public style. Worse yet, with the ballot in hand, or at least in sight, and with northern lawmakers and their Yankee army buddies telling them that they were as good as anybody, African Americans, according to whites, began to act "uppity."[14] Some even began to do the unthinkable, that is to act "like white folks." Anxiety over social equality generated wartime rumors about ice picks, guns, and Eleanor Clubs. "A white woman in every kitchen" was the reported slogan of these Eleanor Clubs. Whites told each other that African Americans would no longer adhere to the rules of the Jim Crow order and step off the sidewalks to let whites pass, move to the back of the bus, or happily accept the worst and most dangerous jobs for next to nothing in pay. Others told alarming stories about African American domestic workers flooding into shadowy unions named after the first lady. Once enlisted, domestics supposedly demanded higher pay, and started to call their bosses by their first names, eat dinner at their employers' tables, and bathe in white people's tubs after work. Then, of course, came wild talk of interracial sex. In this electric climate, a brush became a touch; a glance became a leer. Whites nervously whispered about African American men suggestively squeezing white hands when getting change at stores, whistling at white women, calling them for dates, and sending chocolates to young white girls, just like white boys did. While African Americans registered to vote and left their jobs as domestics for higher paying positions in war-related industries, whites thought they overheard black men say that after the war, "Negroes will marry white girls and run the country."[15]

"I read your article in the newspaper," Bertie Mae Loner of Iva told Eleanor Roosevelt, "where you thought white girls should dance with negroes." Even though she was already convinced that the first lady was "a negro lover," she still could not believe it. "I think it is mighty sorry in you to even ask us to dance with those negroes." Retelling a rumor, Loner said she saw African American women, who "think white people should work for them," carrying a picture of Eleanor Roosevelt. "When our soldier boys return home," Loner told Roosevelt, "the negroes will get the daylights knocked out [of] them if they even talk back to one boy." "We can always bet on our boys," she bragged.[16] As it turned out, Loner was not far off the mark.

During the 1940s, white South Carolinians launched a bloody campaign of terror, reminiscent of Reconstruction, to shove African Americans back into their "place." Greer White accused Louis Nesbitt of talking "very bold . . . in regard to the equality of the two races" and questioning whether black men should volunteer "to fight and die in a white man's war." They also charged him with organizing a mythical Eleanor Club in Spartanburg. Then, Nesbitt tried to register to vote. On November 5,

1942, vigilantes grabbed Nesbitt, drove him across the county line, and whipped him with leather straps.[17]

Uneasy seeing African Americans in uniform, angry whites, especially near military encampments, targeted soldiers for attack.[18] Black political activity and military service also sparked a Klan revival in the state. Even before the war started, Greenville Klansmen, aided by the police, ransacked eight homes in search of a school principal, who was also a NAACP member and head of a local voter registration drive. When the police found the frightened educator armed with a gun, they arrested him for carrying a concealed weapon. Soon after, the white-controlled school board fired him.[19] Two thousand Knights and their supporters, meanwhile, met near Wade Hampton's statue in downtown Columbia in 1941 and listened to speeches by hooded Klansmen about the evils of communism and racial mingling.[20] A couple of years later, the Klansmen returned to the capital. After a short parade, they went on a rampage, burning wood crosses in front of several black churches.[21] According to the FBI, in 1942, male millhands from Anderson, Spartanburg, Ninety-Six, and Greenwood formed chapters of the "Blue Shirts," an organization reportedly similar to the Klan. Following a twilight July meeting in an upcountry brickyard, Blue Shirts fanned out across the region and beat and molested dozens of African American men and women.[22]

White rage took an even uglier turn in the immediate postwar years. A few short months after South Carolinians went "slightly mad" celebrating V-J Day, Isaac Woodward, an African American serviceman anxious to get home to New York after fifteen months in the South Pacific, downed a few drinks and boarded a bus in Augusta.[23] Just after crossing the Savannah River into South Carolina, Woodward and the white bus driver got into a shouting match. When the bus reached Batesburg, a midlands town twenty miles southwest of Columbia, the driver called the local sheriff's officer, saying he needed help with an unruly black passenger. Two lawmen rushed over to the station. They ordered Woodward off the bus, and then dragged him around a corner and beat him. The next day, the veteran could not see. A medical report revealed that a billy club had been shoved into his eye sockets with such force that "both of his eyes were mutilated beyond repair." An all-white jury later acquitted Woodward's attackers. A few months after the decision, a black man was killed in Elko, South Carolina, after he tried to register to vote. Then in 1947 there was a lynching, perhaps the last ever in the state.[24]

Sometime in the evening of February 16, 1947, in one of the black sections of Greenville, Willie Earle got drunk. That was not so unusual. Earle had been drinking a lot since his boss had discovered that he suffered from epilepsy and fired him from his job as a truck driver. Later that tragic night, Earle called for a cab to take him to his mother's house near Liberty. Cabs had long been sites of racial confrontation in the region. They were one of the few places in the South where African Americans could tell whites what to do, and they would listen. A white driver from the Bluebird Taxicab Company, Thomas Watson Brown, picked Earle up around 9:00 P.M. Something happened: a fight, maybe race played a part, maybe Earle said something about a white woman or about African Americans taking over after the war or maybe Brown spit out a racial epithet or made a lewd remark, or maybe nothing happened between them. One thing was certain: the cabbie ended up on the side of a country road bleeding from a deep knife wound. As he lay dying in a nearby hospital, the police picked up Earle and took him to the Pickens County jail.

Word of the knife attack and Earle's arrest spread quickly as one cabbie told another, who told another, and then another. Within hours, fifty men in two dozen cabs were on their way to the jail. The jailkeeper, an older white man worried about his wife's safety, handed over the keys without a fight. He even pointed the angry white men to Earle's cell. They grabbed the twenty-four-year-old African American and drove off into the night. After a fast ride out of the city, they yanked Earle out of the car. They punched him and kicked him. They cracked his skull with a pistol butt, and then they shot him. They shot him again after he was dead. "The bushes around him," wrote a reporter, "were splashed with his brain tissue."

Many people knew that the cabbies killed Earle, but thirty-six hours after the crime, the local police had still made no arrests. Under orders from the United States attorney general, the FBI came to Greenville to take over the case. Agents interrogated drivers. Many of the cabbies admitted that they were there, but all of them denied directly participating in the killing. Several, however, blamed one co-worker or another for Earle's death. Based on this evidence, the state prosecuted twenty-eight cabdrivers and three others including a mill owner's son, who had heard about the crime at a downtown café and joined the mob. Despite graphic testimony detailing the brutality of the murder, the jury of twelve white men—nine mill workers, two salesmen, and a farmer—voted to acquit.

Obviously defense attorneys spoke the same language as the men on the jury. Well known around Greenville as a friend of the working man, John Bolt Culbertson represented several of the accused cab drivers. He told the jury that Greenville was white man's country, and that Earle was a "bad nigger" who got what was coming. "Willie Earle," he pronounced, tapping into white fears of a postwar black crime wave, "is dead, and I wish more like him was dead." The defense team also stirred resentments against the FBI, transforming the agents from dutiful investigators into evil carpetbaggers. Heaping abuse on "northern agitators, radio commentators, and certain publications," another defense lawyer added, "We people get along pretty well until they start interfering with us in Washington." If the FBI stood for a malevolent federal government, then, the thirty-one defendants became every beleaguered white man under attack by the unholy alliance of aggressive African Americans like Willie Earle and pro–civil rights liberals like Eleanor Roosevelt. This argument made sense to the largely white working-class jury.[25]

Little time passed before the violence and mayhem of dark country roads and steamy courtrooms spilled over into the political arena. Elected leaders and candidates for office, however, rarely mentioned African American political mobilization; that would mean recognizing the power of blacks to shape the thoughts and actions of whites. Few talked about the Klan, the Blue Shirts, or cab drivers, either. Highlighting instead themes first previewed by Cotton Ed Smith in 1936 at the Democratic National Convention and then again during the 1938 Senate race, South Carolina politicians described their state as under siege by ruthless Yankees. These sons of Sherman loathed the South and egged on African Americans, urging them to vote even when they did not want to, just to humiliate white men and scare white women. Behind Eleanor Roosevelt's pleas for civil rights, the Soldiers Vote bill, assaults on the poll tax, and the *Smith* decision, Dixie lawmakers saw a well-coordinated replay of Reconstruction.

After a decade in which racial themes could be heard only in the background, the tone of South Carolina politics became meaner and more hateful during the 1940s. Consider the case of Burnett R. Maybank. The Charlestonian was never known as a hard-line segregationist. Yet in the new racial climate of the 1940s, he had to play the race card if he wanted to survive at the polling station. In the 1941 Senate contest, then Governor Maybank said little about the New Deal or labor, but boasted that of all the candidates he was the best prepared to "fight any anti-lynching bill."[26] Following the *Smith* decision, Maybank threatened that South Carolina would do whatever it took to "protect our primaries." Later in 1944, as he prepared to leave for the Democratic National Convention, Maybank told a *New York Times* reporter that white supremacy was *the* issue to be resolved in Chicago.[27]

White supremacy was certainly *the* issue back home in South Carolina. In August 1941, five thousand people gathered in Saluda to celebrate the forty-sixth anniversary of the 1895 Constitutional Convention. The air was thick with heat and humidity. Like in the old days, a band played patriotic songs and soldiers marched in formation. The local American Legion post served everyone heaping plates of barbecue free of charge. Former Chief Justice of the South Carolina Supreme Court Eugene Blease was the keynote speaker. When it came time for the talking, the music stopped and the people put down their plates. Feeling the pressure of the new liberalism and the NAACP's push for civil rights, Blease delivered a furious defense of white supremacy. He charged that the national Democratic Party had given too much encouragement to African Americans in "several places of the country to get his vote." There was danger in this trend, he warned, a danger that the federal government would once again force black voting on South Carolina. Blease ended his speech praising the 160 men of the Constitutional Convention who "wiped out the last vestiges of government forced on South Carolina by the carpetbaggers of the North and the scalawags of the South."[28]

Two years later, Representative John D. Long, who had been a Johnston ally during the highway fight as well as a frequent supporter of labor legislation, condemned "un-American," "agitators of the North" who were "seeking the amalgamation of the White and Negro races by a co-mingling of the races." In the spring of 1944, Long urged his House colleagues to vote for a resolution declaring "our belief in and our allegiance to established White Supremacy as now prevailing in the South and pledging our lives and our sacred honor to maintain it, whatever the cost, in war and in peace."[29] After the measure passed with only a few dissenting votes, Cotton Ed Smith sent a congratulatory telegram, saying, "we are dammed tired of these butterfly preachers who do not know conditions in the South."[30]

The reactionary climate in South Carolina got even hotter after the Supreme Court outlawed the white primary. Sounding the tenor of the times, Richard M. Jeffries, one-time governor and a longtime state senator from low country Colleton County, wrote to a friend: "It seems impossible for us to entertain, even for a minute, the possibility of acquiescing in the voting of Negroes in our primary elections." The reason why, he said was: "[T]he Negro race has not yet developed to the point that it can assume properly this vital function of citizenship." Still if African Americans got the right to vote, "it would not be long before candidates for political offices and factions in the party would be calling upon the Negroes to settle differences between the white people." "In my opinion," Jeffries concluded, casting an eye back to Reconstruction, "we must meet this challenge in the spirit of our fathers and solve the problem for the protection of southern civilization."[31]

Not every white South Carolinian got swept along by the waves of reaction. There were a few homegrown white liberals and integrationists, people like James McBride Dabbs, in the state. Never a large number, these liberals belonged to either the Southern Conference for Human Welfare, the Southern Regional Council, the South Carolina Council on Human Relations, or the Progressive Democratic Party. Committed to ending, or at least adjusting, the Jim Crow order, these people, concentrated mostly in Charleston and Columbia, repeated the arguments of national liberals, saying that the only way to reform the nation was to reform the South, and the only way to reform the South was to get rid of the Bourbons, and the only way to get rid of the Bourbons was to extend suffrage rights to African Americans.[32]

The state's unsteady racial climate also produced some strange hybrids of liberalism. Praised by the *New Republic* as one of the "true liberal leaders of the South," the lawyer John Bolt Culbertson backed African American demands for better schools and expanded civil rights. He was, wrote the British novelist and journalist Rebecca West, "one of the very few white people in these parts who shake hands with Negroes and give them the prefix Mr. or Mrs. or Miss." Culbertson's ties to the CIO further bolstered his liberal credentials. But he also represented several of the Greenville cab drivers accused of lynching Willie Earle and built their defense around vicious racism and twisted analogies to Reconstruction.[33] The South Carolina CIO was another odd liberal hybrid. "Personally," an organizer for the group's textile branch said, "I think the niggers ought to have the right to vote. They're citizens, like everybody else." Yet in the same breath he blurted out that he would not jeopardize his union's standing with millhands by pressing for civil rights.[34]

In the end, the racist diatribes of Maybank, Long, and Smith drowned out the voices of liberalism in the state, even the odd ones. Without question, the reactionary forces in the South put together something resembling a mass movement, one that was clearly bigger, stronger, and more powerful than anything the Southern Regional Council or the Southern Conference for Human Welfare ever imagined for themselves. Following a visit to low country Jasper County just after the war, a *Newsweek* reporter made a similar observation. Hearing the speeches and the lusty applause, he concluded that the South's conservative white politicians "were not stirring up a popular revolt. They were reflecting it."[35]

Olin Johnston was not the kind of man who swam against history. Ambitious to the core, he was the kind of man who amplified and confirmed what people already believed or what they wanted to believe. That's what he did in the 1930s. Sensing workers' identification with the New Deal, he made himself into Roosevelt's messenger. In the 1940s, after a few miscues, Johnston once again tuned into what the majority was thinking. Judging from poll returns, they were thinking about race. That is not to say that labor issues or gender anxieties disappeared, but after 1938, they took a backseat to white supremacy.

Having refrained from playing the race card during the early days of his career, saying that the issue had been settled by Wade Hampton and the red-shirts, Johnston eventually got in line with the shifting tenor of southern politics. His turnabout stemmed not only from the mounting pressures of African American protest, but also from his own dwindling political fortunes. In 1941, Johnston lost a second bid for a United States Senate seat. Just as he did during his 1938 run to unseat Cotton Ed Smith, the millboy-turned-lawyer-turned-politician built his campaign around working-class issues, telling voters that they had a choice between him and his Charleston opponent, or "a cotton mill boy and a wealthy aristocrat." "Cotton mill workers," he insisted on another occasion, "should vote for Johnston if only to prove that the son of a textile worker is as good as an aristocrat." After winning big in the mill precincts and losing another election, Johnston looked to broaden his constituency.[36]

In 1942, Johnston returned to the political victory circle, winning a second term as governor. He made race the central theme of his campaign that year. "Have [I]," Johnston asked, using his earlier reluctance to play the race card to his advantage, "been one to exaggerate the issue of white supremacy?" Now, he warned, threats to the "southern way of life" were everywhere. Promising to put up "new barriers against the invasion of the white party in the South," he proclaimed, "This is a white man's state, and Olin Johnston will always be in there fighting hard as he can to keep it that way." Scratched from Johnston's speeches were his avowals of 100 percent support for the New Deal; in their place came a pledge of allegiance to "South Carolina first, last, and always."[37]

True to his word, once in office, Johnston pursued the politics of white supremacy ahead of his older agenda of the "greatest democracy for the greatest number." In the summer of 1943, Johnston addressed the state's Home Guard. "God didn't see fit to mix them," the governor told the reserves, "and I am tired of people agitating social equality of the races." "If outsiders come into our state and agitate social equality," he warned, "I shall deem it my duty to call upon you men to expel them."[38]

Then on April 4, 1944, the bombshell hit. The U.S. Supreme Court outlawed the white primary. Initially, Johnston said he was "not alarmed" by the decision. But others did panic. They urged, implored, demanded, and begged the governor to do something to save the white primary.[39] Six days later, Johnston called the members of General Assembly back to Columbia for a special session. Addressing the lawmakers, Johnston spoke like a tent preacher; his voice rising and falling with emotion. The text that night was drawn from D. W. Griffith's *Birth of a Nation*; the lesson was the horrors of Reconstruction. "Where you now sit," the governor reminded the packed audience, "there sat a majority of negroes." His voice reaching a fever pitch, Johnston continued, lifting a line or two from Cotton Ed Smith's stump speeches, and embellishing on them:

> The records will bear me out that fraud, corruption, immorality, and graft existed during that regime that has never been paralleled in the history of our State. They left a stench in the nostrils of the people of South Carolina that will exist for generations to come. The representatives of these agitators, scalawags

that called themselves white men and used the colored race to further their own course, are in our midst today, and history will repeat itself unless we protect ourselves against this new crop of carpetbaggers and scalawags who would use the colored race to further their own economic and political gains.[40]

Galvanized by Johnston's savage rhetoric, South Carolina legislators got to work repealing "all laws pertaining to our primaries, thus making the contest a private matter outside the scope of Supreme Court decisions." Over the next couple of days, the "Killbillies," as *Newsweek* nicknamed the representatives, combed through state law books searching for any mention of elections, primaries, and the Democratic Party. When they were done, they had erased 130 laws. "Should this prove inadequate," Johnston vowed at the end of the weeklong session, "we South Carolinians will use the necessary methods to retain white supremacy in our primaries and to safeguard the home and happiness of our people." For now, the white primary had been saved, but not for long; in 1947, Judge J. Waties Waring of Charleston, bravely turning against his region, ruled this legal subterfuge unconstitutional.[41]

Recognized now as an "ardent segregationist," Johnston once again set out on the campaign trail in the summer of 1944, and once again, he sought to topple Cotton Ed Smith. The contest revolved around the question of who could best defend the state's entrenched system of segregation, not the New Deal and other class issues. Slowed by age and a flagging voice, Smith succumbed to his younger, more vigorous opponent. Not long after, as Johnston headed to Washington pledging to defend white supremacy, Smith passed away.[42]

Six years later, J. Strom Thurmond, fresh from his presidential run on the Dixiecrat ticket, entered the Senate race against Johnston. Both men swore their allegiance to Jim Crow and each tried to pierce the other's white supremacist armor. "I am for segregation of the races. God started it and I believe in keeping it that way," the senator bellowed in Florence, "I defy anyone to say that Olin Johnston didn't fight civil rights." At the Newberry stump meeting, Thurmond accused Johnston of sitting by "silent as a tomb" as President Truman integrated the armed services in 1948. "If that's not so, Senator, stand up and deny it!" Thurmond yelled. "That's a lie! That's a lie! That's a lie!" Johnston screamed back. The two candidates almost came to blows. In the end, Johnston narrowly defeated Thurmond.[43] Topping the Dixiecrats' first-man further bolstered Johnston's segregationist standing and made him a leading member of a new breed of postwar southern reactionaries that included arch-conservatives James Eastland and John C. Stennis. So solid were Johnston's credentials on the race question that no one dared to run against him in 1956.[44]

Even as Johnston drifted away from the politics of New Deal liberalism toward the politics of reactionary racism, he remained just about the only politician in South Carolina who stood up for the working man. "I am for the laboring man," Olin D. Johnston told an Aiken stump crowd during his last run for the Senate in 1962, although it could have been 1944 or 1950 or 1956. "I worked in the mills," he said everywhere he went, "my whole life has been dedicated to the working people." After his opponent ripped him for being endorsed by "all those foreign labor bosses," Johnston shot up to defend himself. Thirty years earlier, during his first term as governor, he bragged, he had signed the state's first workers' compensation bill and authorized the establishment of a separate department of labor. "I am proud of my labor record," Johnston declared.[45]

Occasionally during his Senate career, Johnston reinforced his ties to the working class with action. He was one of only a handful of southern senators to oppose the Taft-Hartley Act, a conservative piece of legislation designed to curb trade union power and permit states to enact right-to-work laws. Readily acknowledging the sins of some labor leaders, Johnston nonetheless insisted that the Republican proposal went "too far penalizing . . . those who live by the sweat of their brow."[46]

When Johnston complained about Republican labor proposals, he was doing more than reaching out to his reliable constituency. Crafting a message similar to his New Deal appeal, he spoke in a populist vernacular of the people against the interests, us against them.[47] The big difference was that in the postwar era, Johnston's "them" changed. Leaving the money changers and greedy capitalists alone, Johnston pointed to new threats to working-class whites coming from liberal authorities from above and from aggressive African Americans from below. Meeting in some far-off place, probably Washington, these twin forces of evil, Johnston hinted, plotted to snatch the privileges of whiteness away from millhands. Sounding more like Smith than a New Dealer, Johnston now favored using government power to uphold white supremacy, and maybe to bring a little pork back home, but little else. Again like Cotton Ed, he couched his opposition to government action in the intertwining idioms of race, class, sex, and gender.

Unnerved by African American insurgency, white millhands embraced Johnston's newfound antistatism. For years, they had placed their faith in Roosevelt and centralized authority, but no more. After 1938, millhands mobilized to limit the scope of the federal government's power. That meant voting for politicians, like Olin D., who vowed to uphold states' rights and white supremacy. Racial identity, however, was not the only factor that eroded workers' faith in the power of the federal government. Certainly the many defeats they endured in the state legislature, and on the picket lines through the Great Depression and the New Deal era, soured some on class-based political activism. Throughout the 1920s and 1930s, looking back at one example, textile laborers had demanded government-sponsored workers' compensation. Finally, in 1935, they got their wish, only to discover that the law did not operate in their interests. For all of their hope, imagination, and grit, millhands, as the workers' compensation case illustrated, could not transform their world. Many, in fact, seemed almost politically exhausted from the long fight.[48]

As early as 1939, some millhands voiced their political resignation. "Somehow," explained Columbia's Collie Croft, "I didn't feel like I wanted to vote this time, and I just decided I'd stay at home and pray." Another capital city mill worker said:

> I don't like Roosevelt. Got no patience with him. I'm working hard as ever I did and ain't getting a cent more for it. If I'm going to starve, I just as soon kick my feet up on a dry goods box, get a good book to read, and sit right there and starve.

Few were as bitter as this man. But it does seem that many began to rethink the value of political mobilization along class lines and some decided it was a dead end. Yet class still mattered.[49]

The echoes of the language of labor that reverberated through Johnston's wartime and postwar campaign speeches resonated with workers' continuing concern with class issues. Even after 1938, millhands still complained about wages, workloads, promotions and dismissals, the heat in the factories, injuries, the deadly lint in the air, and being called lintheads. Occasionally they pressed for labor legislation and backed labor candidates for state and local offices. Thousands joined unions and went out on strike. Whether they enlisted with the more conservative AFL or the liberal-leaning CIO or eschewed trade unionism altogether, workers in the postwar period were trying to hang on to what they had gained.[50]

World War II pulled the textile industry out of its depression-era doldrums. Even before Pearl Harbor, orders for material for tents, khaki shorts, mosquito netting, and army-issued baseballs and softballs poured into the state. Mills ran around the clock trying to keep up with demand. As the war kicked other industries into gear, mill owners raised wages in frantic bids to keep their labor forces intact. Things only got better for laborers after the United States entered the war. The conflict put a new shine on textile workers' public image. Portrayed in the past as lintheads and white trash, laborers were described by journalists as patriotic workers doing their part to defeat fascism. Prodded by federal statutes and war production boards and trying to prevent their employees from drifting into other jobs, mill owners raised wages again and again during the war. The labor shortage also presented women with new opportunities to work outside the home. More people at work and more money for each hour of work translated into a dramatic jump in mill people's standard of living.[51]

Even more than World War I, World War II allowed southern mill-hands and their families to enter into the nation's consumer economy.

After saving much of what they made during the conflict, simply because there was nothing to buy, southern workers joined the national postwar spending frenzy. Taking advantage, at the same time, of the G.I. bill, many bought their own homes either in the mill village or just outside of it in newly constructed working-class suburbs. They purchased shiny cars, bright white refrigerators, automatic washing machines, and imitation mahogany hi-fi/radio consoles, and some put away enough money to send their children to college and out of the working class.[52]

By the late 1940s, white millhands were beginning to be people with something to lose and they desperately clung to their corners of the American Dream. Casting aside their older faith in New Deal liberalism, they lined up behind Johnston and other reactionary politicians in an all-out campaign to save segregation. They believed that the wages of whiteness were worth more than the latest promises offered by liberals, and they were not entirely wrong, at least not in the short run. Postwar liberalism, which one observer described as "progressivism shorn of any economic critique," all but abandoned white laborers. Downplaying economic issues while moving civil rights and expanded opportunity to the top of their domestic agenda, postwar liberals offered white workers, according to Numan Bartley, "little aside from contempt and the right to compete for scarce jobs with black workers."[53]

For many poor whites in the postwar period, the key to holding on to their precarious social position was keeping African Americans down. That meant making sure that jobs and suffrage remained racially defined. If liberals prevailed, millhands and people like them—semiskilled, not well-educated, mostly nonunion, white workers—would be forced to compete with African Americans for opportunities that had long been reserved for whites only. Fearing the worst, laborers worried that expanding African American options would increase the labor supply, and drive down their wages, forcing them into lower paying jobs and edging them out of the consumer economy, back into used cars, secondhand appliances, and worn-down neighborhoods.[54]

Millhands embraced a view of democracy similar to their view of the economy. Unlike liberals, who saw democracy as elastic, many white South Carolinians saw it as finite. There was only a fixed amount of citizenship to go around, barely enough it seemed, after 1938.[55] If African Americans were given full democratic rights and allowed to vote in the primaries, then there would be less "democracy" for others. Working-class whites feared that if democracy stopped being racially exclusive, wealthy whites, who they never really trusted, would leave them out.[56] If poor whites were written out of the dominant group, then what would happen? Would they end up like African Americans, cornered into the worst jobs and the worst neighborhoods, despised and humiliated, tortured and exploited? Would someone treat them the way they treated African Americans? Would they end up not being white anymore?

For millhands, African American protest and the new liberalism that started to emerge during the late 1930s jeopardized their lives as white people and participants in the consumer economy. If blacks could vote and work right beside whites in the factory, then whiteness would be meaningless. White workers did not intend to let the whole idea of race and racial privilege evaporate without a fight. They attacked African Americans who attacked their whiteness and they lashed out against politicians who favored easing racial distinctions.

They also talked incessantly of sex across the color line. Interwoven into these discussions of sex were complicated metaphors about race and power. Defining race as natural, as a question of blood, as most white southerners did, meant that interracial sex symbolized an end to racial distinctions. In this coded language, race, then, would no longer matter. Whiteness would no longer matter. Poor whites would no longer receive the economic and social benefits of whiteness. They would be nobodies. South Carolina millhands were not about to give up their whiteness, their jobs, and their status as citizens so easily, especially when the latest chorus of liberalism seemed to offer little in return. Beginning during the war years, therefore, these workers dedicated their political efforts to making a hard fact out of the slippery fiction of race.[57]

NOTES

1. Logan, "Dixie Hospitality," *Opportunity: Journal of Negro Life* 20 (January 1942), 20.

2. *Greenwood Index Journal* and *Spartanburg Herald*, 16 May 1938.

3. Bryant Simon, *A Fabric of Defeat: The Politics of South Carolina Millhands, 1910–1948* (Chapel Hill: University of North Carolina Press, 1998), 188–218, 244.

4. This is a paraphrase of Eldridge Cleaver's famous remark about Rosa Parks. Cleaver is quoted by Harvard Sitkoff, *The Struggle for Black Equality, 1954–1980* (New York: Hill and Wang, 1981), 42.

5. On the highest estimates of NAACP membership, see Interview with Mr. James Hinton, 20 January 1948, Southern Politics, Box 2–Latent Bipartisanism, Folder, The Negro, Used Material, Heard Library, Vanderbilt University. More modest estimates come from Robert L. Zangando, *The NAACP Crusade Against Lynching, 1909–1950* (Philadelphia: Temple University Press, 1980), 171; Miles S. Richards, "Osceola E. McKaine and the Struggle for Black Civil Rights, 1917–1946" (Ph.D. dissertation, University of South Carolina, 1994), 107–9; and Patricia Sullivan, *Days of Hope: Race and Democracy in the New Deal Era* (Chapel Hill: University of North Carolina Press, 1996), 142. See also Edwin D. Hoffman, "The Genesis of the Modern Movement for Equal Rights in South Carolina," in *The Negro in the Depression and War: Prelude to Revolution, 1930–1945*, ed. Bernard Stresher (Chicago: Quadrangle Books, 1969), 193–214.

6. John Egerton, *Speak Now Against the Day: The Generation Before the Civil Rights Movement in the South* (Chapel Hill: University of North Carolina Press, 1994), 428; and Sullivan, *Days of Hope*, 143. See also Morton Sosna, *In Search of the Silent South: Southern Liberals and the Race Issue* (New York: Columbia University Press, 1977).

7. On the national campaign for Double V, see John Morton Blum, *V Was For Victory: Politics and American Culture during World War II* (New York: Harcourt Brace Jovanovich, 1976), 207–20. From South Carolina, see "The Negro Citizens Convention of South Carolina to the South Carolina State Convention of the Democratic Party," 19 May 1942; and A Flier for a NAACP Meeting, 15 March 1942, Voting Rights Campaign, Part 4, Reel 10, NAACP Papers.

8. On eligible voters in Beaufort and Greenville, see Sullivan, *Days of Hope*, 144; Ralphe J. Bunche, *The Political Status of the Negro in the Age of FDR* (Chicago: University of Chicago Press, 1973), 242–45, 421–24; and *Fifteenth Census of the United States*, 1930, Vol. 1, Part 3, Population (Washington, 1931–33), 784–87.

9. Mrs. Lottie P. Gaffney to the NAACP, 25 August 1940, 7 November 1940; and NAACP Press Release, 29 May 1941, Voting Rights Campaign, Part 4, Reel 10, NAACP Papers; and Bunche, *The Political Status of the Negro in the Age of FDR*, 238–47, 425–27.

10. Alan Brinkley, *The End of Reform: New Deal Liberalism in Recession and War* (New York: Knopf, 1995), 10–11.

11. Ibid.; Robert H. Zieger, *CIO: 1935–1955* (Chapel Hill: University of North Carolina Press, 1995), 186; Numan V. Bartley, *The New South, 1945–1980* (Baton Rouge: Louisiana State University Press, 1995), 70–73; and Gary Gerstle, *Working Class Americanism: The Politics of Labor in a Textile City, 1914–1960* (New York, Cambridge University Press, 1989), 289–302, 317–18.

12. On the trends in Washington, see Sullivan, *Days of Hope*, 133–68; Merl E. Reed, *Seedtime for the Modern Civil Rights Movement: The President's Committee for Fair Employment Practice, 1941–1946* (Baton Rouge: Louisiana State University Press, 1991); Blum, *V is For Victory*, 196–98, 212–15; and *New York Times*, 6 September 1942, 14 November 1942.

13. On 1944, Sullivan, *Days of Hope*, 144–49; and Richards, "Osceola E. McKaine," 174–85.

14. On the alleged increase in African American crime, see *The State*, 6 September 1941.

15. Howard Odum, *Race and Rumors of Race: The American South in the Early Forties* (c. 1943; rept., Baltimore: Johns Hopkins University Press, 1997), 22, 57, 62, 63, 64, 115, 117, 122. See also Bryant Simon, "Fearing Eleanor: Wartime Rumors and the Threat of Organized Labor, 1940–1945" (forthcoming, in author's possession). More generally, see Thomas Sancton, "Trouble in Dixie: The Returning Tragic Era," *New Republic*, 4 January 1943, 11–14.

16. Bertie Mae Loner to Eleanor Roosevelt, 3 March 1994, Eleanor Roosevelt Papers, Box 2962, Franklin D. Roosevelt Presidential Library, Hyde Park, New York, (hereafter FDRL).

17. Richards, "Osceola E. McKaine," 119–20.

18. Egerton, *Speak Now Against the Day*, 362.

19. Hoffman, "The Genesis of the Modern Movement," 205–6, 211; Sullivan, *Days of Hope*, 144–45; and Bunche, *The Political Status of the Negro*, 422–23.

20. *The State*, 24, 30 July; 22 August, 1941.

21. See reports from *The State*, 1941. See also Steven F. Lawson, *Black Ballots: Voting Rights in the South, 1944–1969* (New York: Columbia University Press, 1976), 53–54; James Albert Burran, "Racial Violence in the South During World War II" (Ph.D. dissertation, University of Tennessee, 1977), 259; and Harvard Sitkoff, "Racial Militancy and Interracial Violence in the Second World War," *Journal of American History* 58 (December 1971): 661–81.

22. "Survey of Racial Conditions in the United States," p. 256, Official Papers, FDRL.

23. On the war-ending celebrations, see Archie Vernon Huff, Jr., *Greenville: The History of the City and County in the South Carolina Piedmont* (Columbia: University of South Carolina Press, 1995), 384.

24. Egerton, *Speak Now Against the Day*, 362–63, 365; Kari Frederickson, "'The Slowest State' and 'Most Backward Community': Racial Violence in South Carolina and Federal Civil Rights, 1946–1948," *South Carolina Historical Magazine* (April 1997): 180–83. On the rash of killings of African Americans who had voted or participated in early civil rights events in Georgia, Texas, and South Carolina, see Bartley, *The New South*, 76.

25. The best account of the events surrounding the murder and the trial come from Rebecca West, "Opera in Greenville," *New Yorker*, 14 June 1947. See also *Life*, 2 June 1947, 27–29; Huff, *Greenville*, 399–400; Egerton, *Speak Now Against the Day*, 371–73; and Frederickson, "'The Slowest State,'" 188–98.

26. *The State*, 13 August 1941.

27. *New York Times*, 1 April 1944, 21 May 1944, 21 June 1944.

28. *The State*, 17 August 1941.

29. Richards, "Osceola E. McKaine," 159; and Bartley, *The New South*, 12.

30. Richards, "Osceola E. McKaine," 164.

32. Hints of white liberalism in South Carolina can be found in the following places: Press Release, 5 May 1942, Voting Rights Campaign, Part 4, Reel 10, NAACP Papers; and Richards, "Osceola E. McKaine," 160–61.

33. West, "Opera in Greenville," 46.

34. Bunche, *The Political Status of the Negro in the Age of FDR*, 424–25. See also M. L. Woode, President of the Labor Democratic Club of South Carolina, 21 January 1948, Southern Politics Collection, Box 2, Folder–One Party System: South Carolina Piedmont vs. Low Country, Used Material; and Interview with Mr. James Hinton, 20 January 1948, Southern Politics Collection, Box 2–Latent Bipartisanism, Folder, The Negro, Used Material, Heard Library, Vanderbilt University.

35. Egerton, *Speak Now Against the Day*, 484.

36. On the 1941 campaign, see Johnston Speeches, 15 August, 1 September, Johnston Papers, Box 292, Folder, Speeches, 1941, August–September, South Carolina Library, University of South Carolina, Columbia (hereafter SCL); *Charlotte Observer*, 15, 17, 19, 20, 29 August; 3 September, 1941; *The State*, 2, 11 September 1941; *New York Times*, 17, 18 September 1941; and Anthony B. Miller, "Palmetto

Politician: The Early Career of Olin D. Johnston, 1896–1945" (Ph.D. dissertation, University of North Carolina, 1976), 344.

37. Miller, "Palmetto Politician," 359–60, 361–62, 364; *New York Times*, 26, 27 August 1942.

38. Miller, "Palmetto Politician," 387–88, 398–99; *The State*, 17 July 1943.

39. See reactions to the court in *Anderson Independent*, 12 April 1944; *Charleston News and Courier*, 4, 14, 18 April 1944; *The State*, 4, 6, 7 April 1944.

40. John E. Huss, *Senator for the South: A Biography of Olin D. Johnston* (Garden City, N.Y.: Doubleday, 1961), 123–25.

41. "Killbillies," *Newsweek*, 1 May 1944, 33; *The State*, 15–21 April 1944; *New York Times*, 16, 18 April 1944; and Lawson, *Black Ballots*, 49–50.

42. For accounts of the contest see *The State*, 18, 20, 21, 22 July, 3 August 1944; Rodger P. Leemhuis, "Olin Johnston Runs for the Senate: 1938 to 1962," *Proceedings of the South Carolina Historical Association* (1986): 60–62.

43. For more on 1950, see "Olin D. Johnston to Fellow South Carolinians," 26 June 1950, Johnston Papers, Box 304, Folder Campaign 1950, SCL; Leemhuis, "Olin Johnston Runs for the Senate," 62–65; and Nadine Cohodas, *Strom Thurmond and the Politics of Southern Change* (New York: Simon and Schuster, 1993), 206–16. Interestingly, some political observers suggested that African American voters, enfranchised by the *Smith* decision, provided Johnston with his thin margin of victory.

44. Egerton, *Speak Now Against the Day*, 400. Six years later, Johnston did have an opponent, Fritz Hollings. Hollings, however, did not attack Johnston's record on race, but tried to suggest that he was in the pocket of labor. The strategy did not work. It is also worth noting that in the fall of 1962, Johnston faced the first serious Republican challenge in South Carolina since Reconstruction. The candidate was the journalist W. D. Workman, who courted the votes of "country club" Republicans alienated by Johnston's lingering labor ties, along with working-class people fearful of the national Democratic Party's ties to civil rights.

45. For "sound bites" from Johnston speeches, see Luther B. Faggart, "Johnston versus Hollings: The 1962 Democratic Primary for the U. S. Senate in South Carolina" (Seminar Paper, University of South Carolina, 1992), 14–15; and *Charlotte Observer*, 3, 4, 16 May 1962.

46. Huss, *Senator for the South*, 140–47.

47. The continuing resonance of populist language is explored by Michael J. Kazin, *Populist Persuasion: An American History* (New York: Basic Books, 1995).

48. Korstad and Lichtenstein have suggested that "most social movements have a life cycle of about six years." South Carolina textile workers, therefore, lasted a little longer than most. See Robert Korstad and Nelson Lichtenstein, "Opportunities Found and Lost: Labor, Radicals, and the Early Civil Rights Movement," *Journal of American History* 75 (December 1988): 786–811.

49. Mattie Jones, "You Do What You Want To," Life History of Mrs. Colie Croft, 1 December 1939, and Mattie Jones, "The Kellys on William Street," Life History of Reverend Charles M. Kelly, 4 January 1939, Federal Writers Project, Box 30, Folder 326, SHC.

50. For more information on trade unionism, see *Charlotte Labor Journal*, 4 July, 12 December 1940; and *New York Times*, 20 March 1942. Evidence of labor's con-

tinued role in South Carolina politics can be found in the following. Interview with M. L. Woode, President of the Labor Democratic Club of South Carolina, 21 January 1948; and Thomas H. Pope, 12 February 1948, Southern Politics Collection, Box 2, Folder–One Party System: South Carolina Piedmont vs. Low Country, Used Material, Alexander Heard Library, Vanderbilt University; and "Dedication of AFL-CIO Community Building," 9 September 1962, SCL.

51. *New York Times*, 3 August 1941; and Ernest McPherson Lander, Jr., *A History of South Carolina, 1865–1960* (Chapel Hill: University of North Carolina Press, 1960), 208–12. The best account of the rise in working-class incomes comes from Timothy J. Minchin, *What Do We Need a Union For?: The TWUA in the South, 1945–1955* (Chapel Hill: University of North Carolina Press, 1997). For a personal recollection, see the interview in Victoria Byerly, *Hard Times, Cotton Mill Girls: Personal Histories of Womanhood and Poverty in the South* (Ithaca, N.Y.: ILR Press, 1986), 181.

52. Nelson Lichtenstien, *Labor's War at Home: The CIO in World War II* (New York: Cambridge University Press, 1982), 209–21; and Douglas Flamming, *Creating the Modern South: Millhands and Managers in Dalton, Georgia, 1884–1984* (Chapel Hill: University of North Carolina Press, 1992), 233–45.

53. Bartley, *The New South*, 70–73.

54. Others make a similar point; see Kazin, *Populist Persuasion*, 225–29; Robert J. Norrell, "Labor Trouble: George Wallace and Union Politics in Alabama," in *Organized Labor in the Twentieth-Century South*, ed. Robert H. Zieger (Knoxville: University of Tennessee Press, 1991), 249–72. White southerners were certainly not the only group of white Americans trying to protect the privileges of race in the postwar period, see Gary Gerstle, "Working-Class Racism: Broaden the Focus," *International Labor and Working-Class History* 44 (Fall 1993): 33–40; and Thomas J. Sugrue, "Crabgrass-Roots Politics: Race, Rights, and the Reaction Against Liberalism in the Urban North, 1940–1964," *Journal of American History* 82 (September 1995): 551–86.

55. In her fascinating study of anti-Semitism and race in the postwar south, Melissa Fay Greene argues that some poor whites saw democracy in this way. See Greene, *The Temple Bombing* (Reading, Mass.: Addison-Wesley, 1996), 432–33.

56. For evidence of this distrust, see "The Race Question," *(Una) News Review*, 31 July 1936.

57. For the long history of this process, see Grace Elizabeth Hale, *Making Whiteness: The Culture of Segregation in the South, 1890–1940* (New York: Pantheon Books, 1998).

"As a Man, I Am Interested in States' Rights": Gender, Race, and the Family in the Dixiecrat Party, 1948–1950

IN MID-FEBRUARY 1948, the *McComb (Mississippi) Enterprise-Journal* ran an editorial entitled "Time for a Divorce." It told a sad tale of a husband cursed with an unfaithful wife. Although the husband had "built a lovely home and showered [his wife] with his affection and endowed her with his loyalty[,] . . . she commenced running around with Tom, Dick and Harry." Then the editorial continued,

> Then one day Tom, Dick and Harry moved into his home, sat at his table and ordered food from his kitchen and enjoyed every luxury his home afforded. The neighbors looked on with ridicule. They laughed at him. Then one day Tom, Dick and Harry took the husband by the nape of the neck and threw him out into the mud of the street and took over his home, completely. The neighbors looked on with disgust. They had no respect for him. He was without home and standing.[1]

This editorial was not the tale of some unfortunate couple in McComb but rather an allegory to the white South's position in the national Democratic Party during the postwar era. Distressed by President Harry S. Truman's landmark pronouncements on civil rights and fearful that their traditional position of strength within the national party was slowly giving way to the organized efforts of black voters, prominent states' rights spokesmen turned to familial and sexual tales of bastardy, illicit liaisons, jilted lovers, and broken marriages to describe the changing configurations of political power. White southerners' frequent use of familial metaphors and gendered language to explain and justify their relationship to politics and to the national Democratic Party reveals the close interplay of race and gender in southern society and illustrates how the potential loss of political power in the public sphere was intimately linked to concerns regarding disruption of the private sphere. Ultimately, this language tells us much about how white southerners imagined politics, power, and states' rights in the mid-twentieth-century South and in particular about their fears for the destruction of white supremacy. Following the lead of studies of the antebellum and post-emancipation South that probe the connections between the public and the private, and between sexualized and racialized political rhetoric, this essay dissects the language and metaphors of post–World War II southern politics by focusing on the Dixiecrat Party and the presidential election campaign of 1948, and by examining the interplay between this language and political developments in South Carolina during the years 1948 to 1950.[2]

Historians are familiar with the political narrative of the modern South, but few have examined the cultural dimensions of political resistance and change during this tumultuous period.[3] Overshadowed by the furious white response to the United States Supreme Court's 1954 decision in *Brown v. Board of Education*, the Dixiecrat revolt remains the first independently organized regionwide effort by white southerners in the postwar era to defend segregation against federal intervention and increasingly aggressive grass-roots activism. Convinced that the national Democratic Party was fast becoming the mouthpiece of blacks and organized labor, a group of white southern Democrats bolted the 1948 Democratic National Convention. Formally known as the States' Rights Party, and commonly called the Dixiecrats, these Democratic dissenters worked above all to defeat Harry Truman. From February until November 1948, the Dixiecrats developed an explosive language of sex and domesticity to describe the potential horrors of civil rights legislation and black voting as well as to illustrate their declining status within national politics. Like the husband depicted in the *Enterprise-Journal* editorial, the Dixiecrats felt that they had been usurped in their own home. Disempowered and humiliated, their only recourse was divorce.

Anxious over their loss of influence in Democratic politics, Dixiecrats worried that they were losing control in their actual households as well. In South Carolina, home of Dixiecrat presidential nominee Strom Thurmond, concerns about civil rights and white southerners' perceived loss of political power coincided with a movement to legalize divorce. The debate over divorce linked the decline of the family with the end of white supremacy. This intersection of anxieties over the collapse of white supremacy and weakened familial relations revealed itself with particular clarity in the public furor surrounding federal Judge J. Waties Waring of Charleston. Divorced and remarried to an outspoken liberal northerner, Waring, who overturned the state's white Democratic primary in 1947, came to personify the Dixiecrats' worst fears about crumbling racial and gender hierarchies. The melding of Waring's divorced status with his views on race shows how white South Carolinians intertwined gender and racial concerns and ideas about the public and private in their political discussions.

In the public debate that swirled around the opposition to civil rights, the pros and cons of legalized divorce, and the Warings themselves, white southerners returned again and again to the issue of *legitimacy*. A concept with strong sexual connotations, ideas about legitimacy informed southern whites' notions of marriage, sex, politics and race. Local control over domestic institutions lay at the heart of this states' rights ideology. Racial and domestic hierarchies were equally central to white southerners' conception of political autonomy. That is why white South Carolinians fearful of losing power within the Democratic Party characterized themselves as illegitimate children or cuckolds even as they took steps to legitimize and solidify patriarchal family bonds. It also helps to explain why, when Judge Waring opened the political process to African Americans by striking down South Carolina's white primary law, white South Carolinians blamed his rulings on his "illegitimate" divorce and remarriage. The interconnectedness of ideas about the legitimacy of racial and gender hierarchies were indicative of the deep-seated fears white southerners felt at the prospect of black voting and changes in family law. From this point of view, tinkering with white supremacy threatened to tear asunder the broader social fabric by jeopardizing all forms of white male authority.

By the turn of the twentieth century the all-white Democratic Party dominated most parts of the South. Resurrected on the ashes of the Radical Republican governments, the Democrats became the principal instrument through which elite white southerners tried to safeguard the region from federal intervention, hold down poor whites, and keep blacks economically strapped, socially inferior, and politically disfranchised. As the region's most powerful political force, southern Democrats held a decisive position within the national party. Power in Washington was, in turn, key to power at home.[4]

The economic and political changes of the New Deal era and World War II laid the groundwork for the 1948 states' rights defection. In 1936, the Democratic National Convention abolished the two-thirds rule in nominating conventions, a rule that had made it possible for the solid southern Democratic bloc to veto presidential and vice-presidential candidates. The repeal of this rule of procedure eroded white southern dominance of the Democratic Party and left them uneasy and uncomfortable in the national party.[5]

The prominence of African Americans and organized labor in the New Deal coalition amplified the white South's insecurities within a party that was becoming increasingly northern and urban. Although Franklin Roosevelt did not use his position to further the cause of civil rights, his New Deal initiatives aided African Americans nationwide. Roosevelt received 75 percent of the black vote in 1936, a remarkable turnabout from the 1928 election, when the Democratic candidate had received no more than a quarter of the African American vote.[6] Between 1941 and 1944 more than a million southern blacks migrated to northern cities such as Chicago, Detroit, and Cleveland.[7] Unhampered by Jim Crow, these transplants to the

North quickly made their presence felt in national Democratic Party politics. The emerging influence of African Americans in the New Deal coalition unnerved many white southerners.

The war only heightened their anxieties. Responding to pressure from black leaders and voters, in 1941 Roosevelt issued an executive order that forbade discrimination in defense industries and established the Fair Employment Practices Committee (FEPC). It hardly mattered to white southerners that the FEPC had little power to enforce its directives. Mississippi senator John Rankin equated the creation of the committee with the beginnings of a communist dictatorship.[8] Compounding unease, the war-inspired demand for labor opened up new economic opportunities for African Americans. During the 1940s, the Mississippi Delta—locally known as a "planters' heaven"—experienced a 10 percent decline in its rural black population as agricultural workers migrated to cities and towns.[9] Those who stayed behind were less disposed to tolerate ill treatment from white landlords. "The day when a man could protect the grade of his cotton and assume a clean-picked crop by threatening his labor with a single-tree [lynching] or a trace chain [beating] is gone forever," observed one visitor to the region. "The word spreads fast against that kind of planter nowadays and the first thing he knows, he can't get anybody to pick his cotton."[10]

The postwar years did little to soothe the angst of the white South. In 1946, alarmed by a wave of vicious white attacks against black veterans in the South, President Harry Truman created the President's Committee on Civil Rights (PCCR). The PCCR documented a wide range of civil rights abuses, primarily in the southern states. In its landmark 1947 report, "To Secure These Rights," the committee recommended a broad program of civil rights initiatives, including federal action.[11]

Although he did not adopt the committee's recommendations in their entirety, Truman did formulate a civil rights agenda of his own in February 1948. His program represented a bold departure from past Democratic practice. The president advocated a federal antilynching law, anti–poll tax legislation, the establishment of a permanent FEPC, and the prohibition of segregation in interstate transportation.[12] Reaction from the white South was immediate and angry. Many white southerners viewed these measures as the beginning of a general assault on segregation. One South Carolina man wrote to former secretary of state and fellow South Carolinian James F. Byrnes that "in the small towns it's fever hot. People are scared. One man told me that he was much more afraid of Truman than of Russia."[13]

Underlying the white southern response to Truman's initiatives were local political developments. Across the South, whites watched African Americans register to vote after the United States Supreme Court outlawed the white primary. After the ruling black registration jumped dramatically.[14] By 1946, nearly one hundred thousand black Georgians had registered to vote.[15] In neighboring South Carolina, African American voters doubled their registration figures from 1944 to 1948.[16]

South Carolina was, in addition, also home to the Progressive Democratic Party, arguably the most dynamic black political organization in the South at that time. Organized in 1944 and fiercely loyal to the national Democratic Party, the Progressive Democrats organized voter education schools and voter registration drives and justifiably claimed responsibility for the increase in black voter registration. Foreshadowing the Mississippi Freedom Democratic Party's attempt to be seated at the national convention in 1964, the Progressive Democrats sent delegations to the 1944 and 1948 Democratic National Conventions to challenge the seating of the state's all-white delegations.[17] Desperate to stifle these challenges from above and below and to recover their former prominence within national party ranks, a group of disgruntled southerners formed the States' Rights Democratic Party in 1948. The states' rights revolt began in earnest following a pro–civil rights speech by Truman and exploded following Truman's nomination at the Democratic National Convention in mid-July. States' rights advocates assembled in Birmingham on July 17 and nominated Governors J. Strom Thurmond of South Carolina and Fielding Wright of Mississippi as their presidential and vice-presidential candidates. Running on a segregationist platform, the Dixiecrats aimed to capture the electoral votes of the South, and thereby prevent either major party candidate from winning a majority. This would throw the election into the House of Representatives, where Dixiecrats calculated that they had enough support to maintain the regional political and racial status quo.[18]

On the hustings and in private, Dixiecrats explained and understood their role within the Democratic Party in familial terms. William Workman, veteran South Carolina newsman and future Republican, referred to the Dixiecrat insurgency as "the States' Rights motion for divorce in the South's long marriage with the national Democratic party."[19] Arkansas governor, Dixiecrat Ben Laney, saw the national party's support for civil rights as a case of political infidelity, especially painful because "it came from our own people—our own family."[20]

Just as in a real marriage, the South expected certain things from its partner. Above all, white southerners demanded fidelity. Like a husband confronting an adulterous wife, white southern Democrats demanded that the national party choose between them and African Americans. Dixiecrats often described themselves in the role of cuckold. Senator James Eastland of Mississippi warned that Truman civil rights proposals threatened southern whites with political impotency.[21] In May 1948, Strom Thurmond argued that Truman dared to impose black civil rights in the South because he viewed the region as "weak," "foolish," and "meek."[22] Others portrayed the changing relationship between southern Democrats and the national party as a failed love affair. In one sexually charged cartoon, both the Democratic and Republican Party nominees seek to dance with an African American woman who seduces them with the votes she holds in her garter. The South, represented by a diminutive, donkey-faced old maid dressed in nineteenth-century garb, can only watch the seduction from the sidelines.[23]

Displaced as the father in the Democratic family, Dixiecrats likened themselves to unwanted children. Mississippi Dixiecrat J. Knox Huff declared that the Truman Democrats had "reduced the South . . . to the status of illegitimate children at a family reunion."[24] Employing the old southern metaphor for bastardy, William Workman added that the South had been treated as "the red-haired stepchild in national Democratic party affairs."[25] As they toyed with metaphors of subordination, some Dixiecrats went even further and depicted themselves in the position of African Americans. Inverting images of racial control used in the region to keep African Americans in their "place," Dixiecrats spoke of being slapped, gagged, choked, kidnapped, hog-tied, flogged, lynched, and stabbed by national party leaders.[26] Campaign literature often featured a drawing of a stabbing victim to illustrate the South's political dilemma. Sometimes the descriptions bordered on the grotesque. Mississippi congressman John Bell Williams declared that Truman "has seen fit to run a political dagger into our backs and now he is trying to drink our blood."[27]

Having described the betrayal of the national party in such violent terms, Dixiecrats spoke of their redress in the terms of personal honor and vengeance.[28] For Dixiecrats, resistance to civil rights and the federal government became a test of manhood. Although northerners expected the South to "crawl on its belly, submit and beg," white southerners declared they would not take this insult "lying down." "[W]e must be men," one white man insisted, "and not weaklings." Supporting the civil rights policies of the national party was unthinkable for "any red-blooded man," and failure to act on this betrayal would make white southerners "less than men."[29]

Strom Thurmond was particularly well suited to serve as point man in the states' rights crusade. The South Carolinian personified the gendered nature of the region's reactionary political culture. Thurmond won the governorship in 1946 campaigning as the powerful foe of a corrupt political ring. In South Carolina at this time, candidates traveled together from county to county, addressing raucous mass meetings that often stretched on for hours. Thurmond thrived on this type of political debate. Like many of his generation, Thurmond also used his veteran status to his

political advantage. During one gubernatorial speech, Thurmond compared the "scheming, conniving, selfish men" in the South Carolina political ring with the "scheming, conniving, selfish men" who had grabbed
power in Germany, Italy, and Japan. "I was willing to risk my life to stamp
out such gangs in Europe," Thurmond proclaimed. "I intend to devote my
future to wiping out the stench and stain with which the Barnwell ring has
smeared the Government of South Carolina for, lo, these many years."[30]

In 1948, Thurmond effectively combined a fighting spirit with a well-
known penchant for clean living, vigorous physical exercise, and pretty
women. In the gendered discourse of South Carolina politics, Thurmond—a bachelor—portrayed himself as a virile ladies' man. Whether
seen lounging on Myrtle Beach with two attractive companions, or be-
stowing a kiss on a local festival queen, the bachelor governor never shied
away from photo opportunities that accented his masculinity. Congressman William Jennings Bryan Dorn of Greenwood warned his sister
against taking a job in the governor's office. "[U]se your own judgment,"
Dorn advised. "Personally, I had rather you would stay out of Strom Thurmond's office, for your own good if for no other reason. His reputation
and fastness concerning women is nation-wide."[31] Thurmond's bachelor
days came to an end on November 7, 1947, when he married twenty-one-
year-old Jean Crouch of Elko, a former Azalea Festival queen and a secretary in the governor's office. The day before their wedding, the betrothed
governor posed in a handstand for a *Life* magazine photographer. The
caption read: "Virile Governor demonstrates his prowess in the mansion
yard before wedding.[32] In many ways, Strom Thurmond embodied white
southern men's complicated equation of regional political power and male
virility.

Linking together sex and civil rights, family and party, the Dixiecrats
demonstrated how the subversion of one hierarchy ultimately disrupted
the other. At the same time that white southerners contemplated the
Dixiecrats' separation from the Democratic Party, the South Carolina legislature debated whether to abolish the state's fifty-two-year ban on actual
marital divorce. The state's constitution, written in 1895, prohibited divorce. By 1947, South Carolina was the only state in the union that did not
permit couples to sever the bonds of matrimony. Attempts to repeal the
ban had been made in 1916, 1937, 1944, and 1945, but to no avail.[33]

This did not mean that South Carolinians did not divorce. Although
South Carolina did not grant divorces, there was no shortage of divorced
persons or those declared by the federal census as "married, spouse absent"
residing within her borders. Those wishing to seek a divorce simply
slipped across state lines and established a false residency claim in neighboring North Carolina or Georgia where divorces were legal. In 1947, the

General Assembly once again took up the question of divorce.[34] Shrewdly, supporters of divorce presented their plan as a way to strengthen the family. Persons who obtained divorces out of state on false residency information and who later remarried were considered adulterers by law. Any subsequent children that resulted from such a union were thus considered illegitimate, which often threw estates into question.[35] By legalizing divorce, lawmakers sought to bring the practice and law into line. John McMaster, co-author of the resolution, argued that "the sanctity of marriage, the legitimacy of children, and the possession of property" hung in the balance.[36]

In order to win conservative backing for the measure, lawmakers specified four sole grounds for divorce: adultery, desertion, habitual drunkenness, and physical cruelty. Despite strong support, the resolution encountered stiff opposition. Detractors saw any loosening of the bonds of matrimony as a further erosion of masculine privilege. "[Our wives back home] are bad enough now," one representative insisted, "and we had better not be giving them any ideas about divorce." The conservative *Charleston News and Courier* went further. Making a clear connection between "negro rule" and divorce, the paper reminded its readers that South Carolina's Reconstruction government had "repeated the state's . . . historic prohibition of divorces." "[W]hite people," the editors argued, were "for the sanctity of the family."[37] The paper clearly equated broken families with race, and noted that if the divorce amendment were approved, "[d]ivorces in the negro population . . . in the state, will be especially numerous."[38] The protests of the *News and Courier* reveal that whites believed divorce and broken families to be a black condition. Despite the efforts of the Charleston paper, the joint session of the General Assembly approved the resolution in late March 1947. Voters approved the referendum the following year, and Governor Thurmond signed the divorce bill into law in April 1949.[39]

White South Carolinians' concerns about political, racial, and gender hierarchies converged in 1947 and 1948 during the furor over the case of Federal District Court Judge J. Waties Waring of Charleston. In *Elmore v. Rice* (1947) and *Brown v. Baskin* (1948), Judge Waring followed the Supreme Court's precedent in *Smith v. Allwright* and ruled South Carolina's white primary unconstitutional. These actions made Waring a target of abuse and prompted several unsuccessful attempts at impeachment.[40] Waring's personal life fueled the attacks: Judge Waring was divorced. In 1945, his first wife, a Charleston blueblood, obtained a divorce in Florida at her husband's request. A little more than a week later, Waring married Elizabeth Avery, a northern-born divorcee fifteen years his junior. Soon, the Warings were estranged from Charleston society, although it is unclear whether they shunned official society or were themselves ostracized. What is clear is that by the late 1940s, the Warings had become convenient objects of abuse.

Whites attacked the judge's voting rights decisions and railed against Elizabeth Waring's support for civil rights. On January 16, 1950, she addressed the Charleston Negro YWCA and condemned what she saw as the collective social psychoses of white southerners. Southern whites, she believed, were "sick, confused and decadent people . . . full of pride and complacency, introverted, morally weak and low," while black southerners were "building and creating."[41] Mrs. Waring's comments set off a torrent of protest. The Warings told a reporter for *Collier's* that they received obscene phone calls every few minutes for nearly two weeks following her speech.[42] From then on, the Warings suffered endless harassment and abuse in public and in private. Elizabeth Waring's 1950 YWCA speech gave new impetus to the impeachment drive against her husband. Back home in Charleston, Judge and Mrs. Waring received hate mail and harassing phone calls, and their Meeting Street home was vandalized.

In their public and private harangues against the Warings, South Carolinians conflated the couple's divorce and support for civil rights, the breakdown of marriage and male authority, and the collapse of Jim Crow. To many, the Warings' propensity to challenge and undermine the racial status quo was directly linked to the couple's willingness to subvert tradition gender and marital relations.[43] Some claimed Judge Waring's voting rights decisions were a vengeful response to the social ostracism he suffered following his divorce and remarriage. Shunned by polite society, some white South Carolinians reasoned, the judge took out his vendetta by corrupting the all-white primary. "Why did you wait until you took on this second wife before you suddenly became mad at all white people?" an irate letter writer asked. "Did not this course of action [voting rights decisions] occur to you while married previously? Of course it didn't."[44] As this last remark indicates, some white South Carolinians viewed the social compact as composed of interconnecting and naturalized racial and gender components. Many white South Carolinians depicted Waring's divorce as indicative of a more general revolt against hierarchy and morality. One writer characterized Waring's treatment of his first wife as sinful, claiming "[n]ow his sins has a grip on him and he can't shake it off."[45] Others frequently spoke of his "distorted personal life" and his "ungentlemanly" conduct.[46] A chief detractor declared that "a man who disposes of a woman to whom he had been married for 33 years, against her will, and takes another man's wife, whom he sent to Reno, Nevada to obtain a divorce in order that he might marry her himself, . . . and then returns to that State and sits on the bench and passes sentence on people, . . . is morally unfit to serve as Judge."[47]

In a barrage of mean-spirited, hateful letters, South Carolinians suggested that the couple acted the way they did because they were insufficiently manly and womanly. Many believed that Elizabeth Waring's civil rights advocacy cast both her and the judge outside the confines of traditional southern gender roles. By opening the door for black voters to enter whites' political home, and by allowing his wife to deliver civil rights speeches, the judge betrayed his impotency. Unable to control his outspoken wife, Waring became further emasculated. One woman wrote to the judge "to extend to you my profound sympathy in this hour of your humiliation."[48] Another woman admitted that while it was "very sweet" for a wife to mirror her husband's ideas, the opposite was unthinkable. According to this woman, the judge's support of his wife's civil rights advocacy was "revolting."

As for Mrs. Waring, letter writers portrayed her as a sexually dissatisfied home-wrecker unhappy with the legitimate domestic role of the conventional white wife. Some went so far as to suggest that she was black. In a poem written in black dialect, one writer contended that the judge was not "man" enough to satisfy Elizabeth Waring: "Dont let dat ol judge man keep you down too long. Comon up noth honey we'll show you plenty good times."[49] Most letter writers complained that her civil rights activity stemmed from her divorce and marriage to the judge, a union they considered illegitimate. More than one writer accused Mrs. Waring of having "stole" the judge "from his legal wife." One even referred to this alleged marital thievery as "a nigger trick."[50] Ultimately, therefore, attacks on the judge and his wife fused.

White South Carolinians' relationship to divorce—both in a real and a metaphoric sense—was never comfortable or simple. Indeed, many appear inconsistent when they advocate divorce as a means to recapture political potency and racial hegemony while simultaneously vilifying the divorced Judge Waring for his attacks on white supremacy. They drew sharp distinctions between divorce as a selfish and ungentlemanly act. But their seemingly contradictory feelings about divorce are perhaps less important than the link it provides between the public and private worlds of white southern men, a world in which shoring up traditional family hierarchies was critical to maintaining white supremacy. If divorce—political or actual—could serve that purpose, it was a necessary evil.

> Slap us down again, Pres., slap us down again
> Make us take some more Pres., we are mice, not men

During the 1948 campaign, Dixiecrat candidates crisscrossed the South, warning white voters of the dangers of supporting national Democratic Party nominee Harry S. Truman. Voicing his concern over the national party's civil rights platform, the increasing influence of black voters, and the corresponding decline in the power of white southern Democrats, one States' Rights Party backer wrote the song, "The Rebel Yell, 1948." This ditty, he told one southern congressman, was to be sung to the tune of "Slap Her Down Again, Pa!" a song about wife beating. In his revised version, white southern Democrats took the role of the battered wife.[51] Throughout the 1948 campaign, Dixiecrats utilized gendered images and metaphors of powerlessness to illustrate their fears over the threat that potential civil rights legislation and a burgeoning black voting public posed to white male political authority. By describing themselves as battered wives or as illegitimate children, Dixiecrats revealed the critical role that gender played in defending white supremacy in the post–World War II South. If they failed to thwart the political strivings of African Americans, white men worried that they would lose control over their own households. Nothing less than their identities as husbands and fathers were at stake in the battle. This scenario appeared to have come frighteningly to life in the person of Judge Waring, and these notions of patriarchal solidarity infused the debate over the divorce amendment. Perhaps the connections between race, gender, and states' rights advocacy were never so explicitly revealed as in a statement made by a Charleston Dixiecrat. Writing to Strom Thurmond in the wake of the 1948 election, Calvin Holmes declared that, "as a South Carolinian I am deeply interested in everything in South Carolina. As a man, I am deeply interested in States' Rights."[52]

NOTES

1. *McComb (Miss.) Enterprise-Journal*, 17 February 1948.

2. Two recent works which examine the gendered dimensions of southern political culture are Stephanie McCurry, *Masters of Small Worlds: Yeoman Households, Gender Relations, and the Political Culture of the Antebellum South Carolina Low Country* (New York: Oxford University Press, 1995); Laura F. Edwards, *Gendered Strife and Confusion: The Political Culture of Reconstruction* (Urbana: University of Illinois Press, 1997). Although this essay is concerned primarily with the 1948 presidential campaign and its immediate aftermath, it should be noted that the "official" States' Rights organization continued to exist as an organized political pressure group into the early 1950s.

3. For more information on postwar southern politics, see Numan V. Bartley, *The New South: 1945–1980* (Baton Rouge: Louisiana State University Press, 1995), and Bartley, *The Rise of Massive Resistance: Race and Politics in the South During the 1950s* (Baton Rouge: Louisiana State University Press, 1969); Robert A. Garson, *The Democratic Party and the Politics of Sectionalism, 1941–1948* (Baton Rouge: Louisiana State University Press, 1974); Earl Black, *Southern Governors and Civil Rights: Racial Segregation as a Campaign Issue in the Second Reconstruction* (Cambridge, Mass.: Harvard University Press, 1976); and Numan Bartley and Hugh D. Graham, *Southern Politics and the Second Reconstruction* (Baltimore: Johns Hopkins University Press, 1975). On the White Citizens' Councils, see Neil R. McMillen,

The White Citizens' Council Movement: Organized Resistance to the Second Reconstruction, 1954–1964 (Urbana: University of Illinois Press, 1971).

4. V. O. Key, Jr., Southern Politics in State and Nation (New York: Alfred A. Knopf, 1949), 3–12.

5. Monroe Lee Billington, The Political South in the Twentieth Century (New York: Scribner & Sons, 1975), 74; James T. Patterson, Congressional Conservatism and the New Deal: The Growth of the Conservative Coalition in Congress, 1933–1939 (Lexington: University of Kentucky Press, 1967), 75, 97–99.

6. Billington, The Political South, 76–77; Alexander P. Lamis, The Two-Party South (New York: Oxford University Press, 1984), 7. The economic appeal of the New Deal undermined the Republican loyalty of African American voters outside the South, and this shift of northern blacks to the Democratic Party occurred at the same time the black migration from the South was in full swing.

7. Jasper B. Shannon, "Presidential Politics in the South," Journal of Politics 10 (August 1948): 467.

8. George B. Tindall, The Emergence of the New South, 1913–1945 (Baton Rouge: Louisiana State University Press, 1967), 715.

9. James C. Cobb, The Most Southern Place on Earth: The Mississippi Delta and the Roots of Regional Identity (New York: Oxford University Press, 1994), 198.

10. Quoted in Cobb, Most Southern Place on Earth, 203.

11. President's Committee on Civil Rights, "To Secure These Rights": The Report of the President's Committee on Civil Rights (Washington, D.C.: Government Printing Office, 1947), 3–173.

12. New York Times, 3 February 1948. For more information on Truman's civil rights program, see William C. Berman, The Politics of Civil Rights in the Truman Administration (Columbus: Ohio State University Press, 1970). Also see "Memorandum for the President," confidential memo to president file, political file, box 23, Clark Clifford Papers, Harry Truman Library, Independence, Missouri.

13. For general southern reaction, see New York Times, 6 February 1948. M. F. Stack to James F. Byrnes, 6 February 1948, folder 701 (4), James F. Byrnes Papers, Special Collections, Clemson University Libraries, Clemson University, Clemson, South Carolina.

14. Smith v. Allwright, 321 U.S. 649 (1944); Key, Southern Politics, 619.

15. Numan V. Bartley, The Creation of Modern Georgia (Athens: University of Georgia Press, 1990), 201.

16. The State, 27 June 1950. The 1950 registration figure represents about 18 percent of eligible black voters. See Census of Population: 1950, Volume II, Characteristics of Population, Part 40: South Carolina (Washington, D.C.: Government Printing Office, 1952), 27.

17. For the creation of and challenges posed by the Progressive Democratic Party, see Kari Frederickson, "'Dual Actions, One for Each Race': The Campaign Against the Dixiecrats in South Carolina, 1948–1950," International Social Science Review 72 (spring 1997): 14–25. "Meeting of Progressive Democratic Party of South Carolina with Subcommittee of the Democratic National Committee, July 17, 1944" file, and "Proceedings of Credential Committees, Philadelphia, Pennsylvania, July 13, 1948" file, box 1, Democratic National Committee, Records of Meetings, 1944–1952, Democratic National Committee Papers, 1944–1952, Tru-

man Library. For information regarding increase in black voter registration in South Carolina, see *New York Times*, 12 August 1948; *The State*, 27 June 1948; and William P. Baskin, memorandum to South Carolina State Democratic Executive Committee, 11 February 1948, file L647, Edgar A. Brown Papers, 1888–1975, Special Collections, Clemson University Libraries.

18. For the Dixiecrats' strategy and campaign, see Robert A. Garson, *The Democratic Party and the Politics of Sectionalism* (Baton Rouge: Louisiana State University Press, 1974), 232–314; Bartley, *The New South*, 74–104.

19. "Ballot Trouble Caused by Dixiecrats Plagues Truman," *Charleston News and Courier*, 8 September 1948, newsclipping, Bound Volume 1948, p. 171, Workman Papers.

20. *Jackson Clarion-Ledger*, 9 May 1948.

21. *Jackson Clarion-Ledger*, 21 January 1948.

22. J. Strom Thurmond, speech before the States' Rights Democratic Convention, 10 May 1948, *States' Rights Information and Speaker's Handbook* (Jackson, Miss., 1948).

23. Cartoon, file 3241, gubernatorial series, Thurmond papers.

24. *Jackson Clarion-Ledger*, 9 March 1948.

25. "Rice Asks Uninstructed Delegates," *Charleston News and Courier*, newsclipping, 19 February 1948, p. 31; "Bethea Urges South Carolina Democratic Mass Meeting," unidentified newsclipping, 20 February 1948, p. 32; "Real Showdown Will Come in 1952," unidentified newsclipping, 6 August 1948, p. 136; all in Bound Volume 1948, Workman Papers.

26. For example, see *Charleston News and Courier*, 17 March 1948; *Greenville News*, 18 March 1948; *The State*, 11 May 1948; *Anderson Independent*, 10 February 1948.

27. John Bell Williams, speech transcript, 12 February 1948, States' Rights Scrapbook, Mississippi Department of Archives and History, Jackson, Mississippi.

28. For the concept of honor and its historical applications, see Edward L. Ayers, *Vengeance and Justice: Crime and Punishment in the Nineteenth-Century American South* (New York: Oxford University Press, 1984), and Bertram Wyatt-Brown, *Southern Honor: Ethics and Behavior in the Old South* (New York: Oxford University Press, 1982).

29. William D. Workman, "Take Their Stand in Dixie," *Charleston News and Courier*, newsclipping, 15 August 1948; "Jasper Resolution Declares Party Outrages the South," *Charleston News and Courier*, newsclipping, 22 February 1948; "Firm Stand By South for its Principles Urged by Warren," *Charleston News and Courier*, newsclipping, 17 March 1948; "Complete Abandonment of Primary may be Necessary," *Charleston News and Courier*, newsclipping, 10 August 1948, all in Bound Volume 1948, Workman Papers; *Charleston Evening Post*, 18 March 1948; *The State*, 11 May 1948; Strom Thurmond, speech, Wildwood, Florida, 6 September 1948, Speeches, General File, Subseries A, Thurmond Papers.

30. Thurmond quoted in Nadine Cohodas, *Strom Thurmond and the Politics of Southern Change* (New York: Simon & Schuster, 1993), 89.

31. William Jennings Bryan Dorn to Grace Dorn, 25 July 1947, correspondence file, box 23, Dorn Papers.

32. *Life* (17 November 1947), 44–46.

33. John Robert Miller, "A Study of the Change of Divorce Legislation in South Carolina" (Ph.D. diss., Florida State University, 1954), 61–65. See also Janet Hudson, "From Constitution to Constitution, 1868–1895: South Carolina's Unique Stand on Divorce," *South Carolina Historical Magazine* 98 (January 1997): 75–96.

34. *The State*, 30 January, 5 February, 5, 12, 13 March, 1947.

35. *The State*, 30 January 1947; Miller, "A Study of the Change of Divorce Legislation in South Carolina," 35, 61–65. Problems with property transmission to bastard children occurred when the father died intestate. See *Code of Laws of South Carolina*, 1942 (Clinton, S.C.: Jacobs Press, 1942), Volume 4, Part III, Domestic Relations and Property Rights, Title 39, Chapter 164, Article 1, 1029–33; Title 42, Chapter 174, 1201–1203; Title 42, Chapter 175, 1214–1215. The 1940 federal census reported over seventeen hundred families in which the male or female head of household was divorced. The census also indicated that some eighteen thousand families fell under the category in which the head of household was "married, spouse absent." This referred to that group "whose husbands or wives were not living in the same household at the time of the census. These two groups include married heads whose families had been broken by separation (often preceding divorce), immigrants whose husbands or wives are abroad, husbands or wives of persons enumerated as inmates of institutions, and other married heads whose usual place of residence is not the same as that of their husbands or wives, including soldiers, sailors, men in labor camps, etc., and their wives." *Sixteenth Census, 1940, Population and Housing: Families, General Characteristics* (Washington, D.C., Government Printing Office, 1943), 3, 61, 114.

36. *Rock Hill Evening Herald*, 4 February 1947; *The State*, 4 February 1947.

37. *Charleston News and Courier*, 16 March 1948.

38. *Charleston News and Courier*, 21 March 1947.

39. *The State*, 16 April 1949. Also see Leroy M. Want with William D. Workman, Jr., "Divorce—A South Carolina Problem," *South Carolina Magazine* (March 1949): 10, 21, 33–34. Concurrent with their debate over divorce machinery, legislators also considered legislation designed to insure more secure and stable marriages. In January 1949, legislation was introduced which would require a three-day waiting period and a sanity and venereal disease test for couples who wanted to marry. The existing law required only a twenty-four-hour waiting period. *The State*, 23 and 27 January, 1949. The bill's detractors opposed the legislation on the grounds that it would actually prevent marriages. Despite the best efforts of the bill's supporters, the marriage code remained unchanged throughout the 1950s. *Code of Laws of South Carolina*, 1952, Volume 2, Title 20, Chapters 1 and 2, Domestic Relations (Charlottesville, Va.: The Michie Press, 1952), 1079–1100; and *Code of Laws of South Carolina*, 1962, Volume 5, Title 20, Domestic Relations (Charlottesville, Va.: The Michie Co., 1962), 116–22.

40. John Egerton, *Speak Now Against the Day: The Generation before the Civil Rights Movement in the South* (New York: Alfred A. Knopf, 1994), 488.

41. *The State*, 17 January 1950. For more information on Judge Waring, see Tinsely E. Yarbrough, *A Passion for Justice: J. Waties Waring and Civil Rights* (New York: Oxford University Press, 1987).

42. Samuel Grafton, "Lonesomest Man in Town," *Collier's* (29 April 1950): 40.

43. In his recent book on the civil rights movement in the pre-*Brown* era, John Egerton poses the following questions regarding Judge Waring's fate: "Would white Charlestonians have acted more charitably toward Waties Waring if he had ruled against segregation but never divorced his first wife? Would they have ostracized him if he had divorced but not ruled? Would Waring have changed his mind about white supremacy if he hadn't married Elizabeth Avery? The questions are intriguing, but unanswerable." Egerton, *Speak Now Against the Day*, 593. I would argue that these questions are moot. Given the intense overlapping of southern gender and racial mores, one cannot take these as discreet questions.

44. C. C. Phillips to Judge Waring, 27 November [1950?], hate mail file, box 23, series C, Waring Papers.

45. Anonymous to Elizabeth Waring, 20 January 1950, hate mail file, box 23, series C, Judge Julius Waties Waring Papers, Moorland-Spingarn Research Center, Howard University, Washington, D.C.

46. See, for example, James F. Byrnes to Robert S. Allen, 28 October 1950, folder 1390, Byrnes Papers; William Jennings Bryan Dorn to Reverend Fritz C. Beach, 2 August 1948, folder 9, box 112, campaign series, personal papers; and anonymous typed testimonial (probably Dorn), n.d., correspondence file, box 23, public papers, William Jennings Bryan Dorn Papers, 1912–1988, Modern Political Collections, South Caroliniana Library, University of South Carolina, Columbia. Dorn was United States Congressman from Greenwood, South Carolina.

47. William Jennings Bryan Dorn to M. A. [Marion] Wright, 17 August 1948, file 17, box 112, campaign series, personal papers, Dorn Papers.

48. Lena Adams Deshilds to Judge Waring, 18 January 1950, hate mail file, box 23, series C, Waring Papers.

49. Anonymous to Elizabeth Waring, 18 January 1950, hate mail file, box 23, series C, Waring Papers.

50. Anonymous to Judge and Elizabeth Waring, 18 January 1950; Anonymous to Elizabeth Waring, January 1950; Elizabeth B. Munn to Elizabeth Waring, 18 January 1950, hate mail file, box 23, series C, Waring Papers.

51. "The Rebel Yell, 1948," in file 5, box 315, William Colmer Papers, McCain Library and Archives, Southern Mississippi University, Hattiesburg.

52. Calvin Holmes to J. Strom Thurmond, 30 December 1949, folder 3404, gubernatorial series, Thurmond Papers.

Dynamite and "The Silent South": A Story from the Second Reconstruction in South Carolina

"As a follower of Christ," Claudia Thomas Sanders wrote in 1957, "I believe that God is my Father and that all men are my brothers."[1] Even for a wealthy white daughter of South Carolina's low country aristocracy, these words spoke heresy in the last days of Jim Crow, sure to incite ostracism and reprisal. Generations of white dissenters had opposed racial orthodoxy in Dixie. Most of them were so meek that George Washington Cable's hopeful late-nineteenth-century term for them, "the silent South," retained its descriptive power even as it lost its optimistic intent. A handful of what Anthony Dunbar terms "radicals and prophets" always expressed their egalitarian convictions.[2] Lillian Smith, Jessie Daniel Ames, James Dombrowski, Myles Horton, Stetson Kennedy, H. L. Mitchell, Aubrey Williams, Carl and Anne Braden are but a few of the homegrown white radicals who took their stand in Jim Crow's Dixie.[3]

The liberal mainstream of white southern dissidents, however, appeared helpless even to speak, paralyzed by the domestic pressures of the Cold War and ensnared in what one South Carolina liberal called "a grip of fear that freezes the heart and paralyzes the mind."[4] For a few critical days after the United States Supreme Court's *Brown v. Board of Education* decision, southern liberals made halting gestures at leadership that John Egerton has characterized as "tiny shoots of new growth [that] heralded a false spring."[5] But neither *Brown* in 1954 nor the lynching of Emmett Till in 1955 nor the Montgomery bus boycott in 1955–56 sounded the firebell loudly enough to embolden the majority. From his Birmingham jail cell in 1963, Martin Luther King, Jr., sadly concluded that the greatest obstacle to racial justice was not the violence of white bigots "but the white moderate who is more devoted to 'order' than to justice."[6]

Even so, historians of the white liberal South have generally been as gracious as their subjects. Morton Sosna's 1977 *In Search of the Silent South* acknowledges the failings of an earlier generation of upper-class white southern liberals but reminds us that "they, too, had a dream."[7] David Chappell, in his *Inside Agitators: White Southerners in the Civil Rights Movement*, explains the role of white southern dissidents who undercut the segregationist assertion of a monolithic wall of massive resistance.[8] John

Egerton's monumental new study, *Speak Now Against the Day: The Generation Before the Civil Rights Movement in the South*, wisely directs our attention to the missed opportunities of the postwar era, especially the period just after World War II but also to the aforementioned "false spring" just after *Brown*.[9]

Why did long-suffering southern white liberals fail to make the most of such moments of possibility? What follows is a story—only one story, but perhaps an exceptionally telling one—which suggests a partial explanation: that the violent coercion that marked the everyday politics of race in the South and the slim chance of recruiting other supportive whites silenced most potential "race traitors." Behind the violence and hostility, moreover, lay an ever-present sexual politics that defined southern manhood and confined southern womanhood in an often unspoken but always present racial and sexual drama within every southern town.[10] In the life of Claudia Thomas Sanders of Gaffney, South Carolina, these tensions collided and exploded in ways that illuminate the historical knife-edge of sex caste and skin color in the postwar South.

Two postwar African American political landmarks—the victory of the NAACP in the *Brown v. Board* decision in 1954 and the triumph of the Montgomery bus boycott in 1955–56—heralded what C. Vann Woodward has called "the Second Reconstruction."[11] These monuments to African American political perseverance and discipline stood against a backdrop of often violent "massive resistance" by southern white supremacists.[12] In the uncertain years between Montgomery and the founding of the Student Nonviolent Coordinating Committee in 1960, white violence and political repression escalated sharply. The Southern Regional Council issued a report in 1959 which, though far from comprehensive, listed 530 specific instances of racially motivated reprisals in the South from 1955 to 1959: the toll included six African Americans killed; 29 persons—11 of them white—wounded by gunfire; 49 persons beaten or stabbed; 1 black man castrated; 30 homes and 7 churches bombed.[13] "The echo of shots and dynamite blasts," the editors of *The Southern Patriot* wrote in 1957, "has been almost continuous throughout the South."[14] Threats, floggings, gunfire, dynamite blasts, and the lynchings of Emmett Till and Mack Charles Parker seemed to rock all but the most determined civil rights insurgents back on their heels.[15]

White supremacy always had relied upon violence, especially in periods of crisis. In the 1950s, "black leaders forced whites to use violence," Charles Payne writes, "by refusing to yield to anything less."[16] Most of the black insurgents who persisted slept lightly and kept their guns close at hand. *The Eagle Eye: The Woman's Voice*, a black women's newsletter in Jackson, Mississippi, argued in 1955 that "the Negro must protect himself" because "no law enforcement body in ignorant Miss. will protect any

Negro who is a member of the NAACP" and warned "the white hoodlums who are now parading around the premises" of the publisher that the editors were "protected by armed guard."[17] Reverend Joseph A. Delaine, the Clarendon County, South Carolina, NAACP activist who defied reprisals to become one of the plaintiffs in the cases subsumed under *Brown v. Board*, blazed away at nightriders who attacked his home.[18] Amzie Moore, the indispensable 1950s forbearer of the SNCC activists who cracked Mississippi in the 1960s, carried a gun "like most politically active Blacks in the Delta," according to Payne. "His home was well armed, and at night the area around his house may have been the best-lit spot in Cleveland."[19] Medgar Evers, the first NAACP field secretary in Mississippi, Payne points out, "thought long and hard about the idea of Negroes engaging in guerilla warfare in the Delta" of the early 1950s. Evers "kept guns all over the house," and "seldom went anywhere without a rifle in the trunk of his car."[20] In 1957, Robert F. Williams and a group of African American veterans in Monroe, North Carolina, dispatched Ku Klux Klan marauders with a hail of disciplined gunfire and forced the Monroe city council to ban Klan motorcades.[21] "We have been compelled to employ private guards," Daisy Bates, the heroine of Little Rock, wrote to the United States attorney general after her house was bombed in 1959.[22] In a letter marked "NOT FOR PUBLICATION," NAACP executive secretary Roy Wilkins conceded to a friend in 1959 that "I know the thought of using violence has been much in the minds of Negroes."[23] Thus, in the years between the Montgomery bus boycott in 1955 to the Greensboro sit-ins in 1960, the nonviolence of the revolution in the South was more hypothetical than real. With the sit-ins, however, young black southerners launched an aggressive new phase of the black freedom crusade. "We the Union Army," black football players announced as they formed a flying wedge that broke through white hecklers to allow demonstrators to reach the Woolworth's lunch counter in Greensboro on the second day of the movement that would smash segregation.[24] The battalions of nonviolence not only overran segregation but eventually freed liberal white southerners to speak their minds.

Three years before the "Union army" took Woolworth's in Greensboro, late on Monday evening, November 18, 1957, a telephone rang at the Gaffney, South Carolina, home of Claudia Thomas Sanders and her husband, Dr. James H. Sanders. It had been a difficult autumn for the prominent white family. At the invitation of a group of white clergymen, Claudia Sanders had authored one of twelve essays for a pamphlet entitled *South Carolinians Speak: A Moderate Approach to Race Relations*. Her contribution, "This I Believe," made the Christian case for gradual compliance with the Supreme Court's ruling on school desegregation. "We must move *slowly* because we are dealing with human beings within a framework of democracy," Sanders closed her essay. "We must move *surely* because our social conscience and Christian ethics leave us no alternative." After the pamphlet appeared in late summer, hostile letters and threatening phone calls became common at the Sanders house. Dr. Sanders picked up the receiver that November night. Total silence greeted him—not the now-familiar snarl of "nigger lover" or "communist"—not even the click of a caller hanging up.[25]

A mile away, a telephone receiver swayed slowly on its cord in the booth outside Jennings Trading Post. "That is where we tied Mrs. Sanders' telephone up," a member of the Cherokee County Ku Klux Klan recalled. "Boyette called the Sanders home and when they answered, he did not say anything and then left the receiver off of the hook." Given 1950s telephone technology, this silenced the family's telephone line as effectively as if it had been cut. Luther E. Boyette, a thirty-two-year-old white textile worker, walked across the parking lot to his 1954 Oldsmobile and drove to a hilltop graveyard half a mile away. There Robert P. Martin and James Roy McCullough, both textile workers, climbed into Boyette's back seat. The twenty-five-year-old McCullough wedged a wooden nail keg between his feet. It held a homemade device whose main components were a dry cell battery, an alarm clock, and nine sticks of dynamite.[26]

Only a few hundred yards from the cemetery, on the corner of Rutledge Avenue and College Drive, magnolias and live oaks shaded the broad walkway to the stately Sanders home six blocks from the center of town. Gaffney was a county seat town in the Carolina Piedmont. About a quarter of its eight thousand inhabitants were African Americans. Cherokee County was largely agricultural but increasingly dependent on low-wage cotton mill jobs reserved for whites. Just south of the North Carolina state line, the county harbored a proud, hundred-year Ku Klux Klan tradition. J. G. Long of nearby Union, South Carolina—grandfather of the current state senator, John D. Long—had once led Cherokee County horsemen on the largest Ku Klux Klan raid in the history of the South.[27] In 1957, the Carolina Piedmont witnessed a Klan revival led by a charismatic former Baptist tent evangelist named James "Catfish" Cole. The Klan crusade coincided with the closure of several area textile mills, pushing almost five thousand white workers out of their jobs.[28]

Though unemployment in the late 1950s may have fed the Klan revival, black activism in the decades following World War II had already infused the nightrider legacy with new fervor. By the early 1950s, a confusing array of growing Klan groups were carrying out violent acts across the South. Dynamite became their favorite tool; according to a Southern Regional Council report, terrorists bombed the homes of forty black families in the region in 1951 and 1952, probably a substantial underestimate, given that there were eighteen such bombings in Miami, Florida, alone in 1951. These attacks culminated in the Christmas Day dynamite murder of Harry T. Moore, the head of the Florida NAACP and former superintendent of public education, killed along with his wife by Klan terrorists and local law enforcement officers.[29] In Gaffney, an African American grocer who declared his candidacy for the town council in 1952 withdrew after the hooded order issued repeated death threats. On the same day that the Gaffney Klavern packed their dynamite into the nail keg in Luther Boyette's back seat, Mr. and Mrs. Frank Clay, an African American couple in East Flat Rock, North Carolina, were shot and slashed to death in their home after a series of telephone threats; neighbors discovered their bodies after finding a cross smoldering in the front yard.[30] Two days after the dynamite exploded at the Sanders home, a smaller blast shattered windows at the homestead of Lewis Ford, a black tenant farmer who lived ten miles from Gaffney.[31]

Warnings from the Klan in the Carolina Piedmont were not idle threats in the 1950s, even when they targeted whites. In late 1956, Klansmen kidnapped a white high school band director in Camden, South Carolina, and beat him savagely with a piece of lumber. The following week, hooded terrorists shot another white South Carolinian in the chest after condemning his liberal racial attitudes.[32] A week earlier, Klan members hurled what the chief of police called "enough dynamite to blow the place to Kingdom Come" into the Temple Beth-el synagogue in Charlotte, North Carolina; the lives of the forty Jewish clubwomen inside were spared only because the lighted fuse fell out of the bomb.[33]

The imposing columns and wide porches of the Sanders home were almost within sight of Luther Boyette as he huddled with his accomplices. When the carload of Klansmen pulled up behind the house, the soft glow of a television set flickered on the window glass. "We circled the house one time," Martin recounted, "and we came back. We stopped just a little past the driveway. James Roy and myself got out of the car." Boyette wheeled the Oldsmobile around the block while McCullough and Martin performed their errand. "James Roy was carrying the keg," Martin claimed. "He carried it up and set it down beside the house." The alarm clock was set to go off at 2:30. It was now just past ten o'clock.[34]

The Sanders family presented unlikely martyrs in the struggle for racial equality in the South. Claudia Sanders was fifty-six years old, a short woman with brown hair and brown eyes, somewhat dark-skinned and rather pretty. "Her father was a well to do businessman and church and community leader," her son wrote later, "with a rigid Victorian personality. Her mother was the wife expected of such a man."[35] For many years, Colonel John P. Thomas of Charleston had chaired the Board of Visitors at the Citadel, perhaps the most hidebound institution in tradition-steeped South Carolina. His daughter's Carolina pedigree could not have been more proper. Claudia was "related to the Waring, Ravenel, Reeves, Witte, and Thomas families in the Lowcountry," the *Charleston News and Courier* reported, "and connected with many other South Carolina families."[36] Mrs. Sanders orchestrated the autumn bazaar at Gaffney's Episcopal Church of the Incarnation, labored in the ladies' auxiliary at the hospital, and served what the local society page called "dainty refreshments" to the Gaffney Home and Garden Club.[37] The closest she had ever come to "politics," most believed, was the Cherokee County Public Library Board. Called by one newspaper the "soft-spoken mother" of two grown children, recently a grandmother, a less likely insurrectionist would be hard to find. Claudia Sanders, a friend would declare at her funeral, was "a real Southern lady."[38]

Yet, if Claudia Thomas Sanders had been born to Charleston bluebloods, this had also been true of the abolitionist Grimke sisters a century earlier.[39] The oldest of five children, "Claude" grew up as "part mother, as well as big sister," to her younger siblings. As a kind of "family general," her son recalled, "she made decisions for her brothers and sisters, her children and her servants and she expected them followed." Her sister once turned to her at a family gathering and joked, "Claude, you *were* bossy when we were children. When we acted out Bible stories, you were Jezebel and you made me be the dog!"[40]

A graduate of elite Ashley Hall in Charleston, young Claudia Thomas attended Hollins College in Virginia, one of the premier women's academies in the South. Here anthropology and sociology fascinated her. After receiving her diploma, Claudia Thomas studied at New York's Columbia University in preparation for her brief career as a social worker in Charleston.[41] Perhaps it was at Columbia, away from Dixie for the first time, that she began to rethink the racial assumptions of her upbringing. Her passion for anthropology led her to Professors Franz Boas and Melville J. Herskovits, whose work battled the scientific racism prevalent in the early twentieth century.[42] Boas, a fixture at Columbia from 1899 to 1936, attracted many graduate students, including Zora Neale Hurston, with his groundbreaking ethnographic research and his considerable interest in "the homely life of the Southern Negro."[43] While at Columbia, Claudia pursued her intellectual and political interests but kept in touch with her family. In 1924, excited about the presidential election—only the second in which women across the nation were permitted to vote—she announced her intention to cast her historic ballot for Progressive Party candidate "Fighting Bob" LaFollette. Colonel Thomas, a staunch Bourbon Democrat, furious at his twenty-three-year-old daughter's intention to desert the party of her fathers, "saw to it that she didn't get an absentee ballot."[44]

Despite her fury at this paternal high-handedness, Claudia Thomas soon returned to Charleston as a professional social worker. Here she met and married James Henry Sanders, a handsome and affectionate medical intern three years her senior. After he had completed his internship, the couple moved "up state" to Gaffney where Dr. Sanders set up a family practice and bought the large white house at the corner of Rutledge Drive and College Avenue. Claudia bore two children, a boy and a girl, and ruled her household with a gracious but firm demeanor. Flexible and full of fun, Dr. Sanders provided an easy-going counterpoint to his wife's somewhat formal and sometimes prickly personality.

Far from playing the traditional southern patriarch, Dr. Sanders delighted in his wife's willful and occasionally authoritarian character. Once, after "Claude" had given the local barber firm instructions as to how she wanted her toddler son's hair cut, the barber replied, "Okay." Young Jimmy turned to the barber and told him, "My mother doesn't allow people to say 'okay' to her." Dr. Sanders would roar with laughter as he told and retold this story. Another time, the physician turned to his young son and said, "Jimmy, you know that your mother wants to cut down the chinaberry tree in the front yard and you know that I don't want it cut down. What do you think will happen to that tree?" When the youngster answered flatly, "They will cut it down," Dr. Sanders doubled over in loud peals of mirth.

Though the physician poked fun at his wife's sometimes imperious bearing, he respected her judgment and acknowledged her independence. The couple nominally belonged to the Baptist Church and sent the children to Sunday School there. Mrs. Sanders, however, confined her own church activity to the women's organizations of the local Episcopal church. Reserved by nature, intellectual in her outlook, she remained leery of effusive religiosity. When twelve-year-old Jimmy Sanders, after attending a revival meeting, declared his intention to be baptized the following night, his mother asked him why. "I told her that a lot of my friends were joining and I wanted to join with them," he recalled. "She quietly told me that was not a good reason to join the church. After the revival was over, if I still wanted to join she would be happy for me to do so, but that she would not allow me to join during the revival."[45]

Though she had returned to the Bible Belt South to raise her family, Claudia brought with her the world of ideas that she had found at Columbia. The leisure with which she continued to pursue her intellectual life rested at least in part upon the abundance of affordable African American domestic labor. "Mrs. Sanders, you should have been a lady lawyer," the family's black housekeeper delighted Claudia by telling her. "You is always studying your mind!"[46] Active in the American Association of University Women, she hosted a regular discussion group made up of faculty members at nearby Limestone College. At least one participant was a socialist and another advocated "progressive education." Mrs. Sanders read ardently in her spare moments and saw to it that her children were well informed. "My mother read *everything*," her son remembered. She and her husband not only encouraged their children to read, but to think critically about social issues. "They would quietly give me some idea about what they thought," he recalled, "see that I had something to read that gave both sides of an issue and let me decide for myself." Both parents, however, made it unequivocally clear to their children that racial discrimination was wrong.[47]

Tall and heavy-set, courtly but playful in his manner, Dr. Sanders was long on decency but short on dissent. Open-minded to a point that he considered a fault, Dr. Sanders liked to say that the problem with the world was that there were "too many people on the fence—like me." It was good to be able to see all sides to a question, he conceded, but unwavering activists were the ones who made history. Though liberal in his politics, the fifty-nine-year-old doctor advocated "states rights" and defended South Carolina's prerogative to impose a poll tax, even though opposition to the poll tax had long been the one unifying issue for white southern liberals.[48] "He was in favor of more rights for blacks," his son later recalled, "but he was afraid of the federal government taking over too much." Some months before the dynamite bomb ticked beneath his window, Dr. Sanders had suggested to fellow board members at the local hospital that staff members should use the titles "Mr." and "Mrs." when addressing "Negro" patients.[49] Failure to extend this courtesy, he observed, could wound the patient's self-esteem and impair recovery. Voted down by the committee, Dr. Sanders made no further protest. "Quietly, sometimes effectively and sometimes not," his son recalled, "he did what he felt like he could."[50]

In writing her essay, Claudia Sanders joined Episcopal Church "moderates" in an effort to soften segregation. Their adversaries within the denomination characterized these efforts as "the organized, church-financed drive of integrationists within the church to promote the physical mixing of the races."[51] In the 1950s, most white churches in South Carolina edged close to the position that white supremacy was the will of God; one of the state's most prominent churchmen argued that any effort to question segregation was "to mock God," that so-called "moderation" on the race issue was "a compromise with sin," and southerners who advocated integration were "condemning God."[52] Perhaps this view, too, was "moderate" compared to those of Christians in the Mississippi White Citizen's Council, whose children's literature reportedly assured the little ones that heaven would be segregated.[53] In any case, even though conservative Episcopalians organized to prohibit interracial discussion groups or parish human relations councils, a tiny minority of ministers and lay persons began quietly to employ their own interpretation of the Christian tradition to advocate generosity, if not justice, for "the Negro."[54] In the summer of 1957, five Episcopal clergymen solicited essays from a dozen prominent citizens whose views would "steer a course between the excesses of the White Citizens Councils on the one hand and extreme actions of the NAACP on the other."[55] At the recommendation of her local minister, Reverend John B. Morris met with Claudia Sanders and asked her to contribute to *South Carolinians Speak*. This was why Sanders penned her first and only public statement about racial matters, "This I Believe."[56]

Opinions expressed in the twelve essays ranged from those who considered integration "the worst thing that could befall the people of this section" to those who regarded it as an arduous Christian duty. The editors voiced their solicitude for "communication between the two races," but chose an all-white cast of contributors. The central concern of *South Carolinians Speak* was "the right of the individual to freedom of thought, opinion and speech." A new generation of fire-eaters alarmed by the *Brown* decision, said the ministers, sought to "require all South Carolinians to subscribe to their point of view or be ostracized from the community."[57] Guarded though it was, *South Carolinians Speak* represented a voice for civility and an attempt to expand and control the range of acceptable opinion among "moderate" whites.

The real flashpoint of segregationist ferocity was the fear that less rigid racial barriers would open the way to sexual involvement between black men and white women. "We can talk about it all we want to—justice, equality, all that sort of thing, talking," one white Carolinian said to Wilma Dykeman and James Stokely in 1957, "but when it comes right down to it, that's what it's all about: a nigger a-marrying your sister or your daughter."[58] The essayists in *South Carolinians Speak* knew that arguments for "moderation" flew against this gale of sexual fears and therefore almost all of their essays sought to calm the storm over "social equality." John C. Barrington of Dillon, South Carolina, asserted that it "doesn't make sense to claim that removal of legal segregation will mean interracial marriages as is so often expressed in the question, 'Would you want your daughter to marry a Negro?'" Arthur L. King of Georgetown took the same tack, arguing that "the use of Negroes as domestic servants and particularly in relationship to the white children" made the "race-mixing" bombast "too absurd to command the respect of intelligent citizens." Claudia Sanders herself noted that proximity and equality were not the same thing; many white children already attended school among social inferiors of their own race, she pointed out, but this hardly "dooms them to marriages with different backgrounds, different ideals, different ideas of cleanliness and antagonistic religious concepts." A. M. Secrest from Cheraw reassured white readers that segregation by "ability" and "scholastic preparation" could "play a large role in maintaining—for the most part—a de facto segregated school system for years to come." Where these measures did not entirely screen out African American students, Secrest suggested that "school districts may find it wise to separate students according to sex." If Gunnar Myrdal exaggerated in his claim that sex was "the principle around which the whole structure of segregation of the Negroes . . . [was] organized," one cannot prove it by the writings in *South Carolinians Speak*.[59]

"The response of South Carolinians to this book," Reverend John Morris, an Episcopal priest who served as one of the editors, wrote in his summation of the project, "has been overwhelmingly positive."[60] More than a decade later, contributor A. M. Secrest continued to claim that the episode reflected "some vitality in the democratic process in South Carolina."[61] These assessments reflected either self-deception or political discretion: they could hardly have been further from the truth. The best evidence that *South Carolinians Speak* failed to create any discernible political space for "moderation" is that white South Carolina continued to brook no dissent from its coerced consensus of white supremacy.[62]

Several months before the five Episcopalian ministers published the collection of essays, the prospectus for the pamphlet somehow made its way to the desk of Governor George Bell Timmerman, Jr. A grim and vindictive figure who had vowed that "not in a thousand years will the schools of South Carolina be integrated," Timmerman leaked the prospectus to the press in an effort to sabotage the project.[63] All five of the ministers who sponsored the pamphlet soon left their pulpits, joining the ranks of what one wag called the "displaced parsons" of the South.[64] Reverend Larry A. Jackson of Florence hastily accepted a missionary pastorate in Santiago, Chile. Several of the essayists suffered harsh treatment from their friends, family, and fellow citizens. But the Sanders family were the only ones to whom the voice of retribution thundered with dynamite.[65]

To target Claudia Sanders for death by dynamite reflected a peculiar Jim Crow logic. Pretenses of chivalry for "white womanhood" provided the common thread in Ku Klux Klan justifications of racial terrorism. With her essay, Sanders joined a growing number of southern white women whose words and actions betrayed this line of argument. In Charlotte, North Carolina, about forty miles north of Gaffney, a white woman named Nettie Fowler decided in 1957 to begin admitting African Americans to the drive-in movie theater that she owned and operated. Three days before Christmas, arsonists torched her barn and three trucks. A few days later, the terrorists returned with dynamite and blasted Fowler's theater marquee to bits.[66] "Increasingly throughout the South," one journalist observed in 1958, "quietly and usually without fuss, white women—and more particularly white churchwomen—are lining up on the side of desegregation."[67] Anne Braden, whose Louisville, Kentucky, home was dynamited by white supremacists in 1954, felt certain that this was true. "In fact," the veteran activist wrote to a friend in 1959, "all my experience in the integration movement has led me to the firm conviction that the most dedicated and devoted people are women; this applies to both Negro and white women." Not only that, Braden continued, but "we run into so many situations where women are held back from taking the position they want to take by husbands or other poor excuses of the male of the species that I often get to the point where I think if we could just get rid of all the men this problem would be solved overnight."[68]

The "surprising number of women" that the *Gaffney Ledger* reported at a Ku Klux Klan rally the summer before the attack on Claudia Sanders may undermine Braden's assertion to some extent.[69] Nor did upper-class white women always rise above race-baiting as they pursued their own vision of reform. Pleading before the state Judiciary Committee in 1958, delegates of the South Carolina State Women's Clubs suggested that white women were far more qualified to sit on juries than their racial "inferiors," male or female. "As it is now," Sara Livermore told the committee, "I cannot help but feel that the Negro permitted to sit on the jury is more a citizen than I am."[70]

White women in the South, Jacquelyn Dowd Hall writes, "were viewed collectively as the repositories of white racial legitimacy."[71] The protection of white womanhood, "wrought with the crimson that swooned in the rose's ruby heart, and the snow that gleams on the lily's petal," to quote one practitioner of the classic form, provided the central if shopworn justification for white supremacy.[72] A white woman's critique therefore represented a unique threat to Jim Crow. The challenge mounted when it came from a woman of Claudia Sanders' social stature and intellectual ability. Her essay was not only the most "extreme" but the most effective of the twelve included in *South Carolinians Speak*. "This I Believe" mixed literary polish with moral passion. It did not lapse into self-righteousness. Stressing her own "stumbling blocks" of prejudice and the importance of teaching children "that politeness and good manners are for use towards all people," Sanders suggested that "[g]radual desegregation in the schools accomplished by starting with the first grades would seem logical."[73]

Her words were measured and calm, but Sanders had addressed them to a white South reeling from deep racial fears and historically resonant furies. *South Carolinians Speak* appeared on newsstands only a week after President Eisenhower dispatched troops to Little Rock on September 25. This echo of Reconstruction-era federal intervention fanned South Carolina segregationists to white-hot ferocity.[74] A luncheon speaker at the Gaffney Chamber of Commerce, momentarily forgetting two world wars and the Great Depression, referred to "the invasion of Little Rock" as "the worst tragedy in this nation's history in the past hundred years."[75]

"Southerners will not quail in the face of bloodshed if bayonets are directed against them," the *Anderson (South Carolina) Independent* crowed several days before Eisenhower ordered units of the 101st Airborne to Little Rock.[76] After the paratroopers arrived, South Carolina state senator John D. Long—whose grandfather had supervised the lynching of at least eight black men—announced his county delegation's purchase of nine new Browning submachine guns to beat back "any invasion of federal troops."[77] Thomas Waring of the *News and Courier* favored a new secession movement. "All unions are not eternal," he declared. Waring envisioned the day when white citizens would be "fashioning homemade gasoline bombs to hurl at federal troops." The editor justified violent resistance by white southerners because "their only crime is protection of their children and the white man's civilization."[78] C. Vann Woodward writes of the late 1950s in the South: "Words began to shift their significance and lose their common meaning. 'Moderate' became a man who dared open his mouth, an 'extremist' one who favored eventual compliance with the law, and 'compliance' took on the connotations of treason."[79]

The bomb among the flower bulbs and boxwoods outside the Sanders home had been constructed on Sunday afternoon at the Ku Klux Klan headquarters three miles east of Gaffney. James Roy McCullough had brought the dynamite, an alarm clock, a battery, and an electric soldering iron to the "Klavern" in a suitcase. Robert Martin, thirty-five, the father of four small children, provided two electrical blasting caps. The men nestled the explosive charge in the bottom of the nail keg and covered it with nearly two feet of dirt and brick scraps from the yard of the house. The Klansmen placed the battery and the time clock, wired to the dynamite below, at the top of the keg so that the men could easily connect the wires when they planted the device; in this way, they could avoid riding around with a "cocked" bomb in the car. "James McCullough told me they were preparing this time bomb for Dr. Sanders' home," Martin told police later, "because Mrs. Sanders wrote an article in a book about the mixing of the races."[80]

Nine sticks of dynamite, packed in this fashion and properly placed, possessed enough force to demolish the house and kill everyone inside. At 10:25 Monday night, however, moments after Luther Boyette's Oldsmobile raced away, the bomb in the flowerbed stopped ticking. A paper-thin enamel coating on the alarm clock, unnoticed by the bombers, prevented the batteries from igniting the blasting caps. All day Tuesday the nail keg sat unnoticed amid the shrubbery.[81] And yet the murderous plot continued. "The next morning I figured the bomb did not go off," Martin said. "I called Luther Boyette on the telephone, and he said that McCullough was coming down to see me. By the time I had hung up he was there."

While Boyette attended a Klan council in nearby Blacksburg, his accomplices spent the day preparing a second assault on the Sanders family.[82] They planned to toss a smaller bundle of dynamite near enough to the nail keg to set off the original bomb.[83]

In the early evening, Martin and McCullough drove to the farmhouse of John E. Painter, Jr., thirty, another member of the Gaffney Klavern. "We blew the horn and Junior Painter come out," Martin recounted. "We told him we wanted him to come with us and to get some dynamite." Painter went to his garage and unearthed more than a hundred sticks of dynamite, pulled three from the sawdust in the crate and buried the rest back in the dirt floor. Walking to his chicken house, Painter slipped a dynamite cap from its hiding place and climbed into the car with his two friends. Stopping by McCullough's house to obtain a length of fuse and some tape, the men attached the cap and an 18-inch fuse to one of the three sticks of dynamite and taped the bundle tightly.[84]

"We drove from McCullough's house to the Sanders' house," Martin reported. "I was in the front seat." After the car had circled the house once, Martin rolled down his window and reached across the seat with the dynamite. "Junior lit the fuse with a match," said Martin. "I threw it from the car out into the yard." The bundle flew about thirty feet and rolled right up against the brick foundation of the house, almost touching the nail keg. The three men raced away into the darkness. Listening intently for the explosion, they heard only silence. The "invisible empire" struck out again; the fuse had somehow misfired.[85]

Inside the house, family members were oblivious to their peril. Claudia chatted and did chores with her sister, Charlotte McLaughlin of Louisville, Kentucky, who was visiting for a few days. Charlotte's husband Carl watched television while the two sisters washed the supper dishes and folded the laundry. Dr. Sanders had gone out on his second house call of the evening. Returning about ten o'clock, he joined his brother-in-law in front of the TV set to watch "The $64,000 Question."[86] Sometime after nine, Luther Boyette had returned from Blacksburg to check on his bombing crew. He drove to Robert Martin's house alone and took him for a ride in the Oldsmobile. "He asked me if we had done any good," Martin reported without apparent irony, "I told him no." Boyette was determined to try again; since McCullough was working the graveyard shift at the mill, Boyette told Martin, the men would enlist the help of Boyette's brother-in-law, Cletus Sparks. "We drove by Cletus Sparks' house and got him to go with us," Robert recalled. "Boyette already had three sticks of dynamite in a paper sack and already fixed up."[87]

Like his co-conspirators, twenty-four-year-old Cletus Sparks was a textile worker and a member of the Independent Klan. "Me and Cletus was in the back seat and Boyette was driving," Martin said. "We went back to the Sanders home." Sparks struck a match and lit the fuse. This time, Martin jumped out of the car and hurled the dynamite bundle toward the house. It was less than a perfect throw, landing beside the chimney several yards from the original bomb. As Martin clambered into the front seat beside Boyette, the Oldsmobile roared off into the night.[88]

Ninety seconds later, as the Klansmen raced down Chandler Road, they heard the explosion. So did people for miles around. Deafened and stunned, jolted from their chairs, the two husbands imagined for an instant that the TV set somehow had exploded in their faces. Mrs. Sanders kept her composure, but her husband dashed out into the huge cloud of smoke billowing around the house. "I didn't realize how serious it was," he told reporters, "until I went outside and saw the yard filled with smoke." Plaster dust and splinters rained from a gaping hole near the chimney. Broken glass drizzled like sleet. Waving his way through the smoke and the dust, Dr. Sanders saw no one but found a large crater in the earth just beside the chimney. Next to the foundation of the house he found a tightly taped bundle of unexploded dynamite with a charred fuse attached. Claudia summoned the police. Her husband's first words to the investigators reveal the central reality of racial politics in the South of the late 1950s: "We had been expecting something like this," Dr. Sanders told the officers.[89]

It was the chief of police, William Hill, who discovered the original nail keg bomb and ordered everyone away from the house. Someone remembered that R. H. Hines, an explosives engineer from Oklahoma, was visiting Gaffney on behalf of Western Pipeline Construction Company. Hines disarmed the makeshift bomb. He told officers that the exploded dynamite had been ignited with a match rather than a battery; there had been three separate attacks. By the next morning, the South Carolina Law Enforcement Division and the Federal Bureau of Investigation had joined local officers in an effort to locate the would-be assassins.[90]

Editorial reaction from South Carolina's flagship dailies ran full-sail with the prevailing bluster of white opinion. Neither *The State* in Columbia nor the *News and Courier* in Charleston expressed any sympathy for the views or the persons of the victims. Both editorial staffs managed to restrain the high-flown fervor with which they customarily crowed for individual liberty; the effects of terrorism on freedom of speech went almost unmentioned. If the culprits could not be punished, *The State* averred, "at least let's hope there will be no recurrence of this type of crime." Both papers ran small, muted disavowals of violence beneath glowering segregationist lead editorials. "Dynamite is not the way to solve social problems," the editors of *The State* objected faintly, making it clear that Claudia Sanders, not Luther Boyette and his bombers, represented the "social problem" in question.[91]

The primary concern was that such unruly methods might endanger Jim Crow. "Every citizen of South Carolina who believes in maintaining racial segregation," the *Greenville News* opined, should be "shocked and angry" at the bombing. "[Segregation] is not so weak that it cannot stand full examination and thorough debate." The violence, some pointed out, could provoke and mislead outsiders. "If there is *much more* blasting of this kind in South Carolina the whole thing will wind up with this state on the losing end of things," *The State* lamented. "It's the kind of incident that invites criticism, interference, and condemnation." The *News and Courier* blamed the "disorder" on "tension and pressure from outside," an intriguing allegation in light of Claudia Thomas Sanders' impeccable lowcountry lineage. The strongest rebuke that the fiery editor Waring could muster was that the bombings "have a suggestion of racial tension about them that is disquieting to law-abiding persons of all shades of opinion."[92] A Charleston reader condemned the newspaper's response as "an excuse, a justification, an alibi" for the bombing. "Anyone disagreeing with these self-constituted judges," she explained, "runs the risk of having dynamite set off under his house."[93]

Evidence from the Gaffney bombing led straight to what one observer termed "the bedsheet brigadiers who haunt the upper part of the state."[94] Seventeen days after the bombing, the South Carolina Law Enforcement Division arrested Luther E. Boyette, Robert P. Martin, James Roy McCullough, Cletus H. Sparks, and John E. Painter, all of the men who had taken direct part in the attacks. State investigators discovered ninety-six sticks of dynamite still buried in Junior Painter's garage, the box of caps hidden in his chicken coop, and a stack of Klan literature—"The Kloran of the Independent Knights of the Ku Klux Klan"—in the house. A black notebook found in the trunk of Luther Boyette's car contained minutes of Klan meetings and a list of local members, including the names of the accused. The unexploded dynamite found outside the Sanders home and in Painter's garage matched perfectly. Fuses found at both sites were cut in the same distinctive style. The FBI crime lab established that soil found in the nail keg bomb came from the yard of the Ku Klux Klan meeting house.[95]

Detectives could see that the evidential case against the Klansmen was solid. But there was more. During the search of his house, James Roy McCullough asked agent Earl Collins of the South Carolina Law Enforcement Division what kind of sentence he could expect if he were to "admit the whole thing and tell the truth." Beating McCullough to the punch, however, was his Klavern colleague Robert Martin. Immediately after his arrest on December 6, Martin rode to the state capitol at Columbia with investigators and wrote out a detailed, signed confession implicating himself and all of his compatriots. "I have been sick and worried to death ever since [the bombing] happened," he told police. "I feel better now since I have told the truth." The following day, the state released each of the men on $5,000 bond. Martin apparently expected his revelations to state investigators to remain confidential.[96]

Martin and the four men he had implicated made no effort to mask their connection to the Ku Klux Klan. The accused all spoke at a Klan rally in the Lonesome Pine Rodeo Grounds just north of Gaffney on January 11, five weeks after Martin's confession. Hooded, robed Klansmen passed through the crowd collecting money for a defense fund and distributing fliers entitled "She Played With Dynamite," the text of which was a reprinted editorial from a newspaper in nearby Spartanburg. A crowd of about three hundred, two dozen in full Klan regalia, cheered a showing of D.W. Griffith's classic film tribute to the Reconstruction-era Klan, *Birth of a Nation*. "We do not wish Mrs. James H. Sanders any harm," bellowed the orange-robed Grand Dragon of the South Carolina Independent Knights of the Ku Klux Klan to the crowd. "If we could, we would send her back to Africa so she would be with her nigger friends!"[97]

Confession, good for the soul, has an uncanny way of presaging fatal mishaps for the body. Among groups such as the Ku Klux Klan, who live by violence and operate under blood oaths of secrecy, this phenomenon is more pronounced. And so it happened that a few weeks after his confession but before the trial of the Gaffney bombing crew, Robert Martin suffered a tragic, fatal accident. In a two-inch story buried on page 7-B, *The State* reported that an automobile under which Robert Martin was working had fallen and crushed him to death when the jack had given way. "Details of the death were lacking," the newspaper stated. Apparently, none of the other major dailies in South Carolina felt that the mysterious violent death of the sole state's witness in a notorious terrorism trial was newsworthy. "Everybody here pretty much considered it to be a murder," a long-term Gaffney native and local historian recalled. The funeral was set for four o'clock the following Saturday. "Active pall bearers," according to the funeral announcement in the *Gaffney Ledger*, included "Luther E. Boyette, James R. McCullough, Cletus Sparks, and Junior Painter."[98]

On June 30, magistrate I. B. Kendrick ruled the deceased Martin's signed confession inadmissible and dismissed all charges against Luther Boyette and Cletus Sparks. Though the confession had been witnessed by eight police officers and notarized, Robert Martin's death rendered his account of the bombing legal "hearsay." The court also maintained that the Klan membership lists and minutes of meetings found in Boyette's car could not be admitted as evidence. "The state failed to produce any evidence connecting Mr. Boyette and Mr. Sparks with the dynamiting," the magistrate stated. Kendrick bound over the cases of Junior Painter and James Roy McCullough for grand jury assessment of the charges against them. Prosecutor J. Allen Lambright, meanwhile, in a strangely self-defeating move, publicly disparaged the strong physical evidence as "circumstantial" and claimed that his case against the remaining defendants was weak. "I'll have to get together with the State Law Enforcement Division to see what we can do with them," he shrugged.[99]

State Senator John D. Long, who only a month earlier had spent tax money to purchase machine guns to defend his home county from the United States government, represented Painter and McCullough at the trial. The attorney objected strenuously and successfully to any courtroom reference to the Ku Klux Klan and to the admission into evidence of the many written death threats against the Sanders family. So confident was the defense that Senator Long did not call a single witness. Prosecutor Lambright, meanwhile, admitted before the court that the article written by Claudia Sanders "is what caused all this trouble, there isn't any doubt in my mind about that." Lambright even declared his own willingness "to join some organization to preserve the integrity and the segregation of the white race in South Carolina." His only argument with the defendants, the prosecutor argued, was that he "would never dynamite and endanger the lives of innocent people." Apparently Lambright did not mention to the jury that he himself had recently received a scrawled, two-word letter from the Ku Klux Klan—"You're next"—nor is it possible to say with certainty how this message may have affected his handling of the case.[100] The twelve white men of the jury, all citizens of Gaffney or the surrounding area, acquitted the defendants after two and a half hours of deliberation.[101]

Claudia Sanders took an extended vacation in Canada during the trial. No one could blame her for leaving. All of her friends in Gaffney had deserted her. Several members of her extended family had taken pains to let her know that they thought her either wrong-headed or foolish. People she had known all of her life no longer spoke to her. None of the major newspapers in her native Palmetto State defended her right to freedom of speech with any vigor. Her hometown paper featured Ku Klux Klan announcements on the front page, even after the bombing. No public figure of any stature uttered one public word against either the attempt to kill Claudia Sanders and her family or the acquittal of their assailants. The silence was louder than dynamite.

ACKNOWLEDGMENTS

I would like to thank Dan T. Carter, David S. Cecelski, John Cell, William H. Chafe, Raymond Gavins, Glenda Elizabeth Gilmore, Christina Greene, Nancy Hewitt, Perri Anne Morgan, Sydney Nathans, Anne Firor Scott, John Herd Thompson, William L. Van Deberg, and Peter H.

Wood for their helpful readings of various drafts of this essay. I am also especially grateful to Dr. James H. Sanders, Jr., Mrs. Gloria Sanders, and Mrs. Ann Sanders Campbell for sharing family documents, letters, and photographs.

NOTES

1. Ralph E. Cousins et al., *South Carolinians Speak: A Moderate Approach to Race Relations* (Dillon, South Carolina: 1957), 70.

2. Anthony Dunbar, *Against the Grain: Southern Radicals and Prophets, 1929–1959* (Charlottesville: University Press of Virginia, 1981).

3. Jacquelyn Dowd Hall, *Revolt Against Chivalry: Jessie Daniel Ames and the Women's Campaign Against Lynching* (New York: Columbia University Press, 1993, revised edition); Lillian Smith, *Killers of the Dream* (New York: W. W. Norton and Co., 1949); Frank Adams, *Unearthing Seeds of Fire: The Idea of Highlander* (Winston-Salem: John F. Blair, 1975); Stetson Kennedy, *I Rode with the Klan* (London: Arco, 1954); Hollinger F. Barnard, ed., *Outside the Magic Circle: The Autobiography of Virginia Durr* (New York: Simon and Schuster, 1987); Anne Braden, *The Wall Between* (New York: Monthly Review Press, 1958); Morton Sosna, *In Search of the Silent South: Southern Liberals and the Race Issue* (New York: Columbia University Press, 1977).

4. Cousins et al., eds. *South Carolinians Speak*, 29.

5. John Egerton, *Speak Now Against the Day: The Generation Before the Civil Rights Movement in the South* (New York: Alfred A. Knopf, 1995), 616.

6. Dr. Martin Luther King, Jr., "Letter From Birmingham City Jail," in Deirdre Mullane, ed., *Crossing the Danger Water: Three Hundred Years of African-American Writing* (New York: Doubleday, 1993), 638.

7. Sosna, *In Search of the Silent South.*

8. David Chappell, *Inside Agitators: White Southerners in the Civil Rights Movement* (Baltimore: Johns Hopkins University Press, 1994).

9. Egerton, *Speak Now Against the Day.*

10. See Timothy B. Tyson, *Radio Free Dixie: Robert F. Williams and the Roots of Black Power* (Chapel Hill: University of North Carolina Press, 1999).

11. Richard Kluger, *Simple Justice* (New York: Alfred A. Knopf, 1980); Taylor Branch, *Parting the Waters: America in the King Years, 1954–1963* (New York: Simon and Schuster, 1988), 128–205; C. Vann Woodward, *The Strange Career of Jim Crow* (New York: Oxford University Press, 3rd ed.), 8.

12. Numan Bartley, *The Rise of Massive Resistance: Race Relations in the South During the 1950s* (Baton Rouge: Louisiana State University Press, 1969).

13. *Intimidation, Reprisal, and Violence in the South's Racial Crisis* (American Friends Service Committee et al., 1959). See also Barbara Patterson, "Defiance and Dynamite," *New South* 18 (May 1963): 8–11.

14. *Southern Patriot*, Vol. 15, No. 1 (January 1957): 1.

15. For the Till lynching, see Stephen J. Whitfield, *A Death in the Delta: The Story of Emmett Till* (Baltimore: Johns Hopkins University Press, 1991). For the

Parker lynching, see Howard Smead, *Blood Justice: The Lynching of Mack Charles Parker* (New York: Oxford University Press, 1986).

16. Charles M. Payne, *I Got the Light of Freedom: The Organizing Tradition and the Mississippi Freedom Struggle* (Berkeley: University of California Press, 1995), 41.

17. *The Eagle Eye: The Women's Voice* (Jackson, Mississippi), vol. 2, no. 36, (20 August 1955).

18. Kluger, *Simple Justice*, 3.

19. Payne, *I Got the Light of Freedom*, 44. Although there is not yet a book-length portrayal of Amzie Moore, Jennifer Gilbert's "'I Didn't Fail To Tell It': A Biography of Amzie Moore" (master's thesis, University of Wisconsin, 1995) draws upon all the published sources and the Amzie Moore Papers at the Wisconsin State Historical Society to provide an excellent start.

20. Payne, *I Got the Light of Freedom*, 49–51.

21. Tyson, "Radio Free Dixie," 89–90; "Article III Parades, Cavalcades and Caravans," 473–75, *Code of the City of Monroe, 1958*, North Carolina Collection, Louis Round Wilson Library, University of North Carolina. See also Robert F. Williams, *Negroes With Guns* (New York: Marzani and Munsell, 1962).

22. Daisy Bates, *The Long Shadow of Little Rock: A Memoir* (New York: David McKay, 1962), 162.

23. Roy Wilkins to P. L. Prattis, 28 May 1959, NAACP Papers, Group III, Box A333.

24. William H. Chafe, *Civilities and Civil Rights: Greensboro, North Carolina, and the Black Struggle for Equality* (New York: Oxford University Press, 1980), 85.

25. Sworn confession of Robert P. Martin, State of South Carolina, County of Richland, 6 December 1957, in possession of the author; Cherokee County court records, No. 18737, *State of South Carolina v. James R. McCullough and John E. Painter, Jr.*, 6 December 1957; Claudia Thomas Sanders, "This I Believe," in Cousins et al., eds., *South Carolinians Speak*, 69–73; *Charleston News and Courier*, 21 November 1957, 1; *The State* (Columbia, South Carolina), 17 July 1958, 1-D.

26. Martin confession.

27. *Union Daily Times*, "Centennial Edition," 9 December 1950, 2. Allen D. Charles, *The Narrative History of Union County, South Carolina* (Spartanburg, S.C.: The Reprint Company, 1987), 222–26. See also Allen Trelease, *White Terror: The Ku Klux Klan Conspiracy and Southern Reconstruction* (New York: Harper and Row, 1971), 356–58.

28. For the Klan revival led by James "Catfish" Cole, see Timothy B. Tyson, *Radio Free Dixie*, Chapter 6. For the textile unemployment, see Southern Regional Council, "Report on Charlotte, Greensboro and Winston-Salem, North Carolina," 4 September 1957, 11. The report concludes that textile unemployment in the area near Gaffney "may be of great significance in the event that interracial tensions are precipitated."

29. Egerton, *Speak Now Against the Day*, 562; Wyn Craig Wade, *The Fiery Cross: A History of the Ku Klux Klan* (New York: Simon and Schuster, 1987), 276–96.

30. For the East Flat Rock killings, see memorandum to Henry Lee Moon, 29 November 1957, Group III, Box A92, NAACP Papers; *News and Courier*, 21 November 1957, 1.

31. *News and Observer*, 23 November 1957, 1-B; *The State*, 23 November 1957, 1-D.

32. Howard Quint, *Profile in Black and White: A Frank Portrait of South Carolina* (Washington, D.C.: Public Affairs Press, 1958). See also *Charleston News and Courier*, 21 November 1957, 1.

33. *Charleston News and Courier*, 23 November 1957, 1-B; *The State*, 23 November 1957, 1-B.

34. *The State*, 17 July 1958, 1-D; *News and Courier*, 21 November 1958, 1; Martin confession.

35. Dr. James. H. Sanders, Jr., to Tim Tyson, 11 September 1993.

36. *News and Courier*, 21 November 1957, 1-B.

37. *Gaffney Ledger*, 20 March, 5 April 1958.

38. Cousins et al., eds., *South Carolinians Speak*, 69; *Gaffney Ledger*, 28 January 1958, 3; Dr. James H. Sanders, Jr., interview with Tim Tyson, 11 May 1993; *Shelby Star*, reprinted in the *Gaffney Ledger*, 26 November 1957, 4; Dr. James H. Sanders, Jr., to Tim Tyson, 11 September 1993. As Anne Firor Scott has demonstrated, "the Southern lady" had long deployed her respectable ancestry and civic concern as camouflage for social assertion and sometimes even radical politics. See Anne Firor Scott, *The Southern Lady: From Pedestal to Politics, 1830–1930* (Chicago: University of Chicago Press, 1970).

39. Gerda Lerner, *The Grimke Sisters* (Boston: Houghton Mifflin, 1967).

40. Dr. James H. Sanders, Jr., to Tim Tyson, 11 September 1993.

41. Cousins et al., eds., *South Carolinians Speak*, 69; Dr. James H. Sanders, Jr., to Tim Tyson, 11 September 1993.

42. Annette Lopes, office of the registrar, Columbia University, to Tim Tyson, 17 November 1996.

43. See Alan Bullock and R. B. Woodings, eds., *Twentieth Century Culture: A Biographical Companion* (New York: Harper and Row, 1983), 81–82; see also Franz Boaz, introduction to Zora Neale Hurston, *Of Mules and Men* (New York: Harper and Row, 1990), xiii.

44. Dr. James H. Sanders, Jr., to Tim Tyson, 11 September 1993.

45. Dr. James H. Sanders, Jr., to Tim Tyson, 23 August 1993.

46. Ibid.

47. Dr. James H. Sanders, Jr., to Tim Tyson, 11 September 1993.

48. See Sosna, *In Search of the Silent South*. In a sense, this quarrel with the consensus only confirmed Dr. Sanders as a southern liberal, since thorny individualism on all issues was what southern liberals really had in common. According to his family, Sanders simply disagreed that the poll tax was pertinent, because unfair administration of voter tests was what kept African Americans from voting in South Carolina.

49. In the South of the civil rights era, this matter of courtesy titles carried considerable symbolic weight. Dr. Martin Luther King, Jr., mentioned it prominently in his "Letter from a Birmingham Jail." In a speech near Gaffney in November of 1957, Arkansas attorney Amis Guthridge denounced Little Rock editor Harry Ashmore as a Communist agent. His evidence consisted of the fact that "soon after [Ashmore] arrived the paper started mentioning colored women as 'Mrs.' Now some of you may think that is a small thing, but it had never been done

before." Guthrie presented this change of policy as proof of Communist "brain-washing." Although there is no evidence that all present agreed, neither the audience nor the reporters in attendance seem to have regarded the logic as absurd. See *The State*, 21 November 1957, 3-B.

50. Dr. James H. Sanders, Jr., interview with Tim Tyson, 29 April 1993.

51. *Charlotte Observer*, 31 July 1958, 5-A.

52. Judge George Bell Timmerman to Rev. John B. Morris, 29 October 1957, box 1, Reverend John B. Morris Papers, South Carolinia Library, University of South Carolina.

53. *Pittsburgh Courier*, 18 October 1958, 3.

54. Quint, *Profile in Black and White*, 55–70.

55. Prospectus of *South Carolina Speaks*, Reverend John B. Morris Papers. This document is quoted in Thomas D. Clark, *The Emerging South* (New York: Oxford University Press, 1961), 262–63; Dr. James H. Sanders, Jr., to Tim Tyson, 11 September 1993.

56. Reverend John B. Morris to Claudia Sanders, n.d., box 1, Morris Papers.

57. Cousins et al., eds., *South Carolinians Speak*, iv–v.

58. Wilma Dykeman and James Stokely, "Inquiry into the Southern Tensions," *New York Times Magazine*, 13 October 1957, VI–20.

59. Cousins et al., eds., *South Carolinians Speak*, 65, 50–51, 73, 31.

60. William Peters, *The Southern Temper* (Garden City, N.Y.: Doubleday, 1959), 96.

61. A. M. Secrest, "In Black and White: Press Opinion and Race Relations in South Carolina, 1954–1964" (Ph.D. dissertation, Duke University, 1971), 193–94.

62. See, for example, Quint, *Profile In Black and White*. See also Bartley, *The Rise of Massive Resistance*, 230–32, for an excellent account of Governor Timmerman's relentless assault on academic freedom in South Carolina.

63. Bartley, *The Rise of Massive Resistance*, 93–94; Benjamin Muse, *Ten Years of Prelude: The Story of Integration Since the Supreme Court's 1954 Decision* (New York: Viking, 1964), 59; *Southern School News*, August 1956, 9; *Charlotte Observer*, 19 July 1958, 1-C.

64. Secrest, "In Black and White," 192–93, reports that all of the ministers were compelled to leave their pulpits. The "displaced parsons" quip is from Peters, *The Southern Temper*, 98.

65. Clark, *The Emerging South*, 262–63.

66. *Gaffney Ledger*, 9 January 1958, 7.

67. Peters, *The Southern Temper*, 23.

68. Anne Braden to George Weissman, 21 February 1959, Committee to Combat Racial Injustice Papers, Wisconsin State Historical Society.

69. *Gaffney Ledger*, 28 January 1958, 6.

71. Hall, *Revolt Against Chivalry*, 155.

72. Lillian Smith, *Killers of the Dream* (New York: W. W. Norton, 1978), 167.

73. Cousins et al., eds., *South Carolinians Speak*, 72.

74. Bartley, *The Rise of Massive Resistance*, 251–69; for a personal account, see Elizabeth Huckaby, *Crisis at Central High: Little Rock, 1957–58* (Baton Rouge: Louisiana State University Press, 1980).

75. *Gaffney Ledger*, 8 March 1958, 1.

76. *The Independent*, 21 September 1957, 4.

77. *The State*, 7 October 1957, 1-B; Quint, *Profile in Black and White*, 162. For the lynchings supervised by J. G. Long, see Charles, *The Narrative History of Union County, South Carolina*, 222–26. See also Trelease, *White Terror*, 356–58.

78. Secrest, "In Black and White," 217–18. Reverend John B. Morris Papers, notes of conversation between Morris and Thomas Waring, 1957, indicate that Waring had said, "I would fight, too. If it was necessary to use machine guns, I'd use them. I'd throw Molotov cocktails at the tanks."

79. C. Vann Woodward, *The Strange Career of Jim Crow*, (New York: Oxford University Press, 2d rev. ed., 1966), 166.

80. *Gaffney Ledger*, 23 November 1957, 1; Martin confession.

81. *News and Courier*, 21 November 1957, 1; *Gaffney Ledger*, 23 November 1957, 1.

82. Martin confession.

83. *Gaffney Ledger*, 23 November 1957, 1; Cherokee County court records, No. 18737, *State of South Carolina v. James R. McCullough and James E. Painter, Jr.*, 6 December 1957.

84. *The State*, 4 January 1958, 1-B; *Charlotte Observer*, 16 July 1958, 1-B and 28 June 1958, 1-B; Martin confession.

85. Martin confession; *The State*, 21 November 1957.

86. *Gaffney Ledger*, 21 November 1957, 1; *The State*, 21 November 1957, 1; *Charlotte Observer*, 19 November 1957, 5-C; Dr. James H. Sanders, Jr., interview with Tim Tyson, 15 June 1993.

87. Martin confession.

88. Ibid.; *News and Courier*, 20 November 1957, 1.

89. *Gaffney Ledger*, 21 November 1957, 1; *The State*, 21 November 1957, 1; *The Record*, 20 November 1957, 1; Quint, *Profile in Black and White*, 170–73; *News and Courier*, 20 November 1957, 1.

90. *Gaffney Ledger*, 28 June 1958, 1 and 21 November 1957, 1; *The State*, 21 November 1957, 1; *The Record*, 20 November 1957, 1; *News and Courier*, 20 November 1957, 1 and 21 November 1957, 1; Quint, *Profile in Black and White*, 170–73.

91. *The State*, 23 November 1957, 4-A.

92. *News and Courier*, 23 November 1957, 8-A, emphasis added; *Greenville News* editorial, reprinted in *Gaffney Ledger*, 26 November 1957, 4.

93. Harriet P. Simons to *News and Courier*, 26 November 1957, 14-A.

94. Quint, *Profile in Black and White*, 170–73.

95. *Gaffney Ledger*, 28 June 1958, 1; *Charlotte Observer*, 28 June 1958, 7-A; Max Wallace interview with Tim Tyson, 18 September 1993; *The State*, 15 July 1958, 1-B, and 17 July 1958, 1-D.

96. *News and Observer*, 7 December; 1957, 2.

97. *Gaffney Ledger*, 7 January 1958, 1; *Gaffney Ledger*, 14 January 1958, 1.

98. *The State*, 28 February 1958, 7-B; Dean Ross interview, 14 August 1993; *Gaffney Ledger*, 1 March 1958, 1.

99. *The State*, 1 July 1958, 1, and 18 July 1958, 1; *Charlotte Observer*, 28 June 1958, 7-A, 29 June 1958, 1-E.

100. *Gaffney Ledger*, 12 December 1957, 1.

101. *The State*, 17 July 1958, 1-D, 18 July 1958, 1 and 7-A; *Gaffney Ledger*, 12 December 1957, 1; *Charlotte Observer*, 16 July 1958, 1-B, and 17 July 1958, 11-A. Several state investigators reported receiving similar letters.

Afterwords

Portraying Power

THE VALUABLE ESSAYS in this book allow us to see southern politics in a new way. While the authors speak in distinct voices and explore diverse subjects, each essay attempts to expand the boundaries of what we consider "political." In doing so, they follow a goal pursued by historians of many other times and places in recent years. The manifestations of power now appear broader than any formal government, extending far beyond Election Day and embracing people without formal political influence. The desire to understand that power has animated histories stretching from ancient Rome and early Africa to revolutionary France and nineteenth-century China to contemporary Latin America and the Middle East.

The American South might appear an unlikely place to launch that search. Politics in the region have seemed quite straightforward, the property of reactionary white men armed, as a Mississippian put it in 1890, with lies in their mouths and shotguns in their hands. The South between the years of emancipation and the end of segregation might well seem the last place to look for a complicated and subtle political history in which the apparently powerless played significant roles.

Historians of the South in earlier decades, when a different political history defined the New South, could not have imagined a book such as this. Those historians sought to trace the lineage of the South they knew, a South of politically enforced segregation and a heavily restricted electorate. Written in a time when electoral politics sound only in minor keys, the essays in *Jumpin' Jim Crow* do not concentrate mainly on partisanship. The crucial political battlefields in this book are not the editorial page, the ballot box, and the smoky room, but the household and the street. We see politicians not on the hustings or in office but in failed crusades, vigilante groups, and photo ops. The political history of the New South in this book is a history of guerrilla warfare, its battles fought in the shadowy corners of the region, hand-to-hand and in close quarters, any victories hard-won and transient.

If there is a common interpretation that emerges from these pages, it might look something like this: the walls that had defined a stable southern political realm of white male voters collapsed after the Civil War. With the dislocation of emancipation and Reconstruction, the political sphere demanded much reckoning with and allowed some openings for people from the bottom and edges of the antebellum social order. Fundamental

questions about racial identity, gender identity, economic identity, historical identity, and regional identity became embroiled in electoral politics.
Deep struggle continued beneath the surface even as violence and fraud
strangled the democratic promise, as parties collapsed into cynical coalitions and as dishonest constitutions and voting laws exiled black men and
silenced women.

Southern politics after formal segregation, these essays show, continued
to churn. The South became the site of tangled tensions and conflicts;
electoral politics often seemed a thin and distorted surface of more profound struggles. The Democrats and the Republicans switched places and
economic change arrived with powerful effect, but the consequences of
centuries of inequity endured. The roots of injustice and inequity ran not
only into the ballot box and textile mill, but also snaked into mass culture,
consumption, sexuality, and violence. Those roots extend much deeper
than partisan ideology and complicity, to the very heart of who southerners have been and are. The new story is an even more harrowing vision
of the South than the one put forward by older political history.

This new history, unlike revisionism in other facets of history, does not
attack its predecessors. The polite iconoclasts of this book gratefully acknowledge the books, articles, and dissertations that have chronicled, in
state after state, the winners and losers, the leaders and ideologies. These
essays seldom attack that history, seldom argue that descriptions of white
male political conflict were flawed on their own terms. Rather, the challenge goes deeper: the new political historians see electoral history as only
a part of the story, perhaps even the least interesting part of the story.

These essays cannot help but stand as a challenge to the most established
form of postwar southern history. Once overt electoral conflicts are defined as only a subset of the larger political sphere, those conflicts cannot
possess the same explanatory power (or fascination or professional prestige) they have exerted since the inception of professional history of the
New South. Although the new southern political history does not deny the
importance of the electoral politics of white men, it sees politics-as-usual
as a struggle for the spoils after the deeper politics of household and race
have been quelled. The politicians who have occupied center stage in so
many books speak lines here that are important mainly for their language,
a language deeply embedded with metaphors of gender and race.

These essays also tend to diminish the questions of class and interest that
so animated earlier historians of the New South. The older southern political history put struggles over economic power at the center. Politics appeared as the embodiment of desperate fights between classes and regions.
That earlier history drew much of its power from the scale of the issues
that appeared at stake: industrialism versus agrarianism, East versus West
and South, the future versus the past. The essays in this book, by contrast,

do not give material life a starring role. The most telling economic conflicts take place at the point of consumption rather than at the sources of production. The men and women in this book are, by and large, well-to-do and well educated.

Whereas the old political history made region one of its basic themes, region here appears as a given. A close attention to place is seldom a defining category in these essays even though many of them are local studies. It could be argued, however, that place is the most salient political force in the United States. It is place that organizes politics, that gives shape and boundary to fights over race, gender, religion, federal power, capitalist development, and everything else. Voters of all descriptions tend to vote more like their neighbors than like people of their same gender elsewhere. Black Americans calculate their interests from the vantage point of their neighborhoods and states as well as from their racial identity. The volatile issues of abortion, guns, and education follow the contours of region more than any other social demarcation. Regions shape social identities, and regions are defined in part through electoral politics. The old history and the new come full circle, connecting and reinforcing one another.

Written with passion and erudition, these essays introduce us to themes that traditional political history ignored, themes that do not fit into the categories in which that history was written. As a result of the bold essays in *Jumpin' Jim Crow*, we can glimpse a new southern political history that will let us see power more fully, in more of its dimensions and implications. The challenge facing us now is to combine the brilliant possibilities of this new political history with the proven strengths of the old, fusing language and action, culture and power, boundary and center. The prospect is exciting indeed.

Reflections

As I READ these essays, I could not help wondering what identifications and passions draw these particular authors to these subjects. We know that curiosity drives the writing of history, but what drives curiosity? Why "the South"? Why race and gender, with class as a relatively muted theme? Why politics? And to what end? What political solutions follow from this "new political history"? How can we use this work—in Joyce Appleby's words—to help us "think better, live richly, and act more wisely"?[1]

My own curiosities about the past have tangled roots, so tangled in fact that I couldn't dig up and dissect them all if I tried. I grew up in Oklahoma, a place that is sometimes in and sometimes out of southern history, as the ever-moving boundaries between North and South grind and shift. Michele Wallace, in *Invisibility Blues*, comments on "the unwillingness of 'American history' to include Oklahoma in its big picture. It's like one of those nuclear dump sites," she says, "some place nobody wants to know anything about."[2]

To me, it is the psychic rim where the South meets the West and Midwest. One branch of my family wandered up from Texas to farm in "Little Dixie," the cotton growing, biracial corner of the state; the other came from Kansas to open a dry goods store. No southern state had more home-grown socialists than Oklahoma nor a more multicultural, multiracial past. The man for whom my hometown is named, for example, had run away from North Carolina, lived with the Chickasaw Indians in Mississippi, married a Chickasaw woman, and was driven west to Oklahoma on the Trail of Tears. That, however, is not at all the history I learned in the Oklahoma public schools. It was only when I escaped to graduate school at Columbia University in the 1960s that I heard those stories, and it was also at Columbia that I became aware of the mark of region in a way that I had never been before.

I remember my first sight of Manhattan: those blazing skyscrapers, that confusing subway ride, the cacophony of sound, the colonnaded gateway through Columbia's cliff of granite walls. I had no idea that I was repeating a defining moment in countless American lives: as an arriviste in the city of wild promise, alone but not lonely, reveling in orphanage, full of hope, and entirely innocent of what might lie ahead. What I found, in New York in the wake of the civil rights movement, was that southernness tended to override the nuances of geography and class. I could as easily have been a planter's daughter from Mississippi as a border state sharecropper's grandchild. To my professors and fellow students, I was simply a "Southerner," with all the baggage that identity entailed. It was hard to pass as a serious scholar but easy to claim a perverse glamour, the glamour of the outsider who speaks from "the South," a terrible yet culturally resonant place. By the time I decided to come back to the South in the early 1970s, I saw it with an expatriate's eyes. "The South" seemed both familiar and frightening, and I felt an identification with the region that was half chosen and half imposed.

For me, writing about the South as a southerner—and perhaps especially as a white southern woman—has at times been a source of what I can only call anguish, however overwrought that term may sound. First, there was the anguish I shared with generations of white southern intellectuals before me: the ache of writing about a homeland that has such a dark and bloody history, a region, moreover, that has played the role of internal colony in the American imagination: the backward, evil, or romanticized "other" in a country certain of its innocence, superiority, and power.

This anguish had a gender dimension, which had to do with writing about the South as a woman and never feeling quite welcome at home. I knew that it would be naive to expect human beings to give up a professional monopoly willingly. Yet gestures of exclusion and marginalization from male colleagues always took me by surprise, perhaps because it seemed so obvious to me that woman scholars and women's history were bringing to the study of the South the spark of new life it needs. Not so long ago, I could count on one hand the male writers of southern history who took gender seriously in their own work and cited and taught the work of their female colleagues. Neither women nor women's history were welcomed warmly into the house of southern history—but of course they fared little better elsewhere and worst of all, not in the South and West, but in the Ivy League.

What strikes me when I look back at my own work is that all of the women I've written about have been in some sense unintelligible, incommensurable within the traditional narratives of southern history: Jessie Daniel Ames, the Texan who deliberately and ironically donned the white gloves of the southern lady; the rebel girls of Elizabethton, Tennessee, who represented an incipient southern modernism rendered invisible by assumptions about the backward South; white textile workers, who are so firmly saddled with redneck racism and antiunion individualism that any attempt to tell their story as a gender story just doesn't compute; O. Delight Smith, a working-class hero who risked everything for love; Katharine Du Pre Lumpkin, whose "narrative of racial conversion" hid as much as it told.[3] I've always been drawn to women on the margins, exiles, internal exiles; women who resist assimilation into conventional narratives;

women whose place in Southern history can be established only with a fight.

Reading *Jumpin' Jim Crow* made me realize how much southern history has changed and how much of my old sense of uneasiness has fallen away. I was struck by the poise of these essays, their lack of defensiveness, their calm certainty that the work of gender matters. I was also struck by the way they bring both men and women, masculinity and femininity, into the house of history and link them so persuasively with race, southern history's central theme.

These essays are, in many cases, retellings of old stories that cast those stories in a fresh light. In other cases, they radically shift the focus of historical attention, by lifting the curtain from private life, for example, or by gendering the production of social memory. They find new meaning in the most quotidian of artifacts and significance in silences, fantasies, and changes of heart. They do not fit easily into existing models of feminist or racial politics, and, as always, it is in the interstices between old models and new stories that we find new directions for historical research, new questions that will beget new historical truths.

This anthology shows the traces of a diffuse postmodernism, in its interest in discursive struggles, its denaturalization both of race and of racism, its challenge to dichotomies (here the private interpenetrates the public, segregation does not bring separation, politics takes place in the heart as well as at the polling place), but it does so without foreswearing history's irreducible empiricism, its dependence on the materiality of evidence, the conviction that its subject is "real," however dependent on language, however constructed that reality may be. Moreover, these essays do what the functionalist tendencies of postmodern often preclude: they pinpoint power, ascribe agency, and show not just how society replicates itself but how it can change. For that reason, these essays, as Vincent Harding has put it, "beckon to us, open spaces for us, help us figure out how we might go on."[4] *Jumpin' Jim Crow*, moreover, bears witness to our need for narratives of the past that help us grapple with the present, the need that makes writing history such a privilege even if it is sometimes laced with pain.

NOTES

1. Joyce Appleby, "The Power of History," *American Historical Review* 103 (February 1998): 1, 12.

2. Michele Wallace, "Invisibility Blues," in *Invisibility Blues: From Pop to Theory* (London: Verso, 1990), 99.

3. Katharine Du Pre Lumpkin, *The Making of a Southerner* (New York: Alfred A. Knopf, 1946). "Narrative of racial conversion" is Fred Hobson's phrase: *But Now*

I See: The White Southern Conversion Narrative (Baton Rouge: Louisiana State University Press, forthcoming).

4. Vincent Harding, "More than Rights and Race: The Southern Freedom Movement as a Basis for Democratic Renewal," conference on "Black and White Perspectives on the American South," University of Georgia, Athens, Ga., 29 September 1994.

The Shoah and Southern History

SOMEDAY African Americans and Jewish Americans may disentangle our-selves from one another, but that time hasn't arrived quite yet. I won't talk here about all our sundry engagements and exasperations, but one subject draws us together: Old Country trauma. For blacks, the worst Old Coun-try is the slave and segregationist South; for Jews, it is Europe, encapsu-lated in the Shoah (Holocaust) of the Nazi era.

Usually slavery and the Shoah keep their distance. But in the mid-1990s a best-selling young author's highly publicized comments brought Euro-pean and southern history together. The controversy swirling around Daniel Jonah Goldhagen, a Harvard political scientist, riveted my atten-tion. Building on the work of historians such as Christopher Browning, Goldhagen's 1996 book, *Hitler's Willing Executioners: Ordinary Germans and the Holocaust*, disputes the common wisdom that a few evil men or bureaucratic automatons caused the Nazi genocide of European Jews.[1] In-stead, Goldhagen insists that ordinary Germans willingly slaughtered Jews. Goldhagen attributes this willingness to kill to the steady stream of what he calls "eliminationist" anti-Semitism circulating in Germany since the late nineteenth century. By World War II, he argues, "ordinary" Ger-mans killed Jews openly and shamelessly, convinced that they were doing the right thing. Even as the war was ending in obvious Nazi defeat, Gold-hagen points out that German soldiers forced starving, diseased Jewish prisoners on otherwise purposeless "death marches."

Hitler's Willing Executioners describes face-to-face murders in graphic detail and includes such intimacies as a photograph of a policeman shoot-ing point-blank a mother holding her child. Germans from all walks of life, Goldhagen says, "tortured and degraded Jews with zeal and energy." As though proud of the slaughter, assailants photographed the carnage, creat-ing images that sometimes capture wives and girlfriends looking on.

Gory souvenirs remind me of similar but southern images: the charred, tortured black body, often naked, often burned beyond recognition; the proud perpetrators, posing like big-game hunters beside their victim; the crowd staring at the body, looking straight into the camera, sometimes bearing the smiles that greet a camera in happier circumstances. Like Goldhagen's ordinary Germans, these ordinary white southerners docu-mented their deeds for the benefit of lovers and friends.

I read *Hitler's Willing Executioners* with one eye on the American South, where white supremacy found its own willing executioners. The parallel between Nazi Germany and the American South also occurred to Daniel Goldhagen, although he was defending himself historiographically. Criticized for his portrayal of German culture as rooted in anti-Semitism, Goldhagen replied that writing about the mechanics of the Holocaust without focusing on the virulence of German anti-Semitism "would be like writing a book about American slavery without writing about racism and saying, 'So let's write about the way the plantations were organized.'"

Hmmmm. Unfortunately, that is precisely the way too many books on southern history deal with slavery: by and large, American historians still write as though slavery were incidental, not central, to the American past. Considering how rarely racism appears in scholarship as a fundamental constituent of American and southern society, it seems clear that both the history and the historiography of the Shoah can illuminate the history and the historiography of the American South. These two great tragedies of the modern era share a host of horrendous similarities: the racialization of vulnerable people, dehumanization, legal discrimination, segregation, captivity, forced labor, humiliation, cruelty, gratuitous violence, intense bodily and psychic torture. In the aftermath of the Shoah, these resemblances struck Stanley Elkins and inspired his adventurous analysis, *Slavery*.[2] Deeply influenced by Freud, Elkins advanced some excellent points and opened up new interpretive possibilities for southern history. But he made uncritical use of the Sambo stereotype and disregarded black people's own strengths and coping mechanisms (such as families and religion). On Elkins' prototypical southern plantation, the master/father—not the slave child's own parents—engendered the slave/child's psyche. Elkins' depiction of an ego-less slave Sambo quite rightly provoked enormous outcry—against both his conclusions and his methodology. *Slavery* not only doomed psychoanalysis as a tool for southern history, it also made anathema comparisons with the Holocaust. To this day, neither the theory nor the comparison has recovered from *Slavery*. This is a pity.

In my work on Gertrude Thomas, Sojourner Truth, and southern violence I have tried to bring some of the intensely personal attributes of Holocaust historiography—real hurt, real blood, real trauma—into the history of American slave society. After much excellent scholarship on Post-Traumatic Stress Disorder, child abuse, sexual abuse, and personal violence, historians are in a stronger position than a generation or two ago to make sense of both the psychological and physical injuries of slavery. Both Freud and contemporary psychological theory can help us write better southern history. Once we can write the words "trauma" and "slavery" in the same sentence, we will have enriched our understanding of slavery's human costs, for enslavers, enslaved, and bystanders. Already Wilma King, *Stolen Childhood: Slave Youth in Nineteenth-Century America*, has made excellent use of late-twentieth-century Balkan conflicts to illustrate the costs of slave children's lives in the perpetual war zone of slavery.[3]

When historians and other Americans face the fact that violence undergirded southern society after emancipation as before, we will be better able to measure the weight of institutionalized hatred. Racism will no longer appear as an individual, personal flaw, but rather as a way of life, as an ideology. The everyday racism of ordinary people will come into view. The very ordinariness of racism—in this case, southern racism—needs to be faced and admitted. When this omnipresence penetrates southern historiography, our overall estimation of the basic meaning of southern history will change. Southern history will look more like the history of the Shoah.

NOTES

1. David J. Goldhagen, *Hitler's Willing Executioners: Ordinary Germans and the Holocaust* (New York: Alfred A. Knopf, 1996).
2. Stanley Elkins, *Slavery: A Problem in American Institutional and Intellectual Life* (Chicago: University of Chicago Press, 1959).
3. Wilma King, *Stolen Childhood: Slave Youth in Nineteenth-Century America* (Bloomington: Indiana University Press, 1995).

Contributors

EDWARD L. AYERS is the Hugh P. Kelly Professor of History at the University of Virginia and Executive Director of the Virginia Center for Digital History, an institute dedicated to crafting and teaching history in new media. His books include *The Promise of the New South: Life After Reconstruction*, which was a finalist for the National Book Award and the Pulitzer Prize, and which won prizes for the best book on southern history and on the history of race in America. He is an editor of the *Oxford Book of the American South*, and an author of *American Passages: A History of the United States*. His current work is "The Valley of the Shadow: Two Communities in the American Civil War," which will be published on CD-ROM.

ELSA BARKLEY BROWN teaches in the History Department and the Center for Afroamerican and African Studies at the University of Michigan. She is an associate editor of the two-volume work, *Black Women in America: An Historical Encyclopedia*. Her articles have appeared in *Signs*, *Sage*, *History Workshop*, and *Feminist Studies*. Her current research concerns African Americans in post-emancipation Richmond, Virginia.

W. FITZHUGH BRUNDAGE is professor and chair of the Department of History at the University of Florida. He is the editor of *No Deed But Memory: Essays on History and Memory in the South* (forthcoming), and is currently working on a study of black and white historical memory in the South from the Civil War to the present.

JANE DAILEY is assistant professor of History at Rice University in Houston, Texas. She is the author of *Before Jim Crow: The Politics of Race in Post-Emancipation Virginia*, and is currently writing a book on miscegenation and racial identity.

LAURA F. EDWARDS is an associate professor in the History Department at the University of California at Los Angeles. She is the author of *Gendered Strife and Confusion: The Political Culture of Reconstruction* and *Scarlett Doesn't Live Here Anymore: Women and Southern Society in the Nineteenth Century*. She is now working on *The Politics of Private Life: Law, Culture, and Power in the Antebellum South*.

KARI FREDERICKSON is assistant professor of History at the University of Alabama. She received her Ph.D. in history from Rutgers

University in 1996. She is the author of a forthcoming book on the Dixiecrats and is the former editor of the *Florida Historical Quarterly*.

GLENDA ELIZABETH GILMORE is professor of History and African American Studies at Yale University. She is the author of *Gender and Jim Crow: Women and the Politics of White Supremacy in North Carolina, 1896–1920*. She is currently at work on a study of domestic race relations in an international context tentatively titled, *The Second Civil War: The South, the Nation, and the World, 1915–1955*.

DAVID F. GODSHALK is an assistant professor of History at Shippensburg University. The recipient of a 1993–1994 Andrew W. Mellon Postdoctoral Fellowship at Emory University, he is currently completing a book manuscript on the Atlanta race riot of 1906.

GRACE ELIZABETH HALE is the author of *Making Whiteness: The Culture of Segregation in the South, 1890–1940*. She teaches the history of the American South and twentieth century American cultural history in the Corcoran Department of History at the University of Virginia. Her current project, "Your Fantasy, My Freedom: Identity and Politics in Postwar America," explores the origins of our modern conception of identity and contemporary debates about identity politics in the artistic and social movements and popular culture of the period between 1945 and 1975.

JACQUELYN DOWD HALL is the Julia Cherry Spruill Professor of History and Director of the Southern Oral History Program at the University of North Carolina at Chapel Hill. She is the author of *Revolt Against Chivalry: Jessie Daniel Ames and the Women's Campaign Against Lynching*, and coauthor of *Like a Family: The Making of a Southern Cotton Mill World*. She is currently writing a book about Katharine Du Pre Lumpkin, Grace Lumpkin, and the politics of historical memory.

STEPHEN KANTROWITZ was born and raised in Brookline, Massachusetts, and is currently an assistant professor of History at the University of Wisconsin at Madison. He is the author of *Ben Tillman and the Reconstruction of White Supremacy*.

NANCY MacLEAN is associate professor of History and African American Studies and Charles Deering McCormick Professor of Teaching Excellence at Northwestern University. The author of *Behind the Mask of Chivalry: The Making of the Second Ku Klux Klan*, she is now writing a social and intellectual history of affirmative action in employment titled, *Of Jobs and Justice: Affirmative Action and American Life Since the Sixties*.

NELL IRVIN PAINTER, author most recently of *Sojourner Truth: A Life, A Symbol*, is the Edwards Professor of American History and Director of the Program in African-American Studies at Princeton. Her current research concerns whiteness and beauty.

BRYANT SIMON, associate professor of History at the University of Georgia, is the author of *A Fabric of Defeat: The Politics of South Carolina Textile Workers, 1910–1948*. Currently he is writing a book about the rise, fall, and tentative re-emergence of Atlantic City, New Jersey, after World War II.

TIMOTHY B. TYSON is the author of *Radio Free Dixie: Robert F. Williams and the Roots of Black Power*. He teaches History in the Department of Afro-American Studies at the University of Wisconsin at Madison. He is currently working on a book about African American freedom movements in the twentieth-century South.

Index

0439